THE OSS IN BURMA

MODERN WAR STUDIES

THE OSS IN BURMA

Jungle War against the Japanese

TROY J. SACQUETY

UNIVERSITY PRESS OF KANSAS

Published by the University Press of Kansas (Lawrence, Kansas 66045),
which was organized by the Kansas Board of Regents and
is operated and funded by Emporia State University,
Fort Hays State University, Kansas State University,
Pittsburg State University, the University of Kansas,
and Wichita State University

Library of Congress Cataloging-in-Publication Data

Sacquety, Troy J.
The OSS in Burma: jungle war against the Japanese /
Troy J. Sacquety.
pages cm. — (Modern war studies)
Includes bibliographical references and index.
ISBN 978-0-7006-2018-0 (pbk. : alk. paper)
1. World War, 1939–1945—Burma. 2. World War, 1939–1945—Secret
service—United States. 3. United States. Office of Strategic Services.
Detachment 101 4. Burma--History—Japanese occupation, 1942–1945. I.
Title.
D767.6.S27 2013
940.54'867309591—dc23
2012045114

British Library Cataloguing-in-Publication Data is available.

Printed in the United States of America

10 9 8 7 6 5 4 3 2 1

The paper used in this publication is recycled and contains 30 percent postconsumer waste.
It is acid free and meets the minimum requirements of the American National Standard for
Permanence of Paper for Printed Library Materials Z39.48-1992.

This book is dedicated to all veterans of Detachment 101, be they American, British, or Commonwealth, and especially the Kachin. You met unknown challenges in a far-flung land with ingenuity and initiative. The bond that you forged in the jungles of Burma remains as strong today as it was then. For that you have my deepest respect.

Contents

A photo section appears following page 90.

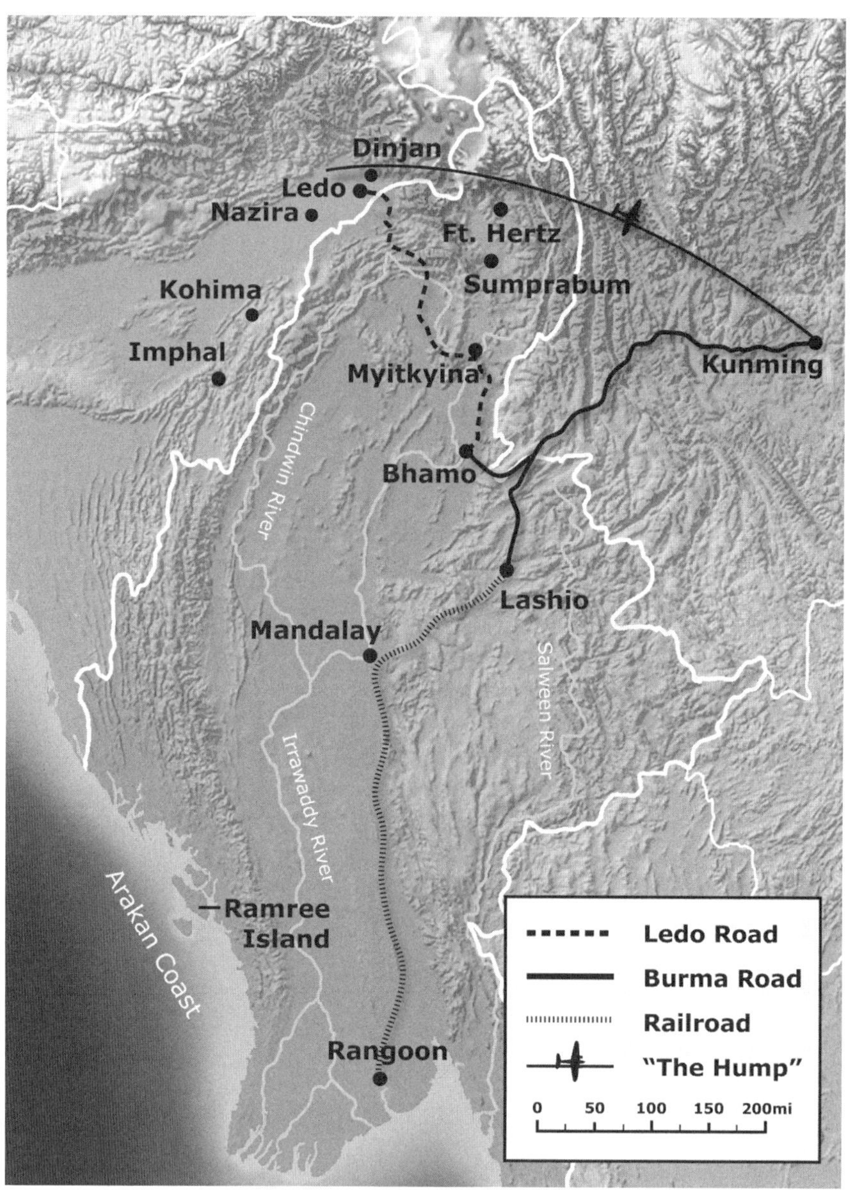

Burma. Map by Daniel W. Telles

Acknowledgments

First I need to thank my family for their support over the long hours. My wife, Mary, my son, Jackson, and my daughters, Emily and Laurel, allowed me the time to write. My parents, Roger and Shirley Sacquety, encouraged my study of history from day one. And my grandfather, Chester Wilson, a WWII and Korea veteran, inspired my love of history.

The OSS veterans and their family members have been invaluable. OSS veteran Elizabeth McIntosh and Detachment 101 members Marje Luce and Sam Spector got me started. Oliver Trechter, Allen Richter, Dennis Klein, Brian Ferry, Zach and Agnes Ebaugh, Walter Mess, Danny Mudrinich, Elton Archer, Oscar Milton, Sam Schreiner, Harvey Sussman, Herb Auerbach, Peter Lutken, Bud Banker, Carl Eifler, Red Ryder, Glenn Moehring, Paula Helfrich, Joe Lazarsky, Rich Kranstover, Dick Hamada, Ace Ellis, Blain Hedrick, Jim Ward, John Breen, Bernard Brophy, and Penny Hicks provided much material. Art Reinhardt, Caesar Civitella, Andy Mousalimas, Art Frizzell, and John Hamblet also provided support and advice along the way. V-Force veteran James Fletcher provided much information on that unit.

I wish to thank my colleagues who at one time or another helped as well: Michael Krivdo, Kenn Finlayson, Charles H. Briscoe, Jared Tracy, Dan Telles, Laura Goddard, Pedro Feliciano, Alejandro Lujan, Earl Moniz, Betty Rucker, Toni Hiley, and Carolyn Rheams. At the National Archives I would have been lost without the steadfast help of archivists Timothy Nenninger and the late John Taylor. A giant thank you goes to Larry MacDonald, who was a guiding hand for years. I also want to thank historians John Chambers, Patrick O'Donnell, Mark Van Rhyn, and Joey Dujon for their support. In particular, I want to thank my mentor Brian M. Linn, without whom this project would have never started. Lastly, I need to thank R. P., J. P., J. P. J., and J. B., without whom I could never have kept focused enough to put pen to paper. You were literally there from start to finish. Thank you!

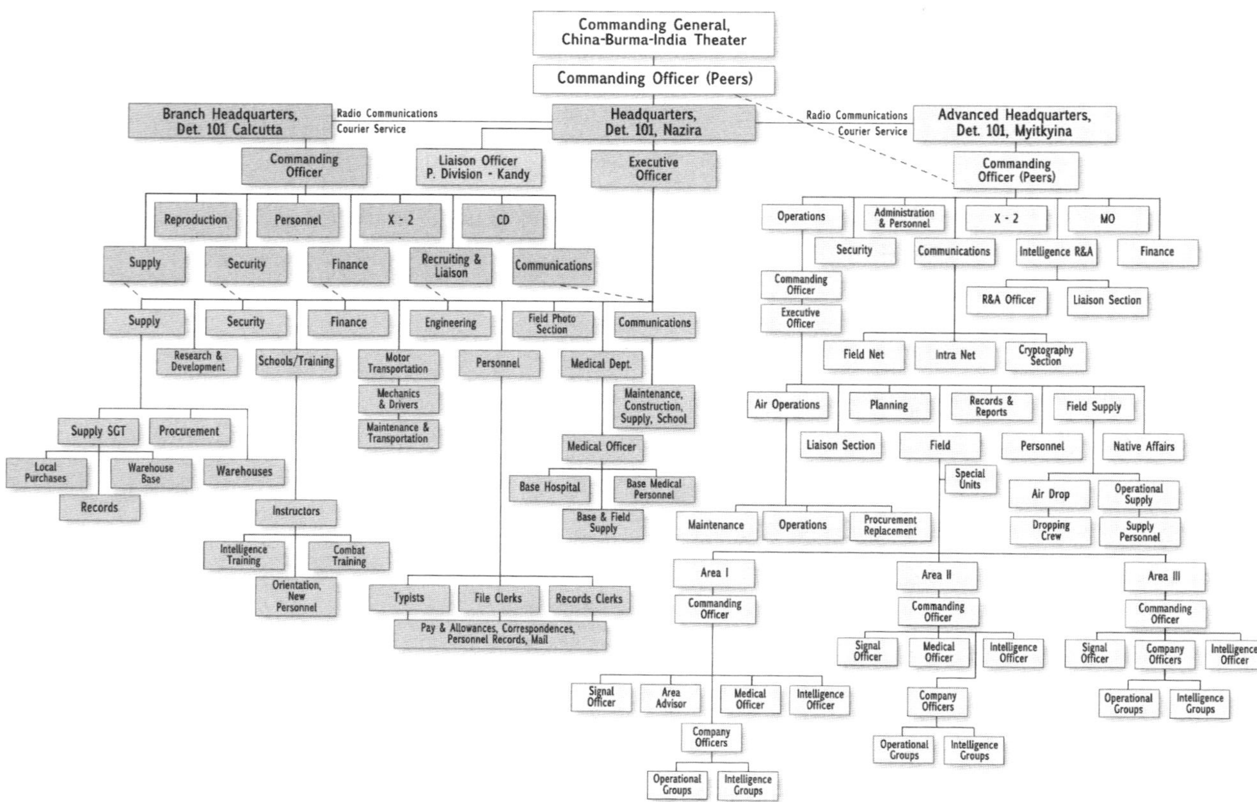

Detachment 101 organization, November 1944

Commonly Used Acronyms

AFL	Burmese Anti-Fascist League
AFU	Arakan Field Unit
ALFSEA	Allied Land Forces South East Asia
AOR	area of responsibility
ATC	Air Transport Command
CAS	British Civil Affairs Service
CBI	China-Burma-India Theater
CIA	Central Intelligence Agency
CIC	U.S. Army Counter Intelligence Corps
CIT	combat interrogation team
CMA	Citation for Military Assistance
COI	Coordinator of Information
FEU	Field Experimental Unit
I&R	intelligence and reconnaissance
LARU	Lambertsen amphibious respiratory unit
LCR	landing craft, rubber
MO	OSS Morale Operations Branch
MU	Maritime Unit Branch
NCAC	Northern Combat Area Command
OCNA	Office of the Coordinator of Native Affairs
OCS	Officer Candidate School
OG	OSS Operational Group
OSS	Office of Strategic Services
OWI	Office of War Information
POW	prisoner of war
RAF	Royal Air Force
R&A	OSS Research and Analysis Branch
R&D	OSS Research and Development Branch

SACO	Sino-American Cooperative Organization
SAF	Special Action Force
SA/G	Special Activities, Goodfellow
SCI	special counterintelligence
SEAC	British-led South East Asia Command
SI	OSS Secret Intelligence Branch
SO	OSS Special Operations Branch
SOE	British Special Operations Executive
SOP	standard operating procedure
SOS	U.S. Army Services of Supply
SSO	OSS Strategic Services Officer
SSU	Strategic Services Unit
S&T	OSS Schools and Training Branch
TO&E	table of organization and equipment
USAAF	United States Army Air Forces
USASOC	United States Army Special Operations Command
X-2	OSS Counter-Intelligence Branch

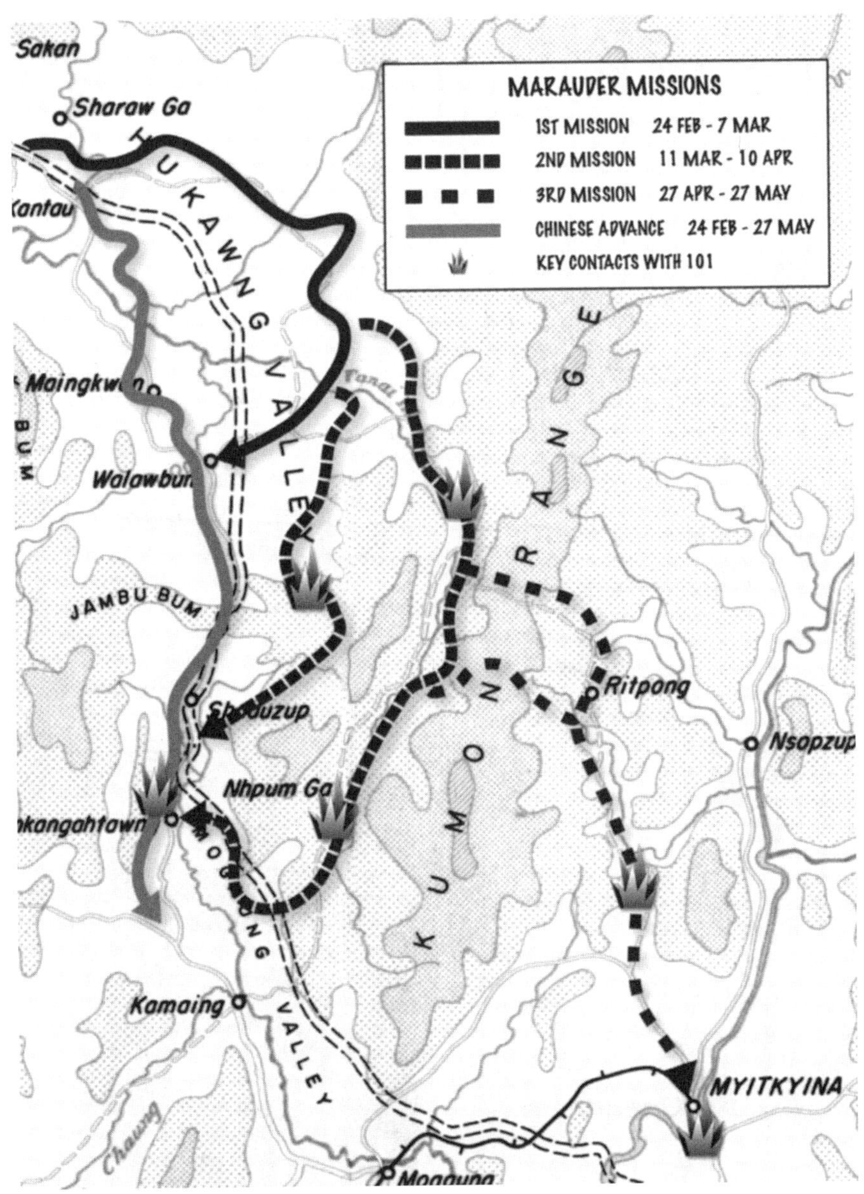

OSS Detachment 101's missions with Merrill's Marauders from the Hukawng Valley to Myitkyina, 24 February–27 May, 1944. Map by Daniel W. Telles

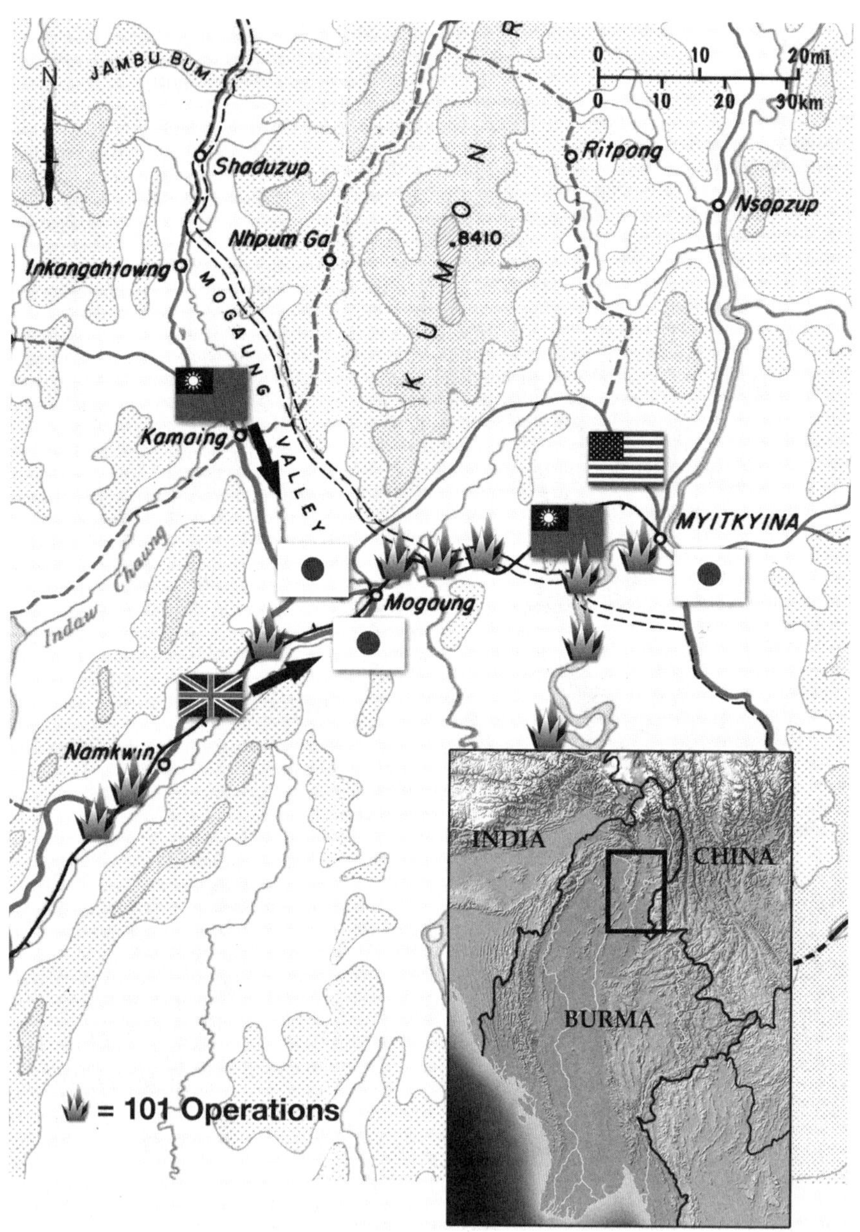

OSS Detachment 101's Myitkyina Campaign, June–August 1944. Map by Daniel W. Telles.

Introduction

I disliked intensely the prospect of a large-scale campaign in Northern Burma. One could not choose a worse place for fighting the Japanese. . . . But, we never succeeded in deflecting the Americans from their purpose. . . . We of course wanted to recapture Burma, but we did not want to do it by land advances from slender communications and across the most forbidding fighting country imaginable.

Winston S. Churchill

Detachment 101 of the Office of Strategic Services (OSS) holds the distinction of being the only OSS unit whose operations were a key component and integral to the conduct of its theater's overall campaign. In part because of its organizational adaptability and unique operational environment, perhaps more than any other unit, Detachment 101 fulfilled OSS director William J. Donovan's image of clandestine units that aided conventional operations through intelligence collection and sabotage.[1] Of the American ground forces that served in north Burma, Detachment 101 entered the field first and left it last. Along the way, Detachment 101 assisted both American ground and air units and several Chinese and British elements with intelligence or screening actions, essentially performing a role in north Burma that covered the conduct of the entire campaign. For its superb performance, the OSS itself assessed Detachment 101 as its "most effective combat tactical force."[2] The OSS went further, adding that Detachment 101 "may well come to be recognized as a model for subversive operations under the same or analogous conditions" and that the original members of Detachment 101 were pioneers "in a type of operation which may well become a classic of modern warfare."[3] Detachment 101's operations were also extremely complex. When the OSS History Office looked to write the story of Detachment 101, some of its historians "suspect[ed] the 101 history is at all odds the most complicated of the several detachments."[4] In part because it fought in the relative backwater of Burma and OSS European operations overshadowed it, Detachment 101 has been unappreciated and previously not received an academic study.

Detachment 101 was one of the first elements formed under the OSS predecessor, the Coordinator of Information (COI). The unit arrived in the China-Burma-India (CBI) Theater in mid-1942 and did not disband until mid-1945. These three years of service in one theater not only allowed Detachment 101 to master the geographical and human terrain in its operational area, but also gave it the longest period of service in any one general locale of any OSS unit. This helped the unit achieve an operational maturity unseen in other theaters.

In a classic unconventional warfare campaign, by mid-1944 Detachment 101 went through what Donovan saw as the three phases of a typical insurgency: infiltration and preparation, sabotage and subversion, and finally guerrilla support to aid conventional units.[5] However, Detachment 101's flexible nature allowed a unique fourth phase: by mid-1945 Detachment 101's guerrillas comprised the only U.S.-led ground combat element in Burma. Detachment 101's path through these phases was not easy, direct, or even intentional. However, the unit's inherent flexibility, due to the situation, lack of resources, and hands-off approach from upper-level commands, allowed Detachment 101's two commanders to mold it into an organization that reflected their personalities.

In late 1942 Lieutenant General Joseph W. Stilwell, the U.S. commander in north Burma, told Detachment 101's first commanding officer, Major Carl F. Eifler, "You have ninety days for me to hear booms from the jungle."[6] Yet, Detachment 101 had no historical operational or organizational model to follow. In addition, once it was in the Far East, Detachment 101 received almost no direction from Donovan and little other than general guidance from Stilwell. Therefore, the men of Detachment 101 had to envision what the unit was to do and then mold it into one capable of handling a myriad of missions. Eifler, bold and impetuous, forged the group into one that believed it could accomplish any task—even if it could not. He focused on high-risk ventures that had the potential to produce dramatic results.

When Detachment 101's far-reaching gambits proved unworkable, Colonel William R. Peers, the second commander, adjusted the unit's mission to that of conducting an unconventional warfare campaign revolving around aggressive intelligence collection and use of indigenous guerrillas to support a long-term north Burma campaign. Through this change in mission, Detachment 101 played a pivotal role in the North Burma Campaign. The unit was so successful that Detachment 101 received a Presidential Unit Citation, one of the few awarded to any specific OSS element, for its later role in conventional-style combat operations in Burma's Shan States. This alone reflects on Detachment 101's ability to adopt new missions.

To succeed through its developmental stages, Detachment 101 adopted an operational structure and role unique even in the unconventional OSS. From a fledgling unit of only twenty-one soldiers in 1942, the unit's guerrilla forces grew to the size equivalent of a light division. As such, Detachment 101 undertook numerous and sometimes noncomplementary missions and had to constantly add to its support elements and adapt its operational structure to meet the changing strategic situation. The structure, mission, and scope of Detachment 101 makes it, in hindsight, a forerunner of the type of operations conducted by today's Special Forces, even if the unit, or even the OSS in general, is not officially recognized in the lineage of any U.S. Army element.[7]

In more modern terms, Detachment 101 functioned much like a Special Action Force (SAF), such as the Eighth SAF in Panama and the First SAF in Okinawa in the 1960s, where capabilities such as Special Forces, civil affairs, special operations support, and psychological operations personnel were closely integrated within one unit. In this regard, Detachment 101 functioned as a combined and joint operations taskforce with its own air, naval, and ground forces, and a multinational complement, all under its control. But operating in Burma was itself complicated.

The American campaign in Burma was one of the most poorly resourced of all operational theaters in WWII and at the end of one of the longest logistics trails of the entire war. Compounded by the difficult operational environment, this meant that the few American ground combat forces that fought in north Burma, Merrill's Marauders and the MARS Task Force, were purposely formed, organized, trained, and equipped to deal with the unique challenges of combat in that theater. Burma was a British colony, and that nation had command supremacy; however, American strategy in the North Burma Campaign centered on keeping China in the war. The Japanese had occupied China's major ports since 1938. This left China with only a tenuous and lengthy overland route called the Burma Road to support its forces with American-supplied aid. With their invasion of Burma early in 1942, the Japanese managed to sever even this link.

With the Burma Road under enemy control, the United States Army Air Forces (USAAF) established airfields in Assam, India, to fly cargo aircraft via the hazardous "Hump" air-bridge through the dangerous Himalayan mountain passes to China. This endeavor was costly in terms of aircraft, cargos, and crews. As a preferred alternative, U.S. planners decided to construct a land route from India to bypass the original Burma Road. Beginning in December 1942, U.S. Army engineers undertook construction on the Ledo Road from upper Assam in India, to cut across north Burma and eventually link up with the path of the original Burma Road at Lashio, Burma. The new route would allow the United States to more efficiently supply the Chinese war effort, which in turn tied down a large part of the Japanese army that would otherwise be available to fight American troops. The North Burma Campaign centered on securing this route, and Detachment 101 played a prominent if unheralded role.

What follows is a study of the operations and organization of Detachment 101. While veterans' memoirs detail what the unit did, this is the first to describe how they accomplished their task. Detachment 101's operations were exceedingly complicated and, though centered in north Burma, involved operations in at least five countries. Therefore, this study does not cover every individual mission or facet of Detachment 101, only those most crucial to the overall story. Because the organization and function of headquarters elements occurred hundreds of miles away and in a virtual vacuum from operations, this study covers the two aspects separately. Detachment 101's constant reorganizations, attention to support elements, and means of incorporating separate OSS functions into its operational matrix were the critical link to sustaining field operations. But first, one has to understand Burma; its peoples, terrain, weather, and history that led up to American involvement there in WWII.

1

Before the Storm

This is Burma, and it will be quite unlike any land that one knows about.

Rudyard Kipling, *Letters from the East*

American soldiers fighting the Japanese in north Burma in WWII experienced the accuracy of Kipling's quote. There, they discovered a wild land about which they knew almost nothing. However, it was not as magical as Kipling made it out to be. North Burma was not a far-flung land filled with romantic adventure. It was a disease-plagued, monsoon-drenched jungle where dangerous creatures abounded. Set in the steep foothills of the Himalayas, the area of operations made for some of the most challenging and wide-ranging terrain ever fought over.

Roughly the size of Texas, Burma has much greater geographical extremes. To the south along the Indian Ocean is the capital city of Rangoon, now called Yangoon. Above Rangoon, the swampy mangrove-lined coast along the Bay of Bengal is the Arakan (now Rakhine State). North from the coast, the terrain is increasingly rugged. The humid subtropical foothills of the Himalayas—often several thousands of feet high—begin in the Kachin hill tracts just past Myitkyina, the capital of Kachin State. Rolling jungle-covered hills immediately become small steep mountains that increase in size and elevation to the north. It was in this location that Detachment 101 operated. Detachment 101 chronicled an example of the difficulty in moving over this terrain in an early 1944 report: "Tilly got lost in the high grass, had to part the grass and fall on it . . . slashed his arms and trouser legs. He then got to the top of a hill and climbed a tree. He got nearly to the crotch and got his hand caught in a bee hive . . . started off through the pit grass. He went right over the cliff 30 feet."[1]

Throughout all this terrain flow several major rivers that bisect the headlands into steep valleys. These rivers, from the west to east, are the Chindwin, the Irrawaddy, the Shweli, and the Salween. The Chindwin flows through the wild Hukawng Valley before joining the Irrawaddy. The longest and most important river in Burma is the Irrawaddy. Formed by the confluence of the N'mai and Mali rivers to the north of the Kachin capital of Myitkyina, it continues south to flow through the strategic cities of north Burma—Myitkyina, Bhamo, and Mandalay—before finally entering the Indian Ocean in a delta that includes Rangoon. Farther east is the Shweli. The major river that is farthest to the east is the Salween. Unlike the others, it is not a tributary to the Irrawaddy. The Salween flows from China, along the border with Thailand, before finally entering the Andaman Sea. Each of these rivers flows through areas inhabited by north Burma's major ethnic groups.

Internally, Burma was hardly unified then, nor is it now. The region encompasses speakers of more than a hundred languages, more than a hundred separate ethnicities, and followers of Christianity, Islam, animism, Buddhism, and Hinduism. Even today insurgencies fueled by ethnic discord plague Burma. For instance, the ongoing Karen struggle for independence started in 1949, soon after Burma's independence from the United Kingdom.[2] The ethnic groups that played the largest roles in Detachment 101 and U.S. Army operations in north Burma were the Burmans, and above all, the Kachin.

The Burmans are the largest and most dominant ethnic group. In WWII they inhabited the most populous areas in southern Burma, made up some 70 percent of Burma's total population, and were predominantly Buddhist. The history of Britain's domination of Burma revolved around this group. In the nineteenth century, British forces in India fought three wars against the Burmans. The first Anglo-Burmese War, in 1824–1826, resulted in the Burmese ceding parts of the country, including the Arakan, to British administration. The second Anglo-Burmese War, from 1852 to 1853, further strengthened the British position. The final and third Anglo-Burmese War, from 1885 to 1887, resulted in British domination and annexation of the entire country.

Although there were occasional minor revolts, until 1937, the British administered Burma relatively peacefully as part of India. However, this was an arbitrary administrative pairing as the two countries have little in common with the exception of certain border areas. Only in 1938 did the British begin governing Burma as a separate colony. The Burmans, however, never forgot their independence nor gave complete loyalty to the British crown. From their ranks sprang a fifth column that would have an active role in the

Japanese invasion and after the war. The story was different in the northern hill tracts.

Despite a reputation of being fiercely independent and ungovernable, the hill tribes of Burma proved to be the most pro-British. This stance assisted the Allies and particularly Detachment 101. There were four main reasons for Kachin loyalty. First was the decades of effort made by British civil administrators before the war. In order to help govern the area, the civil administrators allowed the hill tribes to continue their traditional forms of government, and even encouraged the people to rely on their headmen and councils.[3] Secondly, the Kachins had a militaristic tradition. The British had taken advantage of the ethnic buffer provided by the Kachins between the Burmans and the Chinese and recruited heavily among the tough warrior culture to guard the frontier.[4] Third, regional politics also played a role. Those in the hill tribes were sandwiched between much larger populations of Chinese to the north and Burmans to the south. To many in the hill tribes, the British occupation was ideal. That empire could not exert too much influence in the Kachin home areas, yet it was powerful enough to keep the Burmans and Chinese in check. Fourth, in contrast to the Buddhist south, Christianity had taken hold in the hill tracts. Although many Kachins were animists, Baptist and Catholic missionaries brought their religion into the area and developed rapport. Decades of effort put forth by missionaries paved the way for cooperation. American missionaries had adapted the spoken language, Jinghpaw, into written form. The goodwill of the American missionaries had impressed the Kachins and assisted cooperation with Detachment 101 when it arrived in 1942.[5]

Although other ethnic groups such as the Nagas, Palaungs, and Shans were present in north Burma, by far the most important ethnic group to the Allies was the Kachin. Also known as Jinghpaw, "Kachin" is an umbrella term describing several ethic groups in north Burma and parts of neighboring China. In the Kachin, Detachment 101 had the fortune of finding a warlike and willing ally. The Kachin were far more primitive than the Burmans to the south. They lived in small villages composed of wood and bamboo shacks, or *bashas*. Near and in these villages the Kachin grew their staple crops of rice, beans, and corn, and raised chickens and pigs. The Kachin were also masters of junglecraft, giving them what seemed to the Americans as an almost superhuman power to read the jungle.[6] Having grown up in a severe environment, they did not have great requirements, and they produced what little they needed, including gunpowder. The Kachin possessed incredible stamina and had an effortless capability to walk long distances over steep terrain while carrying heavy loads. The Kachin also knew the area's numerous unmapped trails, and could easily bypass well-traveled roads. With these skills, the Kachin appeared and disappeared from the jungle at ease, proving to be a dangerous foe to the Japanese.

The Kachin were simply ideal guerrilla fighters. According to a 1943 OSS report, "a Kachin with a 'dah' [traditional knife] can be comparable to a whole panzer division in his own country."[7] Many of the Kachins had developed hunting skills from an early age. The Kachins did not fight fair as a Westerner would understand it; however, that was perfectly fine for Detachment 101. For instance, it was not an acceptable fighting practice to the Kachins to hold ground. Rather, hit-and-run ambushes were the norm.

Detachment 101 adapted well to this style of warfare. In a typical ambush, a Detachment 101 group would stake out a position along a road or trail and wait. When an enemy column arrived, a prearranged signal triggered the group to fire. At times, the burst was only long enough to make it through one magazine, or just enough time to throw a few grenades. There was no point in conserving ammunition, as the 101 group did not intend to make a stand, and could always be resupplied by air. Meanwhile, the Japanese often reacted by jumping to cover on the sides of the road or trail. Here they encountered another weapon in Detachment 101's arsenal, the *punji*, which doubled as an outstanding psychological weapon. With the Japanese then reeling in confusion, the guerrillas melted back into the jungle. At this point, as one postwar depiction noted, "nobody covered anybody" as until they reached a prearranged rendezvous, it was "every man for himself."[8] But why Detachment 101 had to fight in Burma deserves explanation.

The Fall of Burma

In addition to the native ethnic groups, Burma was a land of immigrants. Before the war, many Indians and Chinese saw Burma as a frontier for poor workers and entrepreneurs alike to make their fortunes. The immigrants flooded the country, and some created virtual monopolies among arenas of business, in which they would only hire their own. Resentment grew as the immigrants left the Burmans out of the potential economic gains and resultant jobs. By the time that the Japanese attacked in mid-January 1942 internal strife in the south had reached a high point.

At that time, the mood in British Burma was tense. The Japanese invasion came on the heels of a string of British defeats in Hong Kong, Malaya, and

Singapore. The Japanese also forced Thailand into an uneasy alliance and occupied that country.[9] Burma, the gateway to India, was next. When the invasion came, the British did not just lose in Burma. They suffered utter defeat. It was a blow from which London would not recover even after the war, and it sowed the seed for Burma's independence.[10]

The Japanese cut across the Kra isthmus before venturing to Rangoon, with British and Commonwealth forces powerless to stop the advance. Eager to protect their "back door" and lifeline, Chinese forces entered the fray. In all, nine divisions crossed into Burma to protect the one supply route that China had left, the Burma Road. A small U.S. group under Lieutenant General Joseph W. Stilwell arrived to assist, but like the Chinese, it was too late. He arrived just in time to retreat weeks later.[11]

Stilwell led his small group on foot across the hills to India, arriving on 15 May 1942. Furiously, he said, "I claim we got a hell of a beating. We got run out of Burma and it is humiliating as hell. I think we ought to find out what caused it, go back and retake it."[12] However, at the moment, Stilwell had little with which to accomplish this task. His main combat elements were portions of four Chinese divisions that had escaped to India. There, the United States retrained and reformed the Chinese as the X-Force. It provided the bulk of forces under American command in the north Burma campaign. The other Chinese troops retreated back into China proper. Commonwealth military units, although battered, had the discipline and support to more or less make it to India with a semblance of order.

That was not true of Burma's recent immigrant civilian population. Chaos ensued once the reality of a Japanese takeover was apparent to the civilian population. Thousands of non-Burmese refugees tried to make it to safety in India or China. They feared that they would not fare well under the Japanese. Perhaps the hardest hit were the Indians and the Anglo-Indian/Anglo-Burmese. At first, they tried to seek passage by sea. However, once Rangoon fell, the refugees had an even greater struggle to make it out.

The Chinese had it easiest. They ventured north up the Irrawaddy to Myitkyina, where they found transport to China. The Europeans, Indians, Anglo-Indians, and Anglo-Burmans were not so lucky. Despite Burma having long been administered as a part of India, no roads linked the two countries, only rudimentary trails. At first, the journey to India was easy. But soon, roads gave way to paths, forcing those lucky enough to have motor transportation to abandon their automobiles. Then, the rugged mountain passes turned into trails where villages—which offered rest, food, and shelter—were few and far between. Many of the refugees fled through north

Burma, up through the Hukawng Valley and through the steep mountain passes of the Naga hills to safety in Assam. Along the way, however, constant monsoon rains turned the jungle trails into quagmires. Lack of infrastructure, poor sanitation, and eventual disease and starvation led to thousands perishing along the trailside. It was one of the largest humanitarian plights of the era, but has long since been forgotten. As Christopher Bayly and Tim Harper describe in their excellent *Forgotten Armies: The Fall of British Asia, 1941–1945*, "By the autumn of 1942 in the region of 600,000 people had fled from Burma into India by land and sea. Of these, as many as 80,000 may have perished of disease, exhaustion, or malnutrition."[13]

Although difficult, the terrain created a respite. As one American OSS officer later noted, the Japanese were so exhausted by the time they reached the mountain passes into India and so short of supplies that "their mad gallop across Thailand and the flat-lands of southern and central Burma slowed down to little more than a blind stagger at the India-Burma border."[14] Even two years later, American soldiers often came upon the bleached bones of the unfortunate who had not made it into India. It was a grisly greeting to Americans new to a strange land about which most knew nothing. The debacle of the so-called First Burma Campaign provided a preamble that Allied troops would soon come to know; Burma was one of the most debilitating environments in the Second World War for military operations because of the climate, terrain, and endemic diseases.

In this tropical country, temperatures in central Burma exceed 100 degrees Fahrenheit from March through May. From June to September, the monsoon season takes hold with the constant moisture leading to rot, decay, and rust of most equipment. Eifler reported to OSS Washington in June 1943, "A cleaned pistol will develop rust pits in 24 hours, a pair of shoes not cleaned daily will rot in a week."[15] Leeches, mosquitoes, and accompanying diseases—such as malaria, typhus, and encephalitis—prevailed. In his memoir, *Defeat into Victory*, Field Marshall William J. Slim, commander of the British Fourteenth Army, discussed his force's encounters with disease:

> In 1943, for every man evacuated with wounds we had one hundred and twenty four evacuated sick. The annual malaria rate alone was eighty-four per cent annum of the total strength of the army and still higher for the forward troops. . . . At this time, the sick rate of men evacuated from their units rose to twelve thousand per day. A simple calculation showed me that in a matter of months at this rate my army would have melted away.[16]

Americans faced a similar situation in north Burma. In 1943, the rate of malaria in the CBI was 206 cases per 1,000 men per year. After much effort to combat the disease, by 1944 it had only dropped to 167 cases per 1,000 men per year. In special circumstances, the rate could become even higher. Merrill's Marauders, for instance, suffered appalling rates of dysentery, malaria, and scrub typhus during their campaign to seize Myitkyina. By 4 June 1944, out of a force of approximately 3,000 men, they had suffered 1,020 casualties from disease in contrast to 424 reported killed, wounded, or missing.[17]

In just his first month operating in enemy occupied territory, OSS Detachment 101 medical officer Lieutenant Commander James C. Luce reported treating among the local population 103 cases of malaria, 10 of dysentery, 2 of tuberculosis, 100 of scabies, 4 of ringworm, 30 of tropical ulcers, and 27 of gonorrhea, in addition to numerous other ailments.[18] And as another Detachment 101 officer discovered later, the jungle had additional dangers. After describing some of the venomous vipers, Elton Archer said:

> Other varmints also inhabited the jungle floors; the most obnoxious ones were the elephant leeches, which attached themselves to a twig or branch in the path and elongated their bodies and tentacles; sensing the warmth of any human being who passed by, they could slither into an incredibly small space without being detected by their victim, and could attach themselves, even injecting an anesthetic fluid which kept their prey from knowing they were there. In order to get them off, when a person reached the end of a day's march, he had to rub them with salt or touch the lighted end of a cigarette to them. If they were just pulled off, they left the proboscis in the victim and it would continue to fester and cause infection.[19]

It was to this environment that the members of OSS Detachment 101 had to adjust, and even to thrive in it if they were to become successful in their operations in enemy-occupied territory. It was their job to further U.S. policy in regards to China.

With China now under complete blockage, the United States looked for a way to open up a corridor from which to supply their ally. With no overland route remaining, they did so by air. Aircraft flying the treacherous "Hump" route took off from airbases in India, flew over the Himalayas, and landed in China. Although the crews were incredibly brave and daring, the effort was wasteful, in terms of both aircraft and supplies. A second option had more merit.

From Ledo, India, a group of U.S. Army engineers began constructing an all-weather road over incredibly difficult terrain over which Detachment 101 estimated that it took a man thirty days to walk the same distance that a light plane could fly in one hour.[20] Dubbed the "Ledo Road," it was planned to link up with the original Burma Road below Myitkyina, and from there, to China. The trace of this new road, however, was in enemy hands. It was the task of the north Burma campaign to secure it, and Detachment 101 would spearhead the effort.

2

Laying the Groundwork: 1941–January 1943

My observation is that the more the battle machines are perfected the greater the need in modern warfare of men calculatingly reckless with disciplined daring, who are trained for aggressive action . . . it will mean a return to our old tradition of the scouts, the raiders, and the rangers.

William J. Donovan to President Franklin D. Roosevelt

We are something new and definitely unproven in American methods of fighting.[1]

Carl F. Eifler to William J. Donovan

Prior to WWII, the United States had several intelligence organizations, but their efforts were not complementary and focused on the immediate needs of their branch service. Some politicians and military leaders realized that such an arrangement was not adequate if America was drawn into what was rapidly becoming a worldwide conflict. To help remedy this, on 11 July 1941, President Franklin D. Roosevelt appointed World War I hero and Medal of Honor recipient William J. Donovan as the chief of the Coordinator of Information (COI).[2] The COI, renamed one year later as the Office of Strategic Services (OSS), was the first U.S. government entity organized specifically to collect, analyze, and disseminate foreign intelligence. It reported directly to the president.[3] The COI also had the secondary mission of preparing to engage in the subversive, or "black," activities of clandestine warfare. It is this role for which the COI, and later the OSS, is best known. Popular histories have often focused on the OSS from mid-1944 forward, and mythologized this secondary role of special operations.[4] This has led to the OSS being very misunderstood today. The role of clandestine warfare did not come easily for the COI and later the OSS, and the organization experienced tremendous growing pains in 1942–1943. Although the fledgling organization made remarkable strides in a very short time, inexperience often led to dramatic catastrophes, and strained inter-Allied politics hampered effectiveness. Detachment 101 in Burma was no different, and the road to the creation of this capability in the COI was not immediate.[5]

Donovan advocated for a new intelligence organization to better serve the decision-making process of policy makers.[6] He was assisted in these beliefs by his friend Secretary of the Navy William F. Knox. Knox suggested to Roosevelt that Donovan make an unofficial trip to England to evaluate the war situation and the British intelligence services.[7] During his December to 18 March 1941 trip, the British gave Donovan unprecedented access to their bases, including those in Africa. Donovan was able to evaluate firsthand what the OSS later considered its counterpart and mentor organization, the British Special Operations Executive (SOE).[8]

Donovan had an intense personal interest in clandestine warfare and extensively studied SOE's sabotage role. He saw such warfare as an important method to support intelligence gathering to enhance the combat capability of conventional military formations. The future OSS director envisioned that an American special operations element would function in three escalating stages: infiltration and preparation, sabotage and subversion, and finally, direct support to guerrilla, resistance, or commando units. Much in the model of the British commandos, special operations had the added benefit of performing what an OSS-produced history termed "increasing the enemy's misery and weaken his will to resist."[9] After returning from Europe, Donovan wrote to President Roosevelt, "My observation is that the more the battle machines are perfected the greater the need in modern warfare of men calculatingly reckless with disciplined daring, who are trained for aggressive action . . . it will mean a return to our old tradition of the scouts, the raiders, and the rangers."[10]

When Roosevelt appointed Donovan head of the COI, he tacitly gave him the mission to prepare for the possibility of using covert warfare methods. But Donovan could do little in the way of recruiting. After the attack on Pearl Harbor, Donovan again called for the formation of an American special operations force and wrote to Roosevelt on 22 December 1941 that "as an essential part of the strategic plan, there be recognized the need of sowing the dragon's teeth in those territories from which we withdraw. . . . That the aid of native chiefs be obtained, the loyalty of the inhabitants cultivated . . . and guerrilla bands of bold, and daring men organized and installed."[11] With the United States then at war, he could recruit men for special operations, but getting those COI elements deployed for overseas missions was a greater challenge.

In order to prove the value of clandestine warfare, Donovan sought to insert the COI into an active combat theater, but was met with much skepticism. Many senior U.S. Army officers in particular could not understand what role the independent and civilian COI, and later the OSS, could play in their areas of responsibility. They were outright hostile to a clandestine presence. For instance, General Douglas A. MacArthur virtually banned the OSS from his South West Pacific Theater throughout the war.[12] However, Donovan found openings in other theaters, such as the North Africa Theater of Operations. The early COI/OSS operations there opened the way for greater participation throughout the European Campaign. The American effort in Asia, with its lack of resourcing and the desperate need to help the Chinese stay in the war, also held promise for the successful use of clandestine warfare. This was particularly true of Burma.

Creating the Detachment Out of an Undefined Problem

Detachment 101 was one of two special operations units created under the COI, and the only one that served in the same location for the entire war. The "father" of Detachment 101 was Lieutenant Colonel Preston Goodfellow.[13] Then a U.S. Army G-2 liaison officer detailed to the COI, Goodfellow was also the head of Special Activities, Goodfellow (SA/G). Donovan tasked SA/G with organizing and executing "morale and physical subversion, including sabotage, fifth column activities and guerrilla warfare."[14] It was from SA/G, renamed under OSS as the Special Operations Branch, from which the OSS Operational Groups (OG), Maritime Unit (MU), and the Research and Development Branch (R&D) originated. Under Lieutenant Colonel Goodfellow's leadership sprang "Scheme OLIVIA."

Dated 27 January 1942, just weeks after Pearl Harbor, OLIVIA gave the basic outline for Detachment 101. Although the plan did not call for operations in Burma, whose fate was still in doubt, it detailed sabotage operations against "enemy establishments, public utilities and high Axis commanders in the occupied areas."[15] The plan itself had the attention of Donovan. Goodfellow recalled years later that Donovan had "gotten a cold shoulder from the military services" for the types of missions that he wanted the COI to perform and "never did I see Donovan so low in spirits." Goodfellow relented, even though he was going to await "formal acceptance by General Stilwell." Goodfellow told Donovan that Stilwell had shown some interest for a COI group in the China-Burma-India Theater. Donovan was excited. He "insisted that I come in his house for further discussion of the new development. After a glass of sherry and an hour's talk I went home. He phoned me three times that night, the last at 3:00 AM." Once again, Goodfellow was on his way to Donovan's house to discuss Burma further. With that, OLIVIA became a primary project for the COI.[16] After Goodfellow had a discussion with Stilwell, the man chosen to head OLIVIA was Captain Carl F. Eifler.

Captain Eifler, a Pearl Harbor veteran, then commanded a makeshift prison for Japanese civilians in Hawaii. A bear of a man who was later to become a legend in the OSS, Eifler was extremely intelligent, a hard drinker, and a brash, no-nonsense type who overcame obstacles by sheer will and determination. He did not care how the mission was done—or who got the credit—as long as it was successfully accomplished.[17] Eifler had joined the Army in 1921 at the age of fifteen, only to be kicked out eighteen months later when the service discovered his real age. He then became a policeman in Los Angeles for a short while. Just prior to the war, Eifler was an army reservist while serving in the U.S. Treasury Customs Service, where he busted smuggling rings. This experience schooled him in the unorthodox methods of criminals and smugglers. In the Army Reserve he had also met General Stilwell.[18] Eifler accepted the assignment, and made his way to COI headquarters in Washington, D.C.[19]

Activated on 22 April 1942, Detachment 101 was the first special operations unit formed by the COI.[20] This early activation date also makes it one of the earliest American special operations units formed in WWII, predating the First Ranger Battalion and the First Special Service Force. The COI gave Eifler the authority to select a small group of men for overseas service somewhere in the Far East. From a March 1942 conversation with Goodfellow, Eifler understood his area of responsibility (AOR) to be anywhere in China, Korea, Burma, Malay States, Indo-China, Hainan Island, and Japan itself. According to the original OLIVIA, he was to locate his unit near Chungking, China. "I was given a quarter of the world and told to organize it," Eifler later recalled.[21] In addition to planning operations to cover this great swath, Eifler also had to come up with his own operations plan. For the time, Eifler's plans were extremely complex and forward thinking though relatively simple in principle. He was laying the groundwork for a completely new type of paramilitary unit that had no precedent in United States military history. Eifler planned to use

> (1) a small group of officers . . . to contact groups in the War Zone and purchase acts of sabotage. (2) To organize and train an organization to penetrate enemy-held territory and conduct a campaign of directed sabotage to harass the enemy. . . . This organization must be divided into two parts: (1) a section to train agents, (2), an Operations Section. . . . The undersigned intends to . . . contact the Government officials necessary, locate patriotic organizations who have members inside enemy lines, sell myself to the people I intend to use and train them as agents and smugglers. . . . Lines of communication will be developed. The undersigned not only plans to use existing radio equipment but will attempt to develop a new, small set that will better suit the problem as I now visualize it.[22]

Given his set of operating parameters, Eifler had to choose personnel with no clue as to the exact nature or location of his eventual mission. He selected what men he could find who had the necessary language, cultural, or technical skills that would encompass the operating location or methods in which he had the possibility of working. Because the group was so small, each man had to fulfill multiple and often noncomplementary duties. For example, Sergeant Sukyoon Chang served as mess sergeant, an instructor, and liaison to any Korean resistance movements.[23]

Given Eifler's operating plans to employ smuggling methods to insert groups behind the lines, use radios to stay in contact, and support any type of clandestine mission that the group might encounter, he chose personnel with the skills to cover all these requirements. Eifler's experience with smuggling methods came in handy, and he used the contacts gained during his years in the Customs Service to handpick a few men experienced in that field. With regard to recruiting communications personnel, however, he had to rely upon the judgment of others.

Radioman Allen R. Richter was brought into Detachment 101 when Eifler and his deputy, Lieutenant Colonel John G. Coughlin (who outranked Eifler at the time, but such was the COI and later, the OSS) visited the Officer Candidate School (OCS) at Fort Monmouth, New Jersey. The officers asked Richter, who had an extensive background in radios, if he would like to drop out of OCS and join the outfit as an enlisted man for a secret mission. Eifler explained the mission as possibly being in the Far East. He further emphasized that the mission was so dangerous that Richter was almost guaranteed that he would not return home alive. Richter accepted and three days later was on a train to COI headquarters at "Q" building, Washington, D.C.[24] Others, such as William "Ray" Peers, the future Detachment 101 commander, had a far different experience.

Peers did not know Eifler, but was brought in because he knew Coughlin. Peers first met Eifler during his initial interview at COI headquarters. After he "proceeded to crack every joint" in shaking Peers' hand, Eifler then "took a stiletto-type dagger and drove it a good two or three inches into the top of his desk." After a quick briefing, Peers was hooked. He said, "I later took John aside and told him how good it was to be a part of 101."[25]

All told, the original contingent of what the COI termed the "Eifler Mission" consisted of twenty-one officers and enlisted men. At this early stage, the COI had not yet developed the branch structures that would be present in the OSS later in the war. Working within this understanding, however, one can extrapolate the branches represented in the initial contingent by examining the duties for which each man was responsible. One each was involved in administration, photography, medical, research and development, secret intelligence, and special funds; two were in supply; three were in training; and five personnel each were assigned to communications and special operations. Again, each of these men performed a multitude of tasks. Their duties represent the first melding of future specific OSS functions in Detachment 101; however, that these men were in reality all from what would become the SO Branch is significant. This established from the beginning that regardless of a man's branch and training, he performed the duties deemed of the greatest need. The precedent carried through for the remainder of the war.[26]

Detachment 101's blending of roles was not ordinary practice in the OSS. Observers sent from Washington frequently commented on this unique aspect of Detachment 101, such as this example in early 1944: "It is apparent that in all this description reference to SI [Secret Intelligence], SO, OG, etc., is absent. Such branch divisions simply do not occur in the thinking of this unit. There is work to be done, there is a staff to do it, and all are working as OSS/DET. 101 men, doing whatever aspect of the job is feasible, appropriate, and important at the moment."[27] Regardless of the source of the men assigned to Detachment 101, they still had to be trained in COI methods; that, at the time, was a difficult proposition.

Because the country was early in the process of mobilization, in addition to the United States not having a special operations capability, finding instruction in such methods was a problem not faced by later OSS recruits. As the OSS SO history later related, "the so-called guerrillas had no directive; their training had to be done on a purely theoretical basis."[28] The COI gave Eifler's group but a brief training period. Half went to the newly appropriated former Civilian Conservation Corps camp turned sabotage school of Area B, adjacent to what is now Camp David, Maryland, while others went to Camp X, the SOE training area in Canada.[29] The COI men took abbreviated courses on rudimentary sabotage, explosives, hand-to-hand, and firearms. The training was not definitive, but it was all that was available, and, given the rapidity that the COI wanted to get Detachment 101 into action, it was all that was possible.

If the lack of detailed training was not enough, the men of Detachment 101 had little idea about what they were to accomplish. Years later, Peers wrote of that uncertainty:

> A great deal of concern was the fact that being the first American unit of its kind we had no precedent or experience upon which to organize, train and administer such a unit. We had no visualization as to what our base camp should look like. We didn't know how big it should be, what kind of transportation we should have, how we should store our supplies and so on. It was quite obvious that we were neophytes in this business.[30]

In a harried few weeks, the men did the best that they could to gather supplies and prepare them for shipment to the Far East. Detachment 101 was off to war in the Far East.

An advance contingent consisting of Eifler and Master Sergeant Vincent Curl made its way to India by air. The other nineteen men and the supplies left by ship. They had a long voyage ahead of them. The added time gave them some chance to read and study what they could about the Far East. But even then their direction was vague. As Eifler and his group made their way abroad, they had little idea how—or even where—they would operate. Their initial instructions from COI were hazy at best and their operating area ill defined. Not only was Detachment 101's very existence on the line, but so was the reputation of the OSS as a whole. It was only Eifler's sheer will, the group's sense of purpose, and their intense desire to get into action against the Japanese that bonded the group into a cohesive unit.[31]

Deconfliction

Once Detachment 101 arrived in India, Eifler found out that most of what COI Washington had told him was wrong. COI Washington had made almost no arrangements in the CBI for the group. No one in the theater knew of Eifler's mission or had even heard of the COI. Eifler even had difficulty in securing such basics as transportation. At every turn, Eifler found U.S. Army organizations that wanted to absorb Detachment 101—just for the personnel the group represented—but did not want to support the COI unit's mission.[32] Peers wrote later that "it required some mighty shifty tactics on the part of Major Eifler to avoid having us plucked off one by one."[33] To compound the matter, many army officers they met were opposed to Detachment 101's mission. The army officers could not understand that Eifler's men, although military, belonged to a civilian organization, and as such, were paramilitary. Eifler wrote back to OSS Washington that "by most of the old hard bitten regulars, we are not part of the Army, and never will be. We are not regulation and therefore a pain in the neck."[34]

Eifler quickly discovered that he needed an experienced staff or liaison officer to find Detachment 101 a mission in the CBI. One was not available, so Eifler filled the role. OSS headquarters in Washington was of no help and gave very little guidance. This was in part due to the difficulties in communication between India/China and Washington, but Donovan's poor administrative skills did nothing to help the effort.[35] Not only did Eifler have to win over reluctant officers—both U.S. and Allied—but he had to explain to them the unproven subversive warfare mission of the COI. Eifler succeeded admirably in large part due to his insistence to press forward and to accept what missions he could wrangle for his new command so long as they conformed in some way to the COI plan of action.

Eifler met with the CBI commander, Lieutenant General Stilwell. Eifler was under the impression that Stilwell had sent for him by name, having picked him to lead Detachment 101. The instructions given to Eifler by Goodfellow on 20 May 1942 enhanced this impression. They stated that Detachment 101 was "to carry on in the Theater of Operations with the knowledge and consent of General Stilwell."[36] But the instructions were wrong. Stilwell had not called for Eifler, nor did he want him or Detachment 101. Stilwell relayed that he had been asked by COI representatives—who were trying to find any overseas posting for a special operations unit—whom he wanted to lead such a group. Stilwell named Eifler. What Eifler did not know, and what COI headquarters took for granted, perhaps with an added bit of subterfuge, was that Stilwell had responded in the theoretical. He had meant by his reply that *if* the COI sent a group to his AOR then he wanted Eifler, not *that* he actually wanted such a group. This seemingly minor detail, which in reality could have stopped Detachment 101 and its mission cold, has been missed in numerous histories of the OSS.

Despite this misunderstanding, Stilwell remained more receptive to a COI/OSS presence than other theater commanders. He had few other options. The CBI was so resource-starved that Stilwell only commanded a smattering of American aviation units and some poorly led and equipped Chinese troops called the Chih Hui Pu, or Chinese Army in India. It was composed of the reformed 11,000–12,000-man Thirty-eighth and Twenty-second Chinese Divisions and the American-equipped Chinese First Provisional Tank Group.[37] The Thirty-eighth and Twenty-second had been part of the troops supplied by Chiang Kai-shek to help fight the original Japanese invasion of Burma but were forced to retreat into India. There, the United States reorganized, rearmed, and trained the two divisions at the Ramgarh Training Center. Although under Stilwell's command, the Chinese troops were still beholden to the Generalissimo. The result was that Chinese officers often ignored Stilwell's direct orders unless approved by Chiang Kai-shek. This resulted in much frustration on Stilwell's part as well as that of the British, who already regarded the Chinese as untrustworthy. It also made Stilwell understand that he would have to lean heavily upon any American and British forces that might come under his command. Additionally, the only Allied intelligence unit in Burma was the ad hoc British-led V-Force in north Burma.[38] Stilwell needed to decide where Detachment 101 would operate and first sent Eifler to China.

Eifler made fruitless and frustrating inquiries with the Chinese authorities, leading Stilwell to determine that Eifler's group would not operate in that country.[39] The general recognized that Chinese leader Generalissimo Chiang Kai-shek would not allow an autonomous, secret paramilitary unit in his territory. Instead, Stilwell gave orders for Eifler to operate from India into Burma. At first, Stilwell was unclear where he wanted the unit to concentrate its operations. He told Eifler that his unit could do the most good by disrupting Japanese shipping in Rangoon. However, this mission was soon cast aside when it proved impracticable, and it was in north Burma that Detachment 101 began its first operations. According to Eifler, Stilwell said that all he wanted to hear were "booms" coming out of the jungle. Although not reflected in the official record—likely, because the order was verbal—Eifler detailed in his memoir that Detachment 101 had ninety days to make these "booms" happen.[40]

Stilwell's main concern in the CBI was keeping the Hump route open. Japanese fighter planes based at the Myitkyina airfield hampered the flights of the heavily laden unarmed cargo aircraft. This forced American aircraft to fly a longer route at the cost of greater gas consumption and reduced cargo.[41] Stilwell therefore directed Eifler to cut the Japanese lines of communication around Myitkyina to render the airfield ineffective. The mission also had a Machiavellian secondary objective. Such missions might bring about Japanese reprisals on the indigenous population, thereby serving as a brutal form of propaganda that could only help the Allied cause and help dissuade the indigenous population from working with the Japanese.[42]

Eifler also sought to clarify his chain of command with Stilwell. They agreed that Detachment 101 would remain a COI/OSS unit that would serve under the tactical control of Stilwell's headquarters. Initially, Stilwell gave specific directions to Detachment 101. But as the unit entrenched itself in Burma, Stilwell began assigning just strategic objectives and allowed Detachment 101's commanders to figure out the best way to carry out them out. By July 1943, Eifler commented to OSS Washington that Stilwell gave him a "complete hand as far as our unit is concerned. We are practically a little Army on our own. We issue our own orders and, as far as possible, keep care of our own administration."[43] Future commander Peers clarified the situation:

> On the one hand I was assigned to OSS and worked for General Donovan, while on the other, I received orders directly from General Stilwell. We had quite a lengthy exchange of wires with General Donovan on this subject. I pointed out to him that General Stilwell did not want the Washington OSS branches to issue instructions to their corresponding branches in 101; that all instructions must come to me as the Command Officer of 101 and that I, in turn, would issue the necessary guidance to the 101 branch. To facilitate this arrangement we further suggested that a 101 Liaison office be established in Washington to receive all our incoming communications, serve as a processing office for all outgoing communications, and coordinate with other 101 interests in Washington. General Donovan agreed with this recommendation and it was put into effect immediately; we never experienced any other difficulty of this nature. Of all the command arrangements that made Detachment 101 into the highly effective unit that it was, this dual command stands out as the most significant. It was the understanding of both General Donovan and General Stilwell that made it possible.[44]

Technically, Eifler did not have to directly report to anyone in the CBI outside of the COI/OSS command chain, as long as he maintained liaison with Stilwell's command, which would later become the Northern Combat Area Command (NCAC) in Burma. In practice, Detachment 101 served at the behest of Stilwell, but he gave only strategic direction to the Detachment. OSS Washington also continued its benign neglect. It let Detachment 101 run itself with little interference, with only the instructions that "no important operations will be carried out without prior approval" and that the unit was "to operate entirely on your own organizational equipment."[45] Essentially, Detachment 101 was on its own, an arrangement that initially proved confusing, but in practice worked remarkably well. Inter-theater COI and later OSS command channels were a more difficult obstacle.[46]

A joint COI and U.S. Navy effort, formalized in April 1943 as the Sino-American Cooperative Organization (SACO), operated in China under the leadership of Commander Milton "Mary" Miles. Because Miles outranked Eifler, then a major, the military protocol was that Eifler would report through, and be under the direction of, Miles. However, Detachment 101 was the first unit of its type, and the COI did not have much of an overseas presence. Eifler had no precedent to follow, and despite repeated pleas for clarification, COI Washington never informed Eifler whom he was to report to. Miles was also unsure, but eventually solved the bureaucratic issue by telling Eifler that he was far too busy handling Chinese liaison to also handle liaison with the British. Because Burma was in the British sphere of influence, extensive coordination with them was a necessity. Miles therefore gave Eifler—subject to contrary orders from COI/OSS headquarters—operational control of the Burma AOR, and directed him to report through the arrangement worked out with Stilwell. Stilwell responded to Miles, "OK with me. We'll say that Eifler is your man on D.S. [Detached Service] with me—Now if they'll just let us alone, We'll go to work."[47] However, this informal arrangement was not immediately codified.[48] Still, this meant that with few exceptions from the American military/COI/OSS chain of command, Detachment 101 had a free hand in the running its operations and reporting requirements.[49]

OSS and SOE

In spite of the American command arrangement, Eifler still faced failure if the British did not agree to the type of operations he had planned. The British viewed the COI/OSS and Detachment 101 with mixed emotions. On one hand, the Detachment, if successful, could offer more teeth to the minor U.S. effort in north Burma. Stilwell wanted to keep the Chinese in the war and had expended the majority of his effort on running the Hump route. The British saw this as largely a waste of effort and did not share Stilwell's assessment that the Chinese, if led well, could provide valuable and disciplined combat forces.[50] But with the British Empire assailed on all fronts, London could ill afford to spend much in the way of men or materials to retake Burma. Therefore, the prospect of having American help, even if it was a secret paramilitary unit, was a temping one. The British possibly had a secondary motive; the chance of getting increased U.S. assistance. The British were extremely underresourced and sought out U.S. assistance, especially with transport aircraft and logistics. Helping the COI and later OSS might lead to additional U.S. aid.

On the other hand, the British viewed American efforts with suspicion. A large American presence in the former British colony, especially a clandestine special operations group, could undermine Great Britain's status as a colonial power. The Americans had nothing in the way of overseas territories as compared to Great Britain's colonial empire. The United States had the Philippines, but even this possession had been on its way to independence before the Japanese invasion. Many Americans were ideologically opposed to imperialism, a sentiment of which the British were aware. A second issue was of no less importance: an American clandestine effort might not be under direct British control. From the British perspective, American-armed and -trained indigenous guerrillas posed a potential threat to postwar British rule.[51]

Soon after his arrival in India on 20 June 1942, Eifler met with Colin Mackenzie, the commander of SOE in India. Fortunately for Eifler, the meeting was positive and the two agreed to a division of responsibilities. They agreed that as the senior intelligence organization in theater, SOE had first choice in the recruitment of suitable personnel.[52] Mackenzie assigned Major Wally Richmond as the SOE liaison officer to Detachment 101 to ensure the two organizations coordinated their efforts.[53] Both OSS Washington and Stilwell's headquarters eventually concurred on Mackenzie and Eifler's agreement.[54] Indeed, SOE's support proved critical to getting Detachment 101 operational.

The issue of Detachment 101's relationship with the British was not solved at this meeting, and it later came to be a subject of issue in late 1943.[55] By then, Detachment 101 had already conducted independent operations, and both the OSS and Stilwell opposed placing Detachment 101 under British control. Stilwell made it known that if the British insisted, he would discontinue support and ask that Detachment 101 be removed from theater.[56] The threats worked, and coordination was formalized in 1944 through the establishment of P Division, chaired by Lord Louis Mountbatten of South East Asia Command (SEAC). It functioned as a board that discussed Anglo-American intelligence/clandestine operations. In these meetings, deconfliction of OSS and SOE operations was the goal, as well as liaison to inform each party of the other's actions. Although Detachment 101 had assigned British and Commonwealth personnel throughout the war, the organization was always in complete control of its operations.[57]

Finding a Location

Unhindered by higher command influence, Eifler set out to find a base of operations. Detachment 101 needed an isolated location that was near a railroad and river, near the Burma border, but also relatively near a U.S. Army supply depot.[58] Following a tip from the British, and with concurrence from Stilwell's headquarters, he located a secluded location on the grounds of the Assam Tea Estate near Nazira.[59] Detachment 101, then covertly called the U.S. Army Experimental Station with the cover story that it was doing research on malaria, and the tea plantation owners worked out a lease agreement that allowed the Detachment the use of the extensive geographic expanse of the plantation, including the bungalows, and the nearby virgin jungles—in all dozens of square miles. The tea plantation's extensive area was necessary to allow the Detachment to train agent groups independently of others. Compartmentalization was necessary so that agents would not be able to recognize their colleagues if captured; no matter how excruciating the torture, they would be unable to give away any information on other than their immediate group. The Detachment may have drawn this lesson from a Japanese attempt to land saboteurs on the west coast of India. These groups were quickly located and destroyed because they trained as one complete unit, and once one agent was broken, he gave information on all the others.[60]

Another benefit to the tea plantation was its relative isolation.[61] While problematic for liaison with Stilwell's headquarters—nearly 1,000 miles away—it was very close to the eventual operating area. Seclusion also meant that the Detachment could go about its business without a great deal of interference from other military units. The tea plantation offered a large number of servants who could work as cooks, guards, housecleaners, or other help.

Hiring them was necessary, for not to do so would have raised suspicion. But the added benefit was that unburdened by the distraction of daily chores, the elite personnel of Detachment 101 could focus on establishing a school, developing communications, and figuring out how to pay for their clandestine war.

Detachment 101 Sets Up the Jungle School

As it arrived in India, the Detachment needed to learn the operating environment in Burma. Studies compiled by people familiar with the region helped, such as one by noted Burma specialist F. Kingdon Ward in September 1942.[62] Prior to leaving the United States, the group had "purchased all varieties of books to build up a library and talked to anyone who knew anything about the geography and people of the Orient."[63]

The next order of business on the Detachment's priority list was to start a school to train agents. By 8 October 1942, fifteen students, several of them being trained for service in SOE, were under instruction, with the core classes being radio operations, codes and ciphers, signal plans, security, unarmed combat, weapons, demolitions, and junglecraft.[64] From there, the numbers and effort greatly expanded so that by November 1942 there were five separate camps.[65] To ensure confidentiality, agent trainees were given noms de guerre, such as "Skittles," "Robby," "Goldie," or "Parry."[66] Within months, Eifler told OSS Washington that he had fully trained agent groups ready for operations.[67] The instruction at these camps was understandably brief, however, and Eifler had limited manpower to devote to the groups. He assigned three of his men as permanent instructors, while others filled in as required. One of his first requests for additional personnel from OSS Washington was for instructors.[68]

Yet, there was still concern. Despite cooperation with SOE, other liaison obstacles remained, most notably with British and Indian authorities in the Nazira area. Mimicking COI training stateside, part of Detachment 101's training program was to send the students out on extended exercises where they would recommend ways to infiltrate or destroy Allied installations. These forays familiarized students with the intelligence-gathering process, tested their ingenuity, and let the Detachment see how the agents handled themselves under pressure if caught, as inevitably some were.[69] This happened to what would become W group, whose members British officers questioned after apprehending the group. Because the agents were unable to produce any identity documents, local authorities placed them under arrest.[70] The British authorities had a strong suspicion that the agents were intelligence officers working for the Americans, but nonetheless grilled them until OSS personnel showed up to secure their release. Both Detachment 101 and the local British authorities decided that a method of validating agents was necessary, and identification passports became a standard set of each agent's documentation. These remained at base and, in the event of capture, were used as a means of effecting the agent's release.[71] The identifications did little to preserve the secretive nature of the organization, but were necessary because Detachment 101's agent trainees were either Burmese, Anglo-Indians/Burmans, or other locally recruited personnel.[72] Such agents working on behalf of the Japanese might easily be passed off as OSS students.

Part of the documentation needed for the agents of Detachment 101 was proof of their legal status. Therefore, Eifler had a contract drawn up between himself, representing the United States government, and each individual agent.[73] The document guaranteed monetary assistance to an agent's beneficiaries in the event that he died while on a mission. To its credit, Detachment 101 took great pains at the end of the war to honor these ad hoc commitments.

Still, Detachment 101 could not ignore the mundane. Easily overlooked in the excitement, a way had to be found to pay for the unit's operations. Eifler's expenses totaled some $6,400 monthly, most of which was allocated to pay the students and helpers at the training camp. Eifler had brought only $6,000 from COI Washington with him. He had tried to take more—$20,000—but COI Washington balked at the suggestion. COI Washington thought that all Eifler would have to do was wire a request for more money and the funds would be in his overseas account within twenty-four hours. This proved impractical. The remoteness of India meant that Detachment 101 had limited and sporadic communications with Washington. In fact, Eifler counted himself lucky if he received an answer in a week, but it usually took three weeks or more.[74] In addition, Detachment 101's bank, Lloyd's Bank Unlimited in New Delhi, was hundreds of miles away.[75] Even the opening of a second account at the Calcutta office failed to expedite payments.

Finances became a critical problem by the end of 1942. Only an emergency infusion of $50,000 from Stilwell and a temporary loan from the Burma government in exile eased Detachment 101's immediate problems. A disgruntled Eifler wrote to Donovan, "Where would I be if I had to depend solely on your office?"[76]

Captain Robert T. Aitken, the man thrown into the job of finance officer, devised a temporary solution for bringing the banking system closer to Nazira. He created subsidiary accounts to handle the unit's immediate needs. These included ones with the Treasury Office in Jorhat, located some 50 miles from Nazira, and with the Sibsagar Sub-Treasury, about 14 miles from Nazira, as well as with the accounting office at the tea plantation. Detachment 101's financial requirements were diverse and required varying but specific forms of payment, from silver coins to paper bills to opium. Eventually Detachment 101's demands for certain forms of money, such as silver rupees, stripped local locations of their stocks. This caused the Detachment to look for other solutions. In the meantime, however, none of the financial institutions involved, from Lloyd's to Assam Company Limited, asked questions as to why the U.S. Army Experimental Station had odd financial requirements, permitting Detachment 101 to retain at least a semblance of secrecy. The unit still had to develop the means to communicate with its agents in occupied Burma.

Communications

Communications were perhaps the most important problem that the Detachment faced as it tried to determine how best to conduct operations. Through trial and error, the Detachment worked out methods to train and then infiltrate personnel and agents into enemy-controlled territory. Without a long-range, reliable, secure, and portable radio system, however, these agents and groups could not communicate back to Nazira. These groups were effectively worthless if they could not establish communications. They would be unable to pass intelligence back to the Allies, take directions from headquarters, or schedule resupply drops.

The Detachment soon discovered that existing military radios were unsuitable. The sets and their accompanying power source weighed too much, did not have enough range, or could not withstand the harsh Burmese jungles. The Detachment had few opportunities to repair radios once they were behind the lines. In addition to being reliable and able to send messages over a long distance, Detachment 101's radios had to be compact and easily transportable. Because Detachment 101 planned to train indigenous troops—many of whom were illiterate and who did not understand English—as radio operators, the radios also had to be simple to learn to operate under jungle conditions. Due to the remoteness of Nazira, an additional requirement was that they had to be constructed of locally procured materials. Very few supplies arrived, and orders from the United States took months. The Army Signal Corps had priority for radio production, meaning that COI/OSS requirements were filled last. Commercial radio parts could not be obtained on the local market as prices were some 2,000–6,500 percent higher than prewar prices.[77]

Eifler assigned five men, who also had additional duties of handling the coded traffic, to develop the Detachment's radio. Amazingly, they jerry-rigged radios together using tin cans as tuning condensers, housings made from metal plate and lumber, and coils wound out of scrap wire. They even draped antennas over fences or trees, none of which was "good engineering practice," but the home-built radios worked remarkably well.[78] Each radio weighed about 3 pounds, but their batteries added another 35 pounds. Further refinement resulted in a reduction in weight. The first of Detachment 101's groups took the locally produced radios into the field in late 1942 and early 1943.[79] Not only did the sets meet environmental conditions, but they also had longer range than the Detachment originally hoped. Eifler reported to OSS headquarters in December 1942 that the radios could even receive stations in the mainland United States.[80]

Once it developed an appropriate set, the Detachment then had to construct a communications network to handle its planned far-flung operations. This network started with liaison contacts that included daily exchanges with U.S. Army and British networks.[81] On 13 January 1943, Detachment 101 established the first outlying communications hub, radio station "D," in Calcutta under the direction of Captain Harry W. Little. This station eventually became a separate OSS unit, Detachment 505, which was in charge of supplies and procurement for Detachment 101. Because no additional qualified personnel had arrived from the United States, Detachment 101 trained the first complements of its agent school as radio operators in "Camp O," established on 6 January 1943.[82] The new radio operators served both on the field teams and in an expanded liaison network.

Moving toward the First Operations

Eifler's ambition and ideas soon surpassed the twenty personnel available to him. In February 1943, he wrote back to OSS headquarters requesting personnel with the following specialties: finance, medical, communications, technical (to perform what would later be the work of the R&D Branch), photography, and armorers.[83] With this request for more personnel, Eifler made the first steps of moving Detachment 101 beyond an organization that would rely solely on SO personnel to fill in other roles as needed. As it was, Eifler had already begun Detachment 101's Communications, Special Funds (Finance), and Schools and Training Branches.

Eifler wanted to use his experience in the Customs Service to establish smuggling routes to infiltrate agents deep into enemy territory and to extract potential agents and materials. While Eifler's initial planned methods did not work as planned, it is important to keep this concept in mind as one looks at Detachment 101's initial operations. The unit conducted two types of early operations; short- and long-range penetrations. Both types provided valuable lessons that the Detachment used to shape the organization in 1943–1944.

3

Long-Range Penetration Operations

After we had been in operations in Burma for awhile, we took a little time to reflect upon our training. The operations were not developing in the manner which had been expected, based upon the instruction in B Camp or that that the other group had been taught in Canada. It finally became clear that we were operating in an entirely different environment from that upon which our instruction had been founded. Quite logically they had based their instruction upon the situation in the European Theater and to a great extent upon the experiences of the British Office of Special Operations [SOE] and the Commando Forces. Their area of operation was within a highly developed region; economically, sociologically, and militarily. The Burma area of operation was entirely different.

William R. Peers

Operations in 1943 would either make or break Detachment 101. By this time, the unit was established at Nazira and had surmounted its immediate bureaucratic problems. Eifler now concentrated on the very reason why his unit was in the Far East in the first place, to conduct actions against the enemy. This was not an easy proposition. Success or failure of these initial missions would be the determining factor in getting General Stilwell's blessing to allow Detachment 101 to continue operations.[1]

Detachment 101's field operations in 1943 involved short- and long-range penetration operations. Short-range operations, accomplished with a mix of American or Commonwealth personnel, were shallow penetrations into enemy-held territory, usually conducted on foot. While they would be the missions that proved to Stilwell the value of Detachment 101, only long-range penetrations would give the general the "booms" that he wanted within the allotted ninety days.

Long-range penetration operations were conducted hundreds of miles into Japanese-occupied territory with personnel inserted by airborne or maritime means. All operational members (vice support) of these missions were recruited from British or Commonwealth personnel. That alone shows how dependent Detachment 101 was on British support at this early stage. Eifler expended great amounts of effort on the riskier long-range penetration operations to give Stilwell results. Part of the difficulty was that Detachment 101 simply did not know enough about how to conduct operations within occupied Burma, placing great stress on the inexperienced and overworked staff. All of the personnel in the Detachment had multiple jobs and faced a herculean task in accomplishing them. Poor to nonexistent area intelligence compounded the difficulty, as did poorly trained operators who were selected—not trained—to fit the mission. Eifler described his feelings at the time:

> No one knew or could answer the questions that the agents were asking. . . . There was no literature [manuals] we had nothing. A man was trained, and the training that he had was all that he could give the individuals that he was now training. . . . I was plied with questions that I could not answer. . . . I went up to my tent and put I my arms on the desk, and I laid my head down and I cried . . . here I am commanding a unit, teaching individuals what to do behind the lines, and I did not know myself. I got up from that and said never will I be put in that position again.[2]

Although there were some COI/OSS personnel active in North Africa at the same time, the long-range penetration missions of Detachment 101 were the first OSS attempts at strategic sabotage.[3] In contrast to the short-range operations, the early long-range penetration missions of Detachment 101 were almost all total disasters, with only one succeeding out of six attempted. Eifler ignored his group's lack of experience and undeveloped area intelligence in his eagerness to show the value of his organization to Stilwell. In operations of this type, failure equated to the loss of the entire team. These operations, however, also provided some of the most valuable lessons that the Detachment could use to build itself and its subsequent operations. Therefore, in hindsight, the failures were absolutely critical to Detachment 101's evolution. Since short- and long-range operations occurred simultaneously but had no direct influence on one another, they are covered thematically instead of chronologically.

A Group

A Group was the first long-range sabotage mission launched by Detachment 101. This mission created a false sense of operational preparedness, which additional long-range penetration operations subsequently eroded. A Group's mission was strategic. It was to assist American efforts to supply Chinese forces via the "Hump" airlift route by disrupting Japanese air operations from Myitkyina. It would do this by cutting rail lines and blowing bridges south of the city, thereby cutting the inflow of supplies to the Japanese fighter base.[4] It was supposed to "fit into a bigger [operational] picture," and Eifler told the group that "everything depends on the success of your mission as the push has already started."[5] The initial proposed sabotage mission was to destroy several bridges. Ideally, the teams were also to use time delayed charges on the rail lines to trap a train on the lines in both directions, "leaving the two trains helpless to the machine gun fire of the 10th A.F.," according to Colonel Eifler.[6] After that, the group's orders were to stay in enemy-occupied territory and start a guerrilla force.[7]

A Group was composed exclusively of British Commonwealth personnel. Jack Barnard led seven operators: Oscar Milton, Patrick Maddox, Pat Quinn, John Beamish, Aram "Bunny" Aganoor, Dennis Francis, and a Kachin named Saw Judson. Many of the group had worked in the timber or mining industries of Burma for years.[8] Eifler recruited them with the help of Colonel Richmond, the British liaison officer, who knew many of the men personally and who also maintained liaison with the Burma Army and the governor of Burma.[9] Most had prior military service. Jack Barnard, John Beamish, and Pat Maddox came from SOE, while Oscar Milton was on loan from the Burma Army. Four Kachins—Ah Khi, Ahdi Yaw Yin, Yaw Yin Naung, and Lazum Naw—also accompanied the group.[10] Many of those in A Group had made the grueling walk out of Burma with remnants of the Chinese Army in 1942. This prior experience gave the A Group members the necessary backgrounds, including knowledge of the terrain, environment, peoples, and culture, and critical language skills, to survive and operate hundreds of miles behind Japanese lines.[11]

The first major task for A Group was a successful infiltration. The initial plan called for the group to move overland into their operating area from Fort Hertz, then the only British-held outpost in north Burma, where another mission, FORWARD, had recently begun. However, the poor operations security of the British convinced Eifler that the Japanese would discover that the clandestine group—accompanied by its necessary porters—was trying to infiltrate. After all the preparations made, being unable to infiltrate A Group set Detachment 101's morale back. Peers wrote that when the group returned to Nazira,

> things appeared fairly blue. Here we were in a strange land on the other side of the world involved in a type of operation that none of us knew much about . . . the inability to put the group in operation came as a blow to them because they were unable to see much hope for the future. Carl was also affected by it but outwardly he was all optimism and this did much to bolster the spirits of the others.[12]

With no other alternative, Eifler then decided to parachute the group behind the lines—a method of insertion for which no members of Detachment 101 had been trained. The group obtained the loan of Master Sergeant Wayne "Pop" Milligan from the Air Transport Corps to teach A Group how to parachute. After only a few hours of ground instruction with a seat chute—the type used by airplane crews, not paratroopers—the group, though nervous, was ready to jump.[13]

On 5 February 1943, Barnard accompanied an aerial reconnaissance mission to review the drop zone. Two days later, Barnard and Timothy parachuted in safely, although the drop destroyed their radio. After confirming that the recognition panels indicated the area was safe, the remainder of the team dropped in the next day. Despite this being the first jump for the group, all of its members landed without mishap with the exception of one Kachin, who had a few scratches and was dazed for a couple of days.[14]

It took the group several days to sort out their gear and learn more about the surroundings. It was then that they received a radio message relaying that "the big picture has changed."[15] A Group discovered only now that they did not fit into a larger offensive. The group was to go on with their mission of blowing the bridges but was not to recruit a guerrilla force because no Allied push was forthcoming. Milton recalled, "After I decoded a message that Saw had given me, I told Jack the contents." He continued, "For a moment there was silence and then he cursed the Americans and implied that he wished that he was with the British forces."[16]

Despite the unwelcome news, A Group quickly set to its mission of destroying three area railroad bridges. Barnard wrote in his diary, "We had no information on the vulnerability of our target, so our plans were elastic in nature."[17] After creating a rally point where the teams would rendezvous for the walk out once their bridges were blown, A Group split up. Barnard related,

"It was a sad moment when the group broke up, each of us perhaps wondering if we should meet again."[18] Milton, because of his "appearance and size," Timothy, and the four Kachins stayed at the rally point.[19] Wearing disguises so that they would not appear as Allied soldiers, the others began their 40-mile march south. They had to avoid being seen because they were in a Shan area, where the inhabitants were of dubious loyalty.

The agents moved only by night and holed up motionless during the day. Several times they came close to discovery. In one such instance, when children with dogs closed on their position, Barnard wrote, "We only escaped by moving from cover to cover and I can now fully sympathize with hunted animals."[20] The day of the sabotage operation, the group set their time pencils (designed to create a delayed charge) at 4 PM. Since they were 12-hour delays, the charges had to be set before the bridges blew at 4 AM the next day.[21]

As they neared their targets, the three teams split up and moved to their respective bridges. Maddox and Francis went to the Namkwin Bridge, Quinn and Aganoor headed for a smaller bridge 2 miles south, and Barnard and Beamish moved to the main target, the Dagwin Bridge. All appeared to be going well. The three teams reached their objectives on the night of 23 February 1943. Once there, they prepared their demolitions for a timed simultaneous explosion.[22] However, Maddox and Francis, plagued by faulty timers, dropped the Namkwin Bridge too early.

The premature explosion jeopardized the other teams' efforts. Barnard recorded, "A terrific explosion from the direction of Pat's bridge shook the air . . . both of us had jumped to the conclusion that Pat must have accidentally blown himself up." Barnard continued, "We expected the noise would bring the people out—but there remained a deadly silence."[23] They continued as planned, but he and Beamish abandoned their mission when shots rang out. "There was no doubt now, the game was up."[24]

Enemy forces discovered Quinn and Aganoor as they placed their charges. The agents fired on local police who came to investigate the bridge. Soon, the police and local Japanese occupation troops were in pursuit. Quinn and Aganoor split up to increase their chances of escape. Each intended to independently work his way back to the rally point. Barnard heard the action. "The shots were coming closer . . . it is impossible to describe the eerie noise that went up—yelling, dogs barking, and gongs beating. We were surrounded by voices. It would have been foolish to wait any longer . . . we took to our heels." He continued, "The fate of our missing comrades was in the lap of the gods, but I had to assume the worst had happened."[25] What they heard was Detachment 101's first casualty.

Quinn escaped, but Aganoor was captured and presumably killed. Quinn later wrote that a local police patrol discovered them while the two were in the process of getting rid of their explosives. Because the OSS men were dressed like Kachins, the police did not open fire. But "as they came into within range, we emptied our automatics into them, dropping four men, and then ran as fast as we could with the remainder of the patrol giving chase and opening fire on us occasionally."[26] It was then that they split. They had benefited from local confusion.

Fortunately, unbeknownst to the OSS element, the first Chindit operation, a large long-range penetration raid led by British Major General Orde Wingate, was also operating nearby. Because the Japanese presumed the Chindits had caused the bridge demolitions, they did not expand the search for the scattered teams. The OSS benefited from the confusion but also learned the value of better coordination.[27] Peers described it later:

> It was the first inkling we had that a British-Indian Force had entered Burma; . . . we had advised the British authorities on the Imphal front of our planned operation . . . for some reason, they had not considered it necessary to advise us of their plans. When we checked with them and confronted them . . . they were open to admit it and volunteered the information that it was Major General Ord [*sic*] Wingate's Chindit Force.[28]

However, that information did not change the situation that the members of A Group faced on the ground.

Barnard and Beamish made it to the rendezvous camp on the 24th, after speed-marching nearly 40 miles in less than a day. They later described the situation, "we arrived . . . a former shadow of ourselves."[29] They thought that the Japanese had killed or captured the other two groups and that enemy forces were in close pursuit. Without pausing to rest, Barnard, Beamish, Milton, Timothy, and the Kachins gathered what supplies they could carry and beat a hasty retreat. Maddox and Francis arrived on the 27th, and Quinn showed up the next day. From here, Maddox, Francis, and Quinn—minus Aganoor—started their trek north back to Fort Hertz. Both sections of A Group followed the same general trail, but made their way independently to Fort Hertz. They knew that the first outposts of the Kachin Levies, a British-led frontier force, were located on the approaches to Fort Hertz. Maddox's group arrived on 16 May 1943.

Barnard's group was in the lead. In contrast to Maddox's group, it had radio contact with Detachment 101 and received some supply drops. On 7 March, the OSS dropped a note ordering them to stay in the area and provide intelligence based on an urgent and critical need.[30] The Japanese had reinforced the area around Myitkyina in response to the Chindit expedition, and Stilwell's Chih Hui Pu feared that they would make a push north to take Sumprabum. Barnard's group lingered in the area and collected intelligence on targets, roads, and the Japanese military, determined which villages were friendly to the Allies, and assessed the general situation in Burma. His group returned to Fort Hertz on 11 June after eighteen weeks in the field behind enemy lines. Afterward, Barnard and Beamish elected to return to SOE. Wilkinson later cabled back to Nazira that "Jack and the rest feel they have been let down. Say they were fools to risk their lives while others stayed [in] India. Jack has threatened to go to GHQ and raise hell about it."[31] However, several others stayed with Detachment 101, thereby providing Detachment 101 with personnel of great experience. Maddox later parachuted in to take charge of the RED group, and Quinn did the same with PAT in November 1943. Milton chose to lead the OSCAR group that was tasked to rescue downed pilots.[32]

B Group

Despite the fact that A Group was still behind enemy lines and Detachment 101 had received no operational feedback, Eifler felt pressured to launch additional—and increasingly ambitious—operations. Thus, the second sabotage team, code-named B Group, dropped by parachute near the Shan town of Lawksawk, further south of A Group, during daylight on 24 February 1943. Led by Harry Ballard, B Group was comprised of John Clark, Vierap Pillay, Lionel Cornelius, Kenneth Murray, and Cyril Goodwin. All were either Anglo-Burmans or Anglo-Indians recruited from refugee camps in India.[33]

Peers was part of the drop crew on the aircraft. In his book *Behind the Burma Road*, he explained his misgivings about the selected drop zone because it was only a few miles from several villages and the local inhabitants easily noticed the drop aircraft. Assured by Ballard that the group would be fine, Peers approved the parachute drop. Never again would the mission leader have the authority to make the decision to execute a questionable mission. The Detachment 101 staff correctly concluded that a group's leader could not be relied on to make an objective assessment when immediate risk had escalated.[34]

Lawksawk was out of the range of Allied fighters based in India. Therefore, a China-based Army Air Forces C-87 and P-40 fighter escort was necessary. In early 1943, Detachment 101 had only the Army Air Forces for air support. Stilwell's priority—and hence that of the Tenth Air Force—was to fly as much cargo as possible into China over the Hump route. Thus, the request for a single cargo plane had to go through Tenth Air Force command channels to Major General Clayton L. Bissell before it reached Stilwell. Stilwell denied the request because he wanted Detachment 101 to infiltrate groups overland to avoid taxing his limited airlift. Eifler pointed out that A Group had demonstrated that this was not always practical. Stilwell relented when Eifler said that the entire mission—reconnaissance, personnel, and supply drop—could be done by a single mission. Eifler also agreed to bomb Lashio on the return flight. His supply bundle kickers would manhandle twenty 30-pound bombs out of the aircraft over the Lashio airfield to disrupt Japanese air operations. Detachment 101 launched B Group on 24 February to add to the "booms" that A Group had supposedly already made in Burma. At 3:30 PM, they jumped. All landed safely, although Goodwin got hung up in a tree. As the cargo and escort planes circled overhead after the drop, one man waved goodbye. Unfortunately, the men on the ground could not see what Peers saw from the C-87.

> As we made our last pass, we could see a discomforting sight: villagers streaming out in every direction, heading towards the drop zone. I had an aching feeling that the lines looked hostile. I couldn't get it out of my head that they were out to kill. And because of this, I felt it had been a bad decision. As I sat in the plane, I felt miserable about the whole affair and wondered why I had ever got mixed up in this sort of business.[35]

The drop on 24 February 1943 was the last contact Detachment 101 ever had with B Group. Radioman Allen Richter remembered monitoring the radios for a week hoping for the call that never came.[36] On the premise that B Group radios had been damaged in the jump, a B-25 escorted by two P-40s flew up and down the valley on 6 March searching for recognition panels. They were too late. Two days before, the Detachment's radio operators had heard the following Japanese broadcast:

> Rangoon: Unable to take any positive steps in the retaking of Burmese territory, the desperate British Army in India is now resorting to external activities, some of which were frustrated at the very start by the vigilant

> Japanese authorities in Burma and the loyal attitude of the Burmese towards their reborn country. A recent report revealed that a group of six British spies on 23rd February landed by parachute at a certain point in North-Western Burma. Entertaining the idea that any place was safe where there were no Japanese troops, they were greatly shocked when a group of alert Burmese villagers immediately rushed at them. In the struggle that followed, the brave villagers killed three of the spies and captured the rest and subsequently delivered them to the Japanese troops stationed nearby. This recent incident shows that any and all attempts by Britain to win and cajole the Burmese will end in failure and disaster. All the Burmese people from the humble villager to the patriotic leader, realize the danger of John Bull.[37]

Neither Peers nor the rest of Detachment 101 learned what happened to B Group until June 1945.[38]

After Rangoon's capture in May 1945, Peers, then the Detachment 101 commander, sent Lieutenant Daniel Mudrinich to Rangoon to investigate the fate of their lost agents. Mudrinich had to rely heavily on X-2 (OSS Counter-Intelligence Branch) interrogations of Japanese collaborators and friendly locals. Despite Japanese holdouts taking potshots at him, the OSS lieutenant interviewed villagers who had seen the missing agents. At the end of June 1945, the investigations were over and the Detachment's financial officer, George Gorin, and lawyer, Charles Henderson, then settled the pay and provided restitution to the families of the lost agents. What they discovered was the following:

> According to Mudrinich's 1945 investigation, the villagers led the captured survivors of B Group to Lawksawk. On 27 February, the villagers turned them over to the Japanese who imprisoned them in Taunggyi. The captured men provided no information despite being severely tortured for two to three days. In an attempt to convince the rest to talk, the Japanese executed three men—likely Ballard, Goodwin and Hood. The last three prisoners, all in very poor health, were dispatched under heavy guard to Rangoon on 15 March 1943, but there is no record that they ever arrived.[39]

W Group

Without pause for reflection as to what had happened to A or B Groups, Detachment 101 continued to launch long-range penetration missions. Lieutenant General Noel Mackintosh Stuart Irwin, commander of the British Eastern Army in the Arakan region of Burma, asked Detachment 101 for assistance cutting Japanese supplies on the Prome-Taungup coastal road. Any help that Detachment 101 could provide would aid in recapturing Donbiak (Shinkhali).[40] Since the Arakan consists of thick mangrove swamp along the west coast of Burma, W Group (Operation MAURICE to the British) would have to infiltrate by boat. The W Group would be operating even farther south than A or B Groups, and well beyond Detachment 101's area of operations.

Detachment 101 was even less prepared for amphibious insertions than it was for airborne operations. It would be another first for Detachment 101. Unlike A and B Groups, which received some parachute instruction, W Group received no amphibious training. The Detachment had no boats, and the landing party from Detachment 101 had no experience in amphibious operations either.[41] The British naval delivery vessels had to clear the area by daylight to avoid detection and possible attack by the Japanese.[42] The British boats carrying the team and its rubber boats could not carry sufficient fuel internally to support a night reconnaissance of the landing site the night before and return the next night to drop off the team. Eifler requested that the boats carry extra fuel on deck to extend the range of the delivery vessels. The Royal Navy refused the request because carrying fuel externally was against regulations. Eifler asked Vice Admiral Herbert Fitzherbert, the Royal Indian Navy commander, for a waiver. The British admiral did not feel that there was any situation in the theater that warranted a violation of this regulation.[43]

Anticipating that the mission could end in disaster, Eifler, who was himself to be a member of the shore party, wrote a blunt memo. Eifler gave the memo to Lieutenant Colonel John G. Coughlin, his second-in-command, to forward to Donovan if Eifler went missing.

> In the event that we do not come back, I wish to use this report as a reason to Washington why you should have your own boats. . . . If I, at the present time, had my own boats, I would not even consider undertaking this project now. . . . As I stated earlier in this report to you, chances at the present time appear to be against us, but we are going

> ahead. . . . I do not feel that it is right to ask our men to take these unnecessary chances which become necessary in an attempt to coordinate or work with other agencies.[44]

The W Group consisted of six Anglo-Burman/Indian agents: Charles Morrell, John Sheridan, Vincent Snadden, John Aikman, Alex D'Attaides, and Geoffrey Willson.[45] The team finally got ashore after five tries to find a good landing site, near Sandoway, Burma, on the night of 8 March 1943. They had to move, and hide before daybreak, more than 1,000 pounds of supplies.

Because of the time lost in the previous landing attempts, Eifler did not think that the agents would have the time to bury the rafts before dawn. In order to reduce the chances of discovery, Eifler decided to accompany them and swim back to the motor launch with the rubber boats in tow. After the six agents got ashore with their supplies, Eifler told them to get the stuff under cover. When he shook their hands in farewell, he warned them that if discovered, not to be taken alive.[46] That was the last time that Detachment 101 saw W Group, but the drama was not over.

The pounding surf and darkness proved to be nearly insurmountable even for the brawny OSS commander. As he struggled to drag the five rubber boats back through the surf, a wave threw Eifler head first onto a large rock. Dazed, he barely managed to tow the rafts back to the launch craft in time. The injury so disoriented Eifler that he only found the motor launch by the sound of the crew pulling up the anchor chain. It had taken so long to get the agents ashore that dawn was soon approaching, and the boat was preparing to leave without Eifler.[47] W Group marked the beginning of the end of Eifler as Detachment 101's commander. His head injury was severe. Neither prodigious amounts of alcohol nor self-medicating with morphine could dull the constant pain.[48] The injury eventually provided the grounds to remove him from command.

Eifler's handshakes on the beach were the last contact with W Group. Once ashore, the agents hid themselves. The following day, they paid a fisherman to take them to the nearby village of Kyaukpyu. W Group then managed to get to Dawmya, where their luck ran out. Local villagers probably betrayed the group to the Japanese. On 19 March 1943, on a trail near Dawmya, Japanese troops surrounded the W Group agents. Trapped, they followed Eifler's advice and tried to shoot their way out. The group killed one Japanese soldier and wounded another. However, Charles Morrell and John Sheridan lost their lives in the breakout. The remaining four sought cover on a wooded hill nearby. Japanese forces mortared the hill, killing Vincent Snadden. The last three agents escaped by moving into heavier vegetation. On the run, villagers from Natmaw chased and caught John Aikman, who was shot by the headman on 24 March 1943. Three weeks later, the Japanese captured D'Attaides and Willson. They were taken to the prison at Taungup, tortured, and beheaded around 25 April 1943.[49]

Despite having lost contact with B and W Groups and not knowing why they failed, Detachment 101 continued throughout 1943 and early 1944 to launch more ambitious long-range penetration operations further and further south. In south Burma, the populations were not willing to help the Allies. Unfortunately for these groups, Detachment 101 had not taken adequate time to reflect on why long-range missions were unsuccessful.

BALLS, BALLS #1, and REX

The purpose of BALLS, to be parachuted into the Tavoy area, was to provide intelligence regarding roads, enemy order of battle, conditions of the local tin mines, and attitude of local residents, to organize an underground network, and to prepare that network to conduct demolitions.[50] After a prior reconnaissance performed by the group leader, "Mellie" (Joseph Rodrigues), he, along with "Ryk," "Sabu" (Maung Ba Tu), and "Sunny" (Sunny Peters), jumped along the Burmese coast at 2:50 AM, 24 August 1943.[51] After not hearing from the group—and believing that they had not received their equipment due to a ten-second delay on the part of the bombardier in releasing the equipment chutes—the Air Force conducted five reconnaissance sorties between 10 September and 7 October to look for recognition panels.[52] However, no trace of the agents was ever found.

In an effort to find BALLS—which was believed, correctly, to have lost its equipment, Detachment 101 decided to insert BALLS #1. The group went in by the British submarine HMS *Trespasser* on the night of 1 January 1944, and was to use fold boats in order to get ashore. As they were preparing to go, a local fishing vessel discovered the submarine. Rather than shoot at the fishing vessel and attract attention, the submarine took it captive. The 101 agents, Vincent Darlington and Saw Wallace, transferred to that vessel while the original crew was taken prisoner and brought into the submarine.[53] According to the final report, the two agents did in fact make it to shore, and contacted Mellie. Sometime after February 1944 the group was captured, and it is presumed that they were killed by the Japanese sometime before March 1945.[54]

REX was perhaps the most ambitious agent infiltration that Detachment 101 had in this phase of the war. The REX mission was to penetrate into Rangoon to provide intelligence on enemy order of battle, watch Japanese shipping entering and leaving Rangoon harbor, and try to establish an intelligence net that could be later enhanced with more agents. Agents "Rex" and "Rip" dropped into the field on the night of 12–13 November 1943. No contact was ever established, despite several aerial attempts.[55]

The Evaluations

Peers described how the Detachment analyzed these operations:

> "We knew that we were neophytes in this type of business, but we were determined to take advantage of our mistakes and not commit the same error twice if we could possibly avoid it. We set up a procedure of trial and error. As this operation, and succeeding operations, progressed, an account was maintained in minute detail. Each message was analyzed when the personnel returned from the field, they were debriefed and also required to write an inclusive account of their activities, good and bad. By this means, we were able to isolate the sound practices and use them to develop effective operating procedures."[56]

Such a "murder board" was critical to the Detachment's success.

After the consecutive failures of B and W Groups, Detachment 101 had to reorganize, evaluate the limited lessons learned, and train for these future missions. Detachment 101 focused on the A Group operation and its short-range penetration operations. While it had succeeded in dropping only one bridge as opposed to the three targeted, A Group was quite successful. The debriefs from A Group provided extensive intelligence on the attitudes of the local population, economic hardships, locations and patrolling schedules of Japanese troops, and familiarity with jungle conditions. Detachment 101 was able to use this knowledge in its subsequent missions as it inserted forces into the Kachin-dominated area prior to the Allied advance in mid-1944.[57]

One key lesson learned in the long-range penetration operations was to insert a small pathfinder team into the area of operations to conduct a ground reconnaissance before the main body. Detachment 101 did not recognize this lesson until B Group disappeared. Scarcity of air support, the schedule of the drop plane, and allowing the mission commander to make the execution decision doomed that effort. W Group was shackled to the regulations and operating restrictions of the Royal Indian Navy. There was neither a pathfinder team, nor prior reconnaissance, nor boat training. W Group ignored the post-mission note on B Group that called for air reconnaissance of the area of operations beforehand.[58] These lessons later became standard operating procedure (SOP); however, they were too late to help the remaining long-range penetration operations in 1943, the BALLS and REX missions, as well as BALLS #1 in February 1944.[59] After these missions, Detachment 101 no longer took it as a first step to insert whole groups into the south. Instead, "we made it a practice of preceding the group with an agent to obtain and report the lay of the land and to act as a reception party."[60]

Detachment 101 also learned by default the very difficult lesson of overextending its capabilities and the necessity for current intelligence. The successful shallow penetrations in 1943, FORWARD and its follow-on, KNOTHEAD, which are covered in the next chapter, established themselves by walking into north Burma. These missions provided intelligence for bombing targets, built enemy order of battle, and kept the Detachment abreast of the general situation in Burma. These north Burma operations benefited from the help of the indigenous pro-Allied Kachin tribes. Of the long-range penetration missions in 1943, only one, A Group, was in a Kachin area.

Another lesson was to be flexible. The inadvertent splitting of the A Group led to a potential crisis. Thereafter, the Detachment 101 staff had to plan to cover nearly every contingency. This included alternative planning so that the OSS could react proactively should disasters occur.[61]

The fourth and most important lesson learned had a major impact on future operations and helped Detachment 101 grow into one of the largest OSS overseas commands. Eifler realized how critical it was for the Detachment to have its own organic transportation to control the insertion, extraction, and support of teams behind enemy lines. Eifler reported his problems dealing with the Army Air Forces on 6 April 1943. Every Army Air Forces unit—bombers, fighters, and transport—had to have local approvals before Stilwell gave his final approval. Even with permission granted to use Army Air Forces assets, Detachment 101 operations were still bound by their regulations, or by Army officers' indifference or hostility. In trying to insert a team in March, Eifler could not pull the Army Air Forces officer away from a cribbage game long enough to get his attention. This is what Eifler told OSS headquarters in Washington:

> From the beginning . . . I have stated that successful operations should utilize the methods of the smuggler. . . . We are forced at the present time, however, to use military methods that are all wrong for this kind of work. . . . The planes we use are military planes manned by military personnel, operated in a military manner, first thought and consideration being given to equipment . . . our first thought should be given our main equipment and that equipment is a trained agent. He is a tool, a very expensive tool, and his life should be guarded jealously as long as it is in our hands. If he is to be flown into enemy territory, he should be given every chance of a successful landing instead of which, flying under military regulations, he is taken over enemy territory in broad daylight, dropped in daylight along with his equipment. . . . Military planes cannot fly at night. Why, I don't know.[62]

Most of the same frustrations could be equally applied to amphibious insertions.

The other crucial element to Detachment 101 was operational security. Agents and operations exposed themselves to unnecessary risks because personnel who lacked the need to know were involved in operational insertions, resupply, and extractions. Eifler had a solution. He asked for permission to purchase a small fleet of aircraft that could take off and land on short landing fields and be fitted with pontoons if necessary. As for delivery boats, Eifler, the former Customs Service officer, proposed a fast speedboat like those used by liquor smugglers during Prohibition in the United States.[63] Fortunately, Donovan and the OSS staff agreed. By the end of the war, Detachment 101 had its own small air force—unofficially dubbed the Red Ass Squadron after the red-paint tipped tail rudders. These planes proved ideal for insertion and extraction of personnel, able or wounded. Eventually the Red Ass Squadron fleet grew to include Stinson L-1 Vigilants, Piper Cubs (L-4 Grasshoppers), a de Havilland Gipsy Moth, Stinson L-5 Sentinels, a Noorduyn UC-64A Norseman, Stearman PT-17 Kaydets, and a British Spitfire fighter.[64] Detachment 101 also had a small fleet of dedicated USAAF C-47 cargo aircraft to drop supplies. In November 1943, OSS Washington sent a small air-sea rescue boat similar to a PT-boat. By 1945, Detachment 101 would have a small fleet of high-powered boats, as well as a section of OSS Maritime Unit swimmers. But all this was the post-Eifler era.

While Detachment 101 did not successfully apply these lessons to the long-range penetrations of 1943, they did so afterwards. They built on the more successful shallow penetrations in north Burma to expand their utility and to justify organic transportation. It was also fortunate that the Detachment took this direction. By early 1944, recruiting agents from the refugee population in India was no longer worth the effort as they had simply been out of Burma too long to have an accurate enough understanding of area conditions to be able to pass themselves off as locals. Instead, by focusing on shallow penetrations, the group increased their probability of success tremendously. In incorporating these lessons and focusing their efforts in the north where the Kachins could help, by May 1944 Detachment 101 proved to be an effective intelligence-collection unit that fielded a strong guerrilla fighting force that became a thorn in the side of Japanese in north Burma.

4

Short-Range Penetrations Meet Success

The Japs know that [their camouflaged targets] cannot be seen from the air and know they must be designated by somebody on the ground and as a consequence, our people are very much sought after by the armed forces of the Mikado. However, not only do we designate the targets, but we also give them their results.

Detachment 101 report to OSS Washington

In contrast to Detachment 101's long-range penetration operations, its short-range operations were not of the type that Eifler originally envisioned for the unit, nor were they the ones that Stilwell had asked for. They would not provide the strategic results requested, and served only to enhance a long campaign. Although promising little return, they delivered far more than the Detachment ever planned. Their success enabled the Detachment to keep operating into 1944.

Peers wrote in a postwar study that at first Detachment 101 knew nothing about the locale or the operating techniques that they would use. Without the luxury of experience, the leaders of Detachment 101 had to continuously examine their results and change operating techniques. Fortunately, the commanding officer of Detachment 101 had near autonomy and was able to rapidly reinforce success, even if it was unexpected. Operational independence was the key to Detachment 101's developing a systematic approach to how to tackle operations in Burma.[1]

The First Short-Range Effort: Operation FORWARD

At the end of 1942, Detachment 101 was still in its infancy and had only a few more personnel than when it arrived in the CBI the previous summer. Despite a lack of resources, the unit still had to justify its existence and advance operations beyond setting up a base and a training school. One way to accomplish this was to provide Stilwell with intelligence on enemy forces and dispositions in north Burma. Little guesswork was involved for the location of where to start. Operation FORWARD, Detachment 101's first field group, operated from Fort Hertz, the only area in north Burma that the Allies still occupied. FORWARD proved to be a crucial success. Based upon its example, Detachment 101 expanded its operations throughout the area.

Detachment 101 did not intend the FORWARD group to be a separate paramilitary operation. The original intent was for it to be a forward operational base as an adjunct campus to the agent school at Nazira. Eifler thought that closer contact with the Japanese near Fort Hertz would allow agents-in-training to hone their craft and gain experience, giving them a greater chance of success when behind Japanese lines.[2]

The Detachment could spare few personnel, so FORWARD's initial contingent was small. On 28 December 1942, Eifler, Coughlin, Richter, and a few civilian agents made their way from Assam to Fort Hertz. From there, they were to go to Sumprabum, the furthest point in Burma then under Allied control. The group would report on local conditions and study how Detachment 101 could use the area to train agents prior to eventually striking against the Japanese.[3]

The group immediately ran into many problems. The rocky relationship with the British military commander at Fort Hertz proved to be the biggest challenge confronting Detachment 101 in its first attempts at getting into action. This relationship dramatically shaped the efforts Eifler took to conduct independent operations instead of relying on the good graces of the British.

Eifler previously arranged through his SOE liaison that once his small contingent arrived at Fort Hertz, its personnel were not to be identified as Americans and for cover purposes were to operate in British uniform. The British commanding officer of Fort Hertz, Colonel Ralph Gamble, had other ideas. Gamble had blown Detachment 101's cover even before the group arrived. Everyone the group met knew them as Americans, including "even the coolies in the fields."[4] Eifler immediately had the men switch back into American uniforms and adopt the cover of a Tenth United States Army Air

Force (USAAF) radio group that had been expected to arrive. The OSS group then made its way to Sumprabum, where Eifler learned that Gamble believed he had operational control over the mission. This left Eifler with the awkward and unenviable task on 13 January 1943 of directly informing Gamble that such would not be the case. After having given initial cooperation, Gamble then proved himself an obstructionist by refusing quarters, equipment, and most other forms of support. In response, Eifler announced to Gamble that Detachment 101's plan was impracticable and that he intended to withdraw his men.[5]

In reality, the threat was a subterfuge because Eifler did not intend to withdraw. He told Gamble that he would leave a small radio team to report on local conditions. This team would give Gamble all the required cooperation and Eifler might revisit the original plan should conditions merit. Accordingly, on 4 February 1943, Captain William C. Wilkinson and several agents arrived from Fort Hertz to reinforce the small contingent.

The short visit to Fort Hertz had dramatic repercussions. On this trip Eifler got the idea of recruiting Kachins for an unconventional warfare campaign in north Burma. He reported to Stilwell, "After surveying the condition in these hills it is my firm belief that the natives in the Kachin Hills . . . can be united in an effort against the Japanese. I believe it perfectly possible to raise forces in these hills that will be in a position to continually strike the Japanese from their flanks and from their rear."[6] From the aftermath of a Japanese advance on Sumprabum, checked by the British-led Kachin Levies in early January 1943, Eifler also learned the value of Kachin soldiers and their unique fighting techniques.[7]

Wilkinson moved his group south to Sumprabum, where they could fill a gap by furnishing local intelligence. On 8 January 1943, Eifler cabled Stilwell to tell him that his group stood ready to assist the Tenth Air Force by reporting on the weather or other information if necessary. FORWARD also used its secure communications to transmit information from the British back to the Americans. This included sending reports from SOE officer Captain R. W. Reid back to headquarters in India. This simple role filled by the Detachment shaved two to three days off the passing of reports, allowing greater use of the information before it was overtaken by events. The group reported on developments in the area, thereby becoming intelligence collectors in their own right. For example, by the first week of February 1943, FORWARD served as an impromptu air warning station that supplemented the army's chain of stations that reported on Japanese air movements. The group also recruited an ever-expanding cadre of indigenous agents who infiltrated through Japanese lines and reported area intelligence and on Japanese dispositions.[8]

Another opportunity, conducting limited guerrilla operations against the Japanese, had a large impact on Detachment 101. From May to July, the FORWARD group continued to push its operating base ever further south until it reached Ngumla, which was about 50 miles behind the Japanese lines. As early as June 1943, the group had conducted limited sabotage operations and recruited Kachins to send back to Nazira for training as radio operators.[9] In early August, Eifler told Wilkinson to "hit the Jap any way, shape and form that you want to hit him . . . smack him and smack him hard. The more you smack him, the more I'll like it. Use guerrilla tactics on their supply lines and the tactics in which we are supposed to be specialists."[10] By late 1943, FORWARD's operations—compounded by those of the Kachin Levies—had Japanese troops traveling only at night and made them so nervous that they randomly fired into trailside vegetation.[11] Through FORWARD, Detachment 101 began to formulate the type of guerrilla tactics that they perfected by the end of the war. It also learned how to engage key local leaders, and through them, the population.

Operation FORWARD gained local support by conducting impromptu civil affairs missions. In December 1943, Wilkinson reported that he had begun a "campaign" to provide the locals with unobtainable "luxury goods."[12] He requested items such as salt, cloth, yarn, and clothing airdropped to the group, and these were sold at cost. In his July report to OSS chief William J. Donovan, Eifler noted that FORWARD did not have any medical personnel with it and its personnel had suffered from numerous illnesses, including blackwater fever, malaria, and typhoid.[13] In October, Eifler contacted Milton Miles at SACO, who diverted navy doctor Lieutenant Commander James C. Luce to Detachment 101.[14] Luce immediately went into the field and quickly set up medical facilities at FORWARD that he made sure were also available to the indigenous population. He later recalled, "Not having had any previous experience with organization of such a group and knowing absolutely nothing of the terrain over which we would go or the people with whom we would come in contact, it was with considerable misgivings that I accepted the job."[15]

The trade goods and medical efforts proved very popular, gaining FORWARD trust and goodwill from the Kachins. By August, Wilkinson had ten Kachin headmen (the heads of villages) on his payroll and by October employed sixty-two Kachin soldiers.[16] Detachment 101's medical services helped convince the Kachins that they too had access to care if wounded in the field.

Just four months later, FORWARD reported that, given the word, the locals in the area would rise in revolt against the Japanese.[17] FORWARD began to plan for a guerrilla campaign. Luce was able to help with this directly. Luce assumed command when Detachment 101 recalled Wilkinson in December 1943 for another assignment. He now had two roles: chief medical officer in the area and guerrilla leader. Luce, a career naval medical officer who had been wounded on the USS *Maryland* at Pearl Harbor, could not have found himself in a stranger environment. However, he fit very well into the role and served with distinction.

FORWARD found yet another role that greatly increased the support Detachment 101 received from the Army Air Forces. It began to rescue downed aircrew and pilots. This mission grew out of the group's efforts to assist individual Chindits during Orde Wingate's retreat out of Burma in March–April 1943. FORWARD ultimately rescued nine Chindits, one of whom later died.[18] While the Chindit relief mission was limited, the Detachment made it known to the Allied air forces that they now could help rescue downed aircrews. Although this resulted in raised morale and greatly increased cooperation from the Army Air Forces, it did not immediately help the situation on the ground.

FORWARD continued to experience obstruction from Colonel Gamble, such as the refusal of quarters and airlift priorities. In July 1943, the Detachment headquarters reported, "All we get out of Sumprabum and Fort Hertz is trouble," and Peers had previously written in June, "Wouldn't life be sweet if there weren't as many Gambles!"[19] He later recalled that Gamble "was no longer the affable fellow but would often change his mind, and become very demeaning. He was an enigma within a dilemma."[20]

Wilkinson also had to contend with an act performed by one of his subordinates that showcased the darker side of clandestine operations. Having endured excesses by the occupying Japanese troops and their Burman auxiliaries, most Kachins were violently anti-Japanese. Yet, especially early in the war, some Kachins also worked for the Japanese, creating a complicated counterintelligence situation for Detachment 101.[21] In late 1943, one of the SOE men detailed from the British, "Red" Maddox, executed a Kachin villager suspected of being a Japanese spy. Although the situation appeared not to have caused any untoward reaction from the local population, Wilkinson was understandably quite incensed. Detachment 101's position in the Kachin hills was tenuous, and Wilkinson faced the distinct possibility that the Kachins might turn against his group.[22] Detachment 101 could not ignore this warning and lesson lest they lose the rapport so carefully built with the Kachin.

FORWARD was originally to be a group with the limited mission of being an adjunct to the agent training school. Three unique roles, however, that proved critical for the Detachment came out of this first mission: supplying intelligence on enemy targets, rescuing Allied aircrew and lost soldiers, and recruiting Kachins. These add-on missions helped cement Detachment 101 into the American effort in Burma, and defined the unit as it went into 1944. Based on FORWARD's example, the Detachment pushed similar missions into the field.

L Group

Following on the success of FORWARD, Detachment 101 also tried a new type of mission with L Group, the first to penetrate Japanese lines for the sole mission of intelligence collection. Unlike the Special Operations (SO) role of FORWARD, L Group performed much like the Secret Intelligence (SI) role of OSS.[23] While not all missions of this type were profitable, such as the ill-fated HATE Group, the majority of these operations proved to be great successes and resulted in detailed intelligence on Japanese positions and order of battle that resulted into tactical bombing targets.[24]

L Group started when Stilwell requested that Detachment 101 should establish a supply line into Burma from Ledo, where the Ledo Road was then being built. Detachment 101 selected five newly trained native agents for the mission. L Group's leader, agent Skittles, was a natural agent. An ethnic Chinese whose family had lived in Burma and worked as merchants, Skittles spoke four Chinese dialects, as well as Urdu, Hindi, Burmese, and English.[25] The agents met with Major General Raymond Wheeler, commander of U.S. Service of Supply troops building the Ledo Road, who directed them to establish a base at Hkalak Ga in the Hukawng Valley. From there, the group would assist the effort to build the Ledo Road by looking for two missing U.S. officers assigned to V-Force, and help to reconnoiter the front by supplementing the sporadic intelligence reports coming from the Chinese and V-Force.[26] With the promise of additional personnel, the group split once it arrived in the Hukawng Valley. L Group, now composed of Skittles and a radio operator, operated in the upper part of the valley, while M Group had three men and operated in the Taro Valley.

In a true SI-type role, both groups collected intelligence on enemy dispositions, order of battle, and movements in their respective areas by operating some 50 miles ahead of the farthest Allied outposts and reporting developments back by clandestine radio communications.[27] Although their initial mission ended when they found the missing American officers, L Group continued in a similar role under the direction of the KNOTHEAD forward operating group.[28] Although short in duration, L Group demonstrated that it was possible to use native auxiliaries to infiltrate Japanese lines and provide valuable tactical intelligence via clandestine radio communications. In Peer's own admission, the results obtained were "insignificant," but these groups demonstrated that raising guerrilla forces could not be done "along the periphery or front lines. It could only be accomplished well behind the enemy lines and thereafter all our effort was exerted in that direction."[29] Such was the case with KNOTHEAD.

KNOTHEAD

The second short-range penetration operation was code-named KNOTHEAD. Although FORWARD had paved the way, KNOTHEAD made its own contribution, specifically in the recruiting of a Kachin guerrilla force and in mapping the intelligence picture of the region prior to the 1944 Allied offensive. As a group it accomplished both of these missions concurrently and extremely well. The work of FORWARD and KNOTHEAD ensured the Detachment's eventual success in theater. Like FORWARD's, KNOTHEAD's beginnings were humble.

The new Detachment 101 group went to the field to harass the enemy and to gather intelligence following the lack of success achieved by L Group.[30] A subset of KNOTHEAD's mission involved pulling Japanese forces up into the hill tracts so as to allow Chinese forces to more easily advance down the Hukawng Valley.[31] KNOTHEAD had the benefit of being able to learn from FORWARD. Using those lessons, it created an intelligence collection net and raised a guerrilla force almost as soon as it arrived in the field.

The personnel of Operation KNOTHEAD started out from Fort Hertz on 31 August 1943. Led by Captain Vincent L. Curl, formerly Eifler's first sergeant with the Thirty-fifth Infantry in Hawaii, the KNOTHEAD mission consisted of nine men accompanied by porters paid in opium, an acceptable local currency and often the only one that locals would take in payment.[32] Screened by scouts provided by the British-led Kachin Levies, the OSS team arrived near Kawnan an arduous month later, during which several of the men fell ill with malaria. They were also accompanied by Pat Quinn, formerly of A Group, and two agents who pushed past KNOTHEAD to set up PAT, a separate Detachment 101 element.

However, back at KNOTHEAD, 75 miles into enemy-held but extremely rugged territory, Curl had to find a base, arrange for local support, and gather intelligence on Japanese forces in the area. On 10 October, two additional agents parachuted to KNOTHEAD to help form two subgroups to push a radio intelligence network even deeper into Japanese-held territory.

KNOTHEAD's efforts almost immediately bore results that had a long-lasting impact upon Detachment 101's operations. The group's agents contacted Kachin village headmen to arrange for support, intelligence, and security. Whether they were on a payroll or paid per information supplied, these headmen each received between thirty and fifty silver rupees a month or the equivalent in opium. In turn, the headmen helped place other Kachins where they could gather information. In some cases, these agents were employed by the Japanese and used their position to report the disposition of enemy forces in the area to the OSS.[33]

One of the first and most influential Kachins contacted was Zhing Htaw Naw. He was already working for the British and led a Kachin guerrilla group of approximately 150 men that fought the Japanese on account of the depredations committed upon them.[34] Zhing Htaw Naw's men served as "minute men," in that they were not trained nor were they full-time soldiers.[35] Still, the OSS men recognized that Zhing Htaw Naw had the "courage and cunning of a tiger," and he commanded the respect of his fellow Kachins.[36] As such, his support was critical to Detachment 101. Curl worked out an arrangement. Zhing Htaw Naw would provide guerrillas, and Detachment 101 would supply, pay, train, and advise them.

KNOTHEAD's agents soon found a more permanent location for a base at Naw Bum. There, with local support already arranged and an intelligence network started, just as Eifler had already directed FORWARD to do, Curl contracted local labor to construct an airstrip. Following Eifler's intent to use smuggling methods in establishing his organization, KNOTHEAD camouflaged the strip from Japanese observation by using dummy houses that could be lifted off at a moment's notice. With that accomplished, Curl then followed the same pattern established by FORWARD by performing as a civil affairs officer and assisting the local population with their needs.

Like FORWARD, KNOTHEAD had the "benefit" of finding a local populace that required outside assistance. But at the time that the OSS element arrived, that area of north Burma—no doubt influenced by the British withdrawal and concurrent lack of supplies—was facing a famine. Although it could not meet every need, KNOTHEAD arranged for the drop of much-needed staples such as rice, which helped to foster local goodwill.[37] KNOT-

HEAD also had quite a bit of help from Father James Stuart, who arrived as an interpreter on 15 November 1943.[38]

The colleague of Father Denis McAlindon (who helped Operation FORWARD), Stuart was a Columban missionary. As such, he had lived for several years in the Kachin hills and knew the local customs and language fluently. He came as close as an outsider could come to being a Kachin. In short, his experience and willingness to help the OSS proved to be indispensible.

Stuart was one of a kind. Fervent supporters of the Kachin people, after the Japanese invasion, both Fathers Stuart and McAlindon stayed behind to assist the peoples that they had pledged to help. Though the priests were Irish and from a neutral country, the Japanese were extremely wary of allowing a European to live among the native people. The two fathers escaped Japanese internment using their wits and, when required, force. But the threat of the Japanese did not keep them on the sidelines.

Japanese excesses forced the fathers to do more to help their people. Kachin suffering only increased their will to resist and help the people that they came to serve. Father McAlindon gave FORWARD excellent service, though he tended to his people as soon as he could. Father Stuart was different, and as such, played a larger role with Detachment 101. He helped pave the way for local cooperation with the Allies, saving KNOTHEAD months of effort.[39]

Still, having such a friendly environment allowed for a burgeoning network that promised rapid progress. Luck also played a part. This was apparent when a Japanese fighter pilot crash-landed nearby. Zhing Htaw Naw's Kachins captured the pilot. The Japanese airman walked into a Kachin village and was given food. As he sat down to eat, the Kachins "jumped him. His jiu-jitsu almost got him away but they finally tied him up."[40] As the captors led the pilot to KNOTHEAD, Kachins from RED fired a submachine gun over their heads, forcing Zhing Htaw Naw's men to drop the prisoner and run. Then RED reported that it had in fact captured a Japanese pilot. Since RED did not have an airstrip, its guerrillas brought the Japanese pilot back to the control of KNOTHEAD. There, the Detachment had one of its many "tests."

At the time, Detachment 101 did not have any rated pilots despite pleas to OSS Washington to remedy the situation. Eifler had a rudimentary knowledge of flying, and on his own accord had purchased a 1920s-era British de Havilland Moth biplane. The OSS colonel braved the uncharted flight into Japanese-occupied territory to pick up the pilot. As a precaution, the Japanese pilot was drugged for the flight back. In case he woke up and tried to either take control of the aircraft or cause it to crash, a rope was fastened around his neck so that Eifler could strangle the Japanese pilot should the need arise. Eifler flew the Japanese pilot from KNOTHEAD's airstrip on 17 November 1943. The intelligence that the captured pilot provided assisted the Tenth Air Force in targeting Japanese interceptor bases.[41] Eifler's experience with KNOTHEAD's airstrip came in handy.

It was in this environment that Donovan, then in the Far East to view OSS field operations and confer with his commanders, flew into Japanese-held territory on 8 December 1943. Donovan also wanted to evaluate Eifler's suitability of command because he had heard reports that the Detachment 101 commander had been acting irrationally after the B Group insertion. After getting a brief at Nazira, Eifler offered to take Donovan to see one of Detachment 101's field groups. Although it was foolish of Eifler to offer, more inexplicably considering that he was there to evaluate the Detachment 101 commander's fitness to remain in command, Donovan accepted. This was one of the few times that Donovan entered enemy territory. Flying the same antiquated aircraft as before, Eifler brought Donovan in to see KNOTHEAD because it was relatively established and he knew the airstrip. Donovan's observation of KNOTHEAD provided a view of life in the field, and showcased what Detachment 101 was accomplishing with so little. There, in the base so many miles into enemy occupied territory, the OSS chief met the KNOTHEAD staff, Father Stuart, Curl, Zhing Htaw Naw, and several Kachin guerrillas, before Eifler returned them both safely to Nazira.

Although Stuart advised against it due to the amount of natives it would attract, Eifler, backed by Donovan, told the Kachins that Detachment 101 would feed all refugees because they "were the wives, children, and relatives of our own informers and were forced to leave their own villages because they had cooperated with us."[42] Stuart warned that KNOTHEAD could soon experience an influx of as many as 300 refugees, but that number soon reached almost 700. Despite Eifler's and Donovan's assurances, the OSS simply could not supply the amount of food and necessities required to support such a large group. As a result, in January 1944, Stuart led hundreds of the refugees out to Allied lines.

Still, from Detachment 101's perspective the trip was a success. It gave the group a chance to show Donovan firsthand its accomplishments, but it also helped to reinforce Detachment 101's demands. Donovan was "impressed with how much was being done with so little . . . it was not until he saw 101 first hand that he realized the true situation." As a result Detachment 101 began to receive more support from OSS Washington.[43] This included more supplies and personnel. It was after this trip that the group started to receive its own L-1 planes.[44] It was a bit ironic that this trip justified Detachment 101's use of aircraft, because they were already proving their utility to the air force through providing intelligence.

Until KNOTHEAD set up its intelligence network, the U.S. Air Force did not have spotters on the ground in that area to identify targets. Not only did Detachment 101 agents provide targets, but it also conducted bomb damage assessments. After being told of the results, Lieutenant Jenkins, a P-40 pilot shot down and recovered by Detachment 101, "was amazed to find that their routine missions dropping a few bombs down in the mass of trees and green foliage where they were told to, had caused any damage at all, much less blown to bits Jap personnel, petrol, and ammo dumps."[45] Clearly, Detachment 101 had begun to make a difference in supplying intelligence, but also in beginning to wage a guerrilla war.

With Kachin help, Detachment 101 groups were conducting limited offensive guerrilla actions by the end of 1943. Technician Third Grade Tom Moon of KNOTHEAD reported, "Every time they got a chance to knock off a Jap patrol they did it because it was a psychological play."[46] Some of these actions were quite fierce, as evidenced in this 27 December 1943 skirmish near Jaiwa, described in an OSS report:

> The Japs were quite close before our men opened fire. Some Japs fell but they were so close . . . that they rushed our men and hand to hand fighting ensued. Six Japs tried to seize our Bren gun and Sai La fought bravely against odds but was left with only the "locking handle" in his hand. He then grabbed a Tommy gun from one of our patrol, shot 2 Japs in an effort to retrieve his Bren gun. The Japs came to grips with him again, he tried to use his weapon hammer fashion on their bodies but struck a tree and was left with only the butt in his hand . . . [the Japanese] lost 15 killed and 5 wounded.[47]

These successes notwithstanding, the Detachment still had a long way to go before it would be able to assist a major conventional offensive.

Like FORWARD before it, KNOTHEAD greatly assisted the Allied effort in north Burma. Not only did the group supply intelligence, but it also started to form a guerrilla force among a friendly population. Its efforts proved far more effective than the long-range penetration operations previously tried by Detachment 101, and it was the short-range operation that had the lasting impact that influenced Detachment 101's operations for the rest of the war. As 1943 drew to a close, Detachment 101 had several successful short-range penetration operations, and only one long-range one. More importantly, however, the short-range operations helped prove to General Stilwell that Detachment 101 was more viable for providing immediate and valuable tactical intelligence than for conducting strategic sabotage. They also served to enhance the Detachment's clout by providing services where none existed: intelligence on enemy order of battle and locations; tactical bombing targets for the Army Air Forces; and a rescue mechanism for pilots downed while over Japanese-occupied Burma. Even though these operations did not fulfill the intent of those "booms" originally ordered by Stilwell, they succeeded in a far greater fashion than envisioned either by the general or by Detachment 101.

Although the long-range operational failures in 1943 were serious, the Detachment staff learned from the mistakes and used the concepts gained from the shallow penetrations to change their method of operation, develop standard operating procedures, institute necessary training, and most importantly, incorporate the Kachins. Detachment 101 learned the necessity of having current area intelligence and organic transportation assets, and the value of working with trusted and capable indigenous populations. Unbridled enthusiasm gave way to more realistic operational plans that yielded results. But in order to institutionalize what the Detachment learned in the field, it also had to modify its organization in Nazira.

5

Rethinking Operations: The Detachment Evolves, February 1943–January 1944

I have been giving you all that I have and I still don't know where I stand.

Carl F. Eifler to William J. Donovan

From February 1943 until the end of the year Detachment 101 went through considerable organizational change. This reflected the unit's changing focus from conducting sabotage missions behind Japanese lines to encompassing a spectrum of intelligence and guerrilla operations. After a formal agreement in April, Eifler no longer had to report to Captain Milton E. Miles in China. This made Eifler's job easier, but it also left the group unprotected and completely dependent on its standing with OSS Washington and Stilwell. In 1943 Eifler transformed the Detachment into one of greater operational and liaison capacity and laid the groundwork to allow eventual success.[1] As such, the expansion of Detachment 101's activities required it to pay greater attention to its personnel and support elements, and establish far more effective liaison efforts with other units.

The Detachment Reevaluates Its Personnel Situation

Detachment 101's main concern, once it had gained General Stilwell's tentative acceptance to remain in theater, was to acquire additional personnel. Through its agreement with SOE, Eifler had little trouble securing indigenous or Anglo-Indian/Burman recruits, but the additional personnel forced Detachment 101 to expand its training area. By June 1943, Nazira had seventeen separate agent training camps spread out over a 25-square-mile area, accommodating an ever-increasing number of students.[2] By September 1943,

57 students were undergoing radio instruction alone, and with some 150 students in training, the program was at its largest capacity of the entire war.[3] Detachment 101 also had no problem finding workers among the local population. By November it had some fifty Gurkha guards, a like number of cooks and bearers, fifteen to twenty office workers, and six couriers.[4]

These local additions were not enough to meet expanding mission requirements, exacerbated by the widespread nature of the Detachment's operations. For instance, to facilitate liaison, supply, and operations, in March 1943 the Detachment had nine personnel—including its primary officers—spread across modern Pakistan, Burma, India, China, and Bangladesh.[5] The Detachment 101 staff realized the impossibility of undertaking numerous and complex operations without additional OSS personnel. To help the unit, Stilwell approved a table of organization that increased Detachment 101 to fifty-two officers and sixty-nine enlisted men.[6]

The overworked headquarters staff especially needed new additions because they had been swamped with work once the unit began putting personnel into Burma. In February 1943, Eifler's report to OSS Washington relayed that most of his sections were undermanned, that the situation was growing worse, and that it was having a negative effect on operations. Given his new requirements, in February 1943 Eifler called for additional personnel for the following sections: finance (3), recruiting (1), school (31), medical (5), communications (21), administration (3), ordnance (1), and miscellaneous (4).[7] Yet, by September 1943, the original twenty-one man contingent had increased by only twenty-nine OSS personnel out of the sixty-nine requested.[8] Detachment 101 also needed OSS personnel for field operations because though thought impossible in 1942, the unit's efforts had shown that non-indigenous personnel could operate behind Japanese lines.

In addition, many of the new personnel who arrived did not necessarily alleviate the workload because they represented new OSS branches and at least initially served in those functions. For instance, in November, the first Field Photo Branch personnel, a twelve-man contingent led by the Hollywood director turned navy officer John Ford, arrived after a sixty-one-day voyage to record the Detachment's achievements on film. Their efforts eventually enhanced Detachment 101's reputation with OSS Washington, indirectly helping to funnel new recruits to the unit.[9]

But Eifler had additional problems with the morale of the personnel that he already had. Detachment 101's officers were concerned that peers in other units were being promoted above them. The specific incident that triggered resentment was Donovan's promotion of Captain Frank Devlin, Detachment

101's supply officer in Washington, to major. The promotion meant that officers in the field of senior grade had been passed over because slots did not exist within the Detachment for their promotion. Eifler cabled his response to Donovan in the strongest words possible short of insubordination. He said that Devlin's promotion was unacceptable while others lagged behind, and "you created a condition for me that must be corrected."[10] The problems of promotion continually vexed the Detachment.

Finances

The increase in the number of Detachment 101's operations and the expansion of its unit structure meant that its funding mechanisms required more than an officer simply thrown into the role of treasurer. In June 1943, the Detachment asked that the OSS Special Funds Branch designate an officer to handle money for clandestine operations and to pay for locally recruited agents.[11] Lieutenant George Gorin arrived in August to inherit the Detachment's unique finance requirements and to replace the de facto finance officer, Captain Robert T. Aitken. Gorin immediately discovered the group's unique financial challenges. For instance, in 1942–early 1943, silver rupees were an acceptable form of payment among pro-Allied locals in north Burma. But by the end of the year, so much silver had poured into the area that "the people now have more money than they ever had in their lives. Some of them had made more money in this year than they would in their entire life."[12] The result was a scarcity of goods. By late 1943, the indigenous population no longer wanted silver as they had nothing to buy with their newfound wealth. Instead, they wanted opium, or even better, cloth or salt.[13] Peers later said, "It therefore became quite apparent that if we were going to operate in this remote area, we would have to pay the asking price."[14] The demand for these basic goods could be insatiable. For instance, FORWARD reported that the clothes in one goodwill drop—intended to last a month—were gone within half a day.

Yet, the Detachment had to be careful using these items as payment. Wearing Indian-made clothing, or using Indian-produced opium, while in Japanese territory could betray an agent's loyalties, amounting to a death sentence.[15] In places where Detachment 101 could still use silver as payment, only prewar rupees were acceptable, for two reasons. First, an agent could not use newly minted coins while behind Japanese lines as the rupees would immediately give away the agent as being in Allied pay. Second, the populace much preferred prewar coins because of their higher silver content. However, that same higher silver content led the British government in India to withdraw prewar rupees from circulation and declare them no longer legal tender. Reserves were tightly controlled in banks, and Gorin was unable to obtain sufficient quantities. Detachment 101's isolation also hampered Gorin, who found that even if funds existed to pay for operations, the remoteness of the main bank accounts created inevitable delays.[16] Still, by meeting demands for alternative payment—at least in part—the Detachment enhanced the cooperation they received from the locals, itself essential for conducting an unconventional warfare campaign.

Gorin also tracked exactly how much the Detachment spent. In September, the total was some $54,000. Gorin warned Washington that this figure would increase "sharply and without advance notice" and that he could estimate costs associated with training, but not field operations.[17] By December, when the total was $75,000, Gorin reported that Detachment 101's "expenses were increasing at a much greater rate than is our income."[18]

In September 1943, Detachment 101 sent the first samples of Japanese occupation money from Burma and Indo-China to Washington with the request that the OSS make counterfeit examples of these.[19] The next month, Detachment 101 received counterfeit examples back. Although Detachment 101 considered the results quite proficient, it still requested that the production facilities of OSS Washington pay more attention to the proper shading of the counterfeit bills. This was a reflection that the field had a greater operational awareness than their stateside headquarters.[20]

Communications and Coding

The dramatic growth of Detachment 101's radio network throughout 1943 led to the over-tasking of the already seriously undermanned Communications section staff. The Detachment's communications network started with the initial radio stations set up at Nazira, FORWARD, and those that were part of the mobile insertions such as A and L Groups. In addition, the Detachment expanded its network to include daily exchanges with the U.S. Army and the British. Since no additional communications personnel had arrived from the United States, Detachment 101 trained the first complements of its agent school as radio operators. These personnel allowed Detachment 101 to expand its radio networks to twenty-nine field stations by December 1943.[21]

However, the overworked communications and coding (or cryptography) staff was soon approaching its breaking point. One of the few replacements, Samuel A. Schreiner, drafted into the OSS as a civilian in India, said that when he arrived,

> I was sitting besides Sgt. Jack Pamplin and helping him plow into a stack of double-transposition messages that never got done. I almost never got back up again. Pamplin, who became one of my best friends in life, double-crossed me as soon as he could and left me holding the message bag at headquarters . . . traffic was so heavy that there was one period of more than 30 days when I didn't have time to set foot outside the headquarters compound at Nazira.[22]

In one fifteen-day period in March 1943, the radio personnel handled 135 messages composed of 9,377 character groups—jumbled letter groups read as words when decoded—and contact had been established with twenty-seven radio stations.[23] By July, the message traffic had increased to an average of 25 messages and 1,200 groups a day, or for over a fifteen-day period, 375 messages with some 18,000 character groups. Radio contact alone took fourteen-and-a-half hours a day. For the most part a single person accomplished this as all other radio operators were on operational assignments or training prospective agents. The communications personnel at Nazira had to make do, and each worked a daily schedule of sixteen to eighteen hours. This presented the serious problems of leaving messages unanswered or not following proper tradecraft as the communications and coding personnel cut corners to reply to all incoming messages.[24] Additional communications personnel were critical.

In August, the group had a respite with the arrival of the monsoon, and messages for the month slackened to 710 messages and 31,945 character groups. At this time, the chief of the Communications section estimated that he would need 145 personnel to handle post-monsoon operations.[25] Yet, in September, only eighteen military and civilian personnel were available to cover the communications needs at Nazira. All were working twelve to fifteen hours a day, seven days a week, and the pace of communications had increased to an average of more than 40 messages a day. This made a monthly average of 1,254 messages composed of 67,828 groups.[26] By November, the group had their largest amount of traffic to date, with 1,426 messages and 91,927 groups, producing such a hardship on the communications personnel that Detachment 101 decided to split its radio hubs.[27] Thereafter, lesser-volume transmitters broadcasted to a new training area set up at Gelakey, India, to reduce the impact on headquarters.

The Communications section also had to continue to improve its homemade field radio equipment. Operations had shown that the ever-present high humidity caused condensation inside the sets. Major Phillip Huston wrote in September 1943 that "after a short time of non-use in this climate, [an iron power transformer] is so full of dampness that to turn the equipment on for use is almost certain to burn out the transformer."[28] The sets had to be not only waterproof but also as robust as possible.[29] The group received some valuable feedback from Oscar Milton, of A Group. He relayed that an operator had to be thoroughly familiar with how to fix their set, but also that the batteries had to be light enough to permit their being carried long distances over rugged terrain.[30] In November, the Detachment also received its first OSS-produced radios, the SSTR-1 and SSTR-5 sets, as well as experimental charcoal burners to supply power.[31] It was an improvement, because the Communications section was the single most critical rear element for field operations. Without them, the field groups could neither send their intelligence nor receive supplies or direction.

Developing Liaison

Because the personnel of A Group were surprised to learn of the Chindit operations already taking place in their operating area, the Detachment learned the importance of developing closer liaison with other units. By far, the most important liaison efforts that the Detachment developed in 1943 were with units of the U.S. Army Air Forces (USAAF). These efforts began as mundane but helped increase the role for Detachment 101. For instance, in November, the Fourteenth Air Force asked if Detachment 101 was reporting on weather conditions.[32] Eifler took notice. By December, Detachment 101 used its agent and radio network to report weather information three times daily to the Fifty-first Fighter Group. Even though surrounded by the Japanese, the PAT group managed to place an agent on a hill 10 miles from the Myitkyina airfield.[33] Using binoculars, this agent reported when Japanese aircraft used the field, including the daily schedule of enemy planes taking off and landing.[34] Not only did this warn cargo aircraft flying the Hump, but it also helped to ensure USAAF cooperation when a Detachment drop aircraft required fighter escort.[35]

Detachment 101 took liaison a step further when, under the direction of

Major Aiken and Captain Chester R. Chartrand, the group set up an Intelligence section to keep track of all the field intelligence reports received.[36] The section routed individual reports to the appropriate end user and produced a daily intelligence summary. Originally, Detachment 101 intended the summary for outlying OSS groups, such as Detachment 101's supply and personnel processing depot in Calcutta, India, but also made it available to the British Fourteenth Army.[37] The demand for intelligence grew so that by September 1943, Nazira had two regular radio communication schedules with the British, four each with the U.S. Army and Air Force warning networks, and with naval observers in China and India. Eifler also maintained liaison with Stilwell's headquarters.[38]

The local liaison efforts with the British worked well, but presented problems at a higher level. Eifler complained in July that the British "were still interfering—the politicals now instead of the military," because they were concerned with Detachment 101's individual liaison efforts with specific British groups rather than through higher headquarters.[39] The British reasoned that Detachment 101 was purposefully doing this to divide any potential opposition, but in reality, it was the most expedient process.

However, the setting up of P Division eliminated the misunderstanding by formalizing an arrangement through which all SOE and OSS submitted operations for review. P Division gave Detachment 101 greater visibility into what was occurring in Burma because it now had access to the reports and lessons learned of SOE. However, the downside to P Division was that its establishment represented a British desire to bring Detachment 101 under their control.[40]

The QUADRANT conference at Quebec 19–24 August 1943 worked out the P Division arrangement.[41] According to the agreement, P Division would be a joint Anglo-American panel to deconflict clandestine operations in South East Asia. Both the Americans and British would have a maximum of three "voters" each and in all cases an equal quorum.[42] A British staff officer Special Forces and a U.S. deputy would coordinate SOE and OSS operations.[43] But neither the OSS nor Stilwell accepted the subordination of Detachment 101 under the British.[44]

The initial theater arrangements for P Division occurred in New Delhi in late 1943. The OSS representative, Lieutenant Colonel Richard P. Heppner, relayed Detachments 101's operational plan to the assembled members on the P Division panel, and at times that information could be very basic.[45] Heppner, unlike the other American representative, believed that the P Division agreement allowed Detachment 101 to remain autonomous.[46] Heppner reasoned that Stilwell, as the Chih Hui Pu commander, was not under the direct command of Lord Mountbatten, the South East Asia Command (SEAC) commanding officer.[47] The British thought differently because Burma was in their sphere of influence.

From Detachment 101's perspective, the arrangement for P Division was confusing and far from ideal. Detachment 101 and Stilwell feared that the arrangement allowed the British to control clandestine operations in north Burma.[48] British actions enhanced this fear in the very first P Division meetings. In early November, a senior American representative to P Division, Lieutenant Commander R. L. Taylor, wrote to General Wedemeyer about a potential "crisis in OSS relations with the British."[49] In a meeting, the British had not honored the terms of the P Division arrangement and instead stacked up the British and Indian government representation to eight as opposed to representation by just three Americans, forcing the OSS into an untenable position. An irate Heppner fired off a letter of complaint in which he called P Division a "committee [that] does not represent coordination of OSS but rather its complete subjugation." He further relayed, "I am a firm believer in team play and cooperation. At the same time I possess a certain amount of pride in nationality which causes me to rebel at treatment as manifestly arbitrary as this."[50] Even at lower levels, P Division was confusing. As late as December 1943, Peers, then the transitional commanding officer of Detachment 101, wrote, "The thing that is not clear in my mind is who is 'P' Division?"[51]

P Division's final arrangement was agreed upon when Donovan arrived on a site visit in November 1943.[52] Thereafter, Detachment 101, unlike Detachment 404, soon to be set up in Ceylon, was not in practice under SEAC direction. Detachment 101 would coordinate its operations with SOE, as Eifler had already agreed to do, but would not be under SOE or SEAC control. In return, Donovan created Detachment 404 in Ceylon as an OSS element under SEAC's direction. In June 1944, Peers became the P Division coordinator for Burma, thereby allowing him total operational control over clandestine operations in north Burma.[53] Eventually, however, instead of going to every meeting, Peers appointed a staff officer to P Division to represent Detachment 101.

In spite of these higher-level dealings, cooperation between Detachment 101 and the British continued at the local level. The British opened up their arsenals and equipment stores for reverse lend lease. In this manner, a representative from Detachment 101 was able to visit the Small Arms Factory at Ishapore, India, to evaluate British clandestine-operations weapons. These results were due to the liaison Eifler had already achieved with SOE and its representative with Detachment 101, Wally Richmond, who continued procuring additional British and Commonwealth personnel for detached service to Detachment 101.[54]

Supplies Remain a Problem

As the Detachment continued to expand through 1943, supplies continued to be lacking. In part this was because the war in Europe took precedence, and in part because Detachment 101 was at the end of a limited logistics line and attention from OSS Washington still was not adequate. To combat the situation, Detachment 101 detailed Lieutenant David E. Tillquist to Karachi in present-day Pakistan with hopes that he could prevent losses in this port city of supplies intended for Nazira. Other units there tended to steal Detachment 101's equipment after painting out the identifying mark—Task Force 5405-A—and substituting their own. In July, Peers stated to OSS Washington that it was best to ship equipment along with new personnel who could double as escorts, saying "regardless of how carefully a box is marked, if the identification is ripped off, the box belongs to the first person to claim it."[55] Detachment 101 supply officers arrived at a solution by having OSS Washington mark each crate coming into theater for Detachment 101 with a green diagonal cross.[56] This practice was refined and later applied as standard to all OSS shipping.[57]

OSS Washington still made mistakes providing supplies that the men in Detachment 101 could not comprehend. For instance in July, 1,000 M-1 carbines arrived with only one box of ammunition, prompting an incredulous Eifler to reply, "The shipment of carbines was gladly received, but thus far, they are of little value as only one box of ammunition has arrived. This ammunition is not available in this theater at present."[58]

Using the local economy for supplies did not provide much relief either. In June, Peers reported that the markup on food items commonly available in the United States often exceeded 300 percent. In the short time the Detachment had been in India, the price of rice had risen from $1.40 per 80-pound bag to $11.50.[59] In September, Peers reported that despite the Detachment's anticipating future needs, the local merchants' prices "are just one leap ahead of us. Most of their prices are beyond reason, but their attitude is one of indifference, if you don't pay the price, someone else will."[60] The increase in indigenous personnel added to the Detachment's woes, because many local recruits had unique dietary requirements.

In August, supply problems somewhat eased because Captain Harry W. Little, Detachment 101's supply officer in Calcutta, arranged for the group to draw supplies from U.S. Army Services of Supply (SOS) stocks. While this helped with common food supplies and sundries, it did not alleviate all of the Detachment's requirements. Vehicles remained a problem and could not be obtained through local SOS connections. By late 1943, the five jeeps that Detachment 101 brought with them in 1942 all needed extensive repairs, but no parts were available. Lack of communications equipment likewise remained a problem. As late as September 1943, Detachment 101 could outfit only four agents due to a lack of enough batteries for their radios.[61]

Likewise, the SOS connection could not help Detachment 101 acquire mission-specific items, such as oddities like .58 caliber model 1861 Springfield muskets, acquired in September 1943 for use by the Kachins, who preferred the single-shot muskets to more modern weapons.[62] Other items included articles produced by the OSS R&D Branch, whose existence initially was unknown to Detachment 101. For instance, in September 1943, the unit learned of a new OSS-produced medical kit only after seeing one with a navy lieutenant en route to China. Until this time, Detachment 101 had been producing such kits in an ad hoc fashion to supply to their agents.[63] Thereafter, Detachment 101 requested notification of all OSS-produced equipment. Field reports enhanced the need for these notifications. At FORWARD, William C. Wilkinson, said, "There were many situations which showed a definite need for OSS special items."[64]

November and December marked a dramatic improvement in the supply situation. Washington began to give the unit a higher priority. In one shipment alone, the group received a 63-foot boat and crew, four jeeps, the Field Photo unit and equipment, twenty additional personnel, and 50 tons of communications equipment, arms, ammunition, and rations.[65] Reflecting on the increased operational tempo and attention from Washington, the unit reorganized the supply section to be more simple and efficient. The first improvement entailed building four supply warehouses. The section then categorized supplies into most frequently used and infrequently used items. They placed the most frequently used items in the primary warehouse, which doubled as the section office. Another warehouse served as the receiving shed for new supplies, the third was used for bulk and infrequently used items, and the fourth as the parachute packing facility. The addition of five new personnel assisted operations and even permitted Peers the time to design an improved container for dropping supplies that was then manufactured in Calcutta and shipped to Nazira.[66]

New Additions to Detachment 101

The early operational failures in 1943 owed much to the lack of organic transportation assets. The Detachment had been unable to obtain aircraft because the War Department would not allow the OSS to ship planes directly to Eifler.[67] Instead, the aircraft had to come out of Stilwell's allotment. Since Stilwell's primary concern was transporting supplies over the Hump, the chance that the Detachment could draw aircraft away from this activity was virtually nonexistent.

The solution to this problem began in June when the OSS-trained Free Thai group arrived in theater. Originally assigned to Detachment 101, the Free Thai were reassigned by OSS to China just two weeks later.[68] The Free Thai brought three light Piper Cub airplanes with them, but none of them could attain sufficient altitude to surmount the Hump. At Eifler's insistence, the commander of the OSS Free Thai Unit, Lieutenant Nicol Smith, agreed to turn the planes over to Detachment 101.[69] At the end of October, the first dedicated pilot for Detachment 101, Sergeant George W. Stanford, was on his way from Washington.[70] That month, the Detachment also picked up a 1920s-era Gipsy Moth biplane. This was a lucky occurrence as soon after its procurement, Eifler managed to crash one of the Piper Cubs behind Japanese lines.[71]

Detachment 101 also received its first boats in 1943. In July, Eifler was already discussing his specific needs with OSS Washington for a fast "smuggler's boat."[72] In anticipation of receiving boats, in September 1943 Detachment 101 began construction of a small naval base at the mouth of the Brahmaputra River in India.[73] The first boat, a 63-foot air rescue craft named the *Miami*, arrived on 23 November. Its crew readied the boat over the next few days, but the boat had not even been tested nor was the fuel consumption known. Still, Eifler immediately pressed the *Miami* into a reckless but successful mission to rescue nine crewmen of a B-24 downed near Rangoon that ensured cooperation from a very grateful Tenth Air Force.[74]

Although it was not an internal capability, Detachment 101 gained one other valuable asset at the end of 1943. Through their extensive liaison efforts with the USAAF and the goodwill generated by the extraction of downed Allied pilots, Detachment 101 acquired increased use of C-47 cargo aircraft for air-dropping operations. This had an impact. In September and October, Detachment 101 conducted only two air drops, both to Operation FORWARD. In November, Coughlin suggested that the Detachment form its own air operations section to handle an ever-increasing tempo.[75] The addition of parachute-qualified Lieutenant Thomas Riley further assisted operations. Thereafter, the Detachment made improvements to manage its supply requirements and tried to ensure that an OSS member was on each drop aircraft.[76]

Air drops conducted with C-47s and proper drop crews represented a tremendous step for the group and a portent of how it would standardize its operations for the remainder of the war. The beginnings were shaky, especially when Detachment 101 had to parachute in Kachins, many of whom had never seen an airplane, much less jumped from one. Because conditions were rudimentary and planes scarce, OSS personnel could do little more than instruct the natives how to jump out and land.

KNOTHEAD's Jim Tilly recalled one such occasion when Detachment 101 readied a group of Kachins for insertion. All of the other members had jumped, and it was the last one's turn. He headed for the door with eyes like a "wild stallion." He went out, but

> "turned in mid-air and grabbed the static line before it had reached its length. The slipstream slammed him against the side of the ship. He hung on for dear life, rat-tat-tatting against the aluminum side of the C-47. With pursed lips, wild eyes and a determination that I think I can call admirable, he inched his way up the static line, little hand over little hand . . . until we were able to reach out, catch him, and pull him in. You never saw such a happy smile . . . he and I were both wild with glee. I dusted him off, turned him around, and while both of us were still ecstatic, I booted him ten feet straight out."

The Kachin had a perfect parachute opening.[77]

Another difficulty with parachuting native personnel had to do with their light weight. One of Detachment 101's soldiers joked that had nothing been done to compensate for the lack of weight, "a ninety-pound Kachin would drift in [a parachute] for a week." The solution involved adding extra weight, so the Detachment 101 men "draped the Kachins like Christmas trees with bandoliers of ammunition. When they went out, they went down."[78]

In the period through November to mid-December alone, the air operations section of Detachment 101 conducted eighteen air drops, dropping some 84,000 pounds of supplies. Although sometimes numerous air drops were conducted during the same sortie, that total represented a 900 percent increase over the previous two months. Detachment 101 reported in December, "There is no doubt . . . that [our] services to the Air Corps are recognized . . . and the reason why we enjoy [their] full cooperation."[79]

Although Detachment 101 had become a more reliable organization poised to contribute significantly to the U.S. effort against the Japanese in Burma, Eifler's days with the unit were numbered, and his stress began to show. Luce recalled one instance when Eifler browbeat the men of Operation FORWARD. While the others took it, Luce recalled that

> when he commenced to cuss me especially, I told him just exactly what I thought. . . . A change came over Eifler and he complained of being upset because of not being physically well. Such an escape mechanism might have worked with non-medical personnel but it didn't take much medical training for one to know that Eifler's aberrations of behavior were due to his own excesses [with alcohol and other drugs]. When I told him this, he shut up.[80]

This was from an officer who on meeting Eifler for the first time said that he had a "voice that would dwarf a circus barker into insignificance."[81]

He had been crucial in getting the Detachment started in 1942, but Eifler's command style had also run its course. One Detachment 101 member, in comparing Eifler's leadership style to his successor, William R. Peers, described how each would demolish a building. "Ray [Peers] would carefully remove each brick and end up with neatly stacked piles; whereas, Carl [Eifler] would get a Bull Dozer and level it—NOW. Both would achieve the objective, but in a different manner."[82] Peers expanded on this:

> Carl represented one extreme; he wanted to get things going fast, to extend operations to the utmost and hoped resources would become available. . . . I felt we should learn our lessons well . . . in other words, learn to walk first and run later . . . it was better to do a small, limited job concentrating the resources and do it well rather than trying to do a lot of things and not do any of them properly.[83]

Eifler's recklessness and impetuosity made him unsuitable to remain in command of a rapidly growing organization in need of professionalization. As the unit gained more success and its operations became more complicated, Detachment 101 needed a greater level of reliability. Eifler's lack of success in pushing the long-range penetration operations gave an indication that the unit needed more careful operational planning. Although Peers was speaking about a compromised mission, he could just as well have been speaking about Eifler's command style: "It seemed to me we were moving a trifle too fast. . . . We were getting into something we were not yet prepared to do."[84]

In June 1943, Eifler asked Donovan to come out to evaluate Detachment 101 so that he could get a better understanding of Detachment 101's problems and efforts.[85] Donovan came in November, with the veiled mission of evaluating the Detachment 101 commander's mental state, but nonetheless immediately accepted Eifler's invitation to visit one of the groups that was behind Japanese lines. In a foolhardy move, they flew in the Gipsy Moth to visit KNOTHEAD.[86] Afterward, the OSS chief went to China. When he stopped back at Detachment 101 in December, Donovan ordered Eifler to relinquish command for medical reasons and to return stateside to recover.[87] Donovan briefly placed Coughlin in charge of Detachment 101 before making him the strategic services officer (SSO). Coughlin then turned the unit over to Peers.[88] Yet, Detachment 101 had seen the end of an era when Eifler left.

Colonel Eifler had played a critical role in the Detachment. He was impulsive and reckless, but he also set out to succeed regardless of the amount of effort required or the obstacles. His friendship with Stilwell had gained Detachment 101 a place in Burma and had allowed the unit to stay despite its early setbacks. Largely through his unceasing liaison efforts, Eifler had built the unit from nothing into a group that was capable of conducting shallow penetration operations and that was beginning to assert control over its own operational assets. Under his direction, the group evolved from an SO-only function into one that had begun to encompass other OSS branches and capabilities. In particular, the Communications section became critical to the functioning of the unit, for without it, Detachment 101 would have been useless. In addition, this section was responsible for what was at first merely the forwarding of intelligence, but later became collection. As tactical intelligence became important to the USAAF's bombing campaign, Detachment 101's original SO function took a back seat.

Given that Detachment 101 had stepped into a largely unknown operating environment—and was a pathfinder entity in its own right—ongoing operations shaped the group's direction, and Detachment 101 adapted its organization/operations to events as they occurred. Yet, in this critical period for Detachment 101, the group started to capitalize on its strengths. Under Peers's command, the lack of direction from either Stilwell or Donovan allowed Detachment 101 to exploit its new direction. Peers melded Eifler's ideas with his own and expanded upon the size, structure, and utility of the Detachment. Peers's early months of command were critical as Detachment 101 braced itself for the Myitkyina Campaign.

6

Peers Takes Over: Detachment 101 Comes of Age, January–May 1944

At the time our resources were already stretched to the breaking point and little had been done toward carrying out Stilwell's directive. Moreover, his directive was oriented strictly toward Northern Burma and both John [Coughlin] and I felt it would be best initially to do a small limited job in that area and do it properly.

William R. Peers

Colonel Eifler's necessary initial audaciousness that bordered on recklessness gained Detachment 101 a foothold in the CBI, but Lieutenant Colonel Peers was responsible for re-forming the unit into an effective organization that enhanced the U.S. effort in Burma. Like Eifler, Peers was largely left to his own devices in running Detachment 101. Technically Peers should have reported to Donovan through Colonel John G. Coughlin, the CBI strategic services officer. But, according to Peers, Coughlin "gave me absolute free rein."[1] Peers's efforts streamlined Detachment 101 into one capable of supporting a conventional campaign in north Burma.

Although taking much from his former commander, Peers quickly phased out Eifler's brash operational style. These methods had left a mark on Detachment 101, though perhaps not a positive one. One person who visited Detachment 101 soon after Eifler departed remarked to Donovan that he found "a bunch of desperados who know that sooner or later they are going to be hunted down but hope to sell their lives as dearly as possible when the time comes."[2] Peers combated this attitude by replacing potentially high return but exceptionally risky operations focused on specific objectives with ones aimed at four broader goals: securing information on Japanese military movements and intentions; locating targets for the USAAF; rescuing downed USAAF personnel; and fomenting guerrilla warfare.[3] Peers transformed Detachment 101 into a far more reliable force that developed a reputation for doing the seemingly impossible.

Peers built on the foundation Eifler had established. Although the majority of Eifler's long-range penetration operations had failed, Peers reinforced the shallow penetrations, which had mostly exceeded expectations. To enhance Detachment 101's effectiveness, however, he needed to reconfigure the Detachment's force structure. He strengthened the core areas of personnel, schools and training, liaison, and communications. Peers also sought to "get the organization decentralized" so that each element could function more independently.[4] In response, Stilwell developed greater confidence in Detachment 101. As one senior OSS observer remarked several months after Peers took over, "I do not think that the OSS could be in a stronger position in any theater than is the 101."[5]

Indeed, Stilwell had to rely on the relatively inexperienced OSS outfit for his most audacious attempt: the seizure of Myitkyina. In February 1944, Stilwell called Peers and Northern Combat Area Command's (NCAC) OSS liaison officer, Major Chester Chartrand, to a meeting. There, in a rain-soaked hut, the OSS officers met with Stilwell and his son, Colonel Joseph Stilwell Jr. The Army officers wanted to know what Detachment 101 had done up to that point and what it was planning to do.

Peers accurately explained that 101 was "just getting over the initial growing pains."[6] With about thirty OSS men, Detachment 101 was running six bases (FORWARD, OSCAR, DROWN, PAT, KNOTHEAD, and RED) in occupied territory and was organizing Kachins to serve as intelligence collectors and guerrillas. However, Stilwell needed more and directed Peers to increase Detachment 101's guerrilla strength to some 3,000 because he needed intelligence and ambushing actions to support the upcoming offensive and to keep the Japanese off balance. Stilwell did not tell Lieutenant Colonel Peers how to do this, as long as "we can depend on their information."[7] In turn, Peers did not tell his field commanders how to accomplish the task and gave them only broad directives.

Then, Stilwell asked Peers what he needed. The answer was more personnel, arms, and ammunition to supply the guerrillas; better and more frequent access to drop aircraft; and shipping priorities for supplies that were caught up in the long supply channels to the CBI. Stilwell immediately met these requests. In addition to giving Detachment 101 several U.S. Army officers who had newly arrived in India, Stilwell transferred the bulk of the American personnel in the British V-Force to Detachment 101. This gave Detachment 101 an immediate trained cadre of five officers, thirty enlisted men, and forty

Kachins. The addition of the V-Force personnel gave Detachment 101 much more than additional operational capacity. As a plus, many of the Americans previously on loan to V-Force came from the 988th Signal Service Battalion and now served as additional radio operators. Former V-Force personnel brought with them a great knowledge of the Burmese jungles and peoples, and in some cases fluency in the Kachin language. The personnel addition coincided with the establishment of an operations center at Nazira that helped coordinate the field groups and increased the utility of Detachment 101's intelligence.[8]

Detachment 101 kept building its field units to increase their intelligence gathering and guerrilla potential. By January 1944, Operation FORWARD had all the roads north of Myitkyina under observation and had agents working in Myitkyina and Bhamo. By February 1944, Detachment 101 had produced a detailed order of battle of Japanese forces in the Myitkyina area. It was important that Detachment 101 had the time to learn the area and gain the trust of the local inhabitants prior to assisting conventional Allied forces during the drive on Myitkyina. Beginning in March, the OSS shifted its priority from supplying intelligence on the Japanese to assisting Allied forces as they strove to secure north Burma and the eventual route of the Ledo Road. This involved assisting both British Major General Orde C. Wingate's Chindits and Brigadier General Franklin D. Merrill's GALAHAD force.

After he returned from his initial Chindit expedition in 1943, Wingate set out to train a second force, dubbed the "Special Force." Although its six brigades were known officially as the Third Indian Infantry Division, Wingate's long-range penetration group retained the Chindit name. This second Chindit force entered Burma in two phases. Brigadier General Bernard E. Fergusson's 3,000-man Sixteenth Infantry Brigade entered Burma on 5 February 1944 at the start of a 360-mile march to their rally point at Indaw. The USAAF First Air Commando Group, under Lieutenant Colonels John R. Alison and Philip G. Cochran, was a specially created unit with fighters, light bombers, transports, liaison aircraft, gliders, and helicopters. It brought the main body of nearly 9,250 Chindits behind Japanese lines to a strip codenamed BROADWAY, south of Myitkyina, during the night of 5 March as part of Operation THURSDAY. Incidentally, this was the same drop zone used by A Group in 1943.

Shortly after Wingate died in a plane crash near Imphal, India, on 24 March 1944, Major General William Slim, the British Fourteenth Army commander, transferred the Chindits to General Stilwell. They cut the Japanese lines of supply to Myitkyina from the south but took heavy losses. By the time the Chindits withdrew to India in August 1944, they had suffered 1,400 killed and 2,500 wounded.[9]

Brigadier General Franklin D. Merrill commanded the GALAHAD force, or 5307th Composite Unit (Provisional), popularly known as Merrill's Marauders. It was essentially a light infantry regiment of 3,000 personnel formed from volunteers; veterans of Guadalcanal and New Guinea, jungle-warfare specialists from the Panama Canal Zone, and soldiers from units in the United States. Like the Chindits' use of mules, mule transport carried ammunition and food supplies air-dropped by the 10th USAAF. The Marauders, like the Chindits, proved to be one of General Stilwell's few reliable units.

The Marauders began their war in north Burma on 24 February 1944. Their mission was to attack the Japanese Eighteenth Division from the rear because the Chinese divisions, fighting in the Hukawng Valley since October 1943 and keeping the main enemy force occupied, had proved unable, or unwilling, to defeat the Japanese. However, disease, fatigue, and combat severely weakened the Marauder battalions as they maneuvered behind enemy lines. Before capturing the Myitkyina airfield on 17 May 1944, the Marauders were already down to 50 percent effectives. Marauder volunteers had the impression that they would withdraw after ninety days in the field. However, when the Chinese failed to capture Myitkyina, Stilwell chose to keep his only American conventional force in the field. By the end of May, the Marauders were evacuating seventy-five to one hundred men daily because of disease. Stilwell admitted in his diary on 30 May that "GALAHAD is just shot."[10] That meant that the majority of the forces encircling Myitkyina were Chinese. Stilwell needed Detachment 101 to augment conventional Allied units and serve as a maneuver element. This was the strategic situation in the first few months of Peers's command. Things were chaotic and he was pulled in numerous directions, "Sometimes working at the hectic pace we were, one becomes so involved in trying to keep up with the day to day necessities that one loses sight of the objectives; commonly referred to as not being able to see the forest for the trees."[11]

Existing Force Structure

Although no longer Detachment 101's commander, Eifler did not cut his ties to the unit. Eifler took his characteristic energy to OSS Washington, where he ensured that Detachment 101 received more personnel than ever before.

The additional personnel increased morale in Detachment 101. The personnel most in demand at this stage were communications personnel and administrative types, particularly typists, who were needed to generate reports, compile plans, and essentially keep things running at Nazira. Also needed were supply personnel, mechanics, and drivers. Detachment 101 needed these support troops to allow headquarters to devote its efforts to operations. The recruiting of indigenous agents continued unabated, and Wally Richmond's replacement, Major Coffey, secured Anglo-Burmese agents in Calcutta. The largest remaining need was for medical personnel, with spaces available for twelve doctors and fifteen enlisted medics or pharmacists' mates. At the time, the Detachment had a little over 600 military and civilian personnel, not counting guerrillas and agents.[12]

The operations of three sections in particular, MU, Finance, and Field Photo, expanded rapidly in this period. Flush with their recent success of rescuing nine aircrew downed deep over Japanese-controlled waters, the fledgling MU section had ambitious plans. It wanted to use the *Miami* as a training vessel and acquire two specially modified PT boats and a 42-foot launch to conduct arms resupply, perform clandestine insertions, attack Japanese coastal traffic, and undertake rescue work.[13] The group managed to obtain just one extra boat before April 1944.

Undeterred, the MU section strengthened their relationships with the British maritime component of SOE and with captains of smaller British naval vessels. These connections helped the OSS crews discover the pitfalls of navigating along the Burma coast and provided access to current weather reports. The group also discovered then that there were no suitable locations for an MU base along the India or Burma coast during the monsoon season. The head of the MU section, Ensign William Shepherd, suggested to Peers that the group move to Ceylon, where the OSS was in the process of setting up what later became Detachment 404.[14] Peers allowed the transfer, but expected the group to be back operating on the India/Burma coast after the monsoon. Even though colocated with another OSS group, the section remained part of Detachment 101.[15]

The Detachment's Finance section also saw increased activity. Because of irregularities and potential graft on the part of formerly assigned British personnel, it had the additional duty of accounting for the previous period.[16] As an example, Gorin estimated the monthly operations of FORWARD—employing 107 OSS and indigenous personnel—as requiring 9,000 rupees of new silver, 4,000 of old, 50 gold sovereigns, and 30 seers (a seer is about two pounds) of opium.[17] By May, increased operations raised the cost of running the Detachment to some $150,000 per month, or almost $2 million in 2011 dollars.[18] Additional personnel allowed the Finance section staff to reduce their individual duties. Now, one sergeant assumed duties as a cashier, another as an accountant, and still another as a dispersing agent. Showing a remarkable improvement, the Finance section's greatest need was having enough office supplies.

Peers used his Field Photo section as a method to visually show OSS Washington the work being accomplished by Detachment 101 and to put faces to names that appeared in reports. The section shot multiple rolls of film from enemy-occupied territory as part of a project to document Detachment 101's operations. They also began shooting motion pictures to send back to OSS Washington, which in turn used them for propaganda and training films.[19]

The Detachment's supply situation improved. The Detachment finally received new vehicles, needed because, Peers claimed to Donovan, he had "probably the oldest running jeeps in India," ending the report with "Our transportation is old and these roads simply beat them to death."[20] In January Detachment 101 added four new jeeps, three weapons carriers, two command cars, two trucks, a station wagon, a sedan, and a motorcycle to the motor pool.[21] But additional vehicles created another headache, as they required hard-to-find mechanics and nonexistent spare parts, leaving no way to fix the vehicles when they broke down.

By February, supply problems eased and the U.S. Army SOS provided items every two days by train from Calcutta or by truck from Chabua. Even so, some items remained hard to obtain, including ordnance, photographic materials, spare parts, generators, radio equipment, and specific OSS-issue items.[22] The acquisition of a warehouse in Chabua in April improved supply by allowing the Detachment to take advantage of the SOS stocks held there. Detachment 101 reported that their supply requests to SOS were "deserving of attention and we usually receive their best."[23] By May, the chief medical officer at Nazira, Major Archie Chun Ming, summed it up when he wrote, "We are still able to supply men in the field adequately in spite of the rapid expansion of personnel. Our ability to do this can be credited to good planning."[24]

Having supplies at Nariza was one matter, but getting it to the field was another. Captain Sherman P. Joost, newly in charge of the Detachment 101 Air Drop section, reported that the facilities were "extremely inadequate," but that "in all fairness . . . they being a new outfit . . . and already overburdened with their so-called regular customers," that the section was severely overworked.[25] He reasoned that if Air Drop reduced its duties to just rigging parachutes to drop loads and preparing staples like rice, salt, and sugar, then the section would run much more efficiently. The Detachment also moved two officers and a radio operator to Dinjan Airfield to be colocated with the USAAF cargo squadrons. These officers secured aircraft, arranged flight schedules, briefed the aircrews and pilots, put previously packed items on the planes, and accompanied the drops. They helped to ensure that each group received its correct supplies and that constant coordination was maintained with the two main units that helped in the Detachment's dropping operations: the Second Troop Carrier Squadron and the Rescue section of the Air Transport Command.[26] The aircrews—all experienced and skilled volunteers—were given a security brief and told never to reveal the location, cargos, or personnel dropped.[27] First Lieutenant Joseph E. Lazarsky, who commanded the Air Drop section in early 1944, worked at the Second TCS headquarters at Dinjan. "I stayed with them, and I ate with them. My relationship with the 2nd troops was so good . . . we became priority, number one."[28]

He also described the flights: "The jungle looks all the same from up above. But, even where it was bad [no landmarks], I knew where [our] guys were." The OSS personnel on the ground were to signal the drop aircraft if they sighted any Japanese fighter aircraft in the area. Otherwise, the unarmed drop aircraft would have been sitting ducks if intercepted. Should Japanese aircraft be spotted, the drop aircraft turned around, because it was "not worth it . . . you get your ass shot down and that's it," said Lazarsky.[29] Peers recalled, "If the weather was clear, there were zeros, and if the weather was too bad, there was little chance of being able to get into the drop zone. What we were looking for was bad weather, but not too bad."[30]

Even so, it was hazardous duty. Staff Sergeant "Bud" Banker, an armorer pressed to serve as a first-time kicker, recalled one incident:

> The pilot tilted the airplane to help get the cargo out because it was quite heavy. When that happened, we were on our own. We had to hang on with our arms. One of the kickers got his foot caught [in the cargo] and he starting to go out of the plane. I reached out and was lucky. I grabbed him around his waist belt and held on for dear life. He could have been pulled out of the door. We had no parachutes because they would have been in the way. At the last minute his foot released from the cargo.[31]

The Air Drop section soon had other things to worry about. On 18 January, the group experienced Detachment 101's single worst disaster when a flight of Japanese Zeros shot down three C-47 cargo aircraft while on a dropping operation to FORWARD, killing most of the aircrew and all of the OSS personnel. This included a Navy pharmacist mate who was preparing to jump in, a field photo photographer, and the head of the Air Drop section.[32] The disaster had immediate consequences. FORWARD did not get another supply drop for nearly a month, forcing them to live off of the land.[33] Even though supplies were low to nonexistent, Luce continued providing medical care to the locals, accomplishing, in the parlance of a later war, his best to win hearts and minds. He reported that he was "astounded by the response of the natives to the advent of medical care" because they automatically expected the Americans to provide it.[34]

Despite the work Luce was doing, his team could not work without supplies. Although the USAAF helped where and as often as it could, it did not meet all the Detachment's needs. Drops at this time averaged some 85,000 pounds a month, with the realization that they would rapidly increase throughout 1944.[35] By March, it had already risen to 137,057 pounds. April's total was 200,000 pounds. This included food and medical drops covering the needs of hundreds of indigenous refugees who were fleeing from the Japanese advance in central Burma and away from the Allied offensive in north Burma.[36] The total rose to 250,000 in May.[37] An increase in available aircraft was helped by the Detachment's contributions to the north Burma Allied offensive and its greater liaison efforts with the USAAF. Peers knew that he could rely on limited support from the USAAF but that this would dwindle when the campaign for Myitkyina was in full swing. The Detachment estimated that by September 1944 its needs would be around 500,000 pounds dropped per month, so air drop became a primary concern.[38] This required that the Air Drop section look at how it functioned. Since air drop was so important to Detachment 101, air-dropping itself deserves an explanation.

Despite what field group a member of Detachment 101 served in, or whether he supported the field from the rear, the link to all was the Air Drop section. At one time or another, many of the men in 101 served on at least one air drop mission because the demand for flights and the "kickers" needed to throw out the cargo outstripped the personnel available. Air drop was one of the core sections in Detachment 101 that allowed the field work to continue without interruption. For Detachment 101, however, paradoxically, air drop was also the unit's most dangerous assignment, despite not having the field's added dangers from disease, the jungle, and the Japanese.

The rugged, trackless, jungle-covered terrain that dominated north Burma and a lack of roads made aerial resupply necessary. The venerable

Douglas C-47 Skytrain was the main resupply aircraft. Developed as the prewar DC-3 airliner, the C-47 became the U.S. Army's major troop carrier in WWII and remained in service long after the war. For special missions, the Detachment used the small, fast, .50 caliber-armed North American B-25 Mitchell medium-bomber, but the smaller cargo capacity limited its usefulness.

Air-dropping brought with it a high financial cost, in part because most of the parachutes were not recoverable. Although they were expensive, American-made silk, or more likely nylon or rayon, parachutes performed best. Only delicate or critical items such as ammunition, radios, and medical supplies were dropped using these parachutes. Because Detachment 101 had to rely almost exclusively on air drop, Detachment 101 had to find a cheaper way to sustain its operations. The unit often substituted much cheaper locally produced parachutes made of jute (burlap) to make air resupply as economical as possible, especially when some heavy loads individually required more than one parachute. Lieutenant General William J. Slim, commander of the British Fourteenth Army, described why his force also decided to use jute parachutes. Since the war in Burma was at the bottom of the priority list for just about everything, and because the world's jute was grown in India (now Bangladesh), it was easy for the military to work with the cloth manufacturers. Within a month, they had designed a prototype parachute made entirely of jute that proved to be "eighty-five per cent as efficient and reliable as the most elaborate parachute," at a twentieth of the cost.[39] NCAC also found an easy-to-produce, sturdy, cheap, and ideal solution in the "country basket." This was a burlap-covered bamboo basket that cost less than $4 to make and was capable of holding 450 pounds. Secured to a parachute with heavy ¾-inch ropes, several could be kicked out in a single drop pass.[40] Using these methods showed that forces in Burma, including Detachment 101, adapted to and solved their problems.

Still, aerial resupply came at a high cost. American nylon parachutes alone cost $72 in 1945 (nearly $900 in 2011 dollars). Even using burlap parachutes, the cost to drop a ton of supplies—without including the average flight rate of $1,285 per sortie (more than $16,000 in 2011)—was $1909.65 (nearly $24,000 in 2011 dollars). Free-dropping supplies—not counting the sortie cost—was only $94.07 (nearly $1,200 in 2011).[41] Considering that NCAC alone parachuted some 30,000 tons of supplies, free-dropped another 33,000, and air-landed 90,000 tons from April 1943 to March 1945, it was an expensive, but necessary, enterprise.[42] Detachment 101 also had to properly pack supplies to be air-dropped.

Air drop personnel put gasoline in 55-gallon drums, padded them with sacks of rice hulls, and then secured the load to a parachute. They also repackaged unbreakable and bulky items, such as rice, clothing, salt, or animal feed, for free-dropping. For rice, they sewed a half-full sack weighing 35 pounds into a second burlap bag to prevent it from "exploding" on impact. Still, the kickers had to be especially careful during free-drops because an errant sack could easily demolish an indigenous hut, or *basha*, or kill personnel and pack animals. That occurred often enough to mention. Although most Allied troops tried to get under cover during a free-drop, Lazarsky, who served as an air drop officer with OSS Detachment 101 in early 1944, recalled, "You had to really train the Kachins that rice is coming down . . . don't try to catch it or you would be digging your own hole." Nevertheless, he recalled that the Chinese tried to steal what they could from air drops and often were "out there trying to catch the rice." When they "succeeded," as was sometimes the case, the soldier did not live very long to "celebrate," because the rice falling at that velocity literally crushed him.[43] A typical drop, however, is as follows.

On 9 March 1944, as the FORWARD group sat down at dusk to eat, the airplanes came over. Second Lieutenant Daniel Mudrinich wrote in the group's daily log, "They had a little trouble at first as they were circling way east of us. Finally the third [C-47] appeared and he saw our fires and panel. He let go with a free drop which went well over drop ground. I finally got over with a flashlight and beckoned them. . . . It took over 30 minutes for the entire drop to come down. All hands worked until 10 PM," to collect the supplies.[44] By noon the next day, Mudrinich reported that their loads had been stored away but that "everyone was tired as hell."[45]

Even with the increased effort, however, some of the field groups got impatient with the Air Drop section and complained often: "It should be logical enough to understand that a man who wears a 9 or 10 canvas shoe can not wear a 5 or 6. . . . I further suggest that the supply force try wearing shoes two or three sizes too small. . . . I think it's damn foolishness to drop a bunch of junk in the jungle that cant [*sic*] be used."[46] Personnel responsible for resupplying the field units took these comments seriously and frequently adjusted their operations as a result.

Major Raymond T. Shelby, in charge of the nascent Operations section at Nazira, responded with the following, "Don't mind speaking your mind when you don't receive specific quantities of food, equipment and so forth, give us hell . . . that is our sole existence to get you people what you need . . . so don't spare us one minute . . . we don't consider any of your requests or wires as complaints but as suggestions so we can more adequately serve."[47] Shelby's and others' efforts did not put a stop to negative complaints from the field, such as "every fucking time .30 Cal or .303 ammo is dropped . . . the opening shock of the chute rips open the container. And we search the field for loose ammo."[48]

In February, Peers requested that OSS Washington permanently assign an armed heavy aircraft to Detachment 101's dropping operations. Although the Detachment had an allotment from the USAAF of twelve planeloads per month, increased Japanese air activity forced the supply drops to be done at night, and the drops required increased protection of anywhere from nineteen to seventy-four fighter escorts monthly. Peers wanted a B-25 medium bomber, complete with operating and maintenance crews, and the possibility of a heavy B-24 bomber later. He wrote to Donovan, "This may seem like we are asking a lot but when you are in an unarmed DC [C-47 Skytrain or DC-3] it is no fun, especially when a Zero shows up."[49] Although OSS Washington did not come through, Stilwell's response was welcome. He attached two USAAF C-47s for the "exclusive use" of the Detachment.[50] The group also acquired three L-1 and one L-4 liaison aircraft, along with three pilots and a mechanic on loan from the Seventy-first Liaison Squadron. To assist airborne insertions, Peers directed the opening of a parachute school at Nazira.[51]

To get groups into the field, however, liaison was of paramount importance. Throughout early 1944, Detachment 101 continued to strengthen its relationships with other commands. Thereafter, Peers then focused on recruiting even more indigenous personnel, constructing more base facilities, and increasing training and liaison efforts.[52] All of these liaison efforts represented some of the most important advances that Detachment 101 made in 1944. Through these connections, the group secured greater cooperation from other organizations, tailored OSS support to meet their specific needs, and played a greater role in the Burma Campaign.

Not only did the Air Transport Command (ATC) give Detachment 101 credit for the rescue of several airmen, but the Detachment managed to score another coup. Through its intelligence network, Detachment 101 uncovered the existence of a Japanese radio station near Sumprabum that broadcast false signals to lure American cargo aircraft off course so that they would fly into mountainsides.[53] The ATC then briefed their pilots to avoid the trap. In a further effort to help the ATC and the Tenth USAAF, Detachment 101 stood up the OSCAR group in late February. Its primary purpose was the extraction of downed aircrews.[54] Detachment 101 finalized its plans to help in the north Burma campaign during Donovan's earlier visit. Detachment 101 then sent the plans to P Division for consideration.

While Burma was a relatively minor theater, it had plenty of special operations–type forces. Peers established liaison with every special operations unit operating in north Burma.[55] Notification of the second Wingate operation proved that P Division was now functioning as intended, when, unlike its ignorance of the first Chindit expedition, Detachment 101 learned in advance that Wingate was leading a second expedition as part of a larger Allied campaign. Detachment 101 then made sure that it had liaison with Wingate.[56] The Detachment also established contact with the First Air Commando's commanders, Allison and Cochran, and their initial meeting was "most pleasant and beneficial."[57] The unit then arranged meetings with other commanders such as Colonel Frank D. Merrill, who then had several representatives from Detachment 101 assigned to him.[58] Detachment 101 also established good relations with Colonel Joseph Stilwell, General Stilwell's son, and the NCAC G-2 head.[59] By March, Peers reported, "our present set-up . . . is working very well, especially our relationship with Merrill and naturally with Combat Hq."[60]

In April, the unit formed additional relationships with various intelligence organizations, including the British forward interrogation center at Guahati, India, which held refugees and persons taken prisoner in Japanese-occupied territory. This liaison enhanced Detachment 101's recruiting efforts. Representatives from Detachment 101 also contacted the British intelligence section at Agarapara, which interred captured Japanese agents; the British Ministry of Information in New Delhi, which performed propaganda operations; and the Burma Police Intelligence section.[61]

Detachment 101 still needed adequate communications, and frustrations remained high with OSS Washington's lack of commitment to the Communications section. This caused Peers to write to Coughlin in March that he did not think that OSS Washington understood Detachment 101's communications difficulties, nor was it "interested in finding out." Peers went on to add that "I am fairly well perturbed at . . . having to do more signal work with less men."[62] In January, the Communications section reported that lack of personnel forced it to place half-trained indigenous operators on official circuits and let them finish their training, including in Morse code, "on the job."[63] The next month, Peers reported that "our signal personnel is so limited at present time that the units we are furnishing information have assigned personnel to us to relieve the pressure."[64] The pace of the work continued to grow, and the existing personnel could not handle the extra work. In December 1943, the

Communications section handled a new high for the group of 1,571 messages containing a total of 140,471 individual coded groups.[65] By May 1944, the number of coded groups received exceeded 200,000, up 24,000 from the previous month.[66] To receive these messages, the Communications section at Nazira had seventeen radio operators who handled the message traffic coming in from ten field operators/cryptographers and from the additional personnel posted in liaison positions. These numbers, however, do not tell the complete story.

The procurement and supply of radio equipment likewise remained a problem and limited how many agents Detachment 101 could place in the field. Communications equipment was so difficult to obtain that Peers suggested that new personnel coming to Detachment 101 not bring with them supplies of personal clothing—that could be obtained in theater—but instead carry light radio equipment.[67] By April 1944, some of the communications items that the unit had ordered had not arrived after a delay of eighteen months.[68] The situation had somewhat eased in May; however, spare parts remained problematic. The biggest problem then facing the Communications section was a lack of suitable field generators, which prevented using the OSS-produced SSTR-1 set in the field.[69]

A lack of adequate communications caused problems in the field. In mid-February, KNOTHEAD reported that its radio operator spent five and half hours trying to pass traffic back to HQ. He was likely the victim of a student trainee on the other end. In exasperation, KNOTHEAD asked for another radio operator, but was told "there were none."[70] KNOTHEAD also reported that radio operators at Nazira often sent messages to the field that were undecipherable, and then did not stay on-air to receive a reply. All these occurrences led to extreme frustration in the field. This was compounded by new arrivals to the field groups who said that to avoid embarrassment the locally recruited radio trainees were reluctant to turn over their radios to a more skilled operator. Instead, if overwhelmed, the operators let the follow-on operator receive the message. Such methods were unacceptable.

Despite KNOTHEAD's subsequent recommendations, the Detachment had not solved the problem as late as February 1944. Peers relayed that his Communications and Coding sections were twenty-four hours behind in answering messages, and had committed a few potentially serious errors in missing replies to cables. Peers understood that his communications personnel were not lackadaisical, just seriously overworked.[71] Regardless of the lack of personnel, the Communications section had no choice but to transfer four of its radio operators to the cryptography subsection.[72] The creation of new facilities at Nazira, though an improvement, likewise exacerbated the personnel situation. The increased traffic necessitated a new communications hut complete with improved facilities, receivers, and antennas. The larger building allowed for the installation of new and more powerful transmitters that in turn required the construction of two large antennas of sufficient height to reach Ceylon (now Sri Lanka) and Chungking, China. The facility required new generators and the laying of telephone and electric cable.[73] In an effort to build redundancy into its communications network, the Detachment also looked to older methods. Having reasoned that past operations might have benefited from the capability, the group asked OSS Washington to recruit pigeoneers to allow agents to carry messenger birds with them on drops. Should their radio not survive the insertion, as often was the case, the agents would have another means to contact base.[74]

New OSS Branches Arrive

January 1944 saw the inclusion into Detachment 101's organizational structure of the first non–direct action OSS branches, which represented functions not driven by immediate operational requirements, such as Morale Operations (MO). Originally under the Special Operations Branch, MO was created by OSS as a separate branch in January 1943 to create and disseminate "black" propaganda, although the OSS did not actually finalize MO's directive until later that year. MO had a correspondingly slow start and difficult time establishing itself overseas. The branch was in charge of subversion and psychological warfare activities on a theater-wide scale, and was authorized to conduct tactical propaganda with front-line units.[75]

Following a plan approved by President Roosevelt on 26 May 1942, in June 1943 the Joint Chiefs of Staff authorized OSS a black propaganda function in Burma that would serve to harass the Japanese, encourage Burmese national resistance, and prepare the way for Allied operations.[76] However, the first attempt to add a true MO capability at Detachment 101 was a study paper authored by Lieutenant Commander E. L. Taylor, USN, after Donovan sent him to the group on a fact-finding mission.[77] Although Taylor's proposals were overly optimistic, they made an impression on Peers, who called for OSS Washington to send a dedicated MO officer and staff. Peers envisioned the branch as a "major unit" within Detachment 101, but left it in MO hands to make their inclusion a reality.[78] OSS Washington even had sample propaganda products for use in Burma, but could only forward them to the theater and hope that a staff that was untrained in their use or utility might employ them.[79]

Initially, the MO section of Detachment 101 was marked by the impermanence of its personnel. The first representative of MO intended for Detachment 101 arrived in February, but stayed only long enough to recommend training programs for the jungle school.[80] The next representative, Lieutenant Charles H. Fenn, intended to stay, but higher authorities then sent him to work in China.[81] In the short time he was at Detachment 101, Fenn was a flurry of activity and managed to set up a short MO training segment with the school, affected a working arrangement with the Office of War Information (OWI), and made trips to both NCAC and OSS field groups.[82] In this last capacity, he gave a brief on MO's utility, passed out examples of leaflets, and suggested rumors that groups might spread among the local population.

Under the arrangement enacted by Fenn, OWI agreed to produce propaganda pamphlets and leaflets for Detachment 101 because the OSS group did not yet have production facilities.[83] MO derived its source material from the debriefing of captured Japanese soldiers. The resulting products, sent to the field groups for dissemination, aimed at driving wedges between the ethnic groups in Burma and the Japanese.[84] One product depicted a Burmese knifing a Japanese soldier in the back. Written in Japanese on the leaflet were phrases telling the Japanese how much they were hated, including "We shall kill you, the ants will eat your flesh, the jungle will swallow your bones."[85] Other leaflets told of the damage that the Burmese resistance was inflicting upon Japanese supply lines, even though nothing outside of that performed by the Kachins actually existed. Fenn also used another MO specialty: starting rumors to erode enemy morale.[86] He also had plans to enlarge MO by five personnel, including direct liaison with NCAC and OWI.[87] Upon Fenn's leaving, however, MO was in essence no longer present in the Detachment.

In January, the first representative of the Research and Analysis (R&A) Branch came to Detachment 101 for a familiarization visit.[88] One of the original branches formed by the COI, it employed personnel, such as historians, with research backgrounds and was designed to collect and analyze information. R&A then presented its findings in formal reports to senior policy makers. With its inclusion in Detachment 101, R&A made the transition from strategic-level intelligence to providing tactical-level products for an immediate consumer.[89]

In February, Detachment 101 established regular contact with the main R&A office in New Delhi.[90] In turn, this office furnished a liaison officer to

Detachment 101, Lieutenant Charles Stelle, whom Detachment 101 then sent to be the liaison officer for Wingate. Before being reassigned, however, Stelle presented a case study for how R&A might be of use to Detachment 101, and in particular, to the Secret Intelligence (SI) section. Impressed with SI's weekly summary, Stelle saw that it could be improved with the addition of R&A officers who would cross-reference Detachment 101 reports with intelligence from other sources, such as open-source materials, resulting in all-source intelligence reports. Stelle saw additional ways that R&A personnel could help Detachment 101 better utilize its intelligence collection. He proposed forming an R&A section that could have an impact on a tactical and theater level, by assisting in imagery analysis, cartographic support, compilation of thematic intelligence reports, debriefing of OSS personnel when they returned from the field, prisoner interrogation, liaison, training of personnel in intelligence collection, and operational planning.[91] While this was good planning, nevertheless, there remained deficiencies at the Detachment regarding the handling of intelligence.

Detachment 101 had striven so hard to improve its operational capacity that it ignored the mundane. There were critical shortages of staff personnel, such as typists, to handle clerical matters.[92] The increasing number of intelligence reports required a standardized way of evaluating raw human intelligence. Many of the intelligence reports came from locally recruited agents who tended to exaggerate the numbers of Japanese personnel. By January 1944, the Detachment expected the arrival of OSS personnel who could sift through, evaluate, and compile the reports.[93]

Although merely a renaming of the functions already being performed by Majors Robert T. Aitken and Chester R. Chartrand, Detachment 101 first created the SI section by name in January.[94] The section was responsible for providing the first evaluation, analysis, and dissemination of intelligence reports, and acting as a security manager. In this first role, Detachment 101 made a truly bold move and employed a practice that is standard today. Although it needed more personnel to accomplish its plans, the group set out in its first attempts to determine the intelligence needs of other organizations, as opposed to merely sending along reports as they came in from the field. The SI section reorganized the Detachment's overall intelligence-collection effort into a series of eight geographic areas that allowed it to determine what intelligence report might best fit which non-OSS end user. The result was more-concise reports that NCAC considered so useful and the intelligence so unique that, in addition to receiving the daily radio broadcasts, it detailed a plane each week to pick up the summaries.[95]

Detachment 101 also held conferences with its intelligence consumers to find out their specific needs, enabling it to avoid forwarding intelligence that would be of little utility to a particular organization, while at the same time trying to focus on that organization's unique requirements. To enhance the usefulness of the intelligence reports, Detachment 101 used standard U.S. Army classification markings as opposed to those of the OSS or British.[96] In an additional effort to increase the utility of its intelligence, the SI section established a forward radio operator at Fort Hertz who could transfer information back to Nazira immediately. The SI section also sought to analyze captured Japanese equipment, examples of which the field groups sent back to Nazira.[97]

The second role for SI, of security, was a foreshadowing of what the OSS X-2, the counterintelligence branch, would later perform. Peers cited the lack of physical security as one of his chief concerns when he took command of the unit. Nazira alone had twenty-seven camps spread over an area of 40 square miles, and only forty-five Gurkhas available as guards. The SI section proposed a ground defense force to supplement the Gurkhas and also conduct regular patrols to guard against enemy agents. They would also have a pure counterintelligence role in which they would work to uncover any subversion from within Detachment 101 itself. But, in common with other sections, the SI section's personnel situation would not permit expansion.[98]

As opposed to the SI role, the other main function of Detachment 101 was SO. The element received a makeover in March when the group began to create an Operations section. Peers had not been pleased with what he thought was disorganization under Eifler.[99] Instead, he wanted a central staff, under Major Raymond T. Shelby, that was responsible for handling each group's needs. Shelby's first action was to meet with the commanders of other units with whom Detachment 101 had liaison, namely, the aviation units. Their reception was favorable, and these groups pledged assistance to Detachment 101 when possible.

Peers also ordered the reorganization of the field operations and the decentralization of Nazira's control. It was, according to Peers, "perhaps the biggest single step taken by 101 toward the improvement and expansion of operations during the entire Burma campaign."[100] Instead of directing individual operations, as had been the case under Eifler, Peers split the north Burma AOR into "areas." Each area had a commander, who then had a number of subunits under his control. Area commanders were responsible for operations in their subareas, and served as the first filter for intelligence reports and radio communications. This greatly eased command and control as, in large part, Peers had to direct only area commanders as opposed to a myriad of smaller groups. In turn, the area commanders had greater responsibility and latitude in directing operations. In a nod to the growing importance of Detachment 101's operations, in March Stilwell directed Peers to increase the number of his indigenous troops in north Burma to 4,000. In addition, the inclusion of the V-Force personnel meant that Detachment 101 could create another operating area.[101] The former V-Force area was code-named Operation TRAMP and covered the India/Burma border in north Burma. Combined with FORWARD, KNOTHEAD, and PAT, TRAMP created a fourth operating area for the Detachment.

Peers's spring 1944 reorganization strengthened barely functioning sections, such as Finance and Air Drop, and allowed the group to incorporate new OSS assets. The creation of an Operations section allowed the unit to coordinate its groups effectively and more efficiently develop standard operating procedures. The establishment of a central intelligence staff allowed the group to evaluate, analyze, and disseminate its profuse intelligence collection to the best end user. While OSS Washington had not yet introduced some of its branches to Detachment 101, others, like MU and MO, remained unproven. Nonetheless, they tried to integrate themselves into the unit. MU in particular had gotten off to a great start, but weather and a lack of proper staging facilities slowed its growth. The role of MO, which remained unproven, was more problematic. While its ideas—and the promises—were great, the results were not. It is important to note, however, that the inclusion of MO meant that Detachment 101 was able to look beyond its immediate tactical needs and now delved into operations that might not have an immediate return.

The reorganization also allowed greater reflection on the Detachment's role in the Burma campaign. As Major Shelby, the operations officer, put it in March, "Colonel Peers has for a long time been forced to run the 'Show,' by himself, but now that a few new officers have been assigned to him he is setting the organization up as a Battalion, with different sections and that is going to relieve his mind for the 'Big,' picture."[102] Peers was moving as rapidly as possible to incorporate new OSS branches into the Detachment 101 force structure to give the unit greater utility.[103] He wrote back to OSS Washington in May, telling a prior visitor, who had come to the Detachment when Eifler had been in charge, "You would never recognize the unit at present."[104] For this, Peers deserved the credit.

Detachment 101's first commander, Carl Eifler, views civilian vehicles left behind at Sumprabum during the retreat from the 1942 Japanese invasion of Burma. The photo was taken in January 1943 when Eifler was establishing Detachment 101's first mission, FORWARD, at Fort Hertz. (USASOC)

Eifler displays Kachin *punji* stick. The Kachins planted the *punji* sticks, made of fire-hardened bamboo, at the sides of roads and trails to impale Japanese troops when they dived for cover during an ambush. (USASOC)

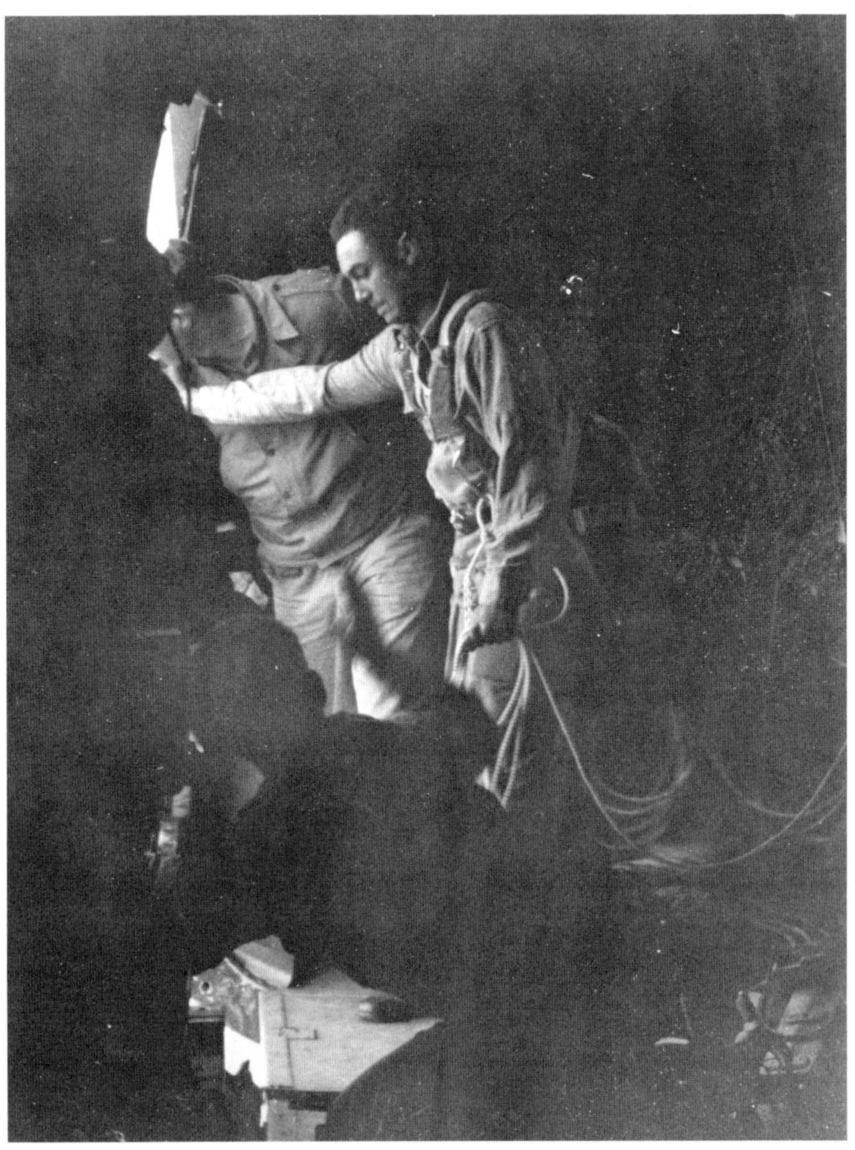

John Beamish prepares to jump into Burma as part of the A Group, Detachment 101's first long-range penetration mission, February 1943. A Group was the only successful long-range penetration mission through early 1944. (USASOC)

The B Group mission on their way to the drop zone. The Japanese captured and executed the entire mission. (USASOC)

James Luce, standing center, with Kachin guerrillas of Operation FORWARD. Luce, a U.S. Navy surgeon, found himself the commander of one of Detachment 101's main guerrilla groups. (USASOC)

Vincent Curl, commander of Operation KNOTHEAD, stands with Kachin leader Zhing Htaw Naw. Zhing Htaw Naw's support of Detachment 101 was crucial to forming a guerrilla force in 1944. (NARA)

One of Detachment 101's first air-sea rescue boats, late 1943. (NARA)

Indigenous radio operators in training. Notice that they are using one of Detachment 101's homebuilt radios and supplying power with a hand-cranked generator. (NARA)

Indigenous recruits learn coding and cyphers. Having secure communications was the key to conducting intelligence and guerrilla operations. (NARA)

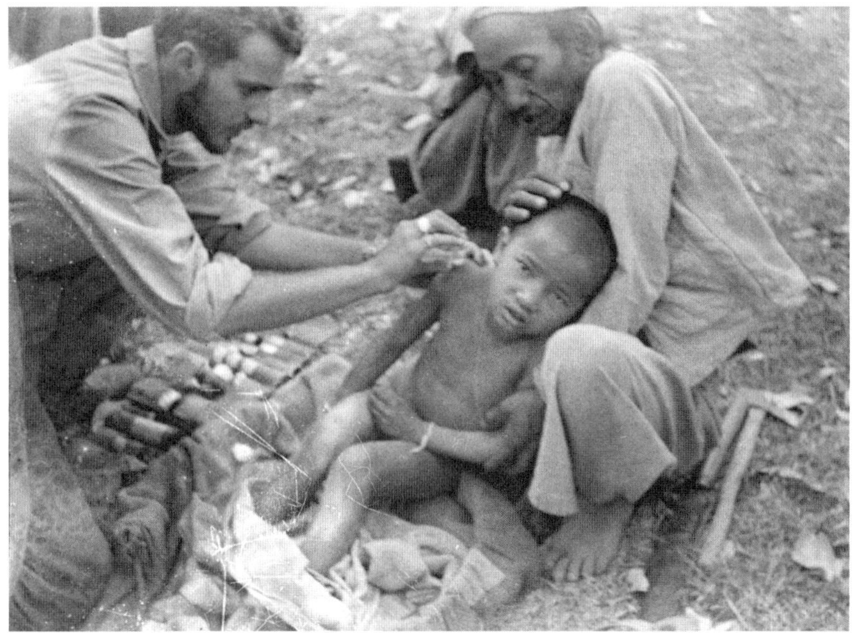

Detachment 101 field groups conducted ad hoc civil affairs missions by providing humanitarian relief that bolstered rapport. Notice the OSS-issued jungle medical kit behind the medic. (NARA)

Detachment 101 headquarters at Nazira, India. (NARA)

This photograph details the difficult terrain over which Detachment 101 parachuted its personnel during airborne insertions. In addition, many of the parachutists had little, if any, airborne training prior to their jump. (USASOC)

Lieutenant General Joseph W. Stilwell (center) confers with Detachment 101 commander, William R. Peers (right), prior to the Myitkyina Campaign. To the left is Joseph W. Stilwell Jr., the NCAC G2. (USASOC)

After receiving Stilwell's directive to prepare for the Myitkyina Campaign, Peers flew into occupied Burma to personally brief his group commanders. Here at KNOTHEAD are Vincent Curl, Lt. Cahill (pilot), Peers, and Father James Stuart. (USASOC)

Chester Chartrand, Detachment 101's liaison officer to NCAC G2 during the Myitkyina Campaign, plots newly arrived intelligence regarding Japanese dispositions on an area map. (USASOC)

One of the most important of Detachment 101's support functions was communications. On the right, Allen Richter sends a message to the field. (USASOC)

Mid-1944, a Kachin guide alongside a soldier from Merrill's Marauders. Detachment 101-provided Kachins served as guides and flank security for the Marauders as they moved to assault Myitkyina. (USASOC)

Getting supplies to the field groups was an unsung task, but also Detachment 101's most dangerous. Looking at the camera is Thomas Riley, killed on 18 January 1944 when the C-47 in which he was riding was shot down by Japanese fighters near Operation FORWARD, north of Myitkyina. (NARA)

Six of Detachment 101's Air Drop Section warehouses at Dinjan Airfield, India. (USASOC)

Air-drop kickers prepare to shove a supply load out the door of a C-47. Notice the homebuilt drop containers, the lack of safety straps, and the man crouching to assist by pushing with his feet. (USASOC)

A supply drop as seen from the ground. The C-47 banks away after a successful drop, early 1944. (USASOC)

A Detachment 101 guerrilla group marching through dense jungle. The Kachins' extensive knowledge of the jungle allowed Detachment 101 mastery over the terrain. (NARA)

Most of the Detachment 101 Kachins in the photo are armed with British Enfield rifles, but the guerrilla on the left has an American Civil War–era Springfield model 1861 rifled musket. Detachment 101 received a shipment of the Springfields because the Kachins could make their own gunpowder and shot. (NARA)

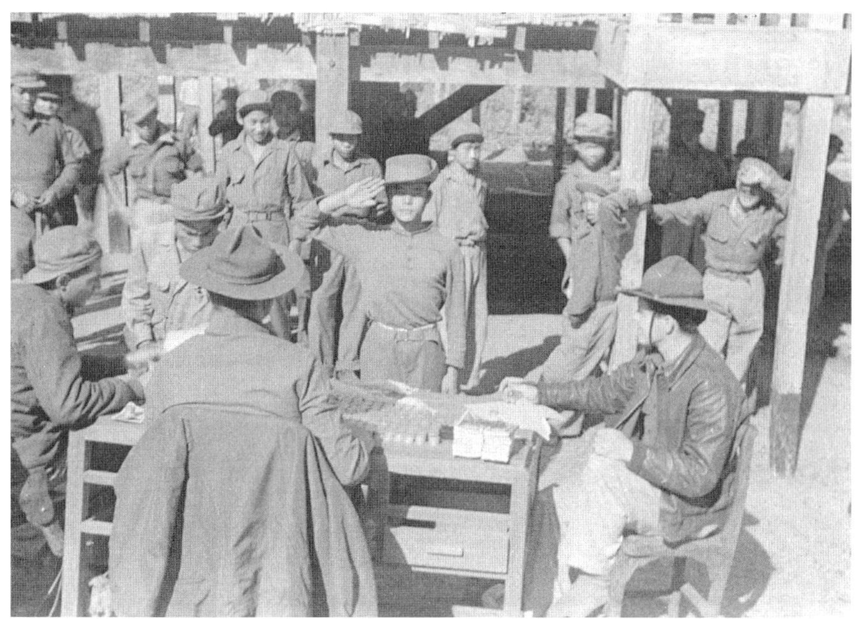

Detachment 101 guerrillas receive their pay, in this case a mixture of silver rupees and paper money. Detachment 101 created its own finance section to handle the unique requirements of clandestine operations in Burma. (NARA)

Newly arrived Operational Group (OG) member Zachariah Ebaugh instructs Detachment 101 personnel in the use of the M9 Bazooka, 1944. Detachment 101's guerrilla groups continually received heavier armament to make up for their lack of artillery. (NARA)

Sherman "Pete" Joost, commander of Operation FORWARD, in his field headquarters during the Myitkyina Campaign, July 1944. (NARA)

A Japanese prisoner receives a field interrogation prior to being flown to allied territory. At the left is the Detachment 101 commander, Charles "the Greek" Coussoule of Area II, while a Nisei on the right translates. (NARA)

Detachment 101 personnel instruct new recruits in the use of the British Bren gun. Because of its durability, weight, and heavy firepower, the Bren was a mainstay of the guerrilla groups. (NARA)

This small group of guerrillas is armed with a Johnson light machine gun, Thompson sub-machine guns, Johnson rifles, and a Bren gun, requiring three different kinds of ammunition. The field groups carried a multitude of weapons, exacerbating supply requirements. (NARA)

Two of Detachment 101's battalion commanders, Lazum Tang and Joseph Lazarsky, illustrate the close comradeship in the unit. (NARA)

The MM Small Combat Team prepares to jump into Burma, January 1945. The small combat team represented the transition of Detachment 101 from intelligence and guerrilla missions to a combat role. (NARA)

A Detachment 101 guerrilla unit on the march in the Shan States, mid-1945. The vegetation is much more sparse and the climate far drier than in the Kachin areas to the north. (NARA)

Detachment 101 found that the majority of its Shan recruits were not as motivated as the Kachins. Here, a group of Shans pile their issued clothing and equipment in dishonor after not wanting to continue operations. (NARA)

A Detachment 101 guerrilla group on the move, mid-1945. In the middle is one of Detachment 101's paratroopers; the indigenous troops mostly march in their bare feet. (NARA)

Indigenous agents under the Secret Intelligence Branch prepare to make an amphibious insertion into Japanese territory in the Arakan, early 1945. (NARA)

The Detachment 101 Research and Development section produced fake vegetables for hiding explosive charges. Detachment 101 agents then set the charges before hiding them in Japanese supply carts. (USASOC)

Two Japanese prisoners await being flown out of the field. To the left is pilot William Hofacker, Nisei interpreter Junichi Buto, agent "Betty," and pilot Vincent Trifletti. (USASOC)

Peter Lutken gives the Citation for Military Assistance (CMA) to select Kachins of his group prior to disbanding. The CMA was a prestigious Detachment 101-specific award that was given only to the best of the guerrilla troops. (NARA)

Kachins celebrate the end of their war with a *manau*, or victory celebration. In keeping with local custom, Detachment 101 held several *manaus* to thank its guerrillas for their service. (NARA)

Peers, in the center, says goodbye to Detachment 101 elements as they pass through Bhamo on their way to China. Within weeks, Detachment 101 fully disbanded. (USASOC)

In 2004, the Detachment 101 veterans dedicated a memorial to their Kachin comrades. Now emplaced on the grounds of the U.S. Embassy in Rangoon, the statue depicts the close working relationship of U.S. soldiers and Kachin guerrillas. (Photo by Paula Helfrich)

7

Detachment 101 and the Campaign for Myitkyina, February–August 1944

Going into swampy jungles to fight the Japanese is like going into the water to fight a shark. It is better to entice him into a trap or catch him on a hook and then demolish with axes after hauling him out on dry land. How then to deceive and entrap the shark?

Winston S. Churchill

Overshadowed in WWII history by events that occurred at nearly the same time, namely, the Normandy invasion and the capture of Rome, the crowning achievement in General Stilwell's North Burma Campaign was the hard-fought battle for Myitkyina. It began in late February 1944 and did not end until the provincial capital fell on 3 August 1944. Capture of the city allowed for a more direct air route to China and its use as a major depot along the Ledo Road. The campaign involved American, Chinese, and British forces, but the participation of the 5307th Composite Unit (Provisional), popularly known as Merrill's Marauders, receives the most attention.

Detachment 101 also played a significant role. Before the Allied offensive had even begun, the unit had thoroughly infiltrated north Burma and was conducting limited guerrilla attacks and collecting tactical and strategic intelligence for the U.S. Army and OSS Washington. Detachment 101 had achieved excellent rapport with the dominant local ethnic group, the Kachins, and became the eyes and ears of the campaign. Detachment 101's service in the Myitkyina Campaign lasted the longest of any Allied organization, and by assisting all of the major Allied organizations involved, it was the only organization involved in all facets of the campaign. More importantly, Detachment 101's service in this campaign highlighted the organization's maturity and its indispensable role to the Allied effort.[1]

Operations in north Burma still involved the complexity of coordinating the forces of three Allied powers that had to compromise if they wanted to succeed against the Japanese. The TRIDENT Conference of May 1943 limited Nationalist Chinese and American forces to operating in north Burma. The British Fourteenth Army (the equivalent of thirteen divisions and seven independent brigades), composed of Indian, British, and Commonwealth units, was in India and the upper Arakan region of Burma preparing for offensive operations in the rest of Burma.

Opposing the Allies were nine Japanese infantry divisions and two independent brigades engaged on three fronts.[2] While the combined Allied forces prepared for the offensive in north Burma, the Japanese Army launched the three-division Fifteenth Army in an attack against India. The Japanese intended for their offensive, Operation U-GO, to capture the British military rail and supply centers in northern India, specifically the towns of Kohima and Imphal. Resupplied from Allied stores, the Japanese planned to push into the Indian plain to cut the Allied logistical lines to north India and Burma, including the USAAF airfields that supplied China. The Japanese hoped that success would stimulate the Indian nationalist movement and prompt a revolt against British rule.

The offensive began in February 1944 with Operation HA-GO, a diversionary attack in the Arakan by the Japanese Twenty-eighth Army. The British defeated it in the Battle of the Admin Box. Undeterred, the Japanese Fifteenth Army advanced on the central Burma front but when they did not capture the British supply dumps, the offensive turned into a battle of attrition that lasted until July. While besieged British and Commonwealth troops relied on aerial supply, the Japanese had paid scant attention to their logistics requirements. Between March and July, British forces under Lieutenant Generals William Slim and Geoffrey Scoones first halted and then decisively defeated the Japanese at the twin battles of Kohima and Imphal. In tatters, starving, and leaving behind their wounded, the Japanese retreated back into Burma. It was a defeat that broke their offensive capability in Burma. With more than 55,000 casualties, this was the largest single defeat suffered by the Imperial Japanese Army to date. Lieutenant General Kotoku Sato, commander of the Japanese Thirty-first Division, signaled to the Fifteenth Army, "our swords are broken and our arrows gone."[3] In a step unthinkable in the Japanese Imperial Army, he retreated contrary to orders. It was against this strategic picture that the Allied offensive in north Burma took place.

Although they considered it a tertiary front, the Japanese maintained a substantial presence in north Burma. The most important was the elite battle-tested Eighteenth Japanese Division, headquartered at Myitkyina. It had achieved a long succession of victories, from the sacking of Shanghai and

Nanking in the late 1930s to the invasions of Malaya and Singapore in late 1941 and early 1942. These last two campaigns had garnered the largest number of British Empire prisoners of war—some 130,000. Like many Japanese units in north Burma, the Eighteenth Division was severely under strength. In January 1944, it had only some 6,300 men, of which only 3,000 remained by late June 1944. The veteran Fifty-sixth Division, also present in north Burma, had also fought in the 1942 invasion of Burma. Elements of the Fifteenth, Fifty-third, and Thirty-third Divisions, and the Twenty-fourth were also present in north Burma. In all, the Japanese Imperial Army had more than 50,000 troops in the area.[4]

Facing this force was an array of Allied units from three nations that comprised General Stilwell's Northern Combat Area Command (NCAC). The Chinese Army in India contributed the well-equipped and trained, but not necessarily well-led, Twenty-second and Thirty-eighth Divisions.[5] The largest American unit was the GALAHAD force under Brigadier General Franklin D. Merrill. Unlike Detachment 101, the three battalions of the Marauders were not thoroughly familiar with the operating environment, but were primarily formed from jungle-trained or -tested troops.[6] Designed after the British Chindits, the 5307th was lightly armed and mobile. Initially its only heavy weapons were mortars, although by necessity the Marauders later added 75mm pack howitzers. The British Chindits were officially the Indian Third Infantry Division and consisted of six brigades.[7] Named after the *Chinthe*, the mythical lionlike beast that guards Buddhist temples in Burma, the second British long-range penetration group was formed around those of the Seventy-seventh Infantry Brigade under Brigadier General Michael Calvert who had survived the first Chindit expedition of February 1943.

The American Tenth Air Force was assigned to support the Allied offensive and provide aerial resupply. Number 1 Air Commando was to infiltrate 9,250 Chindits behind enemy lines, keep them resupplied, and extract wounded personnel. Another 3,000 Chindits of Brigadier General Bernard E. Fergusson's Sixteenth Infantry Brigade walked into Burma. Stilwell's remaining major Allied unit was OSS Detachment 101.[8]

Prior to the Myitkyina Campaign, Detachment 101 had three main priorities: collecting intelligence on Japanese forces and dispositions; rescuing downed Allied pilots; and, least important, conducting guerrilla warfare.[9] The Myitkyina Campaign marked a substantial shift for Detachment 101, for thereafter, guerrilla warfare became equally important a role as supplying intelligence. Detachment 101's involvement in the campaign was in three phases: Phase One (May 1943 until February 1944) was the pre-offensive period, Phase Two (February until May 1944) ended with the Allied capture of the Myitkyina airfield; Phase Three (May to August 1944) ended with the capture of the city and harassing the Japanese retreat.

The Myitkyina campaign built on the Detachment's previous work in north Burma in 1943 and 1944. During this time, the Detachment increased its intelligence-gathering abilities, which was critical to Stilwell and his planners in confirming the state and locations of enemy forces in north Burma. Detachment 101 groups also provided a screen to alert NCAC of pending Japanese counteroffensives. Even in areas where Detachment 101 did not operate, the so-called jungle grapevine provided information on enemy movements and helped to rescue downed Allied airmen. Captain Vincent Curl, in command of the KNOTHEAD group, reported in February 1944, "We have this whole area pretty well organized and if [the pilots] will tell [the Kachins] that they are Americans there is only one chance in a thousand against their being brought to this Hq, or to one of our other units."[10] Detachment 101 groups had also blanketed the area north and west of Myitkyina with agents that sent a constant stream of intelligence to Nazira, India, and from there to Stilwell's headquarters at NCAC. This information ranged from tactical to strategic and included Japanese troop movements and order of battle. The Detachment also radioed map coordinates of targets to the Tenth USAAF, that then bombed them through the jungle canopy. Detachment 101 groups then reported the adverse effect on Japanese morale.[11] This was particularly stinging to the Japanese when the hidden targets could have been found only by ground observation, such as a bridge near Myitkyina that was constructed with its roadbed hidden just under the surface of the water.[12] The combination of intelligence and bombing crippled Japanese transportation so much so that by the beginning of the campaign, only three enemy locomotives remained operational west of Myitkyina.[13]

By recruiting Kachins and other ethnic minorities, Detachment 101 also began to build what would become a considerable guerrilla force of nearly 4,000 by mid-1944. Curl went a step farther by incorporating the *Myihprap Hpuing* (Lightning Force) of Kachin leader Zhing Htaw Naw to serve as the nucleus for his offensive operations.[14] Although Zhing Htaw Naw's guerrillas inflicted relatively few casualties on the Japanese prior to the start of the Myitkyina Campaign, they had a great psychological effect. According to a captured Japanese soldier, Japanese patrols did "not mind working in American or Chinese occupied territory but never volunteered for assignments against the Kachins as casualties were always about 50 percent."[15]

As soon as he learned of the upcoming north Burma offensive, Peers tried to demonstrate Detachment 101's utility to other Allied elements in the campaign. He assigned Chief Warrant Officer Robert Rhea and Lieutenant Martin J. Waters as liaison officers to Merrill's Marauders; Lieutenant Charles C. Stelle to the Chindits; and Captain Sherman P. Joost to the First Air Commando. Peers cited Joost specifically for "doing a magnificent job" and building up "OSS in the eyes of General Wingate and Col. Cochran."[16] All groups had Kachin teams to accompany the liaison elements. Captain Chester R. Chartrand of the SI section, at NCAC headquarters, transmitted Stilwell's specific intelligence requests to the liaison elements.[17] He also took raw intelligence "over to Col. Stilwell [the G-2] without delay." His quarters were even right next to Colonel Stilwell's.[18]

On 20 February 1944, Detachment 101 entered Phase Two of the offensive when Curl was ordered to meet with Merrill and offer him the assistance of KNOTHEAD.[19] The slow pace of the Allied advance delayed the meeting, and the first direct contact with Allied forces was on 8 March when runners arrived from Chinese units. Not until 15 March did Curl meet with Merrill, to whom he briefed the local situation. Father James Stuart conducted services for the Marauders and recalled, "when [the Marauders] found out I was a Catholic Priest, quite a number were very anxious for me to go to their bivouac area to hear confessions. . . . I spent all that evening and most of the night hearing the confessions of the men of Col. McGhee's 'B' Battalion." He continued, "I was very glad to have been able to help these men because the battalion was later surrounded by the Japanese and besieged in a Kachin village for 13 days. Many of the boys who came to me that night lie buried there."[20] KNOTHEAD was also of immediate assistance when it arranged to fly one officer and sixty-seven enlisted casualties out of their improvised airstrip by light plane.

Kachin guides provided by KNOTHEAD were invaluable in pointing out the easiest and most direct paths through the area.[21] KNOTHEAD reported that "A group [of Marauders] would be advancing down the trail, when the Kachin out front would spot and point (rather like a bird-dog), since he could not talk to them. They invariably found a Jap position . . . which they never would have seen otherwise."[22] Kachins also had the ability to tell friend from foe as "to the inexperienced eye . . . there is no difference in a Burman and a Kachin . . . a Japanese out of uniform is almost as difficult to recognize."[23] The Kachins also identified friendly villages, river crossings, and potable water sources, while other KNOTHEAD groups positioned further away reported on Japanese troop movements and concentrations facing the Marauders.

Curl's strike forces were also stirring up the Japanese so much so that on 22 February, Stilwell directed the Lighting Force to stop ambushing Japanese patrols so as not to alert them to the upcoming offensive.[24] The order was revoked on 5 March when Lieutenant James L. Tilly, the American advisor with the Lightning Force, was told to disrupt the Japanese "in every way possible."[25] Peers directed Curl to make sure that Tilly had at least a hundred men and to keep Nazira informed of when and where the Lightning Force would attack.

On 6 March 1944, a failed attempt at a roadblock by the Lighting Force heightened Japanese awareness of the guerrilla threat. Retaliation came on 10 March when the Lightning Force ran into a Japanese ambush. The entrenched Japanese troops allowed the Lightning Force to enter their kill zone before firing, but their marksmanship was poor, and the Japanese did not hit a single Kachin. With no other option, the Kachins charged the Japanese and sprayed them with automatic weapons fire. The Japanese counterattacked. The OSS reported, "One Jap thrust his bayonet into the leading Kachin . . . this Myihprap Hpung [*sic*] then smashed his Tommy gun over the [Japanese soldier's] head, and the man beside him calmly blew off the [Japanese soldier's] head with a shotgun . . . another Jap charged, he was brought down with the other barrel of the shotgun."[26] Then, the Lightning Force withdrew to reorganize.

The next day the Kachins routed the Japanese force. The Kachins crept to within 25 feet of the Japanese and so surprised them when they leapt forward to assault that the enemy abandoned their weapons and equipment and fled. The Japanese response was to retaliate on the civilian population. Tilly reported that "One old Kachin was captured . . . he was tortured . . . to reveal our location . . . he did not talk . . . and was put to death with the bayonet."[27] Sporadic actions continued, such as 14 March when two Japanese scouts were fired upon. Although not hit, they were "frightened enouhg [*sic*] to cause them to dive off the trail, and over sheer drop of about 80 feet, where they were killed on the rocks below."[28]

Still, poor communication and the movements of Allied forces were confusing. On 16 March, a Lightning Force patrol was lying in ambush on a trail near Hkawnglaw Hka, when a large body of 200 soldiers approached. Thinking that they were Chinese from a nearby element, the Kachins challenged them using "O.K.," which was one-half of the sign/countersign for the area. The Japanese soldiers responded by raising their weapons, which was "definitely the wrong password."[29] This fight enabled the Marauders, who were also engaged with this force but who did not yet know of the OSS presence, to disengage and slip around the contested area. Chinese forces later relieved the Lightning Force and dealt with the remaining Japanese.

Unsure of the assistance that Detachment 101 could offer, the Marauders refused to rely upon the Kachins at first. Tilly commented that the worse part of this was the "unnecessary nerve strain on the leading American soldiers," who were blazing their own trails and "sweating out Jap fire at every turn."[30] Fortunately, Merrill came to realize the value of working with Detachment 101 and its Kachin guerrillas.

By the end of March 1944, Detachment 101 credited the Lightning Force with 160 Japanese killed. Some 160 Lightning Force Kachins were serving as Marauder guides and scouts, and Merrill conferred several times daily with Father Stuart and Zhing Htaw Naw.[31] Stuart was especially valuable as he spoke fluent Kachin. Despite KNOTHEAD's objections because the group needed him to perform his duties, the Marauders attached Stuart to their command post.

Detachment 101 elements speeded up the Marauder advance by providing so much information on Japanese troop movements that they reduced the necessity of sending out reconnaissance patrols. The Kachin guides became indispensable, and each Marauder battalion had two point guides, while an additional pool of ten to fifteen guides was maintained at the regimental command post. Detachment 101 patrols operated even farther ahead of the Marauders lead element—itself a day's march away from the main body. They improved or cut new trails to allow easier passage for pack animals. Because of their valuable assistance, Peers ordered KNOTHEAD to move further south and to recruit more Kachins.[32]

Peers placed Lieutenant Jack C. Pamplin in command of KNOTHEAD after the OSS recalled Curl. Pamplin visited Merrill at Nhpum Ga at the end of March and reported to Peers at Nazira that Merrill was "quick to realize the actual and potential value of our Kachins" and that he lavished praise on Father Stuart and Zhing Htaw Naw. Pamplin radioed that the Marauders now had the "greatest respect" for the Kachins and their fighting methods. He often heard them say, "I'm damn glad they're on our side."[33] Pamplin also noted that the American forces had come to realize that the organized Kachins had "been just as important a factor in their own preservation as it has been in their success against the Jap forces."[34] It was the Kachin scouts who averted disaster when the Marauders' Second Battalion got behind the Japanese Eighteenth Division.

The Japanese counterattacked the strung-out battalion in force at Inkangahtawng. Detachment 101 scouts twice reported that another enemy force was close and marching up from the south to flank the Second Battalion. Unfortunately, the Marauders thought that the enemy force was actually the Chinese. Warrant Officer Robert Rhea, who "was the only American present who knew our Kachins didn't exaggerate," accompanied an OSS patrol to investigate for himself. He knew that when the Kachins said "there was trouble ahead, well there was trouble ahead," and there was. The already embattled Marauders fell back, looking for a more defensible position.

After pausing at the village of Auche, the Marauders retreated single-file along a steep, narrow 4½-mile trail upon which Japanese had zeroed in artillery fire.[35] The Second Battalion stopped and barricaded itself at the hill town of Nhpum Ga while the Third Battalion was positioned at Hsamshingyang to protect a nearby improvised airstrip and to guard against possible attacks down the trail from the north. Father Stuart reported that some shaken Marauders were consoled by having "someone to speak to who had the time to listen to them and who didn't try to explain to them with a trembling voice and a shaking knees [*sic*] that there was nothing to fear. I was afraid as they were but I kept my mouth shut. Weeks later . . . some of these men . . . came and thanked me for giving them confidence."[36] Then, a message arrived from fifteen Detachment 101 Kachins dug in a mile below the village.

The Americans had withdrawn through them and they wanted to know what to do. Merrill was unhappy that the Kachins had held their ground while his had retreated and sent a platoon of Marauders to relieve them. Father Stuart reported, "Up till then (Merrill) had always been rather friendly with us. After that he was merely polite."[37] Shortly afterward, the Second Battalion was on the defensive.

At the end of March, the Marauders' Second Battalion, one of the three separate U.S. columns, barricaded itself at Nhpum Ga to fight a rearguard action. There the Japanese besieged it for two weeks. The situation became dire, and only airdropped supplies prevented the Marauders from being overrun. Elements of the Lightning Force led by Father Stuart conducted harassing attacks on the Japanese and their cumbersome logistics train surrounding the Second Battalion. This distracted the Japanese sufficiently to enable the Marauders to regroup. On 3 April, the OSS provided a much-needed morale boost when fifty-five Kachins arrived to strengthen the Third Battalion's efforts.[38] Father Stuart relates that upon hearing the news that the Kachins had arrived, Colonel Hunter told him that this was the "turning point" of the siege.[39] The Marauder unit history describes it: "The Kachins were probably of more assistance than anyone realized, by creating in the minds of the Japanese an exaggerated idea of the size of the area held by the Marauders and of their strength."[40] By 9 April, the combined assaults of the Marauders' First and Third Battalions, in addition to the hundreds of Japanese soldiers killed attacking the Second Battalion, broke the siege of Nhpum Ga. The Japanese retreated back into the jungle. The 5307th's acting commander, Colonel Charles N. Hunter (Merrill had been evacuated after suffering a heart attack), praised Detachment 101's Kachins for "saving over two-thirds of Merrill's forces."[41]

Other Detachment 101 forces made significant contributions to the Myitkyina campaign. Lieutenant Charles Stelle, after meeting with Major General Orde Wingate at Imphal, India, was asked to join the Seventy-seventh Brigade. Though Stelle's initial duties were channeling the Chindits' requests to the First Air Commando, Wingate expanded his role.[42] When the first planeload of Kachin guides was lost in a CG-4A Waco glider accident, Stelle arranged to replace them with six Detachment 101 Kachins.[43] On 19 March, they went into BROADWAY, the Chindit landing zone, and were sent on patrol four days later. The Detachment 101 Kachins identified, apprehended, and brought local Kachin collaborators back to British lines, and helped to repulse Japanese attacks.[44] Reverting to his original R&A function and using his knowledge of Japanese, Stelle identified several Japanese units and enemy agents from captured documents. These agents were swiftly dealt with: "A five minute scanning . . . provided a really definitive translation—definitive by reason of the fact that its bearer was shot ten minutes later."[45]

Stelle's most important contribution was liaison between the Chindits and Stilwell. Wingate was loath to send information through channels. In January 1944, Joost, the Detachment 101 liaison officer with the First Air Commando, commented that "abysmal ignorance existed regarding Intelligence and Plans between the Americans and British." Thus, Wingate's liaison officer at NCAC was never "really up-to-date on the plans and position" of the Chindits.[46] Stilwell had no liaison officer with the Chindits, making Stelle the de facto link between the two organizations. In turn, Wingate gave him carte blanche access to their message traffic, and encouraged Stelle to forward what messages he saw fit.

The north Burma campaign was in full swing at the end of March 1944. As the Marauders pressed further into Japanese-held territory, they left KNOTHEAD's area of operations and moved closer to that of Operation FORWARD.[47] Its leader, Lieutenant Commander Luce, was a rare breed. By training, he was a naval surgeon, but he was an equally outstanding guerrilla leader. In an early version of civil affairs, Luce was ordered by Eifler into the area because "he desired to carry to certain native Burmese hills people medicinal care. It seemed that the Japanese had not been taking care of the people and that Detachment 101 was having considerable difficulty in making friends with the native population down behind Japanese lines. It was hoped that by giving the natives something more than the Japanese were willing to offer that better friends could be made more quickly."[48] Luce conducted a medical clinic and gained the trust of, and recruits from, the local inhabitants. On 5 March, much to the incredulity of the locals, he performed a successful brain surgery on a Kachin soldier under the most primitive of conditions. During the Myitkyina operations, Luce commanded eight guerrilla companies and ten radio operators, in all some 1,100 men.[49] They were organized into 154-man companies, and like all the Detachment 101 guerrillas were lightly armed, but their large number of automatic weapons allowed great firepower.[50] Much like KNOTHEAD had done, FORWARD screened the flanks of the Marauders and waylaid Japanese forces moving to confront the separate Allied columns.

Advancing Allied troops, however, overran several of these Detachment 101 groups. In April, Peers reported to Washington that RED (another element led by A Group veteran Patrick "Red" Maddox) and PAT had to "abandon their positions . . . or penetrate still deeper into Japanese-held territory."[51] Moving forward was not a bad strategy. The groups could continue their mission, and as a later Detachment 101 unit found out in 1945, it was a good operational practice.

> The closer you got to your own lines, the denser the concentration of regular enemy troops. . . . What you met deep in enemy territory were police . . . trained to fight one on one . . . two platoons of regular soldiers could have defeated my whole battalion with no difficulty. But one of our platoons of forty men could have defeated a force of over one hundred policemen. And our battalion could have taken on a police force of close to a thousand for at least several hours.[52]

In PAT's case, their move south enabled the group to wreck a Japanese train on the Myitkyina-Mogaung railway on 24 April.[53]

The increased requirements brought on by the Allied move south meant that the Detachment had to organize and get more personnel into the field as soon as possible. Many were radio operators and medics, who were necessary to support the field groups. U.S. Navy Pharmacist's Mate 1/C Lysle Wilson recalled that during his first C-47 trip into Burma, "I realized how much my new job meant. I could visualize one of these very boys in the plane with me, being wounded and everything for his safety on my hands. . . . I made up my mind at that moment to work hard and do my best."[54]

Providing tailored support to the combat forces had drawbacks. In April 1944, Peers relayed to Donovan that intelligence collection took a backseat to the "sharp increase in the actual combat functions of our patrols."[55] Still, there were some intelligence successes. British Brigadier General Michael Calvert asked for two OSS Nisei to help the Chindits exploit the intelligence scored from a tapped Japanese telephone cable.[56] The DAVIS group, operating out of BROADWAY, provided such opportune intelligence on Japanese troop movements that NCAC headquarters told the group to treat all messages as urgent and to send some without taking the time to encode them.[57]

May 1944 saw Detachment 101 further assisting the Allied offensive. FORWARD commenced clearing villages to the east of Myitkyina and on 10 May staged a successful diversionary attack east of Myitkyina to shield the Marauders' advance from discovery. The attack tied down three Japanese battalions to the loss of three Kachins killed. On 15 May, FORWARD's Kachins directly assaulted the village of Sadon, killing half of the sixty-five defenders and suffering three killed and twelve wounded before withdrawing.[58] The Kachins sniped at the defenders until 29 June, when they took control of the town.[59]

Particularly active in Detachment 101's role to take Myitkyina was a RED subgroup under Lieutenants William J. Martin and William F. Hazelwood. As a result of the Second Battalion's losses at Nhpum Ga, the Marauders could no longer continue operations under their original organization. General Stilwell reinforced the Battalions with Chinese troops. Colonel Hunter's First Battalion with the addition of the 150th Regiment from the Fiftieth Chinese Division became H-Force. The Third Battalion, under the command of Colonel Henry L. Kinnison, was reinforced with the Eighty-eighth Regiment from the Thirtieth Chinese Division and became known as K-Force. Detachment 101 helped fill out Lieutenant Colonel George McGee's former Second Battalion. With the addition of 300 Kachins detached from KNOTHEAD, it became M-Force. However, each of the former battalions continued to have assistance from Detachment 101.[60]

As the Marauders made ready for the final leg of the trek to capture the airfield, Martin's element, assisting the H-Force, prepared a resupply drop zone. After that, fourteen-year-old N'Naw Yang Nau led the Marauders along a hidden trail to the Myitkyina airfield on the night of 15 May 1944. Along the way he was bitten by a highly poisonous krait, but he was the only one who knew the local trails. Martin pulled out his poncho, and covering himself and the injured Kachin, pulled out a flashlight to examine the wound. "Sure enough there were two fang marks right behind his toes." Martin sent word back that a snake had bitten the scout and then applied a tourniquet to the leg. "But the [scout's] solution for this while the medics were coming up [was to] dig a hole, pour silver rupees in it, put his foot in there, and bury it. . . . And he would sit there till he either lived or died. So we proceeded to calm him down, dig the damn hole, put a bag of rupees in there . . . put his foot on top, and start to fill the hole back up."

Hunter and the medics came to the front of the column, brushed away the dirt, and tried to suck out the poison. After about forty minutes, N'Naw Yang Nau was "woozy," and unable to walk. He was strapped on Hunter's horse and led the Marauders with "bleary eyed directions."[61] The critically ill Kachin had to walk the last mile but managed to lead the group to their bivouac a mile from the airfield. Martin's group then left to blow up a Japanese train, but unable to get to the tracks in time, infiltrated to the edge of the airstrip and observed the enemy working at night.

The next morning, 17 May 1944, the Marauders followed the route pointed out by the Kachins, and surprised the Japanese—who did not know Allied forces were so close. The surprise was complete, and the combined force quickly captured the airfield. The American liaison officer with the 150th Chinese Regiment reported that "the Japs were completely unaware of our presence. Total surprise could not have been more perfect."[62] The Chinese and Americans quickly captured the airfield, leaving few Japanese survivors. Martin reported that "C-47's were landing on the strip by afternoon."[63] In recognition of Detachment 101's assistance, Hunter wrote to Peers: "Thanks to your people for a swell job. Could not have succeeded without them."[64]

However, Hunter spoke too soon, and what occurred in the next few days after the capture of the Myitkyina airfield was nothing short of a disaster. After the airfield fell, the Marauders were exhausted. Stilwell assigned the task of taking the city proper to the more numerous Chinese troops. They had to regroup. Over the next few days the actions were quite confusing, and the story has been retold in numerous accounts.[65] What is clear is that the Chinese 150th Regiment was given the "honor" of taking the city but bungled the attack. Instead of conducting a pincer movement, the attacking Second and Third Battalions mistook each other for the Japanese and nearly annihilated one another, while at the same time the few Japanese forces present in the city attacked from the rear.[66] The Chinese forces were ordered to withdraw, leaving behind "many dead officers and soldiers, together with more wounded." The American liaison officer to the regiment reported that the devastation was so great that by the time the Chinese successfully withdrew, the Third Battalion had only "18 officers left of 32, and about 290 men out of 598."[67]

The Chinese debacle, compounded with the inability of the Marauders to aid the effort, enabled the vastly outnumbered Japanese to pull in reinforcements from the surrounding area. Within days, the Japanese outnumbered the Allied attackers. The siege of Myitkyina had begun. On the world stage, the seemingly major accomplishment of the capture of Myitkyina's airfield was in just a few short weeks overshadowed by the capture of Rome and the Normandy Landings. Instead, what was perceived as a quick and decisive victory progressed into a slug match for which both sides were ill prepared. Ever adaptable, Detachment 101 continued their operations even before the need for a siege was apparent.

Martin's work was far from over. His group of Kachins remained to scout in the vicinity. Two days after the fall of the airstrip, he reconnoitered the Namkwin bridge, the site of Detachment 101's first operational mission in 1943. Martin's Kachins managed to surprise a section of Japanese troops eating breakfast before attacking the airfield.[68] That same day, Hazelwood was not as fortunate near Charpate, when a Japanese patrol attacked them from behind. Well beyond getting assistance, Hazelwood managed to break contact and after three attempts extricated his wounded.[69]

Even though the Allied siege lines around Myitkyina were porous, once the Japanese were "bottled up" the Allies intended to keep them there. Detachment 101 teams covered escape routes all the way south to Bhamo; FORWARD to the east, PAT to the south, and KNOTHEAD to the west. These groups cleared out Japanese garrisons in the outlying towns and covered the Irrawaddy River, which flowed south past Myitkyina, as well as its tributaries. The Japanese tried to evacuate their wounded by floating them down the river, but soon discovered that the Kachins posted along the banks fired at anything suspicious. The sharp-eyed guerrillas even discovered and killed submerged Japanese troops breathing through reeds and those clinging to logs and hoping to pass as driftwood. The Kachin then recovered the bodies to glean useful intelligence.

To the south, Detachment 101 forces were working with the Chindits. Renamed the Group #10 Operation, that particular Detachment 101 element had grown to encompass four radio teams. Stelle, the assigned liaison officer, returned from the field to join the DIXIE mission, the liaison effort to the Chinese Communists. Other Detachment 101 personnel from Stelle's group remained to recruit locally and formed the MATES, ADAMS, BARNES, and DAVIS groups. These teams reported on Japanese troop movements, engaged in guerrilla warfare, and organized villagers to report on and defend themselves against the Japanese.[70] The intelligence they gathered alerted the Chindits of anticipated attacks and enabled the British force to avoid Japanese formations. Chindit decisions, however, had unintended consequences. Because the group could not carry excess supplies, when the Chindits moved north from Mawlu in late May they abandoned uniforms and weapons that the Japanese then recovered. As a result, Detachment 101 elements repeatedly encountered Japanese patrols "dressed in these British uniforms."[71] Not all groups got into action. Private Tom Davis, leading the DAVIS group, reported on 31 May that he had "shot a mule, a monkey, a squirrel, and a fish, but no Japs."[72]

After the seizure of the Myitkyina airfield, Detachment 101 began Phase Three of the Myitkyina Campaign, which ended in August when the Allies captured the city and secured the surrounding area.[73] Impressed by the results so far, Stilwell told Peers to raise its number of guerrilla forces to 10,000. In order to stay relevant, Peers also ordered his forces further south "to keep our units in positions where they can watch and report on every move of the enemy . . . our information is now supplied to twenty-five military branches . . . which otherwise could not get this intelligence."[74]

Kachin guerrillas, however, served only of their own volition and occasionally, for lack of a better term, deserted. An example of this occurred in June 1944 on the Chinese border to the east of Myitkyina. Japanese troops had withdrawn from the town of Hpimaw because of the pressure at Myitkyina, and Chinese troops had moved in. The Chinese were not liked by the Maru, a minor Kachin ethnicity, because of long standing bad relations. To make things worse, the local populace accused Chinese troops of looting. Luce tried to get FORWARD's Marus out of the area, but during the first day's march south, 110 of them deserted with their equipment and weapons. For the next three weeks, these Marus waged their own war against the Chinese. The Chinese reported 75 of their troops killed, although the number is likely much higher.[75] Regardless, the Allied advance forced the Detachment 101 guerrillas to push further south.

One of the first groups to move south was FORWARD. The advance party flew by light plane 50 miles south to Kwitu, while the main body made the eight-day trek on foot. FORWARD expanded from eight to ten companies. Many new recruits were veterans of the prewar Burmese Rifles, some of whom had fought against the Japanese in the 1942 invasion of Burma before disbanding. Another 2,300 recruits waited to be armed, but the monsoon rains hampered airdrops and prevented them from being equipped. Throughout June, these forces were active deep behind Japanese lines, and were particularly successful ambushing troops trying to escape down the Irrawaddy. In June, FORWARD claimed nearly half of the Detachment's total enemy killed in action, which was 219 Japanese killed and 2 captured. Meanwhile, the guerrillas of PAT blew bridges and cut rail lines south of Myitkyina. Detachment 101's losses for June were five indigenous troops killed and seven wounded.[76]

Detachment 101 continued its policy of conducting for the Allied forces what Peers referred to as "all operations which they are not prepared to undertake."[77] Assisting with this task was the Detachment's small air force, dubbed the Red Ass Squadron, which was formed to conduct observation flights, evacuate wounded, drop supplies, and effect liaison. These planes landed on airstrips hacked out of the jungle or on sandbars and in open fields. Landing these small planes on makeshift airstrips could be harrowing, such as on 6 July in the rescue of the survivors of a B-25 crash some 18 miles from Myitkyina: "The field was a clearing about 600″ long, she looked terrible from the air. There were fox holes on either side (dug by Merrill's Marauders) . . . looking over the whole thing [the pilot] said over the radio 'Well here goes but we're liable to have to walk back to Myitkyina' . . . on the seventh [pass] we dropped in so close over the trees I thought the wings would hit."[78] Because of the small carrying capacity of the plane, the pilot required six trips to evacuate the crew. In the midst of the rescue, the pilot had to make a field-expedient repair to a broken tail wheel.

The Red Ass Squadron relied heavily on their Stinson L-1 Vigilants, calling them "Burma Butterflies." They were ideal for the task because with their size and durability, they could take off of rough airfields, and because they had a larger carrying capacity than the more common Stinson L-5 Sentinel. Although the U.S. Army considered the L-1 obsolete, Technical Sergeant Blaine Headrick recalled that "it was a very safe airplane to fly . . . it had quite a bit of power. . . . I even had three guys in the backseat at one time."[79] Detachment 101 even had one L-1 fitted with pontoons for water landings. This was pressed into service when it assisted in evacuating some forty-nine Chindits from Lake Indawgyi.

However, the relative scarcity of the L-1 made their losses catastrophic. The high use and horrific flying conditions and terrain did not help matters. Detachment 101 regularly had L-1s down for maintenance. In the event of crashes, the group tried to salvage the aircraft. In the event of a total loss,

Detachment 101's mechanics stripped the L-1 airframes of any part that could be used to keep another in the air. Eventually, Detachment 101 had to use the L-4 and L-5. Like the L-1, these aircraft were dependable. Although they were smaller, they were readily available, as were parts. But once Detachment 101 moved its supply bases forward, the size and range became less of an issue.

By July, Detachment 101 was pushing its forces even further south. Stilwell needed information on Japanese dispositions in north-central Burma for the resumption of the Allied push after Myitkyina's fall.[80] Detachment 101 guerrillas used the cover accorded by the monsoons and the subsequent relative inactivity of regular forces. One unfortunate aspect was that patrols were sometimes mistaken for the enemy and attacked by Allied fighter aircraft.[81]

The push south coincided with a reorganization of the operational elements when Detachment 101 headquarters simplified its command and control. Instead of five operational areas, the Allied advance allowed the consolidation of KNOTHEAD and PAT with the teams working in the Chindit area. Detachment 101 redesignated the groups: FORWARD became "Area #1;" PAT and KNOTHEAD became "Area #2;" and TRAMP became "Area #3." The three areas reported directly to the headquarters Operations section. The Communications section also followed suit. Before, individual groups and even teams had independently contacted headquarters or their designated subordinate radio substation. During July, the individual elements routed all communications to their area headquarters. The three area substations then communicated with one forward-based Communications section. This reorganization provided redundancy; the constant relocations of area headquarters forced by enemy action did not sever communications. If any area substation was out of service for more than twenty-four hours, the forward Communications section picked up that area's message traffic in addition to its normal load, until the area substation came back on line.[82] Additionally, the Detachment headquarters set up a chain of aircraft warning stations, as it had done in early 1943 in the Fort Hertz area. This time, instead of providing alerts that Japanese bombers were coming to attack the Assam airfields, the nine stations warned of the presence of Japanese fighter aircraft operating in hunter-killer groups. These stations reported directly to the Allied fighter control center at NCAC.

These organizational changes helped the Detachment increase efficiency. July was even more successful with 259 enemy killed, an indeterminate number wounded, and 26 captured. Area #1, now under the command of Major Sherman P. Joost after Luce returned to Nazira to establish a fifty-bed hospital, established two roadblocks south of Myitkyina: Kazu, 20 miles south; and Dumbaiyang, 40 miles south. In this period alone, Area #1's "D" company killed ninety-four Japanese who were attempting to float down the Irrawaddy from Myitkyina. Area #2 was likewise embroiled in the campaign.[83]

Since much of its former area was now free of the enemy, Area #2 groups moved south and acted as a screening force for the Chinese and Chindits attacking Mogaung.[84] After receiving a message from the worn-out Chindits that if Chinese troops did not arrive in two days then they would pull out, agent Skittles, in charge of an Area #2 unit, ensured that the Chinese met the timetable.[85] He led the 114th Regiment of the Thirty-eighth Chinese Division on a flanking move that completed the encirclement of the town. Since Detachment 101 agents were embedded with both the Chindits and Chinese, they facilitated a link-up. Although the Chindits accomplished much of the fighting, on Stilwell's orders the Chinese officially received credit for taking the town. In response, Brigadier General Calvert signaled in protest, "The Chinese having taken Mogaung 77 Brigade is proceeding to take Umbrage."[86] With Mogaung's capture, the Allies severed the last potential link that the besieged Japanese in Myitkyina had to supply, reinforcement, or relief.[87]

Since the Myitkyina siege lines remained porous, Detachment 101 guerrillas under Lieutenant Lee E. West patrolled the Mogaung-Myitkyina rail line until conventional Allied forces secured it in August.[88] Other Detachment 101 elements, such as that under First Lieutenant Ted U. Barnes, remained to "police up" Japanese stragglers who were "badly organized, badly equipped, and trying to get through to the south. . . . We spent a good deal of our time trying to organize groups to wipe out as many of these Japanese as possible."[89] Even further south, PETE moved in from the west to target the Katha-Mogaung rail line. The group's self-sufficiency was possible because of the capture of three load-carrying elephants and twenty-five oxen, which enabled PETE to carry large quantities of Japanese supplies captured during raids on enemy supply dumps.[90]

In early August, in the middle of the monsoon, the Allies finally took Myitkyina. Despite washed out roads and trails, Detachment 101 continued to harass the Japanese fleeing south from north Burma. The worn-out Japanese still resorted to using the rivers as avenues of retreat, but Detachment 101 covered the east bank of the Irrawaddy as far south as Sinbo. Peers reported to Donovan that this left the enemy "more or less like clay pigeons for our marksmen on the banks." The situation was almost surreal for First Lieutenant James Ward, who simply occupied a balcony overlooking the Irrawaddy and "sat in it [a chair] with a carbine across the knees, fresh fruit and cigarettes within easy reach, fanned by an attractive native girl, and would take pot shots at the Japs who were trying to escape." Martin had another experience, when his group of Kachins spotted a Japanese soldier on the banks of the river that they wanted to capture. But, the soldier "didn't want any part of it" and "fired one round," hitting a Kachin "right in the head," killing him. Martin's Kachins "just blew him [the Japanese soldier] apart. That was the only man I lost in the river blockade." First Lieutenant Thomas B. Leonard's group caught a party of 300 Japanese that were either "bathing or sleeping" on 3 August. They "were completely surprised" and "Little return fire encountered," with 30 Japanese killed for the loss of one Kachin.[91]

The groups in Area #2 accounted for the most damage inflicted in August on the Japanese. Fifteen Allied officers and twenty enlisted men led over a thousand Kachins while fourteen locally recruited radio operators handled communications. This group managed to kill 350 Japanese and capture another 22 at the cost of just a few Kachins.[92]

As Detachment 101 moved south, some of the region assigned to Area #3 fell outside the Kachin tracts, and was the furthest south that non-air-dropped elements had progressed. This became problematic because the Kachin troops had only agreed to fight in their home region. The move south invalidated their contracts, and some went home, but local recruiting refilled the ranks.[93] The new recruits remained able to attack the defeated Japanese forces retreating from Imphal. Peers told Area #3 in August, "headquarters (at Tailum) will [soon] be out of the war as much as Myitkyina is . . . as soon as the Jap flow ceases."[94] That meant the groups had to work their way even farther south in the coming months, risking even more Kachins to leave for home.

August was another record month for Detachment 101, with another 396 enemy killed and 33 captured.[95] Although the group only kept a strict tally of enemy casualties from May to August, this still left them with a total of 1,081 enemy killed, to a loss of 16 Kachins and 30 wounded.[96] The intelligence supplied by Detachment 101 had indirectly led to many more enemy soldiers killed through air action, which had also lowered Japanese morale and expedited Allied ground actions. Considering the small number of American personnel involved, Detachment 101 and its Kachins were a significant "force multiplier" for NCAC.

With the capture of Myitkyina, the Japanese would thereafter be on the defensive. Although its participation in the Burma campaign was not over, Detachment 101 had demonstrated its value to the Allied effort and received several accolades. Major General Howard Davidson, commanding officer of the Tenth USAAF, wrote about the intelligence provided by Detachment 101: "OSS furnished the principal intelligence regarding Japanese troop concentrations, hostile natives, stores and enemy movement. Up to 15 March 1944, some 80% of all combat missions were planned on the basis of intelligence received from this source. Since then the percentage of direct air-ground support missions and missions based upon OSS intelligence now average about 60% of the total."[97]

Detachment 101 had made great progress since their early operations in 1943, but how much had Detachment 101's efforts at reform aided in the campaign? The answer is found in what they accomplished in two areas: operations, and command and control. Following several unsuccessful attempts at long-range penetrations throughout Burma, Peers concentrated on the north. These operations involved less risk of valuable resources and capitalized on collecting tactical intelligence, such as identifying targets for the USAAF and identifying key elements in the Japanese order of battle. Through gaining the trust of and recruiting the Kachins, Detachment 101 was able to ambush Japanese troops, screen the flanks of Allied forces, collect intelligence, and have a ready reserve of guerrilla troops.

The operations in 1943 had benefited Detachment 101. The group was able to thoroughly blanket the area with agents, and these teams had months in the field to learn the operating areas and the local peoples. That the conventional troops of other Allied units involved in the planned offensive were mainly unaware of Detachment 101's efforts mattered little. What mattered is that Detachment 101 was in place, was building intelligence nets, and was recruiting and training guerrillas. Detachment 101 was ready to assist these other major conventional forces when the Myitkyina offensive began in February 1944, and in so doing, became the strategic theater asset envisioned by Donovan when he sent the group to Burma in 1942. This was even more important considering what happened to the other Allied Special Forces–type units employed in the Myitkyina Campaign.

Both the Marauders and the Chindits were wiped out as an effective fighting force even if Stilwell used them long after they had ceased to be operationally effective. Like the Chindits, the Marauders never forgave Stilwell. By the time Myitkyina fell on 3 August 1944, the Marauder battalions were down to company size. As such, the 5307th Composite Unit (Provisional) was inactivated on 10 August 1944. When the Chindits were withdrawn to India in August 1944, they had suffered 1,400 killed and 2,500 wounded out of 12,000 who had gone into the field. Myitkyina was to be the last Chindit mission.

Detachment 101 was the only American or British ground force that participated in the campaign to remain intact and capable of operations as both the Chindits and Marauders were disbanded after Myitkyina fell. The reputation of the Detachment was so good that when the Marauders disbanded, several veterans asked to join Detachment 101. Their experience proved invaluable in the ten bitter months of fighting that lay ahead before the Japanese were finally defeated in Burma in July 1945.[98]

Detachment 101's impact far outweighed the small numbers of personnel it had committed. This was in large part because of the organizational changes made by Peers after he took command. His creation of an SI-like evaluation system enabled his staff to ask the pertinent questions, evaluate its intelligence, and then distribute that information in a timely manner to the Allied force that most needed it. The formation of an operations cell to coordinate all the Detachment's offensive operations was likewise a major accomplishment. For the first time, Nazira could accurately measure its effectiveness, make the necessary changes while maintaining the offensive, and simplify the operations and communications command and control. Also, by having dedicated aircraft under its control, Detachment 101 ensured that its operational groups were supplied when and where needed. This function permitted the large-scale raising, training, and employment of guerrilla forces.

Other reforms of 1944, particularly those not of an immediate tactical need, were less critical. Morale Operations never played a significant role, even though their white-propaganda-producing OWI counterparts had.[99] R&D had not been integrated into the unit long enough to make a measurable impact. X-2, the OSS counterintelligence branch, had little effect on operations.

Perhaps the most important result of Detachment 101's effort in the Myitkyina campaign was that it validated the OSS mission in Burma and ensured continued support from the U.S. Army and OSS Washington. Peers had calculated well in this regard. Detachment 101 sent detailed monthly reports to both NCAC and to OSS Washington beginning in November 1942. In April 1944, however, Peers further directed his field units to keep a detailed daily log of activities, which he then forwarded to headquarters. This hard evidence to OSS Washington revealed how much Detachment 101 contributed to the success of the offensive.[100] One thing, however, was impossible, as the Field Photo section reported: "As for action snapshots, action against the Japs is—almost without exception—always in the dark and cannot be photographed."[101] Nevertheless, the daylight photography stills and movies gave OSS Washington a taste of the Burmese operational environment, and

Peers's efforts to document Detachment 101's activities paid off. If Detachment 101 needed any more reassurance about their intra-theater role, it was an understanding with Stilwell to raise the number of Kachin guerrillas from some 4,000 to 10,000.[102] The Kachin guerrillas had helped swing the hard-fought campaign over to the Allies. As Peers said later, "the presence of the Kachins with the Allied forces tipped the delicately balanced scale in Northern Burma in our favor. Otherwise, it could have developed into an impossible situation."[103]

Postscript

After the war, Detachment 101 received little recognition for their actions in the Myitkyina Campaign. This was inherent by the very nature of their operations, and in addition, the capture of Myitkyina was overshadowed by events in Europe, namely the capture of Rome, D-Day, and the invasion of southern France. However, as the decades passed, setting their place in the historical record became important to several Detachment 101 veterans. Such a stance came to a head with the publication of two books, *The Marauders* and *Stilwell's Command Problems*. Both emphasized the operations of Merrill's Marauders, while not discussing those of Detachment 101. Or, if they did so, it was in unfavorable terms.

In fact, they were late in their protests. The OSS History Office raised objections as early as 17 May 1945 in reference to what would be published by the War Department as *Merrill's Marauders*.[104] Mischa Titiev, the OSS historian detailed to read the draft, commented to his colleagues that "I do feel that the presentation is poor and not always accurate where Detachment 101 of OSS is concerned."[105] As a result, the head of the OSS History Office, Conyers Read, wrote to the U.S. Army historical staff on 27 June 1945. While refraining from commenting on the work as a whole, he said that "it seems to us that the contributions of OSS to the success of the [Myitkyina] expedition have been inadequately presented." In particular, they said that the work failed to "give due credit to Detachment 101" for providing assistance and trained guerrillas to the Marauders and that "it is hard to see how Colonel Osborne could have been unaware of the 'considerable assistance' provided his men by Lt. Tilly and his Kachin guerrillas, since Tilly's movements were carried out under orders from General Stilwell."[106] However, since the book was published, it seems little was done at the time to assuage the OSS's concerns.

Detachment 101 veterans then took issue with another army publication,

Stilwell's Command Problems, published in 1956, in which the authors assert that the GALAHAD staff (Merrill's Marauders) did not know that Tilly's OSS force was in the area due to Detachment 101's "hoarding of information."[107] That statement drew from Charlton Ogburn's *The Marauders*. The comment drew numerous responses, including from Brigadier General Joseph W. Stilwell Jr., formerly the NCAC G-2. He said that there was no hoarding of information and that "the G-2's orders from the CG [Commanding General] were to shove the info to the units."[108] Lieutenant Colonel Samuel V. Wilson, then the Marauders' intelligence and reconnaissance commander, conceded that he was not aware of Tilly's force. However, he also said that "it is almost inconceivable that no one on the 5307th knew of Tilly's existence. In this connection, the undersigned was amazed when performing separate missions for General Merrill, at the amount of detailed intelligence the latter carried in his head." He continued, "To a man, we knew that without the assistance and support of the Kachins, we would have been licked before we even got started, and we recognized fully the vital role of Det 101 providing coherence and direction to this supporting effort."[109]

Regardless of the slight, it is apparent that Detachment 101 has not received its credit due for the effort put forth in the Myitkyina Campaign. Part of this might have to do with the denial of a proposed Presidential Citation for which Detachment 101 was nominated for that campaign.[110] This proposed citation was also supported by Colonel Stilwell.[111] However, it was not to be, and Detachment 101 would not receive a Presidential Citation until 1946 for its actions in the Shan States in 1945.

It still stands that the OSS is given little credit for its efforts in the Myitkyina Campaign. In the American recollection of the Burma campaign, the exploits of Merrill's Marauders, and to a lesser extent, the Chindits, have garnered a far larger share of the public imagination. It remains, however, that the OSS was the only component active in all aspects of the action. As such, it is in this aspect that the history of the north Burma campaign needs to be rewritten to reflect that it was an operational theater in which the use of intelligence and guerrilla forces was an absolute necessity.

8

Peers Continues His Reforms: June–August 1944

I just can't say too much for the kind of people we had. Practically without exception we found that our American soldiers, both officers and enlisted men, were highly adaptable. It took us a little time to get our people broken in to the jungles and that mode of life. But they were resourceful.

Ray Peers

The Myitkyina campaign entered an unplanned phase when the Chinese had failed to capture the north Burma city. This meant that Detachment 101 had to be even more flexible, and forced Peers to again to envision how to position his unit to keep it relevant. His efforts centered on transforming Detachment 101 into an even more effective tactical intelligence collection and guerrilla warfare organization. Once again, Detachment 101 headquarters experienced the greatest change. The early part of the year saw the critical reorganization of the core sections of the Detachment, as well as the inclusion of new OSS branches. Detachment 101 could now begin greater integration of the remaining OSS branches not yet present. In theory, they would improve the unit's ability to wage war against the Japanese in Burma.

Existing Force Structure

The existing elements of Detachment 101 did not remain static. In the period from May to August 1944, the operational elements underwent some of their most dramatic organizational shifts of the war as they rapidly became crucial to the Allied effort. Other elements were not so readily integrated. Although the MO section made progress, it continued to have significant problems. The head OSS officers in Southeast Asia (Peers, Colonel John G. Coughlin,

Major Harry W. Little, and Colonel Richard B. Heppner) arrived at an agreement in May that the first MO printing press would go to Calcutta, where Detachment 101's supply center was headquartered. Getting the equipment and personnel was another matter. By July, the OSS had identified several officers for the post, but secured none. At that same time, and indicative of the lack of effort shown by OSS Washington, Calcutta learned that they were finally to get MO items ordered more than six month previously. By August, the additional personnel still had not arrived, even though plans were made for groups of Japanese Issei (first-generation Japanese immigrants to the United States) to go to Calcutta for translation work on MO material.[1]

While plans—even if delayed—were in place to establish MO at Calcutta, the branch remained nearly nonexistent at Nazira. It had not had continuity of personnel or direction. The Detachment 101 MO section's third director in seven months, Robert Wentworth, had no background in the field, even if OSS Washington recognized that any MO personnel sent to Nazira needed to be for the duration and not as temporary fill-ins. OSS Washington had created an MO unit specifically for Detachment 101, code-named the GOLD DUST team, but it remained in training and would not arrive until late 1944.[2]

Nazira's frustrations with MO were high. Wentworth wrote to his Detachment 303 counterpart, Elizabeth P. MacDonald, "Frankly the whole MO show at Detachment 101 has been completely muffed by the powers that be back in Washington in that they neglected to fill all their promises for both men and material."[3] He later cynically reported, "Due to a lack of personnel and equipment MO activities at Detachment 101 continue to revolve on the problem of how to get things done with only a typewriter."[4]

To compound the problem, MO's relationship had also soured with the Office of War Information (OWI). While willing to print one or two leaflet products a month for the OSS when they were not busy on another project, OWI feared that the leaflets would be traced back to their source. OWI was charged with disseminating truthful information, and being associated with black propaganda would undermine its mission. Even so, just to arrange for the printing of one leaflet, the OSS personnel had to drive some five hours to reach OWI. In an effort to assist, the Detachment 303 MO section in New Delhi reached out and offered to produce propaganda products for Detachment 101, as long as Nazira told them what was needed. Though it could not solve all of MO's needs, the offer was one of the first examples of OSS branch inter-theater cooperation.[5]

The Detachment 101 MO section tried to capitalize on sample leaflets and rumor suggestions sent from OSS Washington. This section also sent out questionnaires to the field to determine their needs and what kind of products might best work. MO also gave new personnel arriving to the Detachment a one-hour lecture on the utility of MO products.[6] This lecture had the alternative purpose of trying to get non-MO personnel to think of material to go in MO products. The MO staff followed up that lecture with another quick briefing for personnel going into the field. In July, the responses came back from the questionnaires sent into the field. The MO section received requests for specific products only from the groups that the section had briefed on MO methods. The groups that had been in the field longer, like FORWARD, were much slower in responding. Clearly, from the MO perspective, their limited briefing of personnel before they went into the field had an effect.[7]

The MO section had to deal with additional problems. Black propaganda was not very effective in the area where Detachment 101's teams were operating because the populations were already largely pro-Allied. As such, the MO section sought to expand its liaison efforts with OWI, because many of the products that could be used in north Burma were white propaganda. An example of the liaison efforts occurred when a field team requested that MO produce a leaflet aimed at trying to keep the local population from moving south with the retreating Japanese. By August, MO's situation was becoming worse. The section was barely functioning and not providing much assistance to the field units. Peers was completely disenchanted, and wrote to Donovan: "The confusion created by this one branch has been greater than all the other branches combined and despite all promises to better the situation it has had a turn for the worse." He further insisted, "An officer for Morale Operations must be sent to this theater at once if that branch is to be represented at Detachment 101."[8] That was not the only branch in a difficult situation at Detachment 101.

The SI section was even worse off than MO. The section had all but been dissolved and its functions relegated to other sections. Its security function split off in July to form its own section that assumed the duties of vetting of indigenous personnel, counterintelligence, censoring of letters, securing of classified material, fire prevention, and physical security of the Detachment's facilities. Unlike the OSS elsewhere, SI's intelligence-gathering function at Detachment 101 had already been absorbed by SO. SI's intelligence function was then given over to R&A, which was coming into its own as an OSS-unique function embedded in Detachment 101's force structure. In June, R&A served to edit and disseminate intelligence material received from the field. The section encompassed the reports in the weekly intelligence summaries, using them to make maps of enemy positions and to brief new arrivals to Detachment 101. Additionally, the team completed surveys of roads in Burma that were passed to the field. R&A also served a strategic function. For instance, in July it answered eleven requests for information and prepared twenty-one maps for OSS Washington.[9] Other OSS branches also brought Detachment 101 to Washington's attention.

Back in Nazira, the Field Photo section was hard at work. They were continuing work on several films, including one on the Myitkyina campaign, and individual photographers recorded multiple aspects of the struggle.[10] To speed production, Field Photo began building a dark room in Myitkyina capable of processing and printing still photographs. Such documentation helped to show OSS Washington the efforts begin put forth by Detachment 101 and the environmental difficulties of operations in Burma. On the operational side, in June, in their first Ceylon-based mission, MU and Field Photo jointly conducted Operation SUGARLOAF II, a seaborne reconnaissance of Simalur Island off Sumatra.[11]

Detachment 101 enhanced logistics by establishing a supply depot at Taro in the TRAMP area of operations and planned to make Myitkyina a base for the storage of radio spare parts. In June, the unit sent two personnel to the airstrip to establish a cache for supplies by unloading cargo aircraft that could not fulfill their drop missions because of weather or enemy activity, rather than have full planes return their loads to Dinjan.[12] This base increased the amount of supplies able to be dropped to the groups in the field. In July, the USAAF allotted Detachment 101 the daily equivalent of 2.3 planeloads of supplies out of their main airfield at Dinjan.[13] With the Myitkyina arrangement, and if the weather allowed and time schedule permitted, additional trips—that did not count toward the daily quota—could be conducted from that airstrip. However, since the fighting from May to August 1944 had largely destroyed Myitkyina, a larger forward base was not feasible. And, in order to build up stocks of critical items back at Nazira, the group once again resorted to the tactic of having incoming personnel individually carry items that they then turned over to supply. Although ad hoc, the method once again worked.[14]

The increase in the operational tempo since the beginning of the year and the end of the monsoon meant that the pace of air drops would increase. The number of aircraft allotted to the Detachment was not enough to support operations, leading the group to request more carrying capacity. In July alone, the group dropped 310,000 pounds of supplies into the field, requiring sixty C-47 loads and four from B-25s.[15] Despite the monsoon rains, August provided no let-up, with 650,000 pounds of supplies dropped out of Dinjan and another 200,000 out of the advance airbase at Myitkyina. This required 102 C-47 flights and 5 of B-25s.[16] As can be seen from this number, the USAAF's commitment to Detachment 101 was not small, nor was the overall cost of the group's operations insignificant. The fast pace of drop operations did have some impact in the field, as one man reported that "machine guns were dropped without ammo belts, [submachine guns] without magazines . . . valuable equipment was destroyed in drops because of careless packing."[17] Other sections had an easier time.

Ironically, the tempo of operations and the rapid pace at which the Allies were pushing forward in Burma made the Finance section's job easier. While they had to pay a much larger number of local recruits, the Allied advance made prewar rupees no longer as critical a necessity.[18] Nevertheless, the cost of operations had increased by August to 470,000 rupees, or nearly $200,000, making plans necessary to forward-base a finance officer at Myitkyina to more effectively and speedily handle the pay of the indigenous recruits.[19]

In terms of personnel, the Detachment was in better shape that it had ever been. OSS Washington ensured that even with the "D-Day pressure on the European Theater" it was doing everything possible to keep men flowing into the Detachment.[20] The personnel situation had so improved that in June, Peers was imploring OSS Washington to send him only men who were adequately trained and physically able to handle the vigor of fieldwork in Burma. This was very different from 1943, when the Detachment begged for personnel of any type. In parachute-qualified personnel alone, it now had twenty officers and nine enlisted men. This was eight more soldiers than were available to the entire Detachment for most of 1942. In July, the table of organization and equipment of the unit stood at 124 officers, 322 enlisted men, and 210 civilians serving at headquarters. This does not count the several thousand indigenous troops and agents serving in the field.[21] This is a dramatic contrast for a unit that had arrived in mid-1942 with only 21 men. But, some deficiencies remained.

One significant problem for the Detachment was its lack of pilots for the liaison aircraft. In August, the unit only had two pilots—and seven aircraft. Detachment 101 had a few additional pilots who were on detached service from the Seventy-first Liaison Squadron, but they could be withdrawn at any time. As a result, Detachment 101 pressed OSS Washington for more pilots.[22]

Local recruitment netted additional personnel. To help secure agents, through its liaison efforts Detachment 101 secured access to intelligence dossiers compiled by the British. The OSS then used the dossiers to vet potential agents for both Detachments 101 and 404.[23] The system was first put to use on a large scale in August when Detachment 404 requested that Detachment 101 assist it with the recruitment of ninety Gurkha guards and six indigenous personnel for operations. In addition, Detachment 101 was in the midst of processing seven agents for itself, nine for Detachment 404, and seven for the Calcutta office.[24] Before the OSS even approached these potential recruits, undercover agents had already investigated their backgrounds to ensure that the potential recruits were not Japanese agents and that they were willing to conduct operational parachute jumps.[25]

Having more personnel required that the Detachment take care of them properly. In July, the unit requested ten additional clerks just to cover the administrative needs and the "tremendous amount of paperwork" of the incoming personnel. To see that the personnel had their professional needs catered to, the group established a citations and promotions board, which held its first meeting in August. This provided a formal way to evaluate personnel and a way to see that individuals received recognition. It was a major improvement, as under Eifler's command, the lack of promotion for field personnel was a significant gripe.[26]

The third change needed was for upgraded medical facilities. At the time, Peers estimated that there was a 25 percent decrease in efficiency because of illness.[27] In July, the group made plans for the establishment of a fifty-bed hospital facility that had surgical, convalescent, laboratory, dental, and X-ray capabilities. One of the main reasons for this expansion was to better care for the increase in malaria cases that more personnel would create. The lack of medical care already shortened to seven the number of days that the staff could devote to each patient, from the necessary ten.[28] To oversee the building and running of the large facility, Peers recalled James C. Luce from command of FORWARD, and once again, he proved instrumental. Through his connections, Luce secured several Burmese nurses previously employed by the famed Burma surgeon Gordon Seagrave. Prior to the hospital's completion, Luce instituted strict methods to prevent malaria infection, including filling in gullies to eliminate breeding grounds and enforcing greater precautions after dusk to prevent mosquito bites.[29]

Like operations, the Communications section was also in a much better position by simplifying the ciphering of messages in such a way that receiving and transmitting communications became easier and faster. Even so, the cryptographic subsection handled 235,000 message groups in August.[30] In line with improvements in encryption, the Communications section as a whole reorganized. It pushed to Gelakey, India, the communications duties of several field stations, as well as reorganized the way that it handled field communications. The section installed a larger transmitter at Nazira, which permitted the section to maintain contact with "all stations regardless of conditions."[31] Although there was still a shortage of spare parts for field sets, supply was somewhat alleviated through coordination with the U.S. Army Signal Corps and an arrival of supplies from OSS Washington. The situation had so improved that August was the first month since 1942 that the Communications section reported that it had enough sets to supply field needs.[32] Other sections also tried to improve their utility.

The training camps, now subsumed under the Schools and Training section, enhanced their link with SO by debriefing individuals returning from the field, and where possible, incorporating the results into training.[33] The camps conditioned troops arriving from the states during a two-week introduction and field instruction course, that incorporated the lessons that the Detachment had learned in the field. This course gave every new recruit a window into each section of the Detachment 101 organization, the ethnicities of Burma, and a general idea of how to live in the field. A multiday jungle hike capped off the course, in which students had to live off the land under field conditions. If possible, the training group arranged a supply drop while out on the hike, thereby doing as much as possible to prepare their students for when they actually went to operations. Detachment 101 considered this course crucial because the staff did not think that OSS training stateside was adequate. Peers wrote to Donovan that he wished to discuss the matter with him when he visited OSS Washington in September. Specifically, Peers mentioned that a parachute group undergoing training at one of the main OSS bases located at Catalina Island, California, would "be in for a rude awakening when they hit Burma. The terrain at Catalina is no more comparable to the jungles of Burma than Central Park is to a sand lot." He suggested that the closest one could get to simulate the terrain of Burma in the United States was to conduct training in the Everglades or the Mississippi bayous.[34]

New OSS Branches Arrive

On 30 May 1944, a partially recovered Eifler briefly returned to Detachment 101, officially for the purpose of showing off newly produced OSS specialized equipment. In reality, he was on a recruiting trip to identify personnel for a secret mission given to him by Donovan, the Field Experimental Unit (FEU).

This was a new group that was to carry out special assignments under Donovan's direction. Instead of introducing R&D devices to the Detachment, as was his cover, Eifler recruited some of Detachment 101's most experienced men. It was not until the next month that the first true personnel of the R&D Branch arrived at Nazira.[35]

Although other branches such as Communications and MU participated in the development of their own specialized equipment, R&D was an OSS-specific branch whose purpose was to develop or contract for specialized weapons and equipment for guerrilla warfare, special operations, and clandestine intelligence collection. The branch also had the mission of keeping track of potentially useful equipment developed by non-OSS organizations. This specialized equipment was of most interest to the SO and SI Branches, and, in popular culture, was much like those devices plied by "Q" in the *James Bond* series. Although it was formed as an independent branch on 17 October 1942, it was not until April 1944 that R&D representatives first went to overseas positions.[36]

R&D got off to a quick start at Detachment 101. With only a two-man staff, the section laid plans to assist the field groups. They established a laboratory and used it to help tackle the problem of how to camouflage radios and equipment so that they might be of more use. In August, the R&D staff was capable enough to develop items for the Air Drop and MO sections of Detachment 202.[37] Items included a booby-trapped exploding parachute container that would appear to have been inadvertently dropped to Japanese troops. The R&D section's only comment on the item was "Won't they be surprised!"[38] At least one case in which it was put to use was on 20 December 1944, when the Japanese overran a drop zone of Area #1's First Battalion.[39]

Instead of ceasing the resupply mission lest it drop into enemy hands, the OSS Air Drop section prepared a supply drop of four containers: two were rigged with pipes filled with plastic explosives triggered with highly sensitive pull devices and surrounded by taped nuts and bolts to act as shrapnel. The drop aircraft was a B-25 Mitchell.

"When R and D drove up to the plane at the strip they handled the containers like eggshells." One of the air drop men, after discovering how the charge was to go off, asked the simple question of what would the opening shock of the parachute do to the charge. R&D did not have an answer.

First Lieutenant Dennis V. Cavanaugh said, "I had a 25-foot length of nylon rope, and after slinging the containers in the bomb-bay, I attached the static lines to the rope and the rope to the airframe. That's why I can tell you about this today." When the drop plane neared the airstrip, the kickers saw the Japanese "waiting and beckoning for the drop. So we dropped. BOOM-BOOM! Both booby-trapped containers exploded when the chutes opened, fortunately behind our plane because of the extra line. A breathless moment passed before the tail gunner responded to our call." He was fine, but, "the back of the plane was full of holes." Since the Japanese could no longer be under the illusion that the American plane was unaware of who held the dropzone, the B-25 swing around and strafed the position. "When the eight forward guns went off, we almost stopped in midair."[40]

Other R&D weapons undergoing testing included an adapter that would allow the M-3 submachine gun to shoot rifle grenades and explosive fake firewood that could be infiltrated into the fuel stocks used by enemy locomotives. Increased to five by August, the staff provided the additional service of teaching a short class to incoming personnel.

Other new branches, such as X-2, the OSS counterespionage branch, were not as well received at Detachment 101. Peers wrote back to OSS Washington that "so far" the section "has done more harm than good."[41] X-2 originated with the British, who had agreed to provide the OSS copies of their counterespionage files and to train agents. In return, the OSS had to form an organization capable of greater security and stricter handling of classified information than was SI. As a result, the OSS established the Counter-Intelligence Division of SI on 1 March 1943. Having counterespionage under SI was not completely satisfactory, so on 15 June 1943, the OSS established X-2 as a separate branch. In part, this separation from SI allowed cooperation with the British without also giving them complete access to SI holdings.[42]

The newly founded X-2 Branch was in charge of managing security procedures, uncovering penetrations of OSS by other intelligence services, and running penetration operations of its own. Of all the OSS branches, X-2 was the most secretive. With few exceptions, at Detachment 101, X-2 was not a branch that could be molded to fit an operational situation, nor were personnel generally shifted into the X-2 section as needs dictated. Although the X-2 Branch was more established in the European Theater, the X-2 station at New Delhi, India, was particularly active. In China, the ubiquitous presence of agents from Chiang Kai-shek's intelligence chief, Tai Li, prevented the X-2 Branch from being very effective. Burma had few such hindrances.

In Detachment 101, X-2's duties primarily revolved around personnel security and uncovering enemy agents. Before the group could concentrate on determining how it could best serve the field operators and OSS Washington, however, it first had to arrive at how it would conduct business at Nazira. Unfortunately, this was not an easy process. Although X-2 had worked out an agreement with the Indian and British governments in February, the actual start of X-2 in Burma was in March.[43] An X-2 representative arrived at NCAC and met with senior members of General Stilwell's staff, including his son. Right at the time that the drive to take Myitkyina was underway, the representative managed to convince NCAC that a serious problem existed with enemy agents reporting on Allied troop movements.[44] NCAC requested that the OSS provide immediate assistance, but the X-2 representative had spoken too soon. Although he had discussed possibilities, he had no solutions, as X-2 had no plans to provide personnel. All that he had managed to do was to raise Stilwell's fears to a fever pitch. Stilwell feared that enemy reporting on NCAC movements was holding up his units. He thought that X-2 had promised a special counterintelligence (SCI) team, but the X-2 representative was unaware that he had made such a promise.[45] On 30 April, Stilwell asked for a five-man X-2 SCI unit and stated that if the OSS did not respond, he would take the drastic step of asking the British for help.[46] When OSS was unable to provide this team, an exasperated Stilwell turned the mission over to the U.S. Army Counter Intelligence Corps (CIC), creating a rivalry that later proved almost crippling to both services.

Stilwell's move was an embarrassment for Detachment 101. Peers reported to OSS Washington that "had it not been for our own very close personal contact with the General, and his staff plus the success of our other operations, our entire program might have collapsed because of X-2's unwillingness to operate as part of our unit rather than an individual branch." He noted that X-2's conduct was not typical for Detachment 101; "The operation of Detachment 101 depends solely on its operation as a unit rather than operating as branches individually."[47] In May, the Detachment 404 X-2 section again warned that there were many security threats from loose-lipped Chinese, Tibetans, or Afghans who might be working for the Japanese.[48] This further inflamed fears that there was a critical need for counterintelligence personnel in Burma and India. At the end of July, the OSS finally named Major George H. White as the X-2 representative to Detachment 101, although he never ended up serving in Nazira.[49]

Peers still allowed X-2 an opening in Detachment 101, and in August, he placed a substitute officer, Lieutenant Robert E. Adams, in Myitkyina under the cover of an engineering officer. Adams bridged the gap until a true X-2 representative, Major Baird Helfrich, arrived from Washington. Peers gave Helfrich a list of suggestions to follow when he arrived, including using Kachins to ferret out Japanese agents among refugees. But in reality, Helfrich had little idea of how he would operate in Burma, or even in which direction X-2 should go. Even more so than MO, X-2 was off to a poor start. OSS branches without an immediate tactical use were difficult to absorb into a unit that was increasingly focused on combat operations.[50]

By August 1944, Peers had eight months of command under his belt. Detachment 101 was barely recognizable as the same organization that Eifler had created. True, some aspects had remained the same. Eifler had instilled a sense of purpose that pervaded the unit until the end of the war, of getting the job done no matter what it took. Peers, however, had made the changes that permitted Detachment 101 to take on these tasks. Included in these changes was the addition of virtually all the major specific branches and functions that the OSS had to offer, as well as an organic air and maritime capacity. While there still largely remained a lack of true branch distinctions, at least in the field, the inclusion of various OSS elements had improved the unit's utility. Especially important were the improvements in the core areas of intelligence dissemination and the operations center. These had permitted the centralized acquisition and analysis of both operations and intelligence, which, in turn, allowed headquarters to better manage both functions. Yet, gone completely was the sense of drama and amateurism that had marked Detachment 101's early days. Instead, Peers had taken the unit as his own and molded it into an organization that had two purposes: to supply intelligence and to conduct guerrilla warfare behind enemy lines.

9

Reorganizing after Myitkyina: September–December 1944

The grouse at OSS was that 101 had cut loose from OSS and had "Jined the Army!"

William S. Shepardson, head of the OSS SI Branch

With Myitkyina finally under Allied control, the Allies congratulated themselves on a hard-fought joint victory, and with the monsoon not yet over, momentarily regrouped to reflect upon the accomplishment. This was not true for Detachment 101. As the unit charged with gathering intelligence and conducting guerrilla warfare behind Japanese lines, it had to continue pressing the enemy and push deeper into its rear areas to aid the Allied capture of Bhamo in mid-December 1944.

The China-Burma-India Theater itself experienced great change. Despite NCAC's finally achieving success, on 18 October, at Generalissimo Chiang Kai-shek's insistence, President Roosevelt recalled Stilwell. With that recall, the United States reorganized the China-Burma-India Theater into two theaters. Lieutenant General Daniel I. Sultan received command of the India-Burma Theater, with NCAC intact. It was his duty was to see that the north Burma offensive continued. Major General Albert C. Wedemeyer was placed in command of the China Theater.

Detachment 101 could neither allow the new strategic situation to negatively affect its operations nor ignore the need to continue to reorganize and rebuild. The Detachment was not a standardized unit in any sense and had a constantly changing table of organization and equipment (TO&E). Its various sections could not remain static, because they faced increasingly greater tasks. They had to improve efficiency while at the same time help to increase the Detachment's overall pressure on the Japanese. As a result, this period was one of rebuilding existing elements, in which OSS Washington slowly addressed the lack of personnel.

At this time, Detachment 101 also began to get a few OSS veterans who had already seen service in Europe. However, for the combat personnel,

> irrespective of how much experience they had had in Europe, we insisted that they had to go through the 101 orientation course. The reasons were quite basic: the terrain, the people, the economy and everything about Burma was entirely different from Europe; the tactics and techniques used in the two areas were as different as night and day; and they were accustomed to operating as individuals and small teams whereas in 101, everything was built around the unit integrity and espirit de corps . . . any personnel who could not be readily assimilated into 101 we shipped to China.[1]

Existing Force Structure

Peers determined that the best way to serve the Allied forces was to have his men take advantage of the monsoon to push deeper into Japanese-held Burma. The moves necessitated a mobile headquarters. Since operations were now even farther from Nazira, the headquarters Operations section was the first to relocate to Myitkyina on 27 September. The Communications section and a representative, Sergeant Edward S. Pendergast, of the Finance section, soon followed. The Red Ass Squadron followed suit and by September had six planes (out of nine total) forward-based at Myitkyina. The R&A section sent a forward party, but did not officially open their Myitkyina office until 24 October. Within months, the only sections remaining at Nazira were non–combat related, such as the school and the hospital.[2]

The move put headquarters elements closer to Detachment 101's operating area, but it also permitted more timely intelligence dissemination. With Myitkyina finally under Allied control, the Operations section could revisit older ideas and incorporate new ones. In October, much like the initial operations under Eifler, it once again tried its hand at long-range penetrations by parachuting three teams of indigenous personnel deep behind Japanese lines. This time, experienced agents made up the teams. Even though most Detachment 101 units by then primarily engaged in guerrilla operations, these teams served to reinforce intelligence collection.[3]

To prepare for the end of the monsoon, Peers extended liaison to even more Allied formations, and assigned Lieutenants Jacob Esterline and William Martin to the Chinese First and Sixth Armies, respectively, and

Lieutenant Roger Hilsman to the British Thirty-sixth Division. Detachment 101 made further arrangements with the British when it agreed that the former TRAMP units would patrol east of the Chindwin, while the Thirty-third Brigade of the Fourteenth Army would patrol to the west.[4] For purely intelligence matters, the R&A section established liaison with the NCAC G-2 Photo Interpretation section.[5] By November, the Detachment had officers permanently assigned to liaison duties with the 124th Cavalry Regiment (U.S.); the 475th Infantry Regiment (U.S); the 5332nd Brigade (U.S.); the First Provisional Tank Group (U.S-Chinese); the Fourth Corps (U.K.); the Thirty-sixth Division (U.K.); SEAC; and the First and Sixth Chinese Armies. Detachment 101 also attached groups of Kachins to some of these units. The 124th Cavalry and the First and Sixth Chinese Armies had an attached Detachment 101 intelligence and reconnaissance (I&R) platoon, while the Thirty-sixth Division and First Provisional Tank Group also had attached agents and guides.

The liaison efforts increased the awareness and use of Detachment 101's intelligence and guerrilla formations, but proved to be such a severe drain on available officers that those already assigned to the field groups had to stay behind the lines longer without replacement. Extended field service helped to create what Peers termed a "relatively large number of cases of mental fatigue" because officers and men were behind the lines "too long according to any and all standards." He noted whereas "Army Combat Units . . . rarely remain over two months in continuous combat before being withdrawn," many in Detachment 101 had been in the field for anywhere from seven to twenty months.[6] Other Detachment 101 sections also had to deal with the high operations tempo.

The Schools and Training section of Detachment 101 did its best to enhance cooperation with the U.S. Army. In September, it furnished instructors to help train an I&R platoon for the 475th Infantry Regiment of the 5332nd Brigade (Provisional) or MARS Task Force. In October, Detachment 101 established a jungle warfare instruction center in Myitkyina for the 475th and a two-week-long course in jungle familiarization for OSS personnel at the forward training area at Taro, formerly occupied by TRAMP. There the newly arrived personnel met "the jungle face to face . . . we rapidly learned how to cope with this strange environment, and not to merely exist, but to enjoy it." Skills learned ranged from "how to butcher a boar, how to remove leeches without leaving the heads in your skin—the many uses of bamboo, from food to utensils, to housing, to weapons."[7] The Schools and Training section also produced instructional booklets, such as primers on how to pick up foreign languages.[8]

In September, the section finished a reorganization. At Nazira, Schools and Training now had twelve different camps that were broken down into the type of personnel they could handle: including one camp each for Americans, Karens, Burmans, Kachins, Shans, Thai, and females. The reorganization included formulating standard operating procedures for incoming personnel. When an indigenous recruit arrived, they were photographed, given a physical examination, sworn into the unit (under the legal penalties of the India Secrets Act), given dental care, and then sent on to the proper training camp.[9] Even dental care had to be carefully administered because work on an indigenous agent had to resemble something that would have been done by a local dentist. This meant that the Detachment 101 dentist had to use local materials and attempt to artificially age his work so that it did not appear as new.[10] The photographs and records of the agents were the start of the Detachment advocating for a series of background checks and a central records repository that would prevent the rehiring of employees already deemed unsuitable by other U.S. government organizations.[11] New personnel in the field meant that enhanced support was necessary.

Previously, Communications reorganized to increase efficiency and laid plans to push its elements further into Burma to support operations. After briefing the field commanders, on 30 September the Communications section at Myitkyina took over all field radio traffic. The move to Myitkyina left only four communications positions at Nazira; one each to work U.S. Army circuits, traffic from southern India (Calcutta), China, and a backup for communications from Chabua, Dinjan, and Gelakey. The lack of intense operations during the monsoon helped ease the initial impact of the shift even if in September the Communications section still handled 217,000 code groups. The move also built in redundancy by having the capacity to cover communications from all field areas, Nazira, the air warning stations, and a backup to take over the communications of any area that might go off the air due to enemy movements. For example, in September, former Area #3 temporarily lost communications because of a minor Japanese push into the area, and in November, a move south by Area #2 resulted in Myitkyina taking over its schedules for three days. Claude V. Wadsworth, the Communications section chief, said, "It worked so smoothly that the field [units] were not aware of the change."[12]

The pigeon section, a subset of Communications, managed to drop its first birds into the field in late September for use as emergency messengers to signal that parachuted agents had landed successfully, or when patrols or agents could not communicate via radio.[13] The use of pigeons entailed some problems as there was a "tremendous temptation" for indigenous troops to "shoot everything that flys [*sic*]—for eating purposes but to date casualties to pigeons from this source has been light." The success rate of the pigeons in returning was 99 percent. The pigeoneers even experimented by having pigeons fly from Myitkyina to Nazira, entailing an arduous fourteen-hour journey of 225 miles over mountain ranges.[14] The MO section used birds that were not up to being used on operations. Not being trained to return, the birds carried a false message designed to fall into enemy hands.[15]

The continued use of pigeons reflected that the Detachment still did not have adequate field radio sets. Those that arrived from the States were unsuitable for the climate and not waterproof. This meant that the Communications section still had to find the time to build its own transmitters for field operations despite the demands of monitoring radio traffic. For October, communications personnel in Myitkyina handled 1,514 messages (94,152 groups), while Nazira handled 2,030 messages (124,003 groups).[16] November's load reflected that communications duties were shifting from Nazira; 2,037 messages (130,216 groups) at Myitkyina as opposed to 52,050 groups handled by Nazira.[17] The increasing level of radio traffic also forced the Communications section at Myitkyina to once again alter how the field groups could contact base. Previously, field groups were on schedules of when they could transmit to base, but field conditions and emergencies did not always permit the behind-the-lines groups to communicate on time. The solution was to issue a common frequency to the field units and to leave it open for emergency traffic.[18]

Fortunately, with operational successes came new personnel. The Communications section was one that greatly benefited from new arrivals, many of which had the benefit of training stateside at OSS training Area C, established for the sole purpose of training communication personnel. By November, they "materially relieved pressure" on the overworked section.[19]

But additional personnel brought with them problems of needing a robust administration system to deal with a rapid influx of personnel. As Peers reported, "There has been a noticeable tightening of regulations and meticulous attention to detail is now required." Nazira also had to reassess how it handled the personnel of other OSS groups. Previously all personnel for Detachment 202 in China first went through Detachment 101 headquarters. With the OSS involvement in China expanding, it was no longer practical for Detachment 101's limited staff to handle the influx, and arrangements were being made for Detachment 202 to process their own personnel.[20]

An additional critical need was for medical personnel. In October, Commodore M. E. Miles of SACO/U.S. Naval Group, China, requested that all the

U.S. Navy medical personnel on loan to Detachment 101 be released and that they be sent to his command within three weeks. As Detachment 101 reported to OSS Washington, this "could not have come at a more inopportune time," as the increased combat nature of Detachment 101's work placed medical personnel in even greater demand. And as units moved deeper into enemy-controlled areas, they found that in order to prevent their own troops from getting ill, the OSS had to treat the local population for such maladies as smallpox. All this required more medical personnel. Yet, while Detachment 101 had asked for them, none had arrived over the previous four months. Demands on the medical department in November were "approximately three times that of any previous month," making even the keeping of adequate supplies on hand difficult.[21]

All the U.S. Navy pharmacist's mates were withdrawn by December and replaced by U.S. Army medical personnel. But the new additions required time to acclimate.[22] However, the fortunate recruiting of four additional nurses who had previously worked for Seagrave eased the burden. Because these nurses were from Burma, they had the additional benefit of helping put indigenous casualties at ease and improving their morale. Improved facilities also helped.

A new fifty-bed hospital at Nazira allowed for major surgical procedures. By November, the increased level of operations—and subsequent casualties—filled it to capacity. December's hospital records reflect the cost of the increased operational activities and the improvement in the medical section's capabilities. The hospital admitted 75 personnel and discharged 45. There were twelve major surgical procedures, ranging from perforated intestines to plastic surgery to treating bayonet, gunshot, and shrapnel wounds. The dispensary treated 186 patients, conducted 131 physical examinations, and performed 481 immunizations, while Detachment 101's dentist saw 216 patients. Medical personnel detailed to the field were likewise busy, with 107 emergency surgeries and 2,596 disease cases treated.[23]

The continuation of the monsoon allowed the Air Drop section a bit of a respite. Even so, in September the group dropped 542,384 pounds of supplies from 120 aircraft.[24] To accomplish this feat, in some instances the drop planes had to make twenty attempts at finding a single field group. The respite ended in October when the letup of the monsoon allowed for a greater number of flights. The total weight of supplies dropped then topped more than 1 million pounds, requiring 217 flights of C-47s and 18 of B-25s that flew out of four airfields. The Detachment now had seven C-47's reserved for daily flights out of Dinjan, and the USAAF allowed one of these to remain overnight at Myitkyina to allow another flight in either the early morning or late afternoon. To save time, Detachment 101 personnel loaded supplies directly from an airfield at Nazira, but it was only an interim solution while the Detachment moved its main supply depots to Dinjan airfield, where it had secured three warehouses.[25]

By forward-basing supplies at Dinjan, the Detachment reduced the time needed to transport materials 110 miles from Nazira. For additional storage, they secured another warehouse at Chalkhoa (18 miles from Dinjan), but had other improvements as well. The Dinjan Air Drop section had two officers and fifteen enlisted men assigned, while two officers and three enlisted men worked out of Chalkhoa. Eight 2½-ton trucks transported the supplies, and by December the section planned to move its Chalkhoa facilities to Dinjan to further reduce the workload. Detachment 202 took over the Chalkhoa warehouse and thereafter worked with Detachment 505 to transit its own supplies over the Hump.[26]

These moves proved beneficial as by December, the total dropped once again exceeded 1 million pounds when 198 C-47 flights and 6 from B-25s dropped 1,132,028 pounds. Ninety percent of that originated from Dinjan. An extra C-47 was secured (for a total of eight) with another on call for night drops, and the USAAF had B-25s available for more dangerous missions. The Air Drop section grew so busy that they had to standardize loads. Still, a field group had the option of ordering heavy armament if surrounded or expecting an attack from the Japanese.

First Lieutenant Dennis V. Cavanaugh recalled that "in the early days you could order about anything you wanted. Radio supply messages looked like a homicidal housewife's shopping list. When the pace speeded up, we had to organize standard drops. You'd place an order for so many soldiers, and the ration was predetermined for the Kachins at least."[27]

First Lieutenant Bernard Brophy based each unit's ration supply on the size of the group and the time since their last drop. "We had a formula for food. We knew how much we had to get in there." He recalled that sometimes "it took a couple of hours" to load each airplane.

> Some of the things would come in already packaged with the parachute on it. Other times we had to put it in boxes or crates, attach the parachute to it, and make sure we had the right weight. You didn't want it too heavy otherwise some of the panels on the chute would blow, come down too fast, smash-up, and ruin the drop. So, we had to be careful about that . . . most of the time everything went fine.

Brophy said that the weight distribution aboard the C-47 was also a concern. "You had to make sure that you had the weight on both sides the same and not too much in the tail. You had to distribute it [evenly] throughout the fuselage so that you had good take offs and good landings." The shorter flights from Myitkyina helped. "It would take maybe six to eight hours off the airdrop time. Guys were only 150 or as close as 25 miles away. . . . It made it a lot easier to get stuff to them," recalled Brophy. Working with competent USAAF crew also helped.

> The pilots were good. They knew how to come into the drop zone and how to maneuver the airplane to keep the tail up, so that the stuff going out the door did not hit the tail. A pilot who was very new at it, well, the stuff going out would hit the tail and [the wind would cause it to] hang there . . . until the pilot slowed the plane down to a point that it would fall off.

Still, there could be problems on the drop missions such as tremendous wind gusts over the mountainous terrain. Brophy recalled, "Sometimes it got a little tricky. You would be carrying a bag of rice and hit a downdraft. The bag of rice would go up in the air and you could hold it up with one finger. On the other hand, you'd hit an updraft and [the rice sack] would weigh 250 pounds. It would pull you down to the floor of the plane." Uncharted areas were also a concern. "You'd be flying into unexplored areas with mountains. On the map there would be a blank space, just plain white. In the middle of that space it would say unexplored. You did not know what was there, so we were a little concerned about that," he said.

If all went well, the pilot activated the jump lights in the rear of the airplane to tell the kickers when to push the supplies out. Brophy remembered:

> The red light meant that you were to get ready and in position. We would check for the panels at the dropzone to see if everything was alright there, and keep an eye on that light. As soon as that green light went on, everything would be pushed out the door. You would have one guy on the left side of the door, one on the right, and one guy with his back [braced] against the opposite side of the fuselage with his feet up against the back of the stuff that you were kicking out the door. I would say 'go' and one guy would push with his right arm, the other guy with his left arm, and the guy in the back would push with both feet. I would usually be [guiding the load] and looking out the door.

The kickers did not have any restraints. "There was [only] a bar on each side. They [the kickers] held on with one hand, and pushed with the other. They went halfway out the door as they pushed. We got used to that, it was no problem," said Brophy.[28] Air Drop had proved its mettle and even received words of support from the field. "The drop people are to be congratulated on the STICK-TO-ITIVENESS whereby they have and will search for an hour in order to make a drop to a cloud-ridden place. This attitude is most appreciated."[29]

With the war in Europe winding down, more assets and personnel became available from that theater. In November officers and aircraft from the famed Carpetbaggers of the 492nd Bomb Group that had supported clandestine efforts in Europe arrived in the Far East. The 492nd was on a fact-finding mission to see if they could assist Detachment 101, specifically offering twenty-five B-24 aircraft modified for night dropping. However, Detachment 101 rejected the offer as the C-47s that they already used were far more suitable, and unlike in Europe, there was no need for exclusive use of night-flying aircraft for covert insertions.[30] Such a rejection would have been unheard of earlier in the year.

Operations also heavily taxed the Detachment's Red Ass Squadron. With only seven operational aircraft, its pilots racked up 506 hours of combat flying to carry 356 passengers, 30 wounded patients, and 24,495 tons of cargo.[31] They conducted twice-daily flights that in addition to other duties, brought to Nazira the paper copies of all communications transmissions handled by the Myitkyina station.[32]

Increased operations also meant more duties for the Finance section, rebranded as the Special Funds section to reflect OSS Washington's organization. An increased number of indigenous personnel elevated the Detachment's operating costs to 620,000 rupees for the month of October. Fortunately, newer recruits were more likely to accept either newly minted silver coinage, or even paper script, lowering the demand for the hard-to-obtain prewar coins. As units pressed deeper into Burma, however, the section had different currency demands placed upon it, including for Japanese occupation rupee notes, examples of which the section sent to OSS Washington for counterfeiting, and for British gold sovereigns.[33] There remained, however, the problem of having enough personnel to make sure that everyone was paid, so the Special Funds section planned to forward-base a finance officer in each of the three operating areas.[34] Additionally, to help ease the burden, beginning in November the Detachment 101 Special Funds section no longer had to account for Detachment 505 in Calcutta.

The way that the Detachment handled intelligence also changed. After having taken over the SI role at Detachment 101, R&A repackaged intelligence reports into products better able to assist end-users. Mirroring its parent branch functions in OSS Washington, the Detachment 101 R&A section not only compiled lengthy reports, but also created specific products, like illustrated booklets on Japanese rank insignia for non-English speakers. R&A personnel enhanced the usefulness of their reports by providing oral briefings when requested to senior personnel of the OWI, the Tenth Air Force, NCAC Headquarters, and several British organizations. The section conducted briefings, lasting from one to six hours, several times a week.[35] R&A assisted operations by being the conduit through which to obtain maps (produced or secured by Detachment 303), and helped the MO section by translating captured Japanese documents. In December, the R&A section was rewarded for its efforts by receiving a 120 percent augmentation in personnel. With more personnel, however, came more work. In addition to a greater number of oral briefings, the section wrote fourteen reports that month, several of which came from X-2–supplied material. Map orders also had increased by 200 to 430 percent, depending on type, since October.[36]

Other branches present in OSS Washington but not yet considered core areas of the Detachment, such as the MO section, also improved as 1945 dawned. The chief of MO at SEAC (Detachment 404) wrote to OSS Washington that at Detachment 101, "MO ended the moment Charlie Fenn was drawn out [in early 1944]."[37] To help remedy the situation, Peers directed Robert Wentworth, the Detachment 101 MO section chief, to travel to New Delhi (Detachment 303) to confer with his colleagues in the hopes that they could assist production. Due to limited resources and its integration into SEAC, Detachment 303's solution was to use British facilities to assist with the translation and printing of MO leaflets. Wentworth made the further step of traveling to Detachment 404 at Kandy, Ceylon, where he arranged to send a small leaflet printing press to Detachment 101, while Detachment 303 handled larger production efforts. This effort switched the Detachment's reliance on the OWI to the OSS. In quite a reversal from the previous period, OWI now pushed to place a representative with Detachment 101, so that the OSS could assist in distributing their products. Weekly liaison meetings with OWI and NCAC facilitated coordination of propaganda in the area.[38] In addition, MO incorporated itself into operations by producing leaflets that contained coded operational messages for field units. Upon discovery, those on the ground used the leaflets to know when they might expect supply drops.[39]

In November, the long-awaited five-man GOLD DUST team arrived in

Myitkyina from OSS Washington. It was the first "complete and self contained" MO unit for the Far East.[40] OSS Washington put the team through "the most intensive schedule" of preparation to make them "the best trained unit MO has ever sent to the field." The preparation included training in MO techniques as well as studying the situation in Burma and Japanese vulnerabilities.[41] The GOLD DUST team brought printing equipment and were conducting black operations within a week of their arrival. Their first product was a pamphlet directed at Burmese soldiers serving with the Japanese forces.[42] By December, the group received two Nisei from OSS Washington to assist in translation. Production delays due to a lack of equipment, however, prevented GOLD DUST from printing their products. But, unlike what had been the case for prior efforts at Detachment 101, GOLD DUST received extensive support from MO Washington, who supplied the team ideas for use in products and rumor campaigns.[43]

The R&D section was firmly established enough to work on less-time-sensitive projects. In October, their two main projects were continuing to develop a way to launch rifle grenades from M-3 submachine guns and how to use mortars and bazookas to distribute propaganda leaflets. Other projects were parachute locators, bazooka-launched illuminating flares, message self-destruction devices, and ground illumination devices to alert encamped field groups that enemies were nearby. As with most of the other sections at Detachment 101, the R&D section's main obstacle was in having enough trained personnel, but it also lacked laboratory space and tools.[44]

The section also continued working on previous projects such as camouflaging explosive devices. This effort was so important that it became a subsection of Detachment 101 R&D. That R&D subsection worked on using water jugs, bamboo, fake rocks and vegetables of plaster, and a bamboo raft to conceal explosive charges. It also worked on using common items, included shoes and belts, as message concealment devices. Other members of R&D busied themselves with preparing smoke devices to identify Detachment 101 units to aircraft flying overhead. This last item in particular was useful as Allied aircraft occasionally mistook Detachment 101 patrols for the enemy.[45]

The X-2 section also found itself on firmer ground. Major Baird V. Helfrich completed his area survey and noted that although the British had made some effort at identifying what were termed "black" (collaborators) and "white" (friendly) citizens, little was done to keep the information current. Helfrich took this as an X-2 mission and coordinated with Detachment 101 and British forces in the operating area.[46] Helfrich quickly came to understand that the task was not going to be easy, noting, "During early October it became apparent that there was no hope of building 'current' blacklists" because the information was dated.[47] His solution was to travel behind the lines, where the information was more readily available. Helfrich then created a form for the field groups to log information on white and black citizens, called "hats," so that upon liberation, collaborators could be separated from loyal citizens. "Black hats" included Japanese collaborators or those who had turned over Allied soldiers and airmen to the Japanese. "Grey hats" were those whose allegiance to the Allied cause was in doubt, while "white hats" were those who had resisted the Japanese, or at the very least, had not aided the enemy. Helfrich tried to get the Burma Civil Affairs Service, the Burma Intelligence Corps, and the Burma Police to help apprehend the black hats. But due to a lack of manpower, funds, transport, and supplies, these organizations had no means of securing collaborators or making use of the population that had remained friendly toward the Allies. This resulted in their having done little background checking into the indigenous personnel employed by the Allies. Helfrich relayed his findings to the NCAC, G-2 head Colonel Joseph Stilwell Jr., who appointed the X-2 chief to cooperate with the CIC to supervise the activation and coordination of combat interrogation teams (CITs), which sorted out and detained black hats to hand over to Burma government officials.[48] CITS were necessary because in the past, and many times even with the CITs, the Kachins summarily disposed of suspected black hats—with or without the knowledge of the OSS—before a trial could be held.

The first of the five-to-seven-man CITs was activated at the end of October. By November, two more CITs were operating, with plans to create three more. Additional personnel came from the MO section, as well as OWI. In November, the CITs interrogated 220 suspects and apprehended 39.[49] By December, the CITs provided Detachment 101's R&A section with almost 60 pounds of captured Japanese and Burmese documents.

The teams also uncovered for the first time in NCAC the existence of the Burmese Anti-Fascist League (AFL), a widespread underground organization opposed to the Japanese occupation that was based in Rangoon. The CITs also discovered that SEAC had been working with the AFL for over a year. CIT #3 exploited the liberation of Bhamo just two days after it fell by searching the city for intelligence (the delay was because enemy mines had to be cleared) and procured six Japanese knapsacks full of enemy documents that it sent to NCAC G-2.[50] Additional CIT duties included reporting on the local situation, as well as collecting weapons from the indigenous population.

A New Organization . . . of Sorts

Supplying intelligence remained a core function of Detachment 101, and by September, thirty-five separate organizations relied upon its reports.[51] In November, Major Chester R. Chartrand, who had been the liaison to NCAC during the Myitkyina campaign, in effect reconstituted the SI section when he returned to Nazira. Much like he had done before R&A had taken over the role of handling actionable intelligence, Chartrand prepared weekly intelligence reports, handled requests for information, forwarded items of interest to the field groups, and briefed NCAC daily. This was done with the help of a large photomontage of the operating area, upon which Chartrand placed intelligence received from the field groups. The NCAC G-3 used this to task the USAAF with their daily targets.[52] Chartrand reported in December that 85 percent of the items in the U.S. Army weekly G-2 summaries originated from Detachment 101 intelligence, as did most of the Tenth USAAF's bombing targets.[53]

Although assisting with the fall of Myitkyina had been the Detachment's focus in 1944, it could not rest after the victory. Not only did the unit have to work in a rapidly changing operating environment, but it also had to rebuild its sections to support the ongoing north Burma offensive. At the same time, the unit's headquarters sections had to become mobile to support the operating elements. Detachment 101's work in the Myitkyina Campaign gave the unit visibility both in Burma and from OSS Washington, translating into more resources. The unit's inherent flexibility allowed it to easily move its base of operations, build on its previous organization, incorporate new assets, and still be able to recruit a larger pool of indigenous troops to support a higher operational tempo.

10

The Last OSS Branches Arrive: January–March 1945

My 101 experience taught me how well troops could do with so little, other than ammunition and weapons, when they needed to. The OSS gave me a general contempt of logisticians—of which I am one. I learned that it takes combat power to stop combat power.

Major General James S. Welch

Although the North Burma Campaign was nearly at an end, Detachment 101 continued to change its force structure, reinforce its sections, and strive to become more efficient. Those sections with an immediate operational utility, such as the Air Drop section and the Red Ass Squadron, continued to be absolutely indispensable to the Detachment's operations. Others, such as the X-2 and R&D sections, could not offer direct enough support to the Detachment's increasing operational focus. Conversely, the MO section finally proved to be effective, an indication that even at this late stage, even if had gotten off to a poor start, a properly led and supported element could make an impact. In this period the OSS Operational Group (OG) Branch as an entity first made its appearance at Detachment 101. However, it could not offer a unique enough role to merit its inclusion as a separate section within the Detachment.

Operations in north Burma were not Detachment 101's only focus. In February it took responsibility for OSS operations along Burma's Arakan coast by renaming Detachment 404's Operation BITTERSWEET as the Detachment 101 Arakan Field Unit (AFU). Like the effort in the Shan States, the Detachment 101 AFU involved a combined operations campaign with organic land, air, and, uniquely, naval elements. Such had Detachment 101's importance become that it had two high-level visits when both Donovan and General Sultan visited in January. For the personnel of the Detachment, this period represented a rapidly changing strategic picture. Despite Allied successes, the OSS still had much to accomplish in Burma, and Detachment 101 had to evolve to increase its effectiveness.[1]

Existing Force Structure

As had happened with the fall of Myitkyina, the rapid pace of the Allied advance once again left Detachment 101's forward headquarters far to the rear, forcing it once again to move. Between 31 January and 1 February, the entire Myitkyina headquarters—including Peers—moved to Bhamo.[2] Called Detachment 101 BA, it had the benefit of having a cow pasture nearby that was used as an improvised airfield. As Peers said, this put "all our activities within a forty minute flight to our two Field Area Headquarters."[3] The unit even closed the jungle school at Taro in February as impractical and moved it back to Nazira.

The Operations section had to account for an increasing number of indigenous recruits, and by January, raised two additional battalions in Area #1 for a total approximate strength of 5,500 indigenous soldiers. But in the same month some 350 Kachins received discharges in Area #2 and went home.[4] The increasing number of discharges meant that the Detachment officers had to have money reserves on hand to maintain morale. Prompt payment helped ensure that serving troops remained, or if they did not, that the guerrillas received honorariums for good service. The Special Funds section provided the Dinjan Air Drop section with a large ready reserve of both paper money and coin silver. Costs for operations alone in January amounted to some 470,000 rupees, while in March, the disbursement funds owed to the guerrillas disbanding in Area #1 contributed to a monthly operating cost of 764,074 rupees.[5] Paying off these troops was the largest single expense handled by the Special Funds section during its existence.[6]

The high operational tempo also caused the Red Ass Squadron to remove from service a number of liaison aircraft for maintenance. Those requiring a major overhaul or repairs went to the Fifty-second Air Service Command at the Jorhat Air Depot. Parts came through the Air Forces, or if the aircraft was a type not in regular use, through the OSS.[7] In January, Detachment 101 only had four L-1s and one L-5. The stress placed on the L-1s was particularly severe, and Squadron commander, First Lieutenant Francis J. Reardon, described some of the planes as having "a total of 7000 hours are [*sic*] on record as far as we can ascertain. That is far above what is termed war weary aircraft. . . . If no aircraft are forthcoming then it is only a matter of time before our planes become useless."[8] The section hoped to secure twelve more replacement light aircraft and more mechanics. Despite the problems, in January, the Red Ass Squadron managed 421 hours of combat flying, in which it transported 30,450 pounds of supplies and 476 passengers to the forward groups, and brought back 146 wounded, 70 of whom were from the 475th Infantry Regiment. One of the pilots, Vince Trifletti, recalled that dangerous mission. As he flew over a 6,000-foot ridge, there were "many fires burning . . . the place was devastated. Every village, every basha was in flames or was a smoldering pile of ash."[9] For its actions, MARS Task Force commander Brigadier General John P. Willey commended the Red Ass Squadron.[10]

In February, the squadron's situation improved. It moved to the new airfield at Bhamo and received new aircraft. The section had seven aircraft at Bhamo, two at Nazira, two L-1's undergoing maintenance, one airplane due to arrive from India, and an unserviceable Spitfire. The section received enough replacement pilots that it ceased relying upon the USAAF liaison squadrons. By the end of February, the squadron flew nearly 413 combat hours, carried 508 passengers, evacuated 43 casualties and 3 prisoners, and flew 31,275 pounds of cargo.[11]

March was a particularly busy month for the Red Ass Squadron as it assisted in the drive to take Lashio. The planes flew in ammunition and equipment, carried out captured documents and wounded personnel, and flew Detachment 101 group commanders to their various battalion headquarters. This ability was fortunate because in one case, it allowed Joost to warn two battalions that were out of radio communication to move because a Chinese unit would soon shell the area with 155mm guns. In the course of conducting these operations, the section reached another all-time high by flying 519 combat hours, carrying 573 passengers, evacuating 38 wounded, and carrying 40,845 pounds of cargo. Joost, commanding officer of Area #1, said that the light aircraft were indispensable to his actions.[12] The Air Drop section likewise operated at full capacity. The total tonnage dropped into the field in January again exceeded a million pounds, with 1,009,674 pounds dropped out of 200 C-47s, 3 B-25s, and a solitary B-24. At the same time, the planes transported 334 personnel and parachuted 47 into the field, including nineteen night drops to infiltrate teams or agents.

The air drop personnel assumed operational control of the assigned aircrews from the time the airplane took off until it had landed. Prior to taking off, the crews—all selected from volunteers based on their experience and skill—were given a security brief and told never to reveal the location, cargos, or personnel dropped. These flights originated from Myitkyina and accounted for a quarter of the total tonnage dropped to Detachment 101 groups that month.[13] During these missions, Detachment 101 assumed the responsibility of navigating the aircraft to the selected location and supplied kickers. This was because the USAAF pilots often could not find the drop zone without assistance. It was discovered after much trial and error why. First Lieutenant Dennis V. Cavanaugh said, "The custom was to go up and give the captain of the ship the coordinates, then go back and sit down. An hour later we'd be lost." The problem, it was discovered, was in the maps that the Army Air Forces used versus the ones used by Detachment 101. "The Air Force maps had 500 foot contour lines, while our one-inch infantry maps had 50-foot contours. And the way our people on the ground hid in nooks and crannies . . . it's no wonder the Air Force couldn't find them. The real problem though, was that most of the pilots really didn't know how to read an infantry map."[14]

The Air Drop section made sure that all its personnel knew how to read the infantry maps. Then, they had a policy of approaching the pilot and explaining that they would in essence provide the navigation. The air drop men told the pilot to fly in a certain direction for so many miles, after which they would guide the plane into the drop zone.

February provided no let up, with 168 personnel transported, 21 parachuted, and 1,482,989 pounds of supplies dropped to the field groups from 261 C-47s, one B-25, 5 B-24s, and 2 C-45s.[15] Even then it was not enough, and the field groups complained about the lack of supplies.[16] As a result, Detachment 101 had to again improve upon its logistics facilities. In January, the group moved from the three warehouses that it had at Dinjan to six of better construction located together and more isolated. One was used for packing chutes and containers, two for arms and ammunition, and the rest for other supplies. The large quantities of ammunition were needed because of the logistician's nightmare of weapons carried by the field groups. This included British .303 caliber Enfield rifles and Bren light machine guns; .45 caliber Thompson submachine guns; .30-06 caliber M1 Garands, M1941 Johnson rifles, Browning automatic rifles, and M1919 machine guns; .30 caliber M1 carbines; and 9mm Sten and Marlin UD-42 submachine guns.[17] To help move the supplies they now had ten 2½-ton trucks, with five personnel at Dinjan and two at Nazira.[18] At Dinjan, the Air Drop section was assisted by nearly seventy Indian laborers.[19] By March, the number of warehouses available at Dinjan increased to sixteen, leaving Detachment 101 with a reserve of

2,225,925 pounds of rations and 1,000,000 pounds of ordnance and quartermaster supplies. This was about a two-month reserve, as in March, the total amount dropped into the field was 1,476,942 pounds, and fifty-six personnel parachuted. The Detachment had ten dedicated C-47s at this time, with other specialized aircraft on call when needed. The drops in March required 249 C-47 sorties, 7 B-24s, and 9 B-25s. Most drops originated from Dinjan.[20]

First Lieutenant Oliver A. Ryder, an air drop officer who worked with the Second Combat Cargo Squadron, said, "I had flown a lot more than the aircrews . . . simply because there was only one of me." Ryder flew so much that the squadron's flight surgeon grounded him because he was tired and worn out after having more than 600 hours of flight time. While hospitalized, Ryder had a Distinguished Flying Cross with Oak Leaf Cluster pinned on his pajamas.[21]

Ryder remembered, "We would take off before dawn. I will never forget that. I would stand between the pilot and copilot to see the beautiful dawn. It was a gorgeous and beautiful sight. They reminded me of sunrises over Nags Head, North Carolina."[22] Ryder described his role in the air.

> I knew the targets, having been there more than they had. I was an aerial observer in a sense. To get to the drop zone you had to recognize certain landmarks, like rivers, landforms, and villages. You simply learned your way to the DZ. [Once] we got over the target . . . it was pretty much up to me. The pilots would fly circles over the area and make runs . . . one, two, three, four. You kind of half-ass knew when to get it out the door. We knew when we were in the target area, and you just give the green light kick signal and out it would go. It was reasonably accurate.[23]

The regularity of the runs enabled him to recognize certain men on the ground. First Lieutenant Daniel Mudrinich "was always standing out on the drop zone. I got to know him as a little black-haired kid. I would stand in the door and have the pilot make another run and wave goodbye and he would wave back. I got to know him through those drops." It was only later at a postwar reunion that the two would meet one another.[24] But even at this late stage, the Air Drop section still had to parachute personnel into enemy-occupied Burma.

First Lieutenant Dennis V. Cavanaugh remembered that jumping was no problem for those with airborne training. However, not everyone had gotten the chance to attend that course. Those "unfortunates" received the night before what the Air Drop section called the "Fort Benning Short Course," which consisted of "tuck in your chin, cross your arms on your chest, bend your knees, and keep your feet together." On jump day this short course did little to ease the tension. In that case, "as the man stood in the door of the plane over the drop zone grasping with white fingers the cold aluminum sides of the opening, the jump master would gently peel his thumbs from the inside of the doorframe and place them next to his fingers on the outside in the breeze." Then, in case the jumper did not go when directed, a "kicker unobtrusively slid in place behind the jumper and curled his legs up, his feet inches from the seat of the jumper's pants, ready in case he hesitated at the bell."[25] For their part, one of the kickers recalled, "I had some slight misgivings about what would happen if the jumper panicked and grabbed me and took me with him. I have to tell you that to this day, I am grateful that, when the signal to jump was given, not one man hesitated for a moment."[26] Another wryly added that "the view of the jungle between your feet was inspiring."[27]

Like many other elements, in January the Communications section prepared to move from Myitkyina to Bhamo, where it had already constructed a series of four 63-foot steel towers arranged in a square. All that was necessary for their use was to drive a transmitter truck underneath them, hook it up, and send messages. Meanwhile, the communications subsection at Nazira handled an average of 4,640 letter-code groups per day. Field sections were equally busy, with Area #1 handling a daily average of 4,390 groups and Area #2, 3,605 groups. The cryptographic subsection was particularly hard hit. Myitkyina handled 3,699 messages composed of 231,687 groups; Nazira had 1,329 messages with 62,675 groups; Area #1 headquarters handled 1,398 messages and 89,579 groups; and Area #2 headquarters dealt with 1,123 messages and 58,467 groups.

Despite the increased operational responsibilities, however, supply to the Communications section greatly improved and became, as the section chief reported, "the best it has ever been." Quantities of the improved OSS-supplied SSR-1H receiver arrived, making it possible for Nazira to stop the production of field radios, thereby removing their "main headache." The wide distribution of one-time pads, a secure cryptographic device because the key remained at base while the code was used once and thrown away, saved time.[28] A trained cryptographer using a one-time pad could encode or decode a short message faster than using an electric code machine, and almost as fast as a code machine on a longer message.[29] The level of traffic from the field only increased in February. Area #1 sent 2,053 messages composed of 114,567 groups, while Area #2 sent 1,344 composed of 66,286 groups.[30] The pace increased again on 9 March, when Bhamo took over the communications duties of Area #1 when that organization disbanded six of its seven battalions.

On 4 January, the pigeon section established a loft in Bhamo. When a radio was down, the pigeons could deliver a message in a half hour while a human messenger would take up to four days.[31] Pigeons were dropped with several agents and supplied to the pilots of the Red Ass Squadron should their planes go down. On 10 January, the section scored a success when several pigeons returned from an agent who could not find his dropped radio or food and was starving, but reported that his area was free of Japanese. This opened the way to send the eighteen-man JACKO combat team on 19 January.[32]

More indigenous personnel meant that the medical section had to expand in order to meet their needs. The first step was to arrange with the 200-bed Forty-fourth Field Hospital at Myitkyina, responsible for the care of Chinese and indigenous troops, to set aside a separate ward to care for less critically sick or wounded Detachment 101 personnel. This represented a vast improvement by reducing the number of casualties coming back to Nazira, and permitted treating those who would not normally receive medical care because of the minor nature of their condition and the distance necessary to transport them. The 821st Air Evacuation Squadron assisted the Red Ass Squadron in transferring indigenous troops to the hospital.[33] With the inclusion of Arakan operations into the scope of Detachment 101, the medical section also arranged for their use the 142nd General Hospital in Calcutta, India.[34]

The hospital at Nazira nonetheless remained busy. January saw sixty-five admissions and twelve surgical procedures, with the laboratory, X-ray facility, dispensary, and dental clinic being correspondingly active. Field medical personnel handled at least 346 surgical cases and cared for at least 6,500 instances of illness. The majority of the cases treated, whether among guerrillas or the local population, were for malaria. But, since medical personnel were scarce, the Detachment only had the bare minimum to ensure that all groups were covered. This meant that medical personnel assigned to Area #2 had to care for an average of 150 men, while those in Area #1 cared for 750. This does not count treating the local population.

Such heavy workloads and a lack of replacements meant that medical personnel became greatly fatigued and increasingly recognized as requiring rest.[35] The medical personnel from former Area #1 who had stayed in the field were having a "strenuous time keeping up with the marked increase in work" during March.[36] Due to an increased combat role for the guerrilla battalions, they dealt with seventeen severe battle wounds, one of which was fatal. Only six out of the fourteen field groups reported their medical load. However, this still amounted to performing 281 surgeries and treating 1,192 instances of disease. Back at Nazira, the medical section was disturbed to find that many of the disease cases were due to soldiers not using mosquito nets or to poor sanitation, particularly in the preparation of food.[37]

On the intelligence side, the R&A section received new personnel and increased its liaison contacts. Relatively few of their personnel, however, had been supplied by OSS Washington as true R&A personnel (in February, it was three out of eighteen). Rather, Detachment 101 assigned soldiers to the section in an ad hoc fashion, but it did not greatly affect the group's performance. By January, the R&A section was in communication with twenty separate organizations, among them several in NCAC, the USAAF, CIC, OWI, and American, Chinese, British, and Indian combat units. These liaison contacts increased the number of required oral briefings to a point that the section chief reported that it was "impossible to keep a record for the month." In January alone, the section wrote thirteen intelligence reports, many of which concerned the location and status of roads and trails in enemy-controlled areas, and filled numerous requests for map and aerial reconnaissance photographs.[38]

In February, an arrangement with the SI section clarified R&A's duties. Thereafter, R&A was responsible for processing "incoming intelligence and [producing] intelligence through interrogation, translation of documents, photo interpretation, and research."[39] The R&A section compiled the field reports, many of which focused on intelligence of immediate tactical use, into finished products that the SI section distributed. Even R&A's longer-range studies at this point concerned NCAC requirements, such as the inadequacies of the Japanese logistic system.[40] The R&A section also obtained the services of one of the air drop kickers to take aerial photography when requested, which was then turned over to Lieutenant Alger Ellis, the newly arrived photo-interpreter.[41] A further utility for the R&A section was operational support, by defining no-bomb areas to the USAAF. Once it received notification that a Detachment 101 unit was in a certain location, the R&A section plotted the information and sent it to the A-2 officer. The section also established a display room to exhibit captured enemy material.[42]

The small SI section anticipated becoming a larger entity in Detachment 101's force structure. Peers recognized that the section was woefully short of personnel and wrote to Donovan in January that although Detachment 101 furnished about 90 percent of the intelligence used by the USAAF and 85 percent of that used by NCAC, it had "only one SI man from Washington during the entire period."[43] The lack of personnel did not go unnoticed in the field. The Arakan section chief complained that "not one item was transmitted to this Hqs between 21 February and 10 March except in the form of weekly summaries which arrive by pouch so late that most of the information has lost its value."[44] By March, minor personnel additions helped SI by sorting through the more than 500 intelligence reports disseminated to various end-users, as well as assisting in the preparation of a short history of Detachment 101.[45] This final project became the focus of the section after March, when it mainly functioned to summarize operational results or to interview personnel returning from the field. Section head Chester Chartrand received assistance in this endeavor from the newly created reports section, comprised of the sole reports officer, Private First Class John I. Howell. Howell compiled lists of accomplishments merely for OSS Washington's benefit. Even in the limited time that he was at Detachment 101, Howell grew frustrated with OSS Washington's lack of direction, writing in his final report in July, "Since I have been here, I have received no word from Washington as to whether the reports were fulfilling requirements or any criticisms that might help to improve them."[46]

Intelligence dissemination improved in February when a direct teletype line was laid to the Tenth USAAF A-2. This enabled Detachment 101 to pass "'hot' information to them within minutes" upon receipt and increased the actionability of the intelligence.[47] Detachment 101 sent additional officers to the First Tank Provisional Group, and established liaison in March with the British Fourteenth Army, the Nineteenth Indian Division, and the Sixty-second Brigade.[48]

It was at this time that X-2 finally paid operational dividends when in January it selected five AFL agents to insert into south-central Burma. X-2 continued creating black lists and in January had a 3,000-name list covering all of north and central Burma. The X-2 section also moved to Bhamo, and although it had an office in the Detachment 101 headquarters, the secrecy of the work necessitated that the main element be located separately. That portion was located in a *basha* some "three to four miles away."[49] This separation underscores the inability of the section to integrate itself into the Detachment's operations.[50]

The section continued to have considerable difficulty with the CIC. Though relations were amicable on the outside, a power struggle existed between the two entities in large part because the two top officers in each did not get along. Peers's influence had an effect, and an X-2 observer related that it was "most gratifying to observe that Colonel Stilwell [NCAC G-2] appears to be backing Colonel Peers and Major Helfrich in placing the responsibility for running the CIT teams [with] X-2."[51] On 17 February X-2 scored a victory when it established firm control over the loosely organized CITs. This was necessary because the CIC was operating under the understanding that the CITs were under their control. As such, on 10 February, CIC personnel removed all intelligence files from the CIT headquarters. The CIC stance was that while "Detachment 101 had admittedly furnished four officers, eleven interpreters, sixty native police with rifles, uniforms, equipment and munitions, critical clothing; equipment and supply needs for the teams; radio communications in all isolated areas; plane transport on any essential occasion," it was still their function and "CIC could and would be glad to carry on alone." However, thereafter the CIC personnel assigned to the CITs reported through and took direction from X-2, which in turn reported directly to Colonel Stilwell. With renewed vigor, the section established a CIT with the British Fourteenth Army as it moved to liberate Mandalay.[52] The CITs even helped to recruit guerrilla soldiers, as in the case of CIT #1, which sent forty-three Shan-Palaung troops to report to the nearest Detachment 101 formation.[53]

Yet, not all—including those in the section—felt that the X-2 mission was entirely worthwhile. One member wrote, "To put it bluntly, I do not feel that I have contributed anything of any value since I arrived at 101." His concern was mainly over the limited nature of X-2 work. The CITs were entirely subservient to the Operations section, and all recruitment oriented toward that purpose. "The 101 show is a unified one and everything is controlled by Operations . . . in actuality all X-2 can do is advise . . . the agents we have recruited . . . primarily to gather combat intelligence or to further guerrila [*sic*] fighting . . . and no one can complain of this since that is the basis for 101's existence." Part of the reason for the lack of ability to accomplish more intelligence gathering was the tentative nature that the OSS had in regard to the AFL. The British were extremely wary of the possibility of having the United States aid any political groups in Burma. As a result, X-2 limited their interactions with the AFL to those of a purely military nature against the Japanese occupation.[54]

Although not as tied into operations as other sections, the R&D section furthered their work on camouflaging items. The first item for January was called War Paint, a kit for soldiers to camouflage their faces so that they could better blend in with the foliage or to darken skin so that one could pass as a local inhabitant. These kits were also being considered as an escape and evasion tool for downed Allied airmen.[55] Still, Peers found the section difficult to evaluate. He wrote Donovan, "Sometimes it appears questionable whether or not the expenditure of personnel and equipment is truly justified. . . . [They] are all industrious and hard workers . . . the only point in question is whether or not there is actually a field of employment for them here."[56]

Much like the X-2 and R&D section, the MO section was trying to contribute to Detachment's 101 operations. Unlike them, however, it had an edge in the well-prepared GOLD DUST team that had arrived in November 1944. In January, the MO section reorganized and the GOLD DUST chief was thereafter responsible for field operations and intelligence collection. Accordingly, he based himself forward. The section deputy, emplaced at Nazira, was in charge of administration, editing, and the production of propaganda products. The section also created a five-person panel to evaluate its propaganda products, with representatives from MO, Operations, SI, R&A, and Detachment 101 headquarters. Additionally, daily meetings of MO personnel contributed to the section working more effectively. With these efforts, the GOLD DUST team rapidly integrated itself into Detachment 101, a welcome development because throughout most of 1944 the section had been unorganized and contributed little to Detachment 101's mission.[57] By February, the MO Branch at OSS Washington ensured that Detachment 101's MO section received enough equipment, personnel, and supplies to be self-sufficient.

On 17 February, MO showed its first true evidence of operational utility. In cooperation with the SI section, the MO section arranged for an agent wearing a Burma Defense Army uniform from the FULLY mission, to turn a briefcase over to the Japanese military police headquarters at Maymyo.[58] The agent claimed that he had found it beside a wrecked vehicle on the Mandalay-Maymyo road. In reality, the briefcase contained orders forged by MO that reversed the Japanese no-surrender policy by declaring that soldiers could surrender if they were cut off, without ammunition, or incapacitated. Agents slipped another copy of these false orders into the headquarters of a Japanese infantry regiment. The MO section followed this with a rumor campaign and an airdrop of leaflets near the Allied lines that purposefully fell on Japanese positions, outlining to Allied troops that they were to treat Japanese prisoners well. OWI followed up with another white leaflet drop showing the surrender order and assuring Japanese troops that they would receive good treatment if they gave up. The British Fourteenth Army was also given copies and thereafter saw a noticeable rise in surrenders after the program's initiation. The surrender order program was not MO's only work in February, as it sent out 24,000 items to the field. There, however, MO's utility was not universally recognized. One field operator struggled with this as he wrote back to Nazira, "I think it will get better as . . . MO prestige increases. It has been a struggle even to convince the officers here that MO can do some good."[59]

Even so, the MO section became increasingly effective in part because it was working hard to establish liaison with as many units—OSS or otherwise—as it could, and put its printing equipment at the disposal of other elements. Within Detachment 101 itself, MO had good relations with SI, R&A, and R&D. This last section helped to produce items, such as forged stamps, to assist MO's work. The MO section also produced a small weekly newsletter called *The Jungle News* that went out to all the field groups, itself an effective way to get the MO message across. Outside of the OSS, MO secured the assistance of the Tenth USAAF, that made available a night fighter for an MO operation.[60]

The MO section became even more useful when, in addition to Nisei and indigenous translators, it gained the assistance of six Japanese prisoners of war (POWs).[61] The MO chief reported that the POWs were "either writing the original Japanese material produced by the unit, or are criticizing Japanese work produced in the shop."[62] This help may have increased the effectiveness of the FRONT LINE SOLDIER campaign, a series of anti-officer leaflets supposedly produced by Japanese noncommissioned officers. The presence of the leaflets found on the bodies of Japanese soldiers near Lashio indicated low morale, as to be caught with them might have been a capital offense.[63] However, the MO section also got reports from captured Japanese soldiers that they viewed the leaflets as propaganda and "laughed at it."[64] Still, MO's situation so improved that when the head of MO Washington visited Detachment 101 in March, he described it as having had considerable problems getting started but added that it had "achieved considerable success in the field. This mission is considered the purest black operation that has been observed in any theater."[65]

New Branches Arrive

Although individual members had previously arrived at the unit, OSS Washington tried to establish an OSS Operational Group at Detachment 101. The OG Branch had been very active in the European theater, but was just starting to get established in the Far East. The multifaceted mission of the OGs was to organize, train, and equip local resistance organizations, and to conduct hit-and-run missions against enemy-controlled roads, railways, and strong points, or to prevent their destruction by retreating enemy forces. Donovan believed that soldiers with the language and cultural background of operational areas could be found among the many ethnic groups in the United States. These soldiers would be inserted as a team into enemy-occupied territory and foster guerrilla groups. Unlike some SO teams in other theaters, the OGs always operated in military uniform. They were trained in infantry tactics, guerrilla warfare, foreign weapons, and demolition, were generally airborne qualified, and had attached medical and communications personnel. A typical OG section had four officers and thirty enlisted men. Individual teams were often half that size.[66]

Their entrée into Detachment 101 would not be as easy as it was for operations in Europe even though they had been sent to Burma for the same purpose: to be a hard-hitting group behind enemy lines. In contrast to the European groups, the Asia OGs lacked language skills and parachute training. In Detachment 101, the OGs were officially known as Unit D, Fourth Contingent, and initially consisted of nineteen officers and seventy-two enlisted men. From there, the Detachment 101 OG formed two combat teams, each broken into two squads. Immediately, the section ran into difficulties. The greatest was that the medical section deemed nearly 10 percent of the OGs as physically unsuitable for field operations. These men either filled in with other sections or were sent back to the United States.[67]

On 18 January 1945, Detachment 101 headquarters announced that the OGs would not serve as a separate unit on the grounds that such a large group behind enemy lines might lead to excessive American casualties. Moreover, the OG personnel needed jungle warfare training, and most were not parachute-qualified. Detachment 101 parceled out the OGs to groups already in the field, until conditions permitted the formation of an actual OG. Meanwhile, the Communications section received the nine OG radio operators and three radio technicians.[68] Other OGs filled in with other sections—sometimes with unharmonious results. The personnel officer who had received some OGs for administrative personnel described them as "bloated with promises and dreams of glory in the field."[69] However, the OG personnel assigned to Detachment 101 gave exemplary service and suffered several personnel killed in action.

Another new element in Detachment 101's arsenal was the Office of the Coordinator of Native Affairs (OCNA). The large number of Kachin troops mustering out of the organization made the addition necessary. Lieutenant

Julian Niemczyk, the officer assigned, made sure that discharged soldiers were paid in full, properly decorated, and given an appropriate mustering-out festival.[70] He recalled:

> I was naturally curious about the job with Detachment 101 that Colonel Ray Peers had for me. He briefed me in the need for a unit that would develop and maintain individual records and handle personnel administration for all the native troops recruited by Detachment 101 . . . It took some time before I thought of the name Office of the Coordinator of Native Affairs (OCNA). To my surprise, Ray Peers bought it . . . the name also seemed to be acceptable to the local British civil and military elements with whom we dealt.[71]

The growing operational level required that the Operations section rethink how it was organized. Previously, it had been in charge of formulating plans, but it realized that this arrangement was not the most effective because separate elements barraged headquarters with various plans in the hopes that one would be approved. The solution was to create a plans section, to which groups submitted potential plans for consideration. This unit was assisted by a weekly briefing from NCAC that detailed future areas of operation and requests for information. The plans section then developed procedures for how to meet NCAC's needs, while the R&A section searched their files to see if they might already have information that would be of use.[72]

Other higher-level changes affected Detachment 101's force structure. In February, the OSS detached Detachment 101's Calcutta base and renamed it Detachment 505, easing Nazira's efforts, as it no longer had to account for incoming and outgoing personnel. The second administrative change was the creation of the Detachment 101 AFU in February. Previously, the AFU was under OSS Detachment 404 and operated in conjunction with the Indian Fifteenth Corps under the direction of SEAC. Because of the confusion with having two OSS elements operating in Burma, Detachment 101 received command of all operations north of Rangoon. As a result, OSS Washington detached the AFU from Detachment 404 and gave control to Detachment 101. By February, the Schools and Training section of Detachment 101 was sending newly graduated agents to the Arakan for operations.[73]

At the end of March all elements that would make up Detachment 101's force structure were in place. But with this, OSS Washington's continued lack of attention was apparent. The OSS focused on the war in Europe so much so that operations in Burma—or even the Far East—were an afterthought. Only Detachment 101's operational successes in 1944 brought attention from Washington. By this time, however, the new arrivals to Detachment 101, such as the OGs, could not bring with them a mission unique enough to warrant the effort of trying to accommodate their particular specialty as a distinct entity. Other late-arriving sections, such as R&D and X-2, also fell far behind. This was because by the time they arrived, or organized themselves in such a way to be able to contribute, Detachment 101's mission was so focused on guerrilla warfare and intelligence gathering that sections were of little utility unless they could directly impact those core functions. A surprise element, however, was the MO section. After a long period of inexcusable ineffectiveness due to lack of attention on the part of MO Washington, the Detachment 101 MO section finally made big payoffs. The intense training and preparation of the GOLD DUST team prior to their arrival was the reason why it was able to contribute to Detachment 101's core missions. Even at this last stage in the Burma Campaign, a section focused on achieving effective liaison and coordination, which did not have internal squabbles and which wanted to assist combat operations, could have a measurable impact on Detachment 101's ability to wage war on the Japanese.

11

The Shan States: August 1944–March 1945

Don't give the Kachin a pair of boots and a heavy machine-gun and expect him to sit down and hold a position. That's not his way of fighting.

Simon "Monocle" Read

Summing it all up, God must have his arms around the Chingpaws [Kachin], plus the fact that the Japs are such damn poor shots. Their luck was fantastic. It was almost impossible to impress upon them any idea of security, and yet it is surprising the small number of casualties they received.

John L. Swift

Strategically, the war in North Burma continued to be a hard-fought campaign that remained on a relative shoestring. In part because of its mission, the condition of worn-down Allied units after Myitkyina, and the monsoon, Detachment 101 was the only Allied formation in contact with Japanese forces south of Myitkyina from August until 15 October.[1] Yet, despite the long-delayed but successful completion of the Myitkyina Campaign, the unit could not pause to rest and refit like the Allied conventional units. In the field Detachment 101 still had to act on its previous, but unwritten, understanding with General Stilwell to increase its number of guerrillas to 10,000. More recruits meant that instead of companies, as had been the case in the Myitkyina Campaign, the area commands organized their guerrillas into battalions. Combined, all this meant that the unit had to work even harder than before to make sure that it stayed deep behind enemy lines. Only in this fashion could Detachment 101 retain the utility that it had demonstrated during the Myitkyina Campaign. The goal remained to clear the trace of the Ledo

Road; however, at this time the strategic picture of the North Burma campaign was far different than it had been prior to Myitkyina.

Japanese forces reeled south in confusion from the combined beatings they had taken in North Burma and from the failed Imphal offensive. No longer capable in holding all of Burma, Japanese actions in North and Central Burma tried to buy time to prop up defenses in southern Burma.

Recognizing that the war had finally turned to their favor, the Allies exploited their advantage. In the west, advancing against the shattered units of the Imphal/Kohima retreat, the British Fourteenth Army reached the Chindwin River by the end of August. In North Burma, NCAC briefly paused, but built up its force. The fighting around Myitkyina and disease had destroyed both Merrill's Marauders and the Chindits. Those Marauders still capable of fighting went to help form a new and much larger long-range penetration unit, known as the 5332nd Brigade (Provisional), but called the MARS Task Force. The MARS Task Force consisted of the 475th Infantry Regiment, the 124th Cavalry Regiment, and the 612th and 613th Field Artillery Battalions, along with smaller support elements. Although the MARS Task Force required more training, it was NCAC's only U.S. Army ground combat force. NCAC also had five Chinese divisions and the British Thirty-sixth Division, which had been detailed to North Burma to help reinforce British prestige among the area's inhabitants.[2]

Since the Thirty-sixth Division was fresh, the British began the renewed offensive first by taking over the Chindit positions. From there, on 15 October, the Thirty-sixth Division pressed south along the rail corridor to Pinwe against increasingly heavier opposition. To the east of the Thirty-sixth Division, the combined American and Chinese forces moved south along the route of the Ledo Road, meeting considerably less resistance. Although the Japanese briefly tried to hold, they could not stem the Allied tide. By mid-December, Bhamo, the objective of the combined Chinese/U.S. force, was in Allied hands. In this action, the Chinese forces showed a remarkable improvement over their efforts at Myitkyina just six months prior.

With the fall of Bhamo, NCAC's goal was to open the route of the Ledo Road, renamed the Stilwell Road at the insistence of Chiang Kai-shek, all the way to China. At the start of 1945, approximately 19,500 Japanese troops remained in the 50 miles of territory that separated NCAC forces from Allied forces in China.[3] In light of the reduced threat in North Burma, in December 1944 the new China Theater commander, General Wedemeyer, recalled two of NCAC's Chinese divisions back to China. Nevertheless, NCAC cleared the land route to China, and the first Allied convoys arrived in Kunming in early February.

Now, all that NCAC had left to accomplish was to make sure that the Stilwell Road was secure. Remaining Japanese forces were close to the road and enough of a threat that they had to be eliminated or pushed south. In addition, the threat that intact Japanese formations posed to the rear of the British Fourteenth Army necessitated that NCAC clear the enemy from the area. NCAC commander General Sultan set his sights on taking Lashio, on the old Burma Road, to cut the lines of supply to any Japanese forces north of that crossroads. Sultan used the MARS Task Force and two Chinese divisions to secure the area. Although the Japanese bitterly resisted, they no longer had the strength to hold.

Chinese forces secured Lashio on 6–7 March while the MARS Task Force harassed Japanese forces retreating from the Chinese advance. After taking Lashio, the Chinese force drove a further thirty miles south to Hsipaw. Meanwhile, on the western portion of NCAC's area of responsibility, the British Thirty-sixth and Chinese Fiftieth Divisions linked up with the British Fourteenth Army close to Hsipaw east of Mandalay. With no remaining gap between NCAC or the Fourteenth Army, the Thirty-sixth Division transferred back to General Slim's command on 1 April.

Slim's forces to the west also made considerable gains in Central Burma. In a blitzkrieg-like move in early March a British armored column penetrated deep within Japanese lines to take Meiktila. This was the first use of an air-ground-armor combination by the British in Burma. The gamble surprised the Japanese, who only had 4,000 defenders to meet a division of regular infantry, an armor brigade, and an additional airlifted brigade. The Fourteenth Army seizure of Meiktila cut off the escape route for Japanese forces in Central Burma, and their savage but uncoordinated counterattacks could not break the Allied hold on the town. The battle for Meiktila was over by the end of March, and with it, the Japanese lost Central Burma.

Further north, other Fourteenth Army forces invested the key city of Mandalay, which the Japanese unwisely tried to hold. By the time they ordered a retreat, the Japanese forces were in confusion. With both these critical areas under Allied control, the Japanese could no longer mount an effective defense of lower Burma. This left the way open to Rangoon. There, the Japanese faced another threat. The XV Indian Corps pressed into the coastal Arakan region. Compared to the fighting that had occurred there from 1942, the XV Indian Corps made rapid progress. In January, the major town of

Akyab fell, and by March, the British conducted an amphibious assault on Ramree Island to secure its use as a base.

Through these Allied drives, Detachment 101 continued to be a crucial element, especially to NCAC. In the field, Detachment 101 units expanded their operations to the south and east, providing intelligence collection, guides, and forces to protect the flanks of conventional Allied units from the Chinese border to the Chindwin River. Detachment 101's guerrilla actions and intelligence assisted the MARS Task Force, the Chinese Thirtieth and Thirty-eighth Divisions in East Burma, and the British Thirty-sixth and Chinese Fiftieth Divisions to the west. Intelligence from Detachment 101 groups also supported the Fourteenth Army's drive while additional agent groups penetrated the southern Shan States.

Although supplying intelligence was still a primary mission, Detachment 101's focus at this late stage increasingly concentrated on guerrilla operations. As a result, Detachment 101's guerrilla groups carried increasingly heavier armaments. They operated ahead of the Allied advance, and greatly disrupted Japanese efforts to counter the offensive. In the ensuing months, Detachment 101 had to constantly evolve its field structure in order to ensure that it met with the changing tactical situation, with the increasing number of guerrillas under arms, and with NCAC's demands.

The Push after Myitkyina

Detachment 101's field operations only increased after the fall of Myitkyina. The demands placed upon the Detachment's officers were so great that those in the field had to remain behind the lines, despite the strain or the amount of time they had been on operations.[4] It was at this time that the group was at its peak in terms of personnel in the field. The OSS had more than 10,000 guerrillas under arms organized into seven battalions, some 60 clandestine long-range agents, and another 400 that operated on a short-range basis. To support this effort, the OSS employed almost 1,000 American and British personnel. The pace was hectic, and, as Peers later said, "it was not all glamorous—much of it was little more than downright hard work."[5]

Detachment 101 field groups were already well south of Myitkyina when the city fell in early August. Their initial mission of supplying intelligence and ambushing Japanese stragglers as they slipped south did not change. Unfortunately, through September the groups also had to deal with the effects of the monsoon. Not only did the constant rain make life in the field miserable, but the monsoons also washed out roads and trails and made aerial resupply difficult. First Lieutenant Thomas Leonard detailed the problems that the lack of supply caused. Even with several hundred Japanese fleeing though his area, "It was impossible to keep road blocks out. The country around was drained of food. On 14th September, 80% of 'L' company deserted and some went home, others went over to Hpumpyen with 'C' company, who had food."[6] Still, despite the difficulties, in August Area #2 reported back to headquarters that they had killed 350 enemy soldiers that month.[7]

The Detachment 101 field groups used the relative lull as a recruiting opportunity. Although Detachment 101 retained the Area alignments, these subcommands reorganized their larger guerrilla elements into battalions. In general, Detachment 101's battalions had approximately 800 men with a headquarters element and four 160-man companies. Each of these companies was further broken down into three 50-man platoons.[8]

The end of the monsoon season in mid-October, combined with the subsequent Allied offensive, meant that Detachment 101's operations increased. At first, this was particularly so for its intelligence operations. The proximity of the Allied airfield at Myitkyina to occupied territory meant that Detachment 101's tactical intelligence was not just for building order of battle. It was also highly actionable, and Allied aircraft often bombed Detachment 101–supplied targets within two hours of the field groups sending out coded messages.[9]

In support of the intelligence mission, the Detachment also revisited older ideas. By using the concept of having an agent in place prior to inserting a team, which was developed after the failed missions of 1943 through early 1944, Detachment 101 infiltrated three teams east of Mandalay and south of Lashio.[10] Detachment 101 tasked these teams with collecting intelligence and serving as a focal point to recruit guerrilla groups as the lines moved closer.[11] Although the importance of intelligence teams lessened as the war progressed, Detachment 101 continued to insert them until almost the end of the North Burma Campaign. According to Peers, on one occasion, the OSS even used a helicopter, a few of which had arrived in Burma.[12] Peers considered the agents "the paramount advantage of Detachment 101. . . . Through this medium much was known of the Japanese strength and dispositions but they, on the other hand, knew little of the activities of Detachment 101."[13] The long-range intelligence supplied by the inserted agents supplemented the tactical agent nets run by the guerrilla units themselves.

In October, Detachment 101's field groups also stepped up their guerrilla campaign. Detachment 101 reported, "Harassing action against the Japs by our ground units coupled with effective air bombing of targets pinpointed by our agents made the entire area north of Myothit . . . untenable for the Japs." These actions helped the Thirty-sixth Division's efforts to seize the area.[14]

But operating as they did so far ahead of the Allied lines and in relatively open terrain meant that the Detachment 101 field groups occasionally had trouble with "friendly fire" from USAAF aircraft. At times, the fighter planes mistook the marching guerrilla columns for Japanese targets of opportunity. The way the OSS got around this problem was to meet with General Davidson of the Tenth Air Force and form sanctuary areas, in which USAAF aircraft could not attack unless specifically given targets by Detachment 101. Each fighter aircraft carried a map of these areas, which was updated as the guerrillas changed positions.[15]

By November, however, Operations section chief Major William E. Cummings reported that the pace of Allied progress was so great that "our units have had difficulty keeping in advance of it."[16] The rapidly retreating Japanese necessitated that the Detachment undertake a more active civil affairs mission in the newly liberated areas. As had been the case in the Myitkyina Campaign, the threat of Chinese guerrillas remained problematic. Thereafter, Detachment 101 established local government until the British Civil Affairs Service (CAS) reasserted control. In the liberated areas, Detachment 101 groups created a forum of ten local headmen to set price controls over goods and to ensure the recognition of newly minted silver rupees and paper money as legitimate currency. Detachment 101 reported that the effort was very successful because the "local people are fairly represented and have an active voice in the management of their own affairs." In addition, the Detachment arranged to parachute unobtainable salt into the area to appease the local population and to help ease the Kachins' apprehensions about whether their families were being taken care of back home.[17] And just a month later, one of the Detachment 101 medics reported that having a "doctor" and medicine "drew patients who walked 5 days just to get attention." The result "consequently spread good will for the organization throughout the state."[18]

In order to deal with the fluid operational situation, Detachment 101 began to train a new type of organization called a "small combat team." Foreshadowing the type of teams employed by special operations in the Vietnam War, these teams were "composed of highly trained Kachin or Burmese groups led by American officers and enlisted men. They will combine firepower and stealth in their operations . . . and try to hit specific targets and possibly establish bases for future large scale operations." Each of these small combat teams was ideally composed of one American and ten indigenous guerrillas.[19]

At this stage, the war was clearly going against the Japanese in North

Burma. November saw the first large-scale instances of Burmese nationals deserting from siding with the Japanese to join the Allied effort. On 2 November in Area #3, fifty recruits armed with Japanese rifles reported for duty. At the same time, several Burmese serving the Japanese Army deserted to join other Detachment 101 guerrilla groups.[20] At first Detachment 101 officers viewed the Burmans with suspicion, but the former enemy troops proved themselves to be excellent guerrilla soldiers. Conversely, at the same time, the first large-scale disbanding of Kachins occurred when Detachment 101 gave those from the north the option of receiving honorable discharges and going back home.[21]

As they moved south, the guerrillas faced increasingly difficult and violent situations. Detachment 101 officer First Lieutenant James R. Ward reported that the guerrillas had somewhat of an advantage because the Japanese "could not compete with the Kachins in firepower for every one of our 150 soldiers had either an automatic or semi-automatic weapon."[22] Still, the field groups made pains to explain that their increasing number of reported Japanese killed was not a fabrication.

> All Detachment 101 figures of casualties are actually counted and probables are not listed. The Kachin soldier when asked about enemy casualties after a skirmish will usually remark that he fired at a Japanese with perfect aim but does not know whether the Jap was killed or was seeking tactical cover. Accordingly Japanese dead are never credited unless the bodies are found or our agents definitely report that a certain amount of dead were carried by their fellow soldiers. Similarly no claim is made of "probables" resulting from mortar fire, booby traps or grenade fragmentation unless the casualty is proven in the above manner.[23]

Ward reported that in more than eight months of operations, his group reported killing 217 Japanese. However, Ward's group believed the number to be much higher, with his Kachin subhadar (an officer's equivalent rank from the prewar Burma rifles that was carried into use in Detachment 101) estimating up to 500 Japanese casualties, and Ward himself, a little lower at 400. This was as opposed to Ward's losses of six killed, nine wounded, and three Kachins missing in action.[24]

The number of enemy reported killed also did not reflect losses from Allied aircraft acting on Detachment 101's intelligence. As an example, based on a field report, on 23 February 1945 eight P-38 fighter-bombers struck a

Japanese target. On the 27th, the same intelligence agent reported that in the attack, the Japanese lost 150 soldiers, thirty horses, two artillery pieces, and two trucks.[25]

No doubt "aided" by the actions of Detachment 101 groups to their rear, Japanese forces continued their retreat from the conventional Allied forces. Detachment 101 reported in December that by "a series of forced marches marked in many cases by almost continuous patrol contacts and skirmishes" its units were able to "form a continuous line" from the Chinese border to the Irrawaddy River.[26] However, here the terrain began to change as the Japanese retreated beyond the jungles of North Burma and into the more barren hills of the Shan States.

The terrain and population change put Detachment 101 at a great disadvantage. The Kachins had long used their knowledge of the jungle to counter the more heavily armed Japanese. However, in the Shan States, the Japanese had the advantage. There the Japanese could more easily use their artillery and motor transport as well as their better-trained and larger infantry forces; things that the less heavily armed and equipped guerrilla groups did not possess. And even if NCAC believed that in the "big picture" the Japanese were planning on evacuating North Burma, Detachment 101 reported, "That ain't what it says in fine print."[27]

One of the first to experience this was Area #1's First Battalion under Captain Joseph Lazarsky in December near Kutkai. Just before, Lazarsky reported an action where "we had destroyed over a dozen trucks using small arms, light machine guns and a bazooka." But, "unknown to us, [the Japanese] brought in 75mm artillery and light tanks, with lots of troops. Our intelligence reported only a company of Japs moving against our camp. There was no mention of artillery or tanks."[28]

Lazarsky planned an attack because he thought that his group could handle a Japanese company. At the end of 1944, large numbers of OGs began arriving to Detachment 101 from the United States. Instead of going into the field as a group, Peers distributed them among preexisting field units. Right at this time, OG Lieutenants Harold J. Berg and Ken W. Stein flew in as reinforcements. On 18 December, Berg went with the guerrilla company under British Captain Simon "Monocle" Reed, who had earned the nickname for wearing that style eyepiece in the field. As their company moved into position, the guerrillas ran into a Japanese machine gun. Berg took a full burst of fire in the chest, and was killed instantly.

Reed, also wounded, managed to drag himself back, but the effect was instantaneous. The Kachins "panicked" and ran, leaving both Berg and Reed behind. Then, the Japanese opened up with the artillery and tanks, and "totally routed most of the rest of the Kachins." The Kachins themselves suffered up to four killed in action and five or six missing. As one of the Kachin officers, Subadar Major Monga Tu, later said, it was not "one of the Kachins's finest hours." The Japanese attack represented one of the times that a Detachment 101 group learned the hard way that "Kachins are outstanding fighters in ambushes and small unit raids, but they are no good at frontal attacks."[29] After coming under attack by an organized Japanese force of some 300–400 soldiers, the First Battalion retreated. Not only did the First Battalion suffer a setback, but it also had to care for 300 displaced civilians.[30] The Japanese suffered far greater losses in the engagement, but the situation reflected a changed operational picture for Detachment 101.

It was also in the Shan States that some of the Kachin troops became less willing to continue to fight the Japanese. Because the Allied advance placed its groups farther south than it had ever operated, increasing numbers of Detachment 101's Kachins wanted to go home. One Detachment 101 officer recalled the mood: "Some of the Kachins chose evacuation to return to their hills rather than fight the enemy in Shan territory. 'Let the Shans fight for their own country' they reasoned."[31] Another Detachment 101 officer reported that his "unit's attitude changed and 'we want to go home' became the universal cry."[32]

A large reason for this had to do with ethnic strife. Although they hated the Japanese, in turn the Kachins did not get along with many of Burma's other ethnic groups, particularly with but not limited to the Shan. Indicative of the problems experienced by the U.S. personnel in the field groups, on 17 February 1945, Peter Lutken wrote to his commander, Pete Joost, that "Kachin-Palaung relations in this area are nothing short of dynamite. We're all getting grey headed trying to keep them from each others throats. And to add to the difficulties when we move out of here we will have passed the last Jinghpaw [Kachin] village."[33] Lieutenant Douglas B. Martin added, "The Kachins in this area had it in for the Palaungs and killed one every time they had a chance."[34]

The Kachins themselves could be a target. An example occurred in mid-March near Mong Tawn with the Second Battalion when the "villagers tried to 'witch' the Kachins by putting 2-anna pieces [a grave insult involving putting small bits of cut-up coins in food] in their rice. The Kachins resented this super-natural black-balling and wished to liquidate the village, but they were restrained."[35] Such cases increased the Kachins' desire to end their participation in the war and go home.

Units in Area #3, although no longer in the main operational area, were the first to be affected by the Kachins' refusals to go farther south. It had an immediate and drastic effect. Area #3 lost so many guerrillas that Detachment 101 ordered it to disband. The group managed to save its "best Kachins," and combined them with Area #2 under Maddox.[36] At the same time, Detachment 101 discovered that its operations in the area overlapped those of the British. As a result, Detachment 101 turned operations west of the Irrawaddy River over to the British.[37]

The discharges did not reduce the action on the ground, and January 1945 represented another increase in the operational tempo of Detachment 101. The Japanese grew more resolute in their defense, forcing the guerrillas to conduct bolder attacks. The Third battalion reported an engagement centered on two Kachins at the village of Hpa ra.

> Each took a bren gun and using as a tommy gun advanced well ahead of the platoon, shooting as they went. This alarmed the Japs who quickly recovered and fixing bayonets made to charge. By this time Naik Myitung Sing [G]awng was wounded in the foot. But when he saw the Japs charging he drew with his right hand, his trusty dah and with his left, his pistol. He warded the first bayonet off with his dah and shot dead the [Japanese soldier]. This way he killed two.

The stand so stunned the Japanese that they briefly held their positions before retreating "in great disorder."[38]

The potential for the war ending in North Burma—no doubt compounded by fears of a postwar disbandment—meant that the OSS needed all the good press it could generate. This push resulted in news correspondents receiving permission to go into the field to observe Detachment 101's operations. One reporter who went behind the lines was George Weller of the *Chicago Daily News* and another was Ralph Henderson, who wrote an article in the *Reader's Digest* describing guerrilla operations that he witnessed in early January: "In a jungle ambush, the Kachins can do terrible things with sharpened bamboos. They fill the bushes on both sides with needle-sharp stakes, cleverly hidden. When a Jap patrol was fired upon, and dived for the timber—well, I hardly like to talk about it. After a few ambushes like that, the Japs never took cover when we fired on them."[39]

But at this time the guerrilla groups also uncovered an older foe, the Chinese. Just as had occurred in the Myitkyina Campaign, armed Chinese exploiting the power vacuum grew problematic. To add to the tension, Kachin guerrillas operating along the border simply did not mix with the Chinese. Such was the case in Area #1, where the Third Battalion had to be moved to the rear just to protect vulnerable Kachin villages from Chinese warlords. "Had this not been done the Kachins in the other battalions would have felt it necessary to leave the battalions and return to the villages to defend their homes and families."[40]

This seemingly minor act created an international incident. On 5 January, a group of Chinese guerrillas crossed the Burma border, raided the village of Lweje, and killed several Kachins. In response, the Third Battalion, led by Lieutenant Thomas Chamales, crossed the border into China and raided several villages in retaliation. The act incensed the Chinese, who investigated the matter and reported that while "both parties have committed wrong," the Kachins plundered and burnt fourteen villages, killed 300 villagers, and left thousands homeless. The Chinese then requested relief for their refugees.[41] In turn, Chamales reported that his group killed forty-three Chinese guerrillas. At the local level, the Chinese and Kachins agreed to keep to their sides of the border.[42] Nothing more was heard until Chiang Kai-shek sent Peers a personal bill for $25 million.[43] Peers later said, "I was quite honored by his request, to think that a U.S. Army colonel would have that kind of money." Peers turned the matter over to NCAC, where it was dropped.[44]

The Kachin remained greatly alarmed about the local situation. In February, they said, "The Chinese have looted and destroyed more in two weeks than the Japanese did in two years." The Kachin also reported that the Chinese told them that their government intended to annex the area, and had already forced the villagers to pay taxes.[45] Because Chinese guerrillas continued to be problematic, Detachment 101 had to leave a Kachin force, the Fourth Battalion, to serve as a home guard and police force, and to prevent the other Kachin forces from deserting to defend their home areas against the Chinese. The Detachment also had to release individual guerrillas from the battalions so that they could go home to protect their families.[46] These Detachment 101 groups remained in place until CAS reestablished control over the area.[47] Eventually, as the OSS pushed south, the British grew increasingly concerned about the guerrillas operating along the still disputed border areas with China. As a result, Detachment 101—no doubt in part to keep the Kachins away from the Chinese—agreed to stay away from these areas in principle.[48] But problems remained.

After the Chinese retained a Detachment 101 agent group and withheld their money and weapons, Detachment 101 decided to withdraw its agents from all areas that the Chinese would soon occupy. Having to leave forces behind reduced the guerrilla force, leaving just the First, Second, Third, Sixth, and Seventh to either train or press the Japanese. The Fourth and Fifth Battalions, the latter under the command of Captain Lazum Tang of the Burma Army, were in formation or serving as police forces and not yet available for operations.

The guerrilla forces faced increasing Japanese resistance as they moved south. Increased Japanese opposition meant that Detachment 101–supplied intelligence became even more critical to NCAC. Detachment 101 recognized that supplying intelligence remained its primary mission, and reported that it was "the only intelligence unit of the Northern Combat Area Command . . . the entire strategic and tactical operations directed by NCAC are based on Det. 101 intelligence reports." Sensing a comparison by OSS Washington, Detachment 101 also noted that "the comparatively small scale of overall American, British and Chinese operations in this theater as compared to the European theater tends to convey a falsely minimized impression of the importance of Det. 101's operations."

In response, in January Peers sought to set the record straight. In addition to casualties inflicted by the U.S. Army Air Forces acting on Detachment 101 supplied intelligence, from 15 October 1944 to 15 January 1945, with less than 1 percent of the NCAC total strength, Detachment 101 inflicted 29 percent of reported casualties.[49] In those statistics, the Chinese, with 76 percent of NCAC's total strength, inflicted 46 percent of Japanese casualties; the Thirty-sixth Division, with 10 percent of the strength, 18 percent; and the U.S. MARS Task Force, with 13 percent of NCAC's strength, 7 percent of the Japanese casualties.[50] Perhaps even more so than during the Myitkyina Campaign, in this period Detachment 101 again achieved Donovan's perceived mission of special operations forces: to be a force multiplier to conventional units.

In turn, Allied conventional units in Burma recognized the utility of Detachment 101. The commanders of the 475th Infantry and the MARS Task Force commended Detachment 101 for it efforts.[51] Perhaps most striking, British Lieutenant Colonel Cumming, Force 136, reported to ALFSEA that

> I had been informed (a) that GOC-in-C [Slim] Fourteenth Army was dissatisfied with Force 136; (b) that he considered they showed no adequate return for the man-power they employed, (c) that they showed up in a poor light in comparison with Det. 101 of OSS who worked on the NCAC front; (d) that he therefore recommended Force 136 ceased to operate in Burma and that the responsibility for the activities behind the enemy lines in that country be handed over to Det. 101 of OSS.[52]

So many organizations relied upon Detachment 101 that it had to increase its field groups while also recruiting more guerrillas. The fast pace of the advance meant that many recruits did not have the luxury of even a month's training as had previously been possible. Such was the case in late January when in response to an imminent Japanese thrust, "600 untrained Kachins and Shans had all available weapons thrust into their hands, were given 30–40 rounds of ammo, a few were given a 5 minute course in the bazooka and they rushed out and forced the Japs back."[53]

On 1 January, Detachment 101 parachuted its first small combat team into Japanese-held Burma. These teams acted almost in the same fashion as a miniature long-range penetration group. The seventeen-man MM team, led by First Lieutenant Billy G. Milton, jumped 40 miles ahead of the Allied advance into the Mogok area.[54] Their mission was to place ambushes on two roads between Mongwit and Mogok, used as a route of retreat for the disorganized Japanese forces fleeing from the British Fourteenth Army. In only a few weeks, the MM team accounted for several hundred Japanese soldiers killed. A second small combat team, named JACKO, parachuted into Burma on 19 January.[55] A third combat team, called LEONARD, parachuted in on 6 March.[56]

Detachment 101's agent groups, themselves even deeper in enemy-held territory than the small combat teams, assisted operations by paving the way with intelligence collection and encouraging local cooperation. An example of this is the evacuation of the Sabwa of Hsenwi, a very prominent Shan leader. Tipped off that Japanese forces were on the way to arrest him, the Sabwa asked Detachment 101 to evacuate him. But when the Sabwa showed up at the airstrip, he had his wives and children, thirty-nine people in all.[57] Their evacuation and eventual return to the area, helped swing Shan support over to the Kachin-centric Detachment 101 groups. The agent groups needed this support to increase their intelligence reporting on local conditions and the road and rail network running to the Thai border.[58] Although by now intelligence was quickly taking a backseat to guerrilla efforts, Detachment 101 continued to insert agent groups far ahead of its battalions. In March alone, Detachment 101 inserted eight agent and combat groups. Of interest, and reflecting Detachment 101's organization, is that the planning and insertion of these missions were undertaken by Detachment 101's S-3 (operations) as opposed to its S-2 (intelligence).[59]

The guerrilla battalions also grew increasingly bold and confident in February. Early in the month, the Second Battalion attacked dug-in Japanese units, albeit with little success. Still, such a move reflects the changing nature of Detachment 101 guerrillas from ambush tactics to direct infantry attacks. At this stage of the war in Burma, Detachment 101's guerrillas were in almost daily contact with the Japanese.

Such a position greatly assisted the conventional Allied forces. For instance, in mid-February, while guarding the flank of the British Thirtieth Division, Detachment 101 guerrillas warned of the presence of a full Japanese battalion forming up to attack. However, Private First Class Temple R. Kennedy reported that "The English foolishly refused to accept" the intelligence. On the 13th, the OSS guerrillas discovered that the Japanese had laid guide wires and signs in preparation for a night attack just 400 yards from their bivouac. On the morning of the 14th, the Japanese hit the Detachment 101 element, which retreated after expending most of their ammo.[60] At this point, the British "changed their minds when they discovered an estimated 1000 Japs in their backyard."[61] As a result, the British pulled out their headquarters before the Japanese could isolate and attack it.[62] Another Detachment 101 officer reported that "when 'our' Japs started shelling them [the British] revised their judgement." According to that officer, in the words of one British major, Detachment 101's warning "saved the division."[63] This instance was also an example of the Japanese stubbornly resisting the Allied advance.

Another case was on 23 February when the Sixth Battalion attacked a dug-in Japanese position. Unable to dislodge the enemy, the guerrillas retreated to a nearby ridge and set up their own defensive position that cut off the Japanese route of retreat. On 26 February, the Japanese assaulted the guerrilla-held ridge in force. Instead of retreating, which was the normal operating procedure for Detachment 101 guerrillas, the Sixth Battalion held its ground and killed nearly eighty Japanese. Low on ammunition, the guerrillas withdrew on the second day with the Japanese hot on their heels. But here the guerrillas' advantage of trading heavy weapons for speed took effect, and they were able to break contact after a four-day battle.

The guerrilla elements also disturbed Japanese defensive plans by destroying enemy supply depots. With their forces spread thin, the Japanese left several of their caches with minimal guarding. Although previously, Detachment 101 groups had found and destroyed smaller amounts of enemy stores, on 22 March the guerrillas hit pay dirt. Guerrillas in Area #2 uncovered a store of enemy ammunition and rations. The guerrillas set demolitions that caused secondary demolitions that continued for three hours after. "The amount of ammunition and equipment destroyed is inestimable," reported Detachment 101.[64] Such actions only increased the bitterness and desperation of the fighting. In late February, the Second Battalion reported a fight in which the Japanese attackers attacking the guerrillas' perimeter forced local men and women to march in front of them. Having no choice, "the Kachins fired anyway," and beat off the attack.[65]

Meanwhile, the Third and Fifth Battalions consolidated their headquarters, creating the First Regiment. Such a large organization would have been unheard of in 1943, when Detachment 101 was still trying to secure an overall mission and support from inhabitants of North Burma. Recognizing the effectiveness of Detachment 101's guerrillas, the Japanese issued orders directing rear-echelon troops to consider themselves front-line soldiers due to the presence of Allied airborne units. In fact, the only units in the Japanese rear areas belonged to Detachment 101 or Force 136.

The Japanese did have one thing correct. Detachment 101's forces were considerable, approaching 10,000 guerrillas. Eight battalions now combated the enemy, two newly recruited east of Lashio and six veteran ones to the west. The veteran battalions placed the Japanese so off-balance with harassing attacks and reporting targets for the Tenth USAAF that Chinese forces following in the wake did not have much of a fight to take Lashio.[66] This particular landmark caused a rift among the guerrillas.

The field groups reported, "Every member of the AKR [American Kachin Rangers] has had one goal in mind since enlisting and that is to take Lashio." Part of this was because Detachment 101 promised many of the Kachins discharges once the city fell.[67] Detachment 101 cleared most of the Japanese from the area and provided intelligence assisting the Chinese advance. One example was a request at 11:00 in the morning from the Chinese on how they could get their tanks across the Namyao River. Four hours later Detachment 101 sent back a report detailing all the local crossing sites, including those that would not support tanks.[68] One of the Americans with the guerrillas reported that Detachment 101 had plans and laid on air support to take the town, but "everyone was irritated" when NCAC ordered them to stand down.[69] Even though Detachment 101 nearly cleared Lashio of the Japanese all by itself, just as had happened in Myitkyina, that honor of taking the city went to the Chinese.

Unfortunately for Detachment 101, Lashio also represented a dramatic change in the nature of its operations. Although about 450–500 veterans decided to stay, most of the Kachin guerrillas turned in their weapons and equipment, received a discharge certificate, and then were flown back to their home areas.[70] Area #1 was particularly hard hit with the demobilization and disbanded six of its seven battalions.[71]

In response, Detachment 101 directed its units to consolidate. No longer was there a distinction between Area #1 and Area #2. Instead, all units reported to Detachment 101 BA at Bhamo. However, by encouraging enough veteran guerrillas to stay, and recruiting a mix of Shans, Chins, and even Burmese, some of whom still wore the uniform of the Japanese-sponsored Burmese Independence Army, Detachment 101 salvaged four battalions (First, Second, Third, and Tenth), with ten variable-sized independent companies.[72] Thereafter, Detachment 101 recruited "those with any sort of background or of any inclination of military training."[73] They also sent out patrols, "all dressed in their best uniforms with shining weapons who would go to villages and say 'join up and be like us.'"[74]

Not only was extensive recruiting of different ethnicities a new experience for Detachment 101, but it was done under less than ideal conditions. Sometimes the new ethnic mix did not work out well because not all were as fierce as the Kachins. Detachment 101 officer Captain Daniel J. Barnwell remembered when that realization hit him. His group was camped near a Japanese position. At about 10 PM, he heard

> footsteps outside and close to our defensive perimeter and so reported in our radio contact. By 2400 hours we could definitely hear Japs all around us and felt that they were trying to get us to fire and reveal our position. By this time we were all talking in whispers on the radio and requested we not be called anymore since even a whisper sounded to us like someone beating a drum. Finally about 0200 hours all footsteps had died away and Gus and I waited for daylight in grim silence. At last daylight came and I looked around but could see no trace of the Japanese. As it got lighter, we could see that nearly all our foxholes were empty and that we did not have more than about ten people occupying the perimeter. It slowly dawned on Gus and myself that all the footsteps and rattling of equipment that we heard during the night was our own Shan going AWOL. . . . It was such an anticlimax that neither Gus nor I knew whether we should be mad or relieved. Upon reflecting that there were about 200 people who had deserted that night, it was decided to face the issue and weed out the unreliable. This was accomplished by lining up all the Shans (about 300) and asking who wanted to go home. About 150 to 175 took up the offer and were disarmed and their uniforms (to include shoes) taken away. The remainder got a raise in pay and in appreciation put on a ceremonial dance that evening.[75]

Detachment 101 officer Walter E. O'Brien elaborated: "There was a period of confusion when we attempted to make fighters out of the Shans. They wouldn't stick with us. We faced a rather nasty scramble in open infantry country when the Shans piled their weapons and left us with only a few Kachins and some Chinese stragglers from the 38th and 50th Divisions."[76] This meant that despite their previous success, Detachment 101's guerrilla formations were not in the best of shape as NCAC moved into its last phase of the Burma Campaign. By this time, however, Detachment 101 was conducting operations on another front as well.

12

The Arakan Field Unit: February–June 1945

All of a sudden, a school of fish hit me, just all over, and I thought that one of those crocs got me. Those salt-water crocs are the most vicious in the world. . . . I kind of sweated that one out.

MU swimmer CBM James R. Eubank

Detachment 101 was known throughout OSS as an organization that ignored branch distinctions and amalgamated its various functions to serve common goals. This allowed the group to slowly become a combined operations unit that was without peer in OSS.[1] In 1945, Detachment 101 was best able to demonstrate this flexibility that had characterized its operations throughout the war. The short-lived Detachment 101 AFU was dubbed with the derogatory name "All Fucked Up," just as the China-Burma-India Theater had been called "Confusion Beyond Imagination." In practice, the name was a misnomer as the AFU represented a true test of Detachment 101's way of war. The AFU integrated various OSS sections into a single autonomous unit, and represented a pioneering use of maritime, ground, psychological, and intelligence components.

While AFU operations did not involve the large guerrilla formations prevalent in north Burma, they reflected Detachment 101's flexibility to adapt to the mission placed before it. Detachment 101 took over a preexisting unit of limited utility and molded it into one with a much broader operational scope. The Arakan offered a different political environment for Detachment 101. Despite working together more closely than was the case in north Burma, relations with the British in the Arakan were not always harmonious. AFU personnel were extremely wary of British attempts either to spy on them or to sway local public opinion away from the Americans. One of the most blatant examples of British-inspired anti-American propaganda was the newsletters printed by the *Rangoon Liberator*. This daily began publication on 13 May and contained a number of articles that praised the British war effort against Japan while downgrading that of the United States.[2] Some of this behavior could be understood. Many Burmans hoping for independence looked to the U.S. for help because, like the civilian population in north Burma, they did not see America as having colonial designs on the country. The Burmese often asked AFU personnel when the Americans were going to help them gain independence from the British.[3] As one OSS operator noted, the British could not help but see that the local population was "pleased" with their liberation by the British, but would have been "wildly enthusiastic" if their liberators had been American.[4]

Another issue that had the potential to split U.S.-British relations was the arming of Burmese political groups, such as the AFL. In their own words, the AFL was "not pro-British, but we prefer the Allies. We are against Fascism."[5] The AFL articulated the Burmans' anticolonial sentiments, that had gotten so bad that the OSS warned its personnel not to go into certain areas lest they be mistakenly harmed because "hatred for the British had reached that point."[6] In discussions with P Division, Peers and Donovan took the stance that Detachment 101 followed throughout the war, that despite the assistance they might offer, it did not arm politically motivated groups. The OSS's only interest was in forming guerrilla groups to fight the Japanese, not in creating a postwar independence movement. Detachment 101 only wanted the intelligence that such groups might offer. Force 136 had the final decision to arm the AFL.[7]

The OSS also had to contend with an entirely different operating environment in the Arakan, which consists of a coastal plain lined with mangrove swamps frequently pierced with tidal creeks, or *chaungs*. The area itself has dense foliage, and an observer from Detachment 404 called it one of the "world's worst battlefields—a combination of jungle, paddy fields [rice], and mountains." A patrol might "come within ten yards of a Japanese patrol without ever detecting it."[8] People of numerous ethnicities lived in the region; being primarily Buddhist or Muslim, they had little in common with the Americans. This was the strategic and tactical picture that Detachment 101 faced in the Arakan.

The Arakan Field Unit (AFU)

The roots of the AFU predate Detachment 101's involvement. Although it had responsibility for the Andaman Islands, India, Indonesia, Malaya, Sumatra, Thailand, and parts of Burma and French Indo-China, the primary mission of SEAC and its subordinate OSS element, Detachment 404, was to see to Burma's liberation. Churchill himself issued this directive.[9] To help accomplish that task, OSS Detachment 404 operated as an intelligence unit supporting the XV Indian Corps. Prior to that, the only intelligence organizations available in the region were the British V-Force and scattered SOE elements.[10] Detachment 404 assisted the XV Indian Corps with long-range intelligence and reconnaissance patrols, while V-Force did the same closer to the main battlefront. Although the OSS was not able to accomplish its long-range mission until Detachment 101 took control, it performed better than V-Force had at short-range intelligence-gathering missions. Because of this, Detachment 404's operational elements focused on surveying potential locations for amphibious assaults behind Japanese lines, while the intelligence component focused on gathering information about Japanese organizations and dispositions.[11]

The AFU began on 10 December 1944 as the Detachment 404 AFU, called by the OSS Operation BITTERSWEET. The initial joint MU and OG constituting BITTERSWEET set up headquarters at Cox's Bazar, in modern-day Bangladesh. BITTERSWEET moved to Camp Ritchie at Akyab, Burma, in January, from where it conducted underwater and shore reconnaissance missions in support of the British advance.[12] Its teams were under strict orders to fire only in self-defense and followed the guidance that the "most successful penetration group is one which never fires a shot."[13]

Other OSS elements followed. In December, a MO section of seven personnel arrived that, by January, was printing a Burmese language newsletter called the *War Mirror*.[14] MO personnel then regularly infiltrated behind enemy lines and gave the newsletter to Allied sympathizers for distribution. Although the section recognized that it was on the operational side as opposed to intelligence, it also assisted X-2 personnel by information gathering.[15]

Originally, the BITTERSWEET X-2 element was going to mimic the operations of Detachment 101's X-2 section by forming two CITs. The AFU X-2 section soon deemed this impractical because the pace of the Allied advance was too fast and decided instead to retain all personnel in one unit and to follow the combat operations by incorporating into the headquarters of the British Twenty-fifth Division. There, they were in place to join the OG section in the unopposed amphibious assault of Akyab Island. Once on Akyab, the group began apprehending black hats and conducting interrogations.[16] In many cases, the X-2 teams found that their best informants were those on the black lists who now wished to ingratiate themselves with the Allies.[17]

Meanwhile, personnel from the SO section worked with the British V-Force so that they could familiarize themselves with its operations.[18]

The AFU's Schools and Training (S&T) section—long held in the rear in other areas—also moved forward to set up a school to train agents close to the areas in which they would work. After briefly setting up on Akyab, the school moved to Ramree Island on 23 January 1945. There, the OSS assessed and recruited several men even though their work was "considered secondary to operations instead of integral to operations."[19]

The AFU SI section was small and headed by an Anglo-Burmese agent, Edward Law Yone. It functioned differently than SI at Detachment 101 in north Burma. Their personnel accompanied the XV Indian Corps on operations, particularly amphibious ones. SI personnel then contacted local headmen and influential persons, as well as conducted interrogations or recruited indigenous agents to establish intelligence networks. The OSS gave prospective agents an abbreviated training course, after which they went on short-range missions to acquire specific information, such as the number and location of enemy personnel, or to apprehend known collaborators to make them double agents.[20] The SI section also infiltrated agents by indigenous watercraft; because of its successes, it became the primary organization to furnish intelligence on the area of the Prome-Taungup Road. This was the same area of the failed W Group mission in late 1943.[21] By the end of AFU operations, the SI section had sent forty-nine named agent operations into the field. Of these, only five were failures and had no further contact with base.[22]

Meanwhile OSS Washington decided that operational responsibility for Burma north of Rangoon belonged to Detachment 101, while areas south belonged to Detachment 404.[23] As a result, on 16 February, Detachment 101 deactivated BITTERSWEET and renamed the element the Detachment 101 Arakan Field Unit. On his first visit to the AFU, Peers placed Major Richard L. Farr in command. Farr, later succeeded in command by Major Charles J. Trees, established his headquarters at Akyab. OG Major Lloyd E. Peddicord and his deputy, MU Lieutenant Commander Derek Lee, commanded the forward section at Kyaukpyu. The AFU was tied into the Detachment 101 command through Detachment 101 BA, which handled the unit's administration and coordination. Detachment 101 established another minor headquarters under 101 BA in Calcutta at the same location as Detachment 505 to handle administration, supplies, and parachute packing. Operations themselves were coordinated through Allied Land Forces South East Asia (ALFSEA).[24]

On his visit, Peers found an "utter lack of coordination between branches."[25] He transferred responsibility for air drop from Force 136 to OSS control, and ordered representatives of other Detachment 101 elements to the AFU. In March, Detachment 101 detailed an officer, who coordinated through Detachment 101 BA (Bhamo), to handle the AFU's financial needs.[26] The R&D section at Nazira assisted Peddicord by working on requests to improve on items such as submachine-gun magazines or methods to carry additional ammunition.[27]

The AFU's R&A contingent, on the other hand, functioned much like Detachment 101's in north Burma. It handled much of the tactical intelligence and compiled weekly summaries. R&A AFU personnel based themselves near the combat elements, including participating in all major actions and amphibious landings, to provide requested information as quickly as possible. In late March, XV Indian Corps commander Lieutenant General Philip Christison commended the AFU for the value of its intelligence.[28]

Now under Detachment 101's command, the AFU's MU and OG sections made several long-range reconnaissance missions for the XV Indian Corps. MU later reported that the two sections operated together with a "minimum of friction, each pulling their own weight on operations."[29] An example of this close cooperation is Operation BOSTON, a MU/OG reconnaissance mission conducted on 20 February 1945 at Foul Island. Because of the importance of the MU and OG sections in the AFU, that mission will serve as a brief case study for the type of operation conducted by these two units and an indicator of how well they integrated their operations.

The mission of Operation BOSTON, a reconnaissance of Foul Island, located about 20 miles off the coast, was finalized on 19 February 1945.[30] Because the AFU's primary maritime craft, the air-sea rescue P-boat, always operated in pairs in enemy waters, P-101, under U.S. Navy Lieutenant Junior Grade Ralph N. Hubbard, and P-564, commanded by Army First Lieutenant Walter L. Mess, received the mission, his last.[31]

A pre-operational checklist was mandatory. First, the twelve-man crew ventilated volatile aviation gasoline fumes from the boats before they got the motors running. That was a chore, "because the oil was so heavy that it had to be electrically heated for fifteen minutes before you could start the engines," said Mess.[32] P-564 was the most heavily laden boat of the two on Operation BOSTON. It carried four kayaks, one LCR (landing craft, rubber), and eighteen additional OSS personnel, while the 63-foot P-101 carried eleven men and its crew.[33] P-564's crew stored the OG equipment forward, next to the two spare propeller shafts, which weighed a ton apiece. Their relative immobility made them ideal stanchions to secure the equipment. "When you are running into the wind and going about 14 knots, you had a pretty good breeze. Things had to be tied down," and one of the few rules—because of all the high-octane fuel onboard—was "No smoking," said Mess.[34]

Managing fuel consumption was critical because Foul Island was eight hours away. "The object was to save gas so we could make it back home," related Mess. Sometimes the boat was run on one engine. Gasoline from the 55-gallon drums on deck was used first, and a garden hose siphoned the fuel into the internal tanks.

Although aerial photographs indicated that the island was unoccupied, P-564 and P-101 waited until dark to approach.[35] P-564's crew readied the swimmer's four kayaks. With an A-frame on the stern, they "swung the [boat] up on it, brought it overboard, and brought it around the side," said Mess.[36] After silently paddling close to shore, Lieutenant Junior Grade John P. Booth and Chief Boatswain's Mate James R. Eubank of the U.S. Coast Guard slipped out of their kayaks into the water to swim to the beach. Seeing no enemy, the swimmers signaled their two kayaks to come ashore and sent a "safe landing" flash of a red light to P-564. Then they split into two reconnaissance parties that moved in opposite directions along the beach. A kayak trailed each from the water as the MU teams sought to determine if there were any hidden enemy positions along the beach before the OG complement landed.[37] When the swimmers returned to the P-564, they reported having seen no sign of the Japanese.[38] It was time for the OGs to go in for a more thorough reconnaissance.

First Lieutenant Louis A. O'Jibway led the OG force. They left the P-boats in three rubber boats: two seven-man LCRs and a two-man LCR.[39] O'Jibway's seven-man LCR landed first and provided security while the others came ashore. Then, O'Jibway divided his force. Sergeant Thompson, Corporals Starkey, Armer, Devereaux, and Privates First Class Kostrevic and Hess stayed on the beach under the command of Master Sergeant Zimmerman. They had an SCR 300 radio to contact P-564. O'Jibway and his team headed to the north, but after 400 yards, they stopped to wait for daylight because it was so dark. At 6 AM, O'Jibway sent Staff Sergeant Krueger and four men to reconnoiter Foul Island's north side. O'Jibway and two men returned to the beachhead, and then checked the south side. They climbed the volcano on Foul Island and noted its geologic features.

While the OGs reconnoitered the interior, Navy Lieutenant John E. Babb and Coast Guard Chief Petty Officer Herman L. Becker kayaked to shore to take beach sand samples.[40] Everyone was back aboard the P-boats by 0935.[41] Meanwhile, the crew of the P-564 took panoramic photographs of the island from the deck.

Mess described how that was accomplished: "We practiced on Ceylon . . . to figure out how to get photographs of shorelines." The best way was to take the charts and figure out where there was enough water depth to allow circumnavigation of an island from a similar distance without running aground. The photographers steadied the cameras on the boat's .50 caliber "gun tubs." P-564 idled at 6 to 8 knots. Cruising at the same speed and distance from Foul Island, it was a simple matter for the photographers to periodically snap their Leica cameras.[42] The only trick was it had to be done at slack tide because P-564 would have been pushed around by the incoming or outgoing tides. A slack tide at either flood or ebb allowed the boat to remain relatively stationary with the currents around the island.[43] Mission accomplished, the two boats headed back to Kyaukpyu.

Operation BOSTON confirmed that Foul Island was not in enemy hands, vital for SEAC's invasion plan of Rangoon in May. The OSS reported the geographic and hydrologic data to SEAC.[44] The mission was a success, as Booth recalled years later: "We weren't there to start a firefight, we were there to get information."[45] Despite successful missions such as this, the MU section suffered from poor environmental conditions and a lack of supplies.

Its swimmers had trained for underwater swimming with the Lambertsen amphibious respiratory unit (LARU), an underwater recirculating breathing device invented by Captain Christian J. Lambertsen. The LARU permitted swimmers to remain underwater for an extended period and emit no telltale bubbles. The *chaungs* that the MUs were to reconnoiter, however, were murky, forcing the swimmers to conduct their reconnaissance missions on the surface. Several other items that the MU swimmers had trained with, such as kayaks, remained at Detachment 404 headquarters at Kandy and arrived only later when operations began to wind down. In the meantime, the MU borrowed equipment from the British, or made do as they could. Because of the lack of material and the inability to perform their mission, the MU personnel often were used for operations other than what they had been trained for, such as locating sea mines, operating a maritime ferry service, and refueling Catalina PBY aircraft at sea. And, with the inability to use the LARUs, it was left for the MU's high-powered P-boats to reconnoiter up the *chaungs* to find the enemy presence. This new method brought with it the added danger of detection and risk if one of the P-boats grounded in uncharted enemy-controlled waters.[46] These boats only had a short range of 500 miles, and because of their noisy, 1320 horsepower V-12 dual engines, had to carry enormous quantities of high-octane gasoline. This left the possibility, as one

MU report said, that "a single incendiary bullet would convert one of these craft into a 70-ton funeral pyre with all hands on board." Using them to slip into an enemy position undetected was "almost out of the question," due to muffled roar of their motors. Yet, necessity dictated that they be used in this fashion.

In March, the AFU began preparations for the invasion of Rangoon. Because there was very little in the way of intelligence being supplied from the city or from lower Burma, it was here that the AFU's shift from support to combat operations to conducting a strategic intelligence mission occurred. This is exactly opposite of what Detachment 101 was doing for NCAC at the time. The AFU's tactical operations continued, but became of less utility. In particular, the MO Section went to great lengths to ensure cooperation with distributing the *War Mirror*. One MO soldier wrote headquarters, "I am the first American in this village . . . it is a custom in a Chin village for every visitor to chew beetle [nut—*sic*] at the headman's house—I am trying to get out of it—no luck . . . I have to take it." Other times, the distribution of the newsletter required bribing local headmen with rupees or opium.[47] The MO section was able to print the newspaper in multiple languages.[48] However, after five weeks, the work came to naught because the British clandestine services were under the impression that MO actions were inciting Burmese nationalism. They forced MO to give up their agent chains at the end of March and use those of Force 136.[49] Thereafter, MO material came from Calcutta instead of the MO forward section at Akyab, which greatly reduced the section's utility in the campaign.[50]

Still, MO had other projects. One, SWAMP ISLAND, was an attempt to get bypassed Japanese personnel still living in the mangrove swamps to surrender. As with any MO operation in the Arakan, the operation had to be cleared with the British. Once it was approved, SI agents helped distribute the leaflets. That section had placed village headmen on its payroll for 50 rupees per month. In return, the headmen distributed MO propaganda and notified the OSS when strangers arrived in their villages. The arrangement also facilitated X-2 efforts to root out suspected Japanese agents.[51] The MO effort was very successful. Agents reported that the Japanese wanted to surrender, but worried about "being shot in the process by Indian soldiers." The mere fact that Japanese were willing to surrender was enough to convince Major General C. E. N. Lomax, the British commander of the Twenty-sixth Indian Infantry Division, to devote more effort to the project.[52]

In line with the AFU's focus on intelligence operations, in late March the OSS withdrew the MU and OG sections, including the P-boats that had been so instrumental in infiltrating personnel. The majority of the OG section went to China to train parachute units under the CARBONADO Plan, the potential seizure of the China coast. The AFU OG had been unique in that it had never received parachute training in the United States, so with Donovan's prodding the British granted permission for the section to go to airborne school at Chakala.[53]

After leaving behind liaison personnel with the XV Indian Corps, at the beginning of April the AFU moved its headquarters forward from Akyab to Kyaukpyu to consolidate personnel and administration. Detachment 101's influence was beginning to show when the AFU reported that "branch consciousness has been submerged in favor of the main mission of this unit. The entire unit is beginning to work together as a team."[54] At the same time, the U.S. Army Engineers created a camp for the S&T section to establish another agent training school where communications personnel instructed agents in signal plans and code. Additional assistance was offered through liaison with the Second Air Commando Group, which offered two L-5 light aircraft.[55] This was fortunate as on 10 April, the AFU received word that on 15 April they would take over all V-Force operations in the area.[56] V-Force had been operating in the area since 1942, but never made deep penetrations into enemy territory nor developed much intelligence on Japanese forces.[57]

In April, the AFU extended their informant networks and interrogated locals with knowledge of the Japanese military. The gathered information helped the SI and R&A elements verify the credibility of their intelligence, and helped ensure that the indigenous informants/agents were not fabricators. The Allies removed those found to be black hats and unwilling to help from the operating areas so that they could not inform the Japanese on Allied clandestine methods. In all, during the month the AFU interrogated ninety-seven locals who were each paid anywhere from 5 to 15 rupees for their information. The AFU estimated that some 50 percent of these interrogations resulted in usable intelligence. The OSS paid regular agents on a scale of 2 rupees per day, with bonuses for mission completion or important intelligence supplied. Much as it had done in north Burma, the SO section also worked to supply intelligence. Under Operation ANNE, it set up a network of village headmen in Japanese-occupied areas who helped to recruit agents. These contacts enabled the AFU to uncover more intelligence in eight days than the "British 'V' Force had gotten out of the same area in the course of two months." With this information, the AFU submitted forty-nine intelligence reports as well as daily situation reports to the British.[58]

Running agents became a standard operating procedure for the AFU through early May. For instance, in early April, the SI section had eight operations in the field. Unlike Detachment 101's operations in north Burma, there had been little time to properly train these agents. Because of their limited training, the intelligence they produced was not as strategic or central to the campaign as had been produced by similar agent groups in north Burma. However, the sheer number of teams going behind Japanese lines ensured that some of these teams produced usable information.[59] By late February, however, the Japanese realized the effectiveness of the OSS's agents and instituted a 5,000-rupee reward for any Allied agent turned over to them.[60]

In April, the MO section mirrored Detachment 101 programs from north Burma for use in the Arakan. EVERYBODY'S DOIN' IT was an adaptation of the false surrender order that MO had used with success in the Bhamo-Lashio campaigns. A follow-on campaign called THE WATER'S FINE emphasized that the Allies would treat Japanese prisoners of war well. Other programs aimed at getting Burmese collaborators to stop helping the Japanese.[61] MO placed great importance on the surrender campaigns in part because in an initial survey of the Arakan front in November 1944 an MO representative reported that a "brisk trade is going on in 'surrender leaflets.' Through a middleman, [an] informant purchased his surrender leaflet very secretively and paid about five rupees for it. The nearer one gets to the front, the higher the price." In April, the AFU reported that they had six Japanese soldiers surrender to them.[62]

In late March, both P Division and Mountbatten approved a new program, called the DAH Plan, that called for stenciling a picture of a Dah—a Kachin sword—on Japanese killed and at the sites of destroyed infrastructure and vehicles. The intent was to goad the Japanese into believing that the multiple minorities in Burma had organized against the occupation and finally "found a common basis for cooperation."[63] Still other themes concentrated on the shoddy construction of Japanese war material, reinforced with Project NATTERJACK, a Force 136 scheme to infiltrate tampered-with Japanese ammunition into the enemy logistics system, where it would explode upon use.

Rangoon

The capture of Rangoon was Britain's main goal in Burma. To the OSS, it represented a valuable intelligence target, as well as a possible staging area from which to launch operations into Thailand.[64] To uncover intelligence from the city itself, SO began parachuting agents into the region.[65] The X-2 section trained a group of two radio operators and three agents at Nazira to parachute into Rangoon. There, they would meet up with a group of thirty men to abduct a "top Ranking" Japanese intelligence officer.[66] Dubbed Operation WINEGLASS IV, the mission dropped west of the city on 30 April but was too late because Japanese intelligence personnel had already fled six days prior. Instead, the group went into Rangoon and provided military intelligence to the British Twenty-sixth Division on its approach to the city and to the Royal Air Force (RAF), who used it to bomb Japanese targets ahead of the Allied advance.

Much as they had in Europe, the OSS decided that to fully exploit Rangoon's capture required the formation of a City Team. In this case, the Rangoon City Team would exploit targets for their intelligence value by securing known collaborators, documents, and prisoners from Japanese military, police, and intelligence facilities. The Rangoon City Team would also seek out intelligence in such locations as government buildings, police stations, telegraph offices, newspaper offices, libraries, universities, and banks. Since the function of a city team was intelligence, it required a heavy concentration of X-2, SI, and R&A personnel, with supplemental OSS elements, such as Communications, Field Photo to copy documents, and OGs for security. Although the British knew that the teams were OSS, the AFU made an attempt to keep their purpose a secret, and adopted the cover of a CIT.[67]

The test for the Rangoon City Team came on 3 May 1945 when it rendezvoused 25 miles from the mouth of the Rangoon River out in the Bay of Bengal, to take part in Operation JEAN, or in British parlance, Operation DRACULA; the occupation of Rangoon. The OSS group, a mixed lot of MO, OG, and X-2 personnel, landed in the city proper at 1630 hours, several hours ahead of the British invasion forces—the first Allied troops in Rangoon. Once in Rangoon, which the Japanese had abandoned, the city team spread out and exploited the area for intelligence. The Detachment 303 R&A section assisted in this endeavor by providing area maps marked with the suspected locations of intelligence targets. Ten days later, the AFU headquarters moved into the city.[68]

The Japanese had destroyed most of their documents, but some remained scattered throughout locations they had formerly occupied. In the brief time between the Japanese withdrawal and the Allied invasion, locals had ransacked and looted the former enemy-occupied buildings. The looters inadvertently scattered documents, making them harder to sort and compile. As one of the OSS officers described, "When our men arrived . . . the papers were usually in ragged heaps, amply intermixed with old bandages, toilet articles, discarded Japanese socks and other miscellaneous rubbish." Despite the added difficulty, by 16 May the AFU had scoured the city and collected numerous documents, including military manuals and papers concerning Japanese business and industry. The work remained for the AFU to sort, classify, and microfilm their intelligence take. To assist in the translation of captured enemy documents, Detachment 101 provided two of its Nisei from north Burma, Lieutenant Ralph Yempuku and Sergeant Richard Hamada.[69]

The MO section set up a production office and arranged with local printers to produce a newspaper. The State Department, however, soon announced that the United States considered the Burma campaign over. With little utility seen in keeping MO in operation, the OSS withdrew the contingent, and only one representative remained to conduct operations into occupied southern Burma.[70]

The X-2 section transferred to Rangoon from Kyaukpyu and reinforced their element in early May. In particular, it wanted to learn more about how Japanese intelligence worked in Burma: their operating procedures, agents, and recruiting methods.[71] X-2 uncovered the existence of sleeper agents of the Minami Kikan (Japanese intelligence organized for the Burma National Army), as well as information on the more well-known Kempeitai (Japanese military police, which also had an espionage function). X-2 was able to accomplish its mission even faster than the British intelligence organizations could establish themselves in Rangoon, which did little to help Anglo-American relations. Embarrassed, the British then required an arrangement in which the X-2 section passed primacy to them. Thereafter, X-2 needed to secure permission from the British before they could conduct interrogations. In turn, the British provided the information they had on the Japanese intelligence network. X-2 determined the Japanese intelligence system in Burma was poor and extremely underdeveloped.[72]

The seven-man X-2 section had several intelligence coups. Chief among these was the acquisition of Japanese diplomatic codebooks.[73] X-2 also discreetly maintained contact with the AFL and used the organization to help further intelligence collection. Helfrich considered the AFL "a gold mine if we are courageous enough to dig for the ore." X-2 considered the contacts so worthwhile that it planned to keep a representative in Rangoon.[74] Meanwhile, the X-2 section terminated the WINEGLASS IV operation, after it had provided valuable intelligence on the disposition of Japanese forces fleeing Rangoon.

Within the OSS, reactions to the Rangoon City Team were mixed. The intelligence production of the Rangoon City Team was impressive, and the R&A section alone managed to secure and process 1,750 enemy documents and more than 1,000 Japanese books, and took 10,000 microfilm frames.[75] The area strategic services officer, John G. Coughlin, as well as Peers, thought the unit performed well.[76] However, several Detachment 404 personnel had an unfavorable impression of the group's work.

Detachment 101 transferred the AFU back to Detachment 404 on 5 June, thus ending 101's presence in South Burma. Peer's impressions of the AFU were mixed. While generally pleased with the group, he had the following to say:

> I will have to admit that from the day I took over 101 AFU . . . it was somewhat of a bugaboo, but I do believe that in the latter phases their work was good. From an operational and intelligence point of view, they were producing good intelligence. . . . From an administrative point of view, it was somewhat fouled up to the very end . . . simply caused by every detachment in the IBT either assigning or attaching personnel to 101 AFU at will . . . this, coupled with the distance between Akyab and Nazira, created a very bad administrative set-up.[77]

Regardless, the results of the individual OSS sections in the AFU were impressive. For instance, from December 1944 to June 1945, the R&A section managed to produce 360 reports totaling 783 pages, while at the same time providing 1,910 map sets for use in the field.[78] More importantly, however, the individual sections functioned very closely and relatively cohesively. Most notable of this was the coordination between the OG and MU personnel. These two groups, while having different specialties, were nearly seamless in their joint operations. The AFU also had the flexibility to adapt to the local situation and to take missions as they came along. The British recognized this, leading the OSS to report that they "do not hesitate to say that the results obtained by the AFU surpass by far those of V Force, the work of whom has been absorbed by our unit."[79]

However, there were faults with the AFU, many of which stemmed from Detachment 404's prior poor management of the MO and MU sections. Detachment 404 sent the MU to Burma to perform a job for which it came unprepared. Its necessary operational equipment had not arrived, and what it had was inadequate. But MU adapted and performed exceptionally. As it was, MU representatives made it to Rangoon to look for a base from which they could conduct operations further south. This was as far as the section got. On 15 June the OSS ordered the MU section in the Far East to disband, grossly mismanaging what could have been one of the most useful OSS elements in the Far East.[80]

More importantly, however, the AFU represented Detachment 101's organizational flexibility. At the time Detachment 101's main focus was supporting NCAC, in which it was undertaking the new role of switching from guerrilla warfare to more conventional operations. It was also less than six months away from total disbandment. The Arakan mission was nearly out of the Detachment's operational range, and far away from its main bases. Yet, the Detachment was able to undertake this new mission in a detached area, while at the same time coordinating with the numerous OSS branches and commands involved. It was also able to establish an entirely different type of organization, a city team, with which it had no experience. That Detachment 101 had the flexibility to juggle concurrent but dissimilar missions at the same time as it was preparing to disband is a testament to the unit's ability to fill roles that other units could not.

13

The Last Months: April–July 1945

The contribution which the Kachin Rangers . . . have made in defeating the Japanese and driving them out of Northern Burma has been out of proportion to their relatively small numbers. Their skill in jungle fighting, in the use of modern weapons of war, their knowledge of the terrain and their fearlessness and desire to drive the invader from their homes has made their service of great assistance to the Allies, the Americans, the British and the Chinese. Without their friendly cooperation, the successful completion of the North Burma Campaign would have been delayed and at a much greater cost to the Allies in men and material. This guerrilla army has every right to be proud.

Lieutenant General Daniel I. Sultan

By April, the war in Burma was going very well for the Allies. Lashio fell to the Chinese in March, as had Mandalay and Meiktila to the British. British forces in the Arakan and central Burma were making a two-pronged drive for Rangoon. NCAC had reached the end of its operational area, and no longer had to cover the British Fourteenth Army's rear. Beginning in March and completed in May, NCAC withdrew the entire MARS Task Force and sent it to China. NCAC's British units reverted to Fourteenth Army control, and Kunming recalled its forces to serve as elite units in the National Chinese Army. This left the OSS as the only ground combat unit, U.S. or otherwise, operating with NCAC.

At the time, Peers planned to move Detachment 101 as an entity to China to serve in the Chekiang area. However, that was not to be because theater-level command had other ideas. Admiral Mountbatten, the SEAC commander, wanted a guerrilla force to remain in Burma to free up the remaining Chinese forces, but also to "maintain guard . . . keeping one zero one

[Detachment 101] or similar unit on such mission would be great economy of force."[1] In turn, General Sultan feared that at least 10,000 Japanese troops could retreat to Thailand and regroup. He wanted Detachment 101 to protect the Stilwell Road by clearing the Shan States.[2] In April Colonel John G. Coughlin, the India-Burma Theater strategic services officer, reported the situation to Donovan.

> I showed your cable to General Sultan and asked him when he thought 101 could go to China. The cable immediately put the General on the defensive. He read the cable, went to the map and showed me what 101 was doing, returned to his desk and read the cable again; went back to the map, returned and read the cable once more. He then explained that he was required to clear the Japs out of the area down as far as the Taunggyi-Loilem-Kengtung road, and 101 was the only unit he had to do it with. He admitted having several Chinese regiments, but stated his orders from the Generalissimo did not permit him to move them south of the area they were in at present.[3]

Detachment 101 would stay in Burma. It was here that Detachment 101 transitioned into its fourth phase of operations by performing more like a quasi-conventional force. Intelligence collection became even less important to Detachment 101 as the unit's new mission was, in Peers's words, to "kill and capture as many Japs as possible."[4] Detachment 101 parachuted in several long-range elements and had numerous agent groups, but they became less valuable as the need for their intelligence ceased or as Allied movements bypassed them.

As Detachment 101 had previously demonstrated, it was highly adaptable. However, its last assignment was costly. The group suffered more casualties, comparatively, during these final months than at any other time of the war. Indeed, as one veteran noted, "With less experienced leaders or without the intimate knowledge of the Burma-style campaign gained through three years of similar operations, the hazards of such an undertaking might have been disastrous."[5]

Field Operations

Sultan's directive placed Detachment 101 in an awkward position; the field units had already told their Kachin troops that they would be disbanding.

Still, Peers had no choice. He allowed the disbanding of all but two battalions (the Tenth under Robert Delaney and First under Major Dow Grones). In the other battalions, those guerrillas who wanted to were allowed to go home. If soldiers volunteered to stay, they would be placed into two new battalions consolidated from the remnants (Second under Lieutenant Colonel Newell Brown and the Third under Major Red Maddox). Locally recruited soldiers, including Burmese and Shan soldiers, then filled in the new units. This led to the most ethnically diverse guerrilla formations ever fielded by the unit.

These troops also faced a new mission for the OSS guerrillas. Instead of providing support to more conventional combat operations, whether they be conducted by American, British, or Chinese formations, the guerrillas were now taking that role upon themselves. Although the guerrillas had the support of the USAAF, they also had to act more as infantry than at any other point in the war. Still it was a challenge to get the guerrillas to act in this manner because they had to change their fighting methods.

No longer would the guerrillas be operating far into Japanese-held territory against mainly support troops. Now, they faced combat veterans from tested infantry units. The guerrillas would also not have the heavy firepower possessed by the Allied units that they had formerly supported. The guerrillas had to remain lightly armed due to their methods of transport and resupply. Moreover, each battalion faced a different set of circumstances and level of enemy oppositions. Therefore, they would have to individually develop their tactics and techniques with no direction from headquarters other than in general orders. The Tenth Battalion probably had the least change as their mission was primarily that of guerrilla warfare. In contrast, the Third Battalion faced the greatest pressure as a quasi-infantry force.

By April 1945, Detachment 101 took the central role in NCAC. It was General Sultan's sole combat force, meaning Detachment 101's remaining four battalions had responsibility for an area of some 20,000 square miles while manning the outpost line of liberated Burma.[6] However, since by then Detachment 101's groups had moved even further south, in a welcome move, they began to recruit Karens. Many of them had prewar military training under the British. By then, the guerrilla groups had a tremendous number of ethnicities and nationalities present, including Kachin, Shan, Karen, Chinese, Burman, Indian, U.S., and British, led by U.S., U.K., Kachin, and Burmese commanders. Internally, the groups were relatively harmonious, even if certain ethnicities kept apart. Despite new recruiting, the last months were marked with continual reorganization and disbanding of guerrilla units as the soldiers, especially Kachins, wanted to end their contracts and go home. Given the increasing combat mission and the need to rely on veteran soldiers, having the Kachins go home could not have occurred at a worse time.

Another problem was the local population. Some ethnicities, including the Kachin, had a score to settle among the local population. This rose to the level of General Slim, the British Fourteenth Army commander. He wrote to Sultan, complaining of "cases of FORCE 101 summarily executing civilian British subjects far behind the lines."[7] Reports came to Slim that relayed "The people in the area said they would prefer the Japanese to return rather than suffer from 101 MISSION."[8]

For their part, the men of Detachment 101 refuted the accusations, calling them "absolutely unfounded," adding "Our soldiers have been instructed at all times to deal fairly with the locals—our success and our lives depended upon swaying the locals to our side."[9] No doubt some instances were genuine, but most were likely cases of Detachment 101 personnel summarily executing Japanese agents. Enemy agents were numerous in the area, which had largely sided with the Japanese. Some of the groups also reported killing locals that had previously turned over Allied personnel to the Japanese, such as one of the groups supporting the British Thirty-sixth Division that found locals who had turned in Wingate's Chindits to the Japanese. The guerrillas "convicted and killed every headman . . . except one."[10] As Roger Hilsman later wrote, "It was the understanding among OSS guerrilla leaders that the senior Allied command in any particular district had the authority to hold a general court and that they, the guerrilla leaders, were by definition the senior Allied commanders."[11] Hilsmen contends that with this understanding, the guerrilla leaders took it upon themselves to order any executions that they might find necessary when they uncovered local Japanese agents.

In May, the Detachment 101 guerrilla groups received the final operational directive from General Sultan. Instead of monitoring the outpost line, now the guerrillas were to clear Japanese-occupied Burma north of the Taunggyi-Kengtung Road and east to Kyusawk. This put them about 50 miles in front of the remaining Chinese units, with other elements as far as 150 miles into occupied territory.[12] In this area resided the remnants of two Japanese divisions, the Eighteenth and the Fifty-sixth, possessing artillery and tanks.

Although the guerrilla units still used their prior tactics, Detachment 101's role in north Burma now made the final transition to the fourth phase. When the increasingly desperate Japanese held, the guerrilla units attacked them head on, while also slipping past them to attack enemy lines of communication. The clashes could be quite fierce, and Detachment 101 racked up a larger number of kills than at any point prior. For instance, in March and April combined, Detachment 101 reported having killed 447 enemy soldiers. At 865, the tally for May 1945 was almost double of the prior two months.

An example of one of Detachment 101's devastating attacks occurred on 17 May. Peers reported that one ambush "consisted of a hundred yards of prima cord stretched along a trail and camouflaged, and with a grenade every three yards. A party of Japs came up the trail in column . . . when they were opposite the booby trap it was set off electronically and at the same time fire was put on the advance guard and the rear guard. Total destruction amounted to eight-five Japs and eleven horses killed. There was no return fire."[13]

The man responsible for the attack was Captain Roger Hilsman Jr., a former member of Merrill's Marauders. He reported that previously his group had blown a bridge nearby the ambush site, then set up the grenades, using a flashlight and its batteries as the trigger mechanism. Unable to cross the destroyed bridge, the Japanese force had to ford the stream and did not expect an attack so close. They marched along the road with fifty soldiers in front of the main body and another fifty in the rear, with the main body walking in columns, two abreast. The guerrillas allowed the advance party though, and a "scout dog in advance of the Japs ran into the first platoon position right up to the lad holding the flashlight. The lad petted the dog and it turned around and went back to the Japs without barking once." Hilsman continued, "Oddly enough [the Japanese] walked along the ditch to the right of the road, their elbows almost brushing the grenades strung out along the bank." Hilsman reported that upon firing the charges, the "middle section did not fire a shot as the grenades wiped out the whole center section of the Jap column."[14] In contrast to Peers's report, the toll for the 17 May ambush was 104 Japanese killed.[15]

Attacks like that drew a response of Japanese forces in excess of 500 men on numerous occasions. These desperate attacks helped raise the number of Detachment 101 members killed in May to 44, as compared to 12 for March and April combined.[16] Occasionally, the battalions uncovered surprises. Such was the case of the Second Battalion, which in late May found numerous Japanese storage depots. One of these had medical supplies of such quantity and quality that they supplied a good deal of 101's need for the rest of the North Burma Campaign.[17]

Although it was clear that the Japanese had nearly lost Burma, even at this late stage some of the locals remained pro-Japanese. In the very least, some, including guerrillas employed by Detachment 101, were unwilling to risk themselves. An example of the lack of commitment to the Allied cause occurred on 5 May when a thirty-man group of Detachment 101's Shan guerrillas lay in wait to ambush a Japanese force of several hundred soldiers. When the Japanese approached the ambush site, "all the Shans, as if prearranged, began coughing so no Japs were trapped." The next morning several of the Shans deserted.[18]

Even so, the fighting remained bitter as the guerrillas boxed the Japanese into a corner. The latter on occasion took out their frustrations on the civilian population. The Second Battalion reported such an instance in mid-May near Loilem. Guerrilla scouts near a Japanese encampment heard laughing and "screams of terrified women. The screaming scared the Shans so much. They took off forcing the two Americans and one Karen jemidar [a native rank] to withdraw to a pre-arranged rendezvous." The guerrillas later found "the cause of the screams—two raped women's bodies shot through the head, the baby of one of the women with its face smashed in and the body of a man."[19] Such a case highlights the no-win situation in which some of the civilians found themselves. An earlier example is recounted in October, when a Detachment 101 group reported that the Japanese killed any Shan who refused to tell where the Americans were, while Detachment 101 patrols later killed those that did.[20]

Part of the bitterness had to do with the "intelligence" war as both the Japanese and the Allies had numerous undercover agents in the area. It was the mission of the Detachment 101 guerrillas to reveal the enemy spies. Although numerous cases occurred right up until the end of the war, an instance in late March gives insight into Detachment 101's difficult counterintelligence mission. Detachment 101's agent Jacko uncovered a man with recent tattoos who passed himself off as a Palaung. He spoke good Palaung, but his traditional tattoos looked recent. When stripped, the "Palaung" wore Japanese underwear. While interrogating him in Palaung, Jacko asked him his name in Japanese. Giving himself an on-the-spot death sentence, the man replied, and thereafter spoke Japanese up until the moment he was killed.[21]

By the last week of May, all but four of the intelligence groups ahead of the guerrilla battalions had been bypassed or absorbed into the battalions themselves. Once absorbed, although the agent groups still produced intelligence, they did so under the direction of the battalion commanders.[22] In addition, the battalions absorbed any of the remaining independent guerrilla companies.[23]

Operations until the end of the war in north Burma in June became even more of a conventional nature, including a combined ground-air offensive. The Second Battalion received orders to clear the Japanese from Loilem. Although patrols found Loilem largely unoccupied, the Japanese had taken up defensive positions to the southeast of the town. There the Japanese had dugouts, many armed with machine guns, which were 6 feet deep and covered with 2-foot-thick logs. This forced the guerrillas to act much like a conventional infantry force and root them out. "Kachin troops sparked the drive which saw raw native guerilla troops push a well-armed force of 300 Japanese soldiers out of well-dug in, log reinforced positions both in the town and the surrounding hills. Aggressive patrols and assaults cleared hill after hill," reported a Detachment 101 officer.

When the Japanese defenses proved too strong for the Second Battalion's mortars and bazookas to crack, the OSS commanders called in air support. The Detachment's own Red Ass Squadron marked the enemy positions by dropping smoke grenades right on top of the bunkers. Then, P-38 Lightning fighter-bombers, based just twenty minutes away in Lai Hka "bombed, and straffed [*sic*] the dug-in Japs out of their holes."[24] Although the Second Battalion succeeded in clearing the Japanese, it lost two Americans and at least six guerrillas killed. This was the highest number of Detachment 101 personnel killed in combat during a single mission.

Operations slowed through June.[25] Detachment 101's guerrillas last had contact with the Japanese on 25 June 1945. All told, in its final phase, Detachment 101 killed 1,246 of the enemy and captured 10. The number of enemy killed was nearly a fourth of that attributed to Detachment 101 for the entire war.[26] The Detachment 101 groups also destroyed or captured an estimated 300 tons of enemy supplies, while furnishing NCAC with 99 percent of its intelligence and aerial targets.[27]

In late June, the Allied commanders decided to cease Detachment 101's field operations on 1 July.[28] Peers arranged with the British Civil Affairs Service (CAS) that they could recruit a police force from the recently charged Detachment 101 guerrillas. Accordingly, on 26 June, CAS officers went to Lawksawk, Lai Hka, and Loilem to take over administration of the area from Detachment 101. It came at the right time. Peers considered that the demands of continued field operations had so stressed his men that "many, even of the stauncher type, are broken mentally as well as physically," and suffered "repeated attacks of dysentery and diarrhea."[29] However, only by having a rear support structure could Detachment 101 function as well as it did in its last few months of operations on two fronts.

The Detachment

Despite its new combat role and the impending defeat of the Japanese in Burma, Detachment 101 still went to great effort to enhance its organization. At no other point in the war did Detachment 101 better demonstrate its inherent flexibility. It undertook numerous and disparate missions while simultaneously preparing for its own deactivation.

Although operations were winding down, it did not mean that Detachment 101's force structure and sections remained static. This included the elimination of an entire section. Peers came to believe that "it is very difficult to draw a line between which is OG and is SO, and anything reported by either of the individual branches is purely eye-wash," and felt that a separate OG section resulted in an unnecessary duplication in communications, supply, administration, and other entities such as medical.[30] In an effort to resolve this problem, in April he transferred OG personnel into the SO section.

To no surprise, Detachment 101's air elements continued to be of great importance. Although operations had slowed since the previous month, in April the Red Ass Squadron flew 655 hours, evacuated 24 wounded, and carried 368 passengers and 22,910 pounds of cargo. Three planes even flew a mission 86 miles into hostile territory—the farthest the squadron had yet penetrated—to bring back three Japanese prisoners. It was but one special use of Detachment's liaison aircraft. The pilots also had their own ideas.

Captain Hugh R. Conklin described his experiences flying as a passenger with the Red Ass Squadron. Reardon, the squadron commander, asked him if he wanted to fly over a Japanese unit that was opposing one of Detachment 101's field groups. Reardon also asked Conklin if he "minded" shooting at the Japanese, to which he responded, "That's what I am paid for." Conklin then described the airplane that he boarded:

> Under the right wing, he [the pilot] had mounted a machine gun [M-3 "Greasegun"] controlled by a lanyard that he gave me to hold. Under the left wing he had a rack which held a few bazooka shells also controlled by a lanyard which I held. At my feet I had a box of hand grenades, and on my lap a box of incendiary grenades. He said that if the Japs had built bashas they would make great fires. He would signal me with his right or left hand when to turn on the machine gun or drop bazooka shells, and that the bombing and strafing run would be first, then I should drop grenades whenever I thought I had a target. . . . We made a successful bombing and strafing run during which I also unloaded a lot of grenades.

> It was particularly satisfying to see some of the incendiary grenades make bulls eyes on the bashas.[31]

The squadron had an additional problem when seventeen new pilots arrived, yet including those under repair, had only fifteen aircraft available.[32] Operations in May declined significantly. The Red Ass Squadron flew 464 hours, evacuated 39 casualties, and carried 177 personnel, but just 8,645 pounds of cargo.[33] This included a strenuous period from 8 to 10 May when a Detachment 101 unit came under a sustained Japanese assault. The Red Ass Squadron reacted quickly and evacuated twenty-five casualties from a makeshift airfield even as it was under attack. In June, the squadron moved from Lashio to an airfield at Lai Hka, where its aircraft were used by battalion commanders to coordinate operations of their far-flung companies, to conduct reconnaissance on Japanese positions, and to mark enemy positions for air strikes. This enabled even closer support to the field units because the aircraft were now only a half hour's flight away. Indicative of its high level of efficiency is the following report; "an enlisted man was shot at 1020 . . . through the rapid and well coordinated evacuation system . . . the soldier was evacuated and met at Bhamo airstrip at 1700 hours . . . about 300 air miles from the site of his injury."[34]

Likewise, in April, the Air Drop section operated at a reduced level with only seven C-47s allotted. The seven-hour round trip to the dropping zones from the main airfield at Dinjan meant that many could only fly one sortie per day. Still, the section dropped 1,196,447 pounds of supplies and parachuted twenty-nine personnel into the field, requiring 229 C-47 sorties and 13 B-25 special missions flown out of the newly finished all-weather airfield at Bhamo. The section recorded its first losses since January 1944 when two C-47s crashed separately with the loss of four OSS personnel.[35] By May, air drop operations were noticeably winding down, and the section dropped only 837,487 pounds of supplies, requiring 183 C-47 sorties and 5 B-25s that parachuted six personnel into the field.[36] In June–July, the section dropped only 841,963 pounds, some of which was clothing, food, and supplies to thank villagers for their assistance. On their return, the drop aircraft stopped at collection points and picked up equipment and arms to bring back for turn-in.[37]

Communications experienced a minor reorganization when the Bhamo section took over communications duties from Area #2 when it disbanded. Area #2's disbanding produced a surplus of radios that, once reconditioned and redistributed, eliminated any shortages. The laying of a cable from Lashio to Bhamo also saved time by allowing the secure sending of unencoded messages. This was fortunate as the section also began to handle communications from the AFU, resulting in a combined daily total of some 175 messages and 11,000 groups.[38] May's total showed the same general level, with 5,388 messages composed of 326,894 groups. The general pace, however, decreased as stations closed and liaison officers returned.[39] The totals for June and July combined reflected the reduction in traffic; 328,566 groups for a total of 6,309 messages.[40] Although the section had adequate radios and receivers, they still worked to develop new and smaller equipment.[41] Other sections, such as MO, also focused their efforts in the tactical situation.

As the Detachment moved into the Shan States, MO managed to distribute 30,730 copies of some twenty-one different leaflets. Many of these exploited low Japanese morale and revolved around surrender themes. MO reasoned that while they could not prove the link, the section's black propaganda efforts may have influenced surrenders. In particular, a group of Japanese soldiers who surrendered had in their hand the MO-produced modification to the no-surrender order. The section reported that one Japanese soldier urgently "sought to bring out that he came within the provisions" of the no-surrender order and "was therefore entitled to the good treatment promised in the leaflet." Because of this possible success, the MO section decided that its best course was to refine the surrender leaflets.[42]

Although the Detachment's function was now more of supporting tactical combat operations rather than strategic intelligence, there remained some successes. During the last month of operations, the long-range agent teams scored a success when a Shan official who had his own police force gave the Detachment 101 team Japanese-furnished passes that allowed the agents to move about in enemy territory.[43] With the war winding down in the NCAC area, the R&A section turned its analytical attention to the Arakan, and in particular, Rangoon. Still, reports came at a hurried pace from the groups under NCAC; 515 reports in total came into the R&A section during April, and the initial interrogations of Japanese prisoners of war and Burmese collaborators kept the interrogators and translators busy. The section also revamped its presentation of reports. Instead of the weekly intelligence summary, on 18 April the section substituted a daily edition. Additionally, the section reorganized by cross-referencing its files to more speedily access numerous analytical subjects.[44] Peers commented to Donovan on Detachment 101's unique arrangement regarding intelligence collection and dissemination.

> The lack of intelligence personnel . . . has resulted in a change from the OSS conception of collection and dissemination of information. . . . SO

> has been and is responsible for the collection of all information, guided in part by requests from one of the dissemination agencies. . . . Previously, with one intelligence officer [Chester R. Chartrand of the SI section], we were able to disseminate all of our tactical information. . . . As a result the R&A section has been developed to handle the dissemination of all information, regardless of type. Therefore, the situation stands, SO collects, R&A disseminates. We would never have had the means to accomplish our intelligence mission if this procedure had not been adopted.[45]

These comments reflect upon the very beginning of Detachment 101, when a lack of personnel forced the unit to use whomever it had to fill those new roles that came along. The OSS did not create Detachment 101 to gather intelligence, but it evolved into a core area that to its end users was perhaps the most useful.

The X-2 section expanded its CITs throughout Lashio and the surrounding region, but recognized that their mission was coming to an end. Contacts with the AFL continued. Coinciding with a leaflet drop to mask the purpose for the presence of a plane, X-2 parachuted the BARK team into Pyinmana on 30 March.[46] BARK, made up of AFL members, supplied tactical information on Japanese forces and movements that X-2 liaison officer Stuart Power then gave to the British Fourteenth Army. X-2 also planned to infiltrate personnel and agents into the Arakan region to kidnap selected enemy personnel and to be of use during and after the securing of Rangoon. CIT teams continued to have success, and in the Katha area alone arrested 152 black hats, of whom Burma government authorities convicted thirty-seven.[47] On 25 May, however, the CIT program was considered complete, and the teams disbanded. Many of the X-2 personnel transferred from north Burma to the Arakan. There, the section organized into two small groups. One section joined the amphibious assault on Rangoon, while the other joined the British Fourteenth Army in the event that element first reached the city.[48]

Detachment 101 Disbands

July 1945 was officially the last month that Detachment 101 was active, but the process of disbanding began in May. By then it had become readily apparent that Nazira was too far away from the action and that the unit no longer needed to train additional agents for operations. The Detachment started to shut down its rear base. The first sections to close, such as MO, R&D, the school, the pigeon section, and the hospital, were those that had little effect on tactical combat operations. Detachment 101 took advantage of the fact that the U.S. Army Services of Supply (SOS) in India had numerous vehicles that it needed to get to China, but no drivers. As a result, SOS turned vehicles over to units that needed to transport personnel and equipment, so long as the vehicles ended up in an army depot in China. The MO section packed up its facilities first and departed for China in the first of four Detachment 101 convoys to travel the Stilwell Road from May to July. The remaining personnel and sections from Nazira not sent to China transferred to quarters near Dinjan. There, sections still needed to support operations, such as a skeleton medical element, continued working.[49]

After Nazira, the next bases to close were Detachment 101 BA and Detachment 101 AFU. Both closed on 6 June and transferred their assets to Detachment 404. Then, the field units disbanded. Locally recruited Shans were discharged on the spot, while other guerrillas were flown to Bhamo, Lashio, and Myitkyina for discharge. The First, Second, Third, and Tenth Battalions were all disbanded by 6 July and paid the guerrillas each a month's salary.[50] Peers wrote to the new IB commander, Lieutenant General Raymond A. Wheeler, who succeeded Sultan on 23 June:

> All of our people rather hated to cease operations at this time, because they felt that in a very short time they could have completed the assigned mission of securing the entire Taunggyi-Loilem-Kunhing road. As it finally ended up, we secured the greater part of it, but did not have control of the city of Taunggyi or the road junction at Hopong, although we had mined the road on all sides at these points. . . . In the closing of operations and the break-down of Detachment 101, we can only add that we have enjoyed our assignment in this Theater. Your predecessors, General Stilwell and Lt. Gen Sultan, have always issued clear-cut mission orders, leaving planning, direction and operation entirely to this unit. With this we have been able to fully employ the imagination and ingenuity of every officer and enlisted man in this entire organization. This task has always been one in which there was a definite feeling of accomplishment, and one in which everybody was eager to devote his full time and energy. It has been most interesting and enjoyable.[51]

The last Detachment 101 field radio station went off the air on 7 July, and thereafter Force 136 accepted responsibility for the remaining agents. Only

Detachment 101's headquarters at Dinjan remained. This was soon turned over to Detachment 206, a supply organization for Detachment 202. Detachment 101 officially closed on 12 July 1945. All that remained were mostly administrative functions, such as the Finance section and legal representatives, who ensured the unit finalized its debts and obligations to its indigenous personnel. This included making final restitution to the families of thirty-eight missing or deceased indigenous agents.[52]

The medical section gave returning field personnel examinations for fatigue, disease, and parasites before sending them to their new assignments. Thirty percent of Detachment 101's personnel had enough time in Burma or a medical reason to return to the United States, while others went to other OSS organizations in the Far East. SO and OG personnel went to Detachment 202. There, they formed the nucleus of several SO teams, such as BABOON 2, GNU, and COW. Several former 101ers also served in the postwar Mercy Mission teams that parachuted at the end of the war into Japanese-held POW camps in China to prevent any harming of Allied prisoners. The eleven teams operated at great peril since many Japanese commands were unaware that the war was over, and they arranged for food, medical care, and the evacuation of the POWs. Many of the Detachment 101 Nisei served as translators on these teams, including for teams CANARY, MAGPIE, and PIGEON. Other former Detachment 101 personnel served on teams ALBATROSS, CARDINAL, DUCK, and RAVEN. In all, 50 percent of Detachment 101's former personnel went to China. The remaining 20 percent of Detachment 101's former personnel went to Detachment 404, where they were involved in operations in Thailand and postwar intelligence missions in the SEAC AOR.[53]

Despite the war in north Burma being almost over by mid-1945, Detachment 101 once again reinvented itself by undertaking the role of conventional warfare. The role did not suit the clandestine organization, yet it still worked. According to one of the battalion commanders, Detachment 101 succeeded only because the Japanese by then were beaten and had poor morale: "If the Japanese in this area had been the same Japs we fought in Northern Burma our force would not have lasted for two days."[54] Yet, it was also the cohesiveness of the Detachment's various sections that allowed for success. Without effective Communications, Air Drop, or liaison aircraft sections, the Detachment never could have completed the mission change.

As it was, the Japanese could still be quite determined and in many cases were better armed than the OSS units were and backed with artillery. This caused the Detachment to suffer during this period its highest casualty rate of the war. In May and June alone, among its indigenous troops, Detachment

101 suffered forty-four killed, thirty-four wounded, nine missing, and twenty captured. The toll was also hard on the American personnel—considering the previous light casualties—with five killed and three wounded in June and the beginning of July. The damage inflicted on the enemy was far greater. From May to June, Detachment 101 units were responsible for killing 1,246 Japanese troops, and they liberated 13,600 square miles of territory.[55] A unit in the process of tearing its own structure and capabilities apart achieved these exceptional accomplishments. It is a reflection of Detachment 101's inherent flexibility that it could adopt a new operational role, that of conducting heavy combat operations, and a new mission in the Arakan, while simultaneously disbanding. Coughlin, the area strategic services officer, wrote to Peers, saying:

> The manner in which you handled Detachment 101 in the closing days, assembling your personnel, discharging and making final arrangements with hundreds of native operators, and at the same time maintaining operation until the last minute, disposing of all the Detachment property, assembling and packing all the records, writing letters of appreciation and goodbye to all the Commanders with whom you have been associated, arranging for the decoration of your deserving personnel, and finally, assigning all your personnel to their various new assignments, was in keeping with the manner in which you have always run that remarkable Detachment.[56]

As a final statement, Donovan received the message, "Ray wanted me to tell you that breaking up 101 broke his heart."[57]

Conclusion

About 99 percent of it is nothing more than downright hard work and common sense. The remaining 1 percent may have little intrigue in it, but that depends upon one's point of view. In Detachment 101 we always tried to do things in the simplest and uncomplicated manner, and it paid off with high dividends.

William R. Peers

Activated in mid-1942 and in operation until July 1945, Detachment 101 had one of the longest periods of service of any OSS group. It was consistently able to change its operational focus and adopt new missions to fulfill Donovan's vision of a clandestine unit that could assist conventional forces. The initial contingent of twenty-one men that arrived in the China-Burma-India Theater in June 1942 bore little resemblance to the group that grew to almost 1,000 OSS personnel and 10,000 indigenous troops in the India-Burma Theater by July 1945. That the group transitioned from a small sabotage-oriented group to a major combat formation in a little over three years is a tribute to the Detachment 101's adaptability. There are several reasons why Detachment 101 achieved success.

First, the lack of oversight over Detachment 101 gave it a flexibility that allowed it to constantly alter its force as the situation and success dictated. Colonel Carl F. Eifler, Detachment 101's first commanding officer, wanted to use sabotage operations against the Japanese forces. His long-range penetration operations, while having the potential of being strategically significant, were beyond Detachment's limited abilities in 1943. Instead, it was the shallow penetrations, such as the FORWARD and KNOTHEAD missions, that allowed Detachment 101 to fill roles that other units could not. Supplying intelligence became one of Detachment 101's core missions and greatly improved its utility to other organizations. Detachment 101 was the "eyes and ears" of NCAC.

When he assumed command from Eifler in December 1943, Lieutenant Colonel William R. Peers took a more pragmatic approach. He reinforced missions like FORWARD and KNOTHEAD while encouraging them to develop a guerrilla capacity. His command style became evident during the Myitkyina campaign when Detachment 101 greatly assisted the Allied effort far beyond what their relative lack of numbers would suggest. When the Allies kicked off the Myitkyina offensive, Detachment 101 supported NCAC's specific intelligence needs and became an effective guerrilla force that devastated the Japanese in their rear areas. Starting at the end of the Myitkyina campaign, guerrilla warfare became Detachment 101's main role in Burma until the end of the war. By this time, Detachment 101 was flexible enough to support two separate campaigns—in the Shan States and in the Arakan—while simultaneously arranging for its own disbandment.

The second factor contributing to the success of Detachment 101 was the freedom to change its command structure to meet evolving mission roles and duties. Much of this ability was due to the lack of direction from higher authorities. At first, this was a severe detriment and caused great confusion and helplessness in 1942 as the unit searched for a mission. Detachment 101, then under the COI, was the first unit of its type under the umbrella of an organization that was likewise the first of its type. It was a pioneering element with no previous example to follow. Moreover, Detachment 101 did not interest OSS Washington enough to warrant the latter's attention. Even though Burma represented one of the first operational theaters for his civilian organization, this practice can be laid on COI/OSS director William J. Donovan, a poor administrator who was far more focused on the war against Germany than the one in Burma.

Once Detachment 101 established its role in the Burma Campaign, the lack of oversight became a hidden strength. With no one looking over the Detachment, its commanders could determine for themselves how to best formulate its organization and operational methods, and they adopted hard-learned lessons more quickly. On the U.S. Army side, General Stilwell's NCAC Headquarters was interested only in results, not in how Detachment 101 achieved them.

Under Peers's direction, Detachment 101 became a proactive, effective, and reliable organization. He reorganized the unit, strengthened critical but undermanned sections, and incorporated new OSS assets. He created an Operations section to effectively coordinate its guerrilla elements and established a central intelligence staff to evaluate, analyze, and disseminate intelligence collection. These changes allowed Peers to focus his attention less on running the Detachment and more on developing it into a larger asset for the

North Burma Campaign. Under Peers's direction, the unit developed a strategic focus by incorporating OSS elements, such as psychological warfare, that did not provide immediate operational returns. Operations were no longer the sole force driving administrative change.

As part of this, Detachment 101 ignored OSS branch distinctions, making it unconventional even within the OSS. This lack of compartmentalization enabled Detachment 101 to better absorb disparate functions into its operations, reinforce those that worked, and ignore those that did not. At first the unit did not plan to follow this model. In 1942 and 1943, Eifler's ambition surpassed his resources. Although all of his men were from the Special Operations Branch, the group had the beginnings of the Communications, Special Funds, and Schools and Training sections.

Increased operational duties, however, again meant that the Detachment had to virtually ignore OSS branch distinctions and assign personnel in an ad hoc fashion to where they were most needed. This allowed the unit to better integrate its separate elements into one operational focus in a coordinated fashion. This was not a preplanned process, as Detachment 101 could make do with only what was available, especially if OSS Washington ignored pleas for personnel.

This was especially true of staffing OSS-specific branches, several of which arrived too late or without enough support to contribute much to the Detachment's operations. Organizationally, all elements that made up Detachment 101's force structure were in place by March 1945. But the lack of attention from OSS Washington remained apparent. New arrivals, such as the OG, did not have a mission unique enough to merit the effort of trying to accommodate their particular specialty as a distinct entity. Other mission-specific sections that arrived late, such as R&D and X-2, assisted only tangentially. One X-2 member put it more succinctly, calling his section "ornaments on a tree not producing much light . . . insofar as original intelligence X-2 would get a D or an F."[1] Only an element able to integrate its efforts into operations, such as MO, had the potential to grow into a main part of Detachment 101. As the OSS later summed up:

> At Detachment 101 representatives of all branches carried on specific projects, but as is usually found under field conditions, results could only be obtained by merging plans, facilities, and personnel for actual operations. Consequently, although originally 101 was composed entirely of SO personnel, much of the credit for its spectacular success must go to R&A, Communications, Services, and in its later days to MO members of

> the Detachment, not omitting the indispensable contributions made by the Kachin tribesmen recruited and trained on the spot.[2]

Third, by concentrating on the unglamorous mission of building liaison with other organizations, Detachment 101 became far more influential and effective than would have been the case for another force of similar size. Like Eifler before him, Peers encouraged liaison with other units. For instance, in the Myitkyina campaign, Detachment 101 was the only element keeping the American and British forces in communication. Peers later reported to Donovan the advantages of Detachment 101's liaison arrangements: "It is believed that one of the outstanding reasons for the assistance and cooperation rendered this Detachment has been through . . . liaison."[3] Detachment 101 also used its capabilities to achieve liaison in other ways. By adopting the role of helping downed Allied pilots and providing the USAAF with target data, Detachment 101 achieved extraordinary cooperation as it secured scarce airlift that enabled it to expand its forces and area of operations. Detachment 101 became so important to the USAAF that by the end of 1944 it boasted that the unit "has rescued so many pilots from the jungle that the total 'dollar value' of such pilots . . . exceed[s] the cost of all Detachment 101 operations."[4]

Fourth and most important, Detachment 101 benefited from the tremendous assistance offered by the indigenous peoples of Burma, particularly the Kachin. Without their indispensable help, the unit could not have acquired its intelligence or carried out guerrilla warfare. In so doing, the Detachment became a model in the postwar period for clandestine operations using indigenous personnel.

The Detachment's success did not come easily or without mistakes. The intense operational focus led the group to underdevelop—or even ignore—important areas, such as administration. One of the Detachment's ranking officers put it succinctly: "A unit of the size and scope of Det. 101 requires a staff . . . willing to devote their time to prosaic, dull administrative duties to further the success of the 'glamorous' field operator, to relieve the Commanding Officer of meddlers and irrelevant minor problems, and to be actively interested in the welfare of the unit as a whole."[5] The lack of administrative personnel produced some negative results, and at times Detachment 101's personnel suffered from low morale because its lack of a staff to submit reports caused soldiers not to receive awards or promotions. As one officer noted, "Many of those righteously, justifiably, and deservedly, have not received recognition because of this deficiency. The theory that units operating in the field do not require a full staff is entirely irroneous [*sic*]."[6]

Though aware of the problem, Peers could do little because of the lack of attention from OSS Washington. He commented, "For a unit to function effectively it must have competent administrative personnel. This Detachment actually handles the administration of what would normally be expected of a Division, with the personnel that would normally service a Company, or at most, a Battalion."[7] It was not all OSS Washington's fault. As a new civilian agency with detailed military personnel, the OSS had difficulty getting its personnel promoted. Still, field personnel felt the effect most because officers and men at OSS Washington were more likely to receive promotions.

Yet, despite the unit's problems, by 1945, the Detachment's accomplishments were considerable. The OSS credited the unit with the following totals:[8]

American airmen rescued	232
Other Allied personnel rescued	342
Known enemy killed	5,447
Enemy killed or seriously wounded (estimate)	10,000
Enemy captured	64
Bridges destroyed	51
Railroad trains destroyed	9
Military vehicles destroyed	277
Supplies destroyed (estimate)	2,000 tons
Supplies captured (estimate)	500 tons
Intelligence furnished to NCAC	90 percent
Targets designated for air action	65 percent,
resulting in	11,225 killed
and	885 wounded

The unit had been able to assemble its disparate OSS Sections into a force that utilized land, air, and sea elements for collecting intelligence, conducting civil affairs, and waging guerrilla and psychological warfare. These assets allowed the unit direction and control over its operations, resulting in the OSS's best combat unit. Although other OSS units provided exceptional service, such as the OSS operational groups in Europe, and SO missions in France and China, only Detachment 101 in Burma was a critical element in its theater. Although the situation Detachment 101 faced in Burma in WWII was unique, the group's organizational challenges, solutions, and method of warfare offer lessons that can be utilized by today's special operations forces.

Postscript: The Lasting Relationships of Detachment 101

We probably have patterned our Special Forces doctrine more after the operations of Detachment 101 than any other single operation of that type. . . . Special Forces is Detachment 101.

Lieutenant General Samuel V. Wilson

It has been fifty years since we left our Kachin friends but we have not forgotten the promise we made to ourselves to help them.

OSS-101 Association

Summing up my experience in the field from a personal point of view I should say that all in all it has been an experience quite unequal heretofore. I have endeavored to learn the Kachin language and learn the people. I have left many true native friends behind, whom I shall long remember.

Pharmacist's Mate Eugene C. Dumond

In many ways Detachment 101 was a model unconventional warfare organization. It influenced U.S. Army Special Forces dating to its earliest days. At the end of the war, the U.S. Army disbanded all of its remaining special operations units. President Harry S. Truman also disbanded the civilian OSS on 1 October 1945. The R&A Branch, widely considered the most valuable OSS function, transferred to the Department of State. Remaining OSS personnel transferred to the War Department's Strategic Services Unit (SSU). Although saving some aspects of SI and X-2, the SSU then dismantled most of the inherited OSS structure, including its special operations branches. Not until the National Security Act of 1947 created the Central Intelligence Agency (CIA) did the United States once again have a civilian intelligence service. However, by this time, the special operations capability that the OSS built through difficult trial and error was long gone.

At the start of the Korean War on 25 June 1950 the U.S. Army realized that it once again needed a special operations capability able to form, train, and lead resistance movements. The champion for this effort was Brigadier General Robert A. McClure, who had led the Psychological Warfare Division under General Dwight D. Eisenhower in northwest Europe in WWII. In the years leading up to Korea, McClure lobbied for the U.S. Army to recreate psychological warfare units. Like Donovan had in the COI/OSS, McClure soon came to see that special operations were linked to psychological operations. He gathered with him five "thinkers" to help. All of them had been in special operations units in the Far East in WWII. These men were Colonel Wendell Fertig and Lieutenant Colonel Russell W. Volckmann, both veterans of guerrilla operations in the Philippines; Colonel Melvin R. Blair, formerly of Merrill's Marauders; Lieutenant Colonel Martin Waters, with service in both Merrill's Marauders and Detachment 101; and Colonel Aaron Bank, who served the OSS as a Jedburgh in France, and the leader of SO team RAVEN in Laos. Together with McClure, these men helped to codify what became Special Forces, formed in 1952 at Fort Bragg, North Carolina, under the U.S. Army Psychological Warfare Center. Like Detachment 101 had done, the mission of Special Forces was to work with resistance groups in time of war.[1]

Peers, then a recognized expert on unconventional operations, led CIA efforts against China from Formosa during the Korean War. To help in this effort, he recruited many of his former comrades, so much so that the CIA's effort there resembled a Detachment 101 reunion.[2] Several of these men stayed in the CIA after Korea and became fixtures in that organization. Peers retired from the U.S. Army as a lieutenant general after being the lead investigator for the 1968 My Lai massacre.[3] Detachment 101 retained military ties as well.

In 1966, only five years after its members received the right to wear the beret from President John F. Kennedy, Special Forces recognized Detachment 101 as one of its forerunners by presenting a Green Beret to the OSS veterans at their annual banquet. Staff Sergeant Barry Sadler, who wrote and sang "The Ballad of the Green Beret," presented the beret to Detachment 101 veterans on behalf of the former NCAC G-2, now commanding officer of the John F. Kennedy Center for Special Warfare, Brigadier General Joseph W. Stilwell Jr.[4] In addition, service in Detachment 101 allows for retroactive qualification for the award of the Special Forces Tab, a symbol of the ties between the OSS and its influence on today's Special Forces.[5]

The United States Army Special Operations Command (USASOC) has recognized Detachment 101 as being one of its legacy units by adding a stone dedicated to Detachment 101 to its Memorial Plaza in 1994. USASOC also hosted two reunions for Detachment 101 veterans. Although it was never an army unit, and as such not officially in the lineage, Detachment 101 developed standards and practices that very much made it a forerunner organization to U.S. Army Special Forces.

A lesser-known legacy of Detachment 101 is that the ties that they forged with the Kachins from 1942 to 1945 did not die with the war's conclusion. The men of Detachment 101 did not allow difficult political circumstances from preventing them from contacting or providing aid to their former comrades. If anything, despite the obstacles their enthusiasm continued unabated. That eagerness was evident even during the war.

In early 1945, Detachment 101's leadership realized that it needed to think about how to appropriately handle the dissolution of the guerrillas. Peers later said, "We wanted to insure that we were doing everything for them we possibly could; it was their war as much as it was ours."[6] In response, Detachment 101 created the Office of the Coordinator of Native Affairs (OCNA) under First Lieutenant Julian Niemczyk.[7] The OCNA was responsible for "records, payments, awards, discharge, and pensions."[8] With a small staff including Detachment 101's only American female employee, Ann Palko, Niemczyk had a huge undertaking. It was up to the OCNA to keep records on all the guerrilla troops hired by Detachment 101, see that they were paid in full when they separated, and see that they received awards for their service. The care that Detachment 101 gave to its guerrillas by creating an office solely for them was reflected in the methodical approach taken by the OCNA.

The OCNA's first action was making a personnel record for each guerrilla. Although this was not complete when Detachment 101 disbanded, the records helped to ensure that the families of killed or injured agents and guerrillas received adequate compensation. This complex task helped Detachment 101 maintain the good will of the native people. However, a far cheaper solution garnered the most appreciation on behalf of the Kachins and built upon Detachment 101's esprit de corps.

The only OSS group to do so for its indigenous troops on a large scale, Detachment 101 contracted in the United States to have several items of insignia made for its guerrillas. Upon disbanding, guerrillas received a paper certificate honoring their service. Those who had distinguished themselves received a shoulder patch or a silver bar embossed with raised letters that spelled "Burma Campaign" upon the face. Each bar cost about $2 to make, but they "were greatly prized by the Kachins."[9] Those who had exceptionally distinguished themselves earned the Citation for Military Assistance (CMA), an award with a unique background.

The CMA emanated from a mistake. In response to a question received from Wilkinson of Operation FORWARD in October 1943, asking what he could promise Kachins in return for their help, he received a cable reading "five/thousand/lbs/rice/per/month/guns/cloth/cma/salt." Wilkinson assumed that "cma" stood for a British decoration that he knew nothing about. He got no help from headquarters when asking what a "cma" was, so he assumed it was a medal, and promised the same to Kachins. Despite the mistake, the Kachins were promised CMA medals, so Detachment 101 could not break the promise.[10]

Since no U.S. decoration called a CMA existed, Detachment 101 had to design and create one. Detachment 101 tasked Major Harry Little in their rear area in Calcutta, India (Detachment 505), to have the medals struck. The result was a silver disk about the size of a silver dollar. One side had an American eagle with the letters CMA engraved underneath. On the back, where the recipient's name was engraved, was a wreath. Finally, the medals hung from a green neck ribbon with three peacocks embroidered with silver thread on each side. The award was striking and a suitable honor for those Kachins who had exceeded themselves in action against the Japanese. Detachment 101 personnel presented in an elaborate ceremony no more than about seventy-five CMA medals total. Although the CMA medals cost nearly $50 each, according to Peers, they "proved themselves worth their weight in gold."[11] The decorations and the presentations showed how much cultural sensitivity and respect Detachment 101's personnel had gained in working with indigenous troops.

Following Kachin custom, upon disbanding, each Detachment 101 field group decided to have a large party, or *manau*. At these gatherings, the Kachins wore their finest clothes, while all the local villagers came out to watch. Food and *laukoo*, a fermented beverage made from rice, were in abundance. The Kachins paraded and then stood in formation while those among them slated to receive the award were called out and given their medals. A select few also got prized shotguns or muzzle-loading rifles with which they could hunt.

Per direction from the British authorities, the Detachment 101 officers then had the Kachins stack and surrender their military weapons. After the conclusion of the *manau*, Detachment 101 arranged to fly the Kachins, often hundreds of miles from home, back to locations nearer to their villages in north Burma. All in all, Detachment 101 had perhaps the most successful demobilization of guerrillas at the end of WWII. Detachment 101 veterans continued to have contact with their former comrades.

In the interwar years, several former OSS men, particularly those who had learned Jinghpaw, kept in sporadic contact with the Kachins. Some of these contacts became the focus of high-level dealings. In 1948, Lieutenant Colonel William "Ray" Peers, the last commander of Detachment 101, interceded with Donovan on behalf of Saw Judson, one of Detachment 101's original Kachins from A Group. In 1947, Judson came to the United States on a scholarship. Because he had little money, several of the former members of Detachment 101 supported Judson financially. However, Peers tried to get Donovan to help Judson obtain official support. Peers also met with several State Department officers to try to arrange for government support for the children of Lazum Tang to come to the United States for schooling. At the same time, another Detachment 101 veteran, Dick Dunlop, tried to establish a school for the Kachins in north Burma.[12]

Not until the Detachment 101 veterans organized themselves into an association did they make a more focused effort to help the Kachin. The Detachment 101 veterans had what could be called their first local reunion in 1947 in New York City. At that time several supported the unsuccessful Jinghpaw War Memorial Act of 1947, an effort to have Congress sponsor building schools in north Burma to help repay the debt owed to the Kachins.[13] Unfortunately, that effort fizzled.

Although some of the veterans met together in the late 1940s, not until 1950 did the Detachment 101 Association as an entity hold what could be termed as its first national reunion.[14] But it was not until 1961 that the Association really took off. In that year, veteran Samuel A. Schreiner sent out the first of regular newsletters for Detachment 101 veterans and their families.[15]

In only a few short years of reunions and newsletters, the attention of the Detachment 101 veterans turned back to the Kachins. As Burma moved through the throes of independence and later military rule, efforts to help the Kachins grew more difficult.[16] The Kachins were not a favored people of the Burmese government and had long resisted its influence. With persistence, the Detachment 101 veterans began to make inroads with Burmese government officials to allow help to go to the Kachin. Several people stand out for their contributions, but one of the first "pioneers" was former assistant secretary of state Roger Hilsman.

A long-held goal of Hilsman's was to develop an educational plan to assist his former comrades. His idea was to create a school and education center based in Myitkyina, with a total cost estimated at $3 million. The Burmese government even donated land in Lashio to be used for the site of an agricultural school.[17] The Detachment 101 veterans thanked the Burmese government for approving the school, writing "This acceptance is accompanied by a sense of gratitude and obligation. It signals the long awaited opportunity to repay an aging debt of honor to the highland peoples of Myanmar, whose invaluable cooperation and active assistance to Allied Forces during World War II contributed so heavily to victory."[18] By using connections garnered in public and private life, Hilsman raised a substantial amount of money, but he could not meet the $3 million goal.

Even so, Hilsman's ideas were infectious. In 1992, wanting to do more for their former comrades, Detachment 101 veterans raised and donated $10,000 for Southern Methodist University's Institute for the Study of Earth and Man, Center for Highland Burma Peoples. The money went toward assisting the Kachin people.[19] Detachment 101 veterans also successfully lobbied the U.S. Congress for additional assistance. In 1996, Congress voted for "not less than $380,000 for crop substitution working cooperation with the Kachin people."[20] The U.S. Department of State soon increased this sum, and in the next few months, the Detachment 101 veterans received the first of $530,000.[21]

The first aspect of the veteran's plan, dubbed "Project Old Soldier," was a crop substitution effort designed to combat the opium poppy trade in the Kachin States by replacing that illicit crop with sustainable agricultural products such as corn. Detachment 101 veterans Peter K. Lutken, Oliver E. Trechter, Mickey S. Kaliff, Stuart E. Power, and Oscar B. Klein spearheaded the movement. They were assisted by Dennis Klein, the son of Oscar Klein. At that time, both Southern Methodist University and Texas A&M supplied agricultural experts at no cost to help the Detachment 101 project succeed. The movement got more impetus when the Detachment 101 veterans arranged for support from the Department of Soil and Crop Sciences at Texas A&M. There, the veterans enlisted the support of Dr. C. A. Edward Runge, later made an honorary member of Detachment 101 in 2001.

By 2001, a total of eighty-four villages with about 2,200 farmers were participating. Local administrators found that two villages had also been growing opium, and these were dropped from the program.[22] The program grew considerably. By 2010, the number of farmers enrolled in the program had risen to 5,400.[23] The program continues as of 2012.

The Detachment 101 Association also started multiple projects aimed at helping the Kachins achieve a higher standard of living. One involved helping to pay the medical bills for some of the aging Kachin warriors, critical because long-term care is difficult to obtain in north Burma and many of the veterans were in dire need. In addition, the Detachment 101 veterans arranged for a full-time nurse to provide once-a-week homecare to Kachin veterans.

Other projects helped the Kachin children. The Detachment 101 veterans donated the money to buy playground equipment. Emplaced in Myitkyina, it gives a place for the Kachin children to play. However, perhaps the most important assistance has been in setting up schools and providing funds for Myitkyina's numerous orphanages. By 2009, the school project, called "101 Schools," had a total enrollment of 268 students from age seven to seventeen undergoing instruction. Nominal tuition was charged only to those who could afford the fee.[24] In total, the cost to run four schools, including rent, supplies, salaries, and utilities, came in at $800 a month. "In terms of demand, we could easily double the size of this program if funding permitted," reported Colonel (retired) Daniel Tarter, who visited the area to check on the status of the program.[25]

Despite the difficult political environment, the Detachment 101 veterans have managed to greatly aid their former comrades and their descendants through nonpolitical programs. Securing funding remains an issue as each year there are fewer veterans remaining to contribute. Still, the programs were wildly successful. Major James McAndrews, then a U.S. defense attaché in Burma, perhaps said it best when he wrote to the Detachment 101 Association in 2003. He said, "Please let your membership know that the members of OSS 101 remain an important part of Kachin society . . . when I talk to vets, they always tell me that, as a member of the Kachin Rangers, they were eager to serve with the Americans because you treated them with the honor and dignity worthy of their warrior race."[26]

That same dignity can be seen on the grounds of the U.S. Embassy in Rangoon. There, emplaced in 2004, is a bronze statue immortalizing the WWII partnership of an American OSS soldier and a Kachin guerrilla. It is a fitting tribute to the bond formed between two different cultures united in a common struggle.

A Note on Sources

A wealth of untapped primary material exists on OSS Detachment 101. By far, the most important of these sources is Record Group 226 (RG 226) in the National Archives II at College Park, Maryland. This record group is composed of the documents of the OSS's predecessor organization, the COI; the OSS; and a few post-OSS records of its follow-on organization, the Strategic Services Unit (SSU).[1]

The OSS records present a unique group among those held by NARA. They are the only records of any U.S. intelligence service open in their entirety, and are also virtually complete. When they were turned over to NARA, the CIA held back only a few reports still deemed of intelligence interest—most of which have been subsequently released—or deemed as having no historical value. This enables one to find a depth of detailed information on the OSS. There are some 2,500 boxes of documents regarding Burma and Detachment 101 alone.

Donovan's personal papers, a subset of RG 226, proved surprisingly limited, having almost no mention of Detachment 101.[2] The records of the China-Burma-India Theater (RG 493) also contained virtually no mention of Detachment 101 or the OSS in general.[3] However, this too is an important discovery. Combined with RG 226, the lack of material in either RG 493 or Donovan's papers confirms how little direction higher OSS commands gave Detachment 101.

Another valuable source is the Detachment 101 Collection in the U.S. Army Heritage and Educational Center at Carlisle, Pennsylvania. Although small, it holds several key documents. Foremost among these is the unabridged draft of what would become Peers's book *Behind the Burma Road*. In addition, Carlisle's collection of the documents of William J. Donovan proved useful, particularly when Detachment 101 veterans argued with authors over assertions they later made that the OSS played a minor role in the Myitkyina Campaign.

Another primary source is the Detachment 101 veterans' group, which has been in existence since 1947, and the families of Detachment 101 veterans. They are the source of many valuable documents and recollections. This includes hundreds of personal letters, decades of the group's quarterly newsletters, and copies of many original notes, diaries, unpublished memoirs, and other records.

These primary sources are more crucial when one reviews the secondary literature. With few exceptions, the literature on Detachment 101 consists mainly of veterans' memoirs. The most important of these are the two books cowritten by the former commanding officers. Thomas N. Moon and Carl F. Eifler cowrote *The Deadliest Colonel*, and Dean C. Brelis and William R. Peers produced *Behind the Burma Road*.[4] Of these, *Behind the Burma Road* is the more valuable because of its greater scope and honesty. Even so, its primary focus is on operations, though not all of these are covered. Other broad treatments include Detachment 101 veteran Richard Dunlop's *Behind Japanese Lines: With the OSS in Burma*.[5] This work is valuable for the personal accounts that it relates, but, like the other works, it focuses on operations. A variety of other veterans' memoirs are narrower in focus. Examples of these include Thomas Chamales's *Never So Few*, Roger Hilsman's *American Guerrilla: My War behind Japanese Lines*, and Dean Brelis's *The Mission*.[6] Similarly, limited press books such as Bill Brough's *To Reason Why*, Thomas Baldwin's *I'd Do it All Again: The Life and Times of Tom Baldwin*, and Harry "Skittles" Hengshoon's *Green Hell: Unconventional Warfare in the CBI*, as well as unpublished ones such as Zach Ebaugh's *The Other Side of War*, offer valuable but focused views.[7]

Until recently, the OSS has escaped substantial academic study. There are no scholarly studies on Detachment 101. On the larger subject of the OSS in Asia, the only scholarly works are Maochun Yu's *OSS in China: Prelude to Cold War*, E. Bruce Reynolds's *Thailand's Secret War: The Free Thai, OSS, and SOE during World War II*, Dixee Bartholomew-Feis's *The OSS and Ho Chi Minh*, and Richard Aldrich's *Intelligence and the War against Japan: Britain America and the Politics of Secret Service*. They offer valuable contributions, but none gives much detail on Detachment 101. The two volumes of *The War Report of the OSS* by Kermit Roosevelt—the official OSS history—and its British counterpart, Charles Cruickshanks's *SOE in the Far East*, are valuable resources, but likewise neither deals exclusively with Detachment 101.[8]

Notes

INTRODUCTION

1. Michael Warner, *The Office of Strategic Services: America's First Intelligence Agency* (Washington, DC: Central Intelligence Agency, 2000), 18.

2. Kermit Roosevelt, *The Overseas Targets: War Report of the OSS*, vol. 2 (New York: Walker, 1976), xvii. A draft of Roosevelt's work was penned by OSS during the war, but the organization's disbandment on 1 October 1945 prevented its completion. Roosevelt returned decades later to the project to finalize its compilation. Although Detachment 101 was the first COI/OSS unit of its type, one of the early SA/G (the predecessor name of OSS SO) chiefs, Lieutenant Colonel Garland Williams, did not want to reveal that to the British. He chose the name "Coordinator of Information Special Unit Detachment 101" to imply that the unit was one of many. Thomas N. Moon and Carl F. Eifler, *The Deadliest Colonel* (New York: Vantage, 1975), 53.

3. [OSS Special Operations Branch history], "This Phase of SO," Folder 4, Box 101, Entry 99, Research Group 226, National Archives and Records Administration, College Park, MD.

4. Robert Warner to William J. Donovan, "History of OSS/IBT," 14 April 1945, F1, B75, E99, RG226, NARA. The OSS History Office was headed by Conyers Read, future president of the American Historical Association. Detachment 101 did produce several histories of their operations. Although far from comprehensive, these can be found at F 74, B 42, E 190, RG 226, NARA and F 1, B 78, E 99, RG 226, NARA.

5. Although not a period publication, the U.S. Army's first postwar manual concerning guerrilla warfare, itself based on the WWII experience, Department of the Army Field Manual 31-21, *Organization and Conduct of Guerilla Warfare* (Washington, DC: Government Printing Office, 1951), 16–18, basically describes these three phases.

6. According to a letter from Carl F. Eifler to Joseph W. Stilwell dated 11 November 1942 (F4, B 76, E 99, RG 226, NARA), it was "I want 'Booms,'" but in later life, Eifler relates the jungle and ninety-day requirement. Regardless, Stilwell placed Eifler under intense pressure to produce quick results.

7. Neither the U.S. Army Center of Military History nor the Institute of Heraldry recognizes the OSS as being in the lineage of any U.S. Army unit. This is because even though U.S. Army personnel were detailed to the OSS, it was a civilian organization, not military. Instead, the Central Intelligence Agency is the organization that draws its lineage from the OSS.

1. BEFORE THE STORM

1. "Captain Tilly with the KNOTHEAD Group," January 1944, Folder 48, Box 38, Entry 190, Research Group 226, National Archives and Records Administration, College Park, MD.

2. The Karens were independent-minded and many were of the Christian faith, an asset to the Allies in trying to get these indigenous groups to work with them. In a tacit agreement, SOE focused most of its recruiting on Karens, making this ethnic group less important to the OSS. Plans were formulated by OSS to try and organize the Nagas along the same lines as the Kachins, but they never took root. A plan to capitalize on the Nagas' headhunting past, and to try to get them to revitalize the practice against the Japanese, can be found in [George?] Devereux to John R. Coughlin, "Assam Headhunters, Immediate Utilization of," 14 April 1944, F 340, B 57, E 190, RG 226, NARA. Nearly every American serviceman who served along the India/Burma border tells tales about the wild "headhunter" Nagas. However, those that actually met a Naga quickly lost their fear and felt quite safe.

3. Shelby Tucker, *Among Insurgents: Walking through Burma* (New York: Radcliff Press, 2000), 34.

4. Christopher Bayly and Tim Harper, *Forgotten Armies: The Fall of British Asia, 1941–1945* (Cambridge, MA: Belknap Press, 2004), 83–85.

5. For more on missionaries in Burma, see Edward Fischer, *Mission in Burma: The Columban Fathers' Forty-Three Years in Kachin Country* (New York: Seabury Press, 1980).

6. For example, there is a plant that grows in the foothills that visibly shrivels when touched. Whereas an American or Japanese would not notice the plant, the Kachin would and instantly knew that others had recently passed by. When the author traveled to Kachin State, Myanmar, in November 2004, he asked about this plant, thinking it only a myth. The Kachin guide immediately stooped down and touched a roadside plant, which instantly shriveled at the touch. Knowledge and careful observation of such a plant would indeed provide instant intelligence that something—animal or human—had recently passed.

7. Agent Robey to Wilky [William C. Wilkinson], "Introduction (Report on Travels)," [early 1943], F 495, B 29, E 154, RG 226, NARA.

8. William Boyd Sinclair, *Confusion beyond Imagination: China-Burma-India in World War II*, book 7 of 10 (Coeur d'Alene, ID: Joe F. Whitley, 1990), 65.

9. For more on the OSS in Thailand, see the excellent E. Bruce Reynolds, *Thailand's Secret War: OSS, SOE, and the Free Thai Underground during World War II* (Cambridge: Cambridge University Press, 2005).

10. For more on the postwar independent movements in the Far East see Christopher Bayly and Tim Harper, *Forgotten Wars: Freedom and Revolution in Southeast Asia* (Cambridge, MA: Belknap Press, 2006).

11. A contingent of the American Volunteer Group, popularly known as the "Flying Tigers," also flew missions against Japanese aircraft from Burma.

12. Joseph W. Stilwell, *The Stilwell Papers* (New York: William Sloane, 1975), 106. For information on Stilwell's walkout see Frank Dorn, *Walkout: With Stilwell in Burma* (New York: Thomas Y. Crowell, 1971).

13. Bayly and Harper, *Forgotten Armies*, 167.

14. Martin J. Waters, "The Operations of a Provisional OSS Platoon, Night Reconnaissance Operations, the Arakan Coast, Burma, Oct. 1944–Apr. 1945" (Advanced Infantry School Officer's Course, Infantry School, Fort Benning, Georgia, 1946–1947), 4.

15. Carl F. Eifler to William J. Donovan, "Report Covering Period June 1 to June 30, 1943, Inclusive," 1 July 1943, F 1, B 65, E 99, RG 226, NARA.

16. Field Marshall Viscount William Slim, *Defeat into Victory: Battling Japan in Burma and India, 1942–1945* (New York: Cooper Square Press, 2000), 177.

17. Charles F. Romanus and Riley Sunderland, *United States Army in World War II: China-Burma-India Theater: Stilwell's Command Problems* (Washington, DC: Center of Military History, 1987), 286, 240; As an aside, in talks with Detachment 101 veterans at their reunions, many relate that they suffered with malaria and its remissions for decades after the war.

18. James C. Luce, "Background, Historical, Military and Political of the Kachin Hills Area," 28 January 1944, original copy in author's possession. The term "behind the lines" will only be used to describe shallow penetrations of enemy territory. In most cases, Detachment 101 operated far into enemy-occupied territory. Therefore, "behind the lines" is a misnomer for activity that takes place 50 or more miles away from friendly lines.

19. Elton W. Archer, "The Sniper," *OSS 101 Association Incorporated Newsletter*, Winter 2003–2004, 4.

20. [Brief Chronology of OSSSU Detachment 101], F 74, B 42, E 190, RG 226, NARA.

2. LAYING THE GROUNDWORK: 1941–JANUARY 1943

1. Carl F. Eifler to William J. Donovan, "Status of OSS Detachment 101," 16 February 1943, F 4, B 76, E 99, RG 226, NARA.

2. Franklin D. Roosevelt, "Designating a Coordinator of Information," 11 July 1941, F 23, B 119A, William J. Donovan Papers, U.S. Army Historical and Education Center (USAHEC), Carlisle Barracks, PA.

3. The OSS reported to the Joint Chiefs of Staff. It functioned much like a separate military service, albeit civilian. One very misunderstood aspect of the OSS is that it was civilian, not military, and that soldiers serving in it were detailees, and were not serving their individual military service.

4. Popular histories often overlook the OSS's primary function: to analyze and disseminate all-source intelligence, not to conduct special operations.

5. For the directive assigning OSS its basic functions, see Thomas F. Troy, *Donovan and the CIA: A History of the Establishment of the Central Intelligence Agency* (Washington, DC: Central Intelligence Agency, 1981), 428. Although Special Operations are what the OSS is best known for, the revolutionary idea—and perhaps the most useful aspect of OSS—of the organization was that of producing all-source intelligence reports. The OSS Research and Analysis (R&A) Branch compiled these reports for the use of politicians, military officers, and other policy makers.

6. For the most recent biography of Donovan, see Douglas Waller, *Wild Bill Donovan: the Spymaster Who Created the OSS and Modern American Espionage* (New York: Free Press, 2011).

7. Roosevelt, *War Report*, 5.

8. OSS Special Operations Branch history, NARA. For greater detail on this trip, see Troy, *Donovan and the CIA*, 36–42.

9. OSS Special Operations Branch history, NARA.

10. OSS Special Operations Branch history, NARA. For a brief account of COI/OSS setting up the Special Operations Branch, see Roosevelt, *War Report*, 70–74.

11. OSS Special Operations Branch history, NARA.

12. General Douglas MacArthur allowed OSS into his theater only in the closing months of the war, after he was made commander of U.S. Army Forces in the Pacific. Even then, all he allowed into his theater was special OSS equipment and its operators. See Roosevelt, *Overseas Targets*, 358.

13. Even in later years, Goodfellow referred to 101 as his "baby." See *101 Association Incorporated Newsletter*, Fall–Winter 1962–1963, 2.

14. Roosevelt, *War Report*, 80.

15. M. B. Depass Jr., "Memorandum for Colonel Donovan: Subject—Scheme 'OLIVIA,'" 27 January 1942, F1, B 4, Goodfellow Collection, Hoover Institute Archives, Stanford University, CA.

16. "A Presence at the Creation . . . M. Preston Goodfellow Dies," *101 Association Incorporated Newsletter* 5, no 5. (Dec. 1973): 5–6.

17. Major Carl F. Eifler, "Report of Action to Date and Request for Instructions," to Colonel William J. Donovan, 24 November 1942, F 49, B 39, E 190, R 226, NARA.

18. Heidi Vion, "Booms from Behind the Lines: An Oral History of the Covert Experiences of the Office of Strategic Services Detachment 101 in the World War II

China-Burma-India Theater" (MA thesis, California State University, Fullerton, 2004), 284–285, 304–305. After the war, Eifler struggled to recover from injuries received in Burma, but managed to finish a career in the Customs Service and earn a doctorate of divinity. He died in 2002 at the age of ninety-five.

19. For Eifler's accounting of his prewar service and recruitment, see Thomas N. Moon and Carl F. Eifler, *The Deadliest Colonel* (New York: Vantage Press, 1975), 1–41.

20. [Brief Chronology of OSSSU Detachment 101], F 74, B 42, E 190, RG 226, NARA.

21. Carl F. Eifler, interviewed by Dr. Stanley Sandler, USASOC History Office, Fort Bragg, NC.

22. Eifler to Donovan, "Report of Action to Date and Request for Instructions," 24 November 1942, NARA.

23. Carl F. Eifler to William J. Donovan, "Status of O.S.S. Detachment 101," 16 February 1943, F 49, B 39, E190, RG 226, NARA. In November 1942, Chang met with Mr. David An, the representative to President Kim Koo of the Korean Provisional Government to discuss the possibility of getting Korean troops serving in the Japanese Army on the side of the Allies. These talks may have been the start of what would later be the NAPKO project under then Colonel Eifler. See "Report from Sergeant Sukyoon Chang," 26 December 1942, F 4, B 76, E 99, RG 226, NARA.

24. Email from Allen Richter to Troy Sacquety, 13 January 2006, in author's possession.

25. William R. Peers and Dean Brelis, *Behind the Burma Road: The Story of America's Most Successful Guerrilla Force* (Boston: Little, Brown, 1963), 39–41.

26. Eifler to Donovan, "Status of O.S.S. Detachment 101," 16 February 1943, NARA. For clarification, the personnel are assigned as follows: Admin: Charles Bruce; Commo: Phillip S. Huston, Allen R. Richter, Jack Pamplin, Donald Y. Eng, Fima Haimson; Field Photo: Irby E. Moree; Medical: Archie Chun Ming; Procurement: Frank Devlin, Harry W. Little; Research & Development: Floyd R. Frazee; Schools & Training: William R. Peers, Vincent Curl, Sukyoon Chang; Secret Intelligence: Chan*; Special Funds: Robert T. Aitken; Special Operations: Carl F. Eifler, John G. Coughlin, William C. Wilkinson, George T. Hemming, John M. Murray, Dave E. Tillquist. 27. Carlton F. Scofield, "Informal Report on Detachment 101," 13 March 1944, General Donovan's personal correspondence, roll 110, A 3304, E 180, RG 226, NARA.

28. OSS Special Operations Branch history, NARA.

---

*Chan is not considered (by the 101 Association) to be one of the original complement according to Allen Richter in a 16 September 2006 phone interview. However, in Moon and Eifler, *The Deadliest Colonel*, 46, a man described as a Eurasian in his fifties was recruited for infiltrating smuggling rings in the Far East. He was known only to Eifler and Coughlin, and later to Peers when he took over command. Since Chan is listed as an undercover agent in Calcutta, it is possible that he is Eifler's "mystery man."

29. For more on Camp X, see Lynn Philip Hodgson, *Inside-Camp X* (Port Perry, Canada: Friesens, 2002). For more on the training given to early COI recruits at Catoctin Mountain Park (near what would later become Camp David) see the excellent work by John W. Chambers, *OSS Training in the National Parks and Service Abroad In World War II* (Washington, DC: U.S. National Park Service, 2008), found online at http://www.nps.gov/history/history/online_books/oss/index.htm, accessed 24 March 2012.

30. William R. Peers and Dean C. Brelis, "Original Draft of Peers-Brelis Behind the Burma Road," 39, Box 1, Detachment 101 Collection, USAHEC.

31. Detachment 101 veterans who knew Eifler all remark on his sheer will to accomplish any task asked of him.

32. Eifler to Donovan, "Report of Action to Date and Request for Instructions," 24 November 1942, NARA.

33. Peers and Brelis, "Original Draft," 53, USAHEC.

34. Eifler to Donovan, "Status of OSS Detachment 101," 16 February 1943, NARA.

35. Troy, *Donovan and the CIA*, 92.

36. Eifler to Donovan, "Report of Action to Date and Request for Instructions," 24 November 1942, NARA.

37. The Chih Hui Pu was renamed the Northern Combat Area Command (NCAC) on 1 February 1944.

38. In April 1942, General Sir Archibald Wavell, commander in chief, India, ordered the creation of a guerrilla element to attack Japanese lines of communication if they decided to continue their advance from Burma into the Assam region of India. This group, recruited from members of the Assam Rifles, Burmese Rifles, and Kachin Rifles, "hill tribesmen," former British tea plantation owners, and workers in the territorial guard, and some detailed American servicemen, came to be known as V-Force. Since the Japanese did not invade further west until 1944, the unit mission became primarily intelligence gathering, weather reporting, and pilot rescue. They maintained a chain of forward observation posts from upper Assam to the northern Arakan, providing protection for the Tenth Air Force and Royal Air Force air warning outposts, while also serving to maintain an Allied presence in the forward areas. This was important to the pro-British indigenous groups who were suffering under the Japanese occupation. The memoirs by V-Force veterans are surprisingly many, including: Ursula Graham Bower, *Naga Path* (London: John Murray, 1952), C. E. Lucas Phillips, *The Raiders of Arakan* (London: Heinemann, 1971), and John Bowen, *Undercover in the Jungle* (London: William Kimber, 1978). For V-Force support to American air warning stations, see Bob Phillips, *KC8 Burma: CBI Air Warning Team, 1941–1942.* (Manhattan, KS: Sunflower University Press, 1992); B.C. Case to G-2 section of Stilwell's HQ, "Dinjan Air Raid Warning and Information Net Work," 12 September 1942, F 499, B 68, E 190, RG 226, NARA, illustrates how little Stilwell's HQ knew about the situation in north Burma, where Detachment 101 would initially operate. Case was sent on a fact-finding mission to ascertain the general

situation in the area. Case appears to have had no knowledge of what V-Force was or that it was operating in the area.

39. The Chinese, in part due to their suspicions of having another country's intelligence service operating in their area, proved to be difficult allies in regards to the OSS. Although the COI and later OSS was present in China from 1942, it was not until late 1944 that they were effective.

40. Eifler to Donovan, "Report of Action to Date and Request for Instructions," 24 November 1942, NARA. While neither Eifler nor Stilwell officially asked Chiang Kai-shek for permission for Detachment 101 to operate in China, given the problems experience by the Sino-American Cooperative Organization (SACO), a group operating in China made up of U.S. Naval Group, China, and OSS, it is likely that, even if Detachment 101 had received permission to operate in China, it would have experienced extreme supply and liaison difficulties. While the OSS was in China early, with SACO and AGFRTS (Air and Ground Forces Resources and Technical Staff), it was not to reach its full zenith until 1945 and only then after the surrender of Germany in May and the end of the Burma Campaign in July. At this time, the OSS was able to concentrate its full resources—including both personnel from Europe and Detachment 101—into its effort with Detachment 202 (China); Eifler and Moon, *The Deadliest Colonel*, 61. The official record, while not giving an exact figure of ninety days, does imply that Eifler was under extreme pressure to prove himself and the new organization to a skeptical General Stilwell. This often-told story of the "booms" is repeated in Richard Dunlop, *Behind Japanese Lines: With the OSS in Burma* (Chicago: Rand McNally, 1979), 109. For a documentary reference to this, see Carl F. Eifler to Joseph W. Stilwell, 11 November 1942, F 364, B 58, E 190, RG 226, NARA; another copy can be found at F 27, B 191, E 92, RG 226, NARA.

41. Charles F. Romanus and Riley Sunderland, *United States Army in World War II: China-Burma-India Theater: Stilwell's Command Problems* (Washington, DC: Center of Military History, 1987), 9–10.

42. "Burma," F 2538, B 192, E 139, RG 226, NARA.

43. Carl F. Eifler to Carl O. Hoffman, 17 July 1943, F 371, B 58, E 190, RG 226, NARA. Copies of Eifler's correspondence from mid-1942 to May 1943 to Stilwell's headquarters can be found at F 499, B 68, E 190, RG 226, NARA. In 1942, the instructions given are very specific. Thereafter, they get less so.

44. Peers and Brelis, "Original Draft," 258–259, USAHEC.

45. L. B. Thompson to Carl F. Eifler, "Letter of Instructions," 15 September 1942, original in Eifler's papers in the author's possession. The author can find little evidence in either the OSS or Army CBI records that Donovan or other OSS Washington authorities tried to manage Detachment 101's activities. Discussions with some of the original cadre of Detachment 101 also lend support to this assumption.

46. The lack of direction from Washington had some drawbacks, especially in the early period. The main concern for the fledgling unit was financial. Detachment 101 started with an allotment of $288,000 for its first year of operations, but OSS

Washington did not send the funding when needed. In Eifler to Donovan, "Report of Action to Date and Request for Instructions," 24 November 1942, NARA, Eifler complained that he had no money with which to conduct operations. To combat the shortfall, the personnel of the Detachment had all dug into their own pockets and contributed their pay to keep the unit running. This situation was cabled to Washington in Carl F. Eifler to William J. Donovan, "Report of Actions to Date and Request for Instructions," 26 December 1942, F 27, B 191, E 92, RG 226, NARA. Pleas to Washington were unsuccessful. Only a $50,000 emergency infusion from General Stilwell saved the unit from running out of funding. Documentation of the transfer of the funds from Stilwell to Eifler can be found in Joseph W. Stilwell, "Transfer of Funds for Military Intelligence Purposes," 15 December 1942, F 364, B 58, E 190, RG 226, NARA. As late as February 1943, Eifler was still trying to clarify his command arrangement with OSS, Stilwell, and Miles. See Carl F. Eifler to William J. Donovan, "Status of O.S.S. Detachment 101," 16 February 1943, F 49, B 39, E 190, RG 226, NARA.

47. Cable text contained in Eifler to Donovan, "Report of Actions to Date and Request for Instructions," 26 December 1942, NARA.

48. Eifler to Donovan, "Status of Detachment 101," 16 February 1943, NARA.

49. Eifler to Donovan, "Report of Action to Date and Request for Instructions," 24 November 1942, NARA. For more on SACO, see Roy Olin Stratton, *SACO: The Rice Paddy Navy* (New York: C. S. Palmer, 1950). From the OSS perspective, SACO was a disaster. As soon as this was apparent, the OSS allowed the effort devoted to SACO to slip, and established Detachment 202 in its stead. For this perspective, see Roosevelt, *Overseas Targets*, 419–428.

50. Romanus and Sunderland, *Stilwell's Command Problems*, 56.

51. Richard J. Aldrich, *Intelligence and the War against Japan: Britain, America and the Politics of Secret Service* (Cambridge: Cambridge University Press, 2000), 102–103, 146–147; E. Bruce Reynolds, *Thailand's Secret War: The Free Thai, OSS, and SOE during World War II* (Cambridge: Cambridge University Press, 2005), 51.

52. Eifler to Donovan, "Report of Action to Date and Request for Instructions," 24 November 1942, NARA. Another copy of the agreement with SOE can be found in F 197, B 23, E 165, RG 226, NARA. Eifler also submitted his operational plans to Mackenzie in writing. This can be seen at Carl F. Eifler to Colin Mackenzie, "Dear Mackenzie," 22 Oct 1942, F 499, B 68, E 190, RG 226, NARA. For a discussion of the activities of SOE in the Far East, see Charles Cruickshank, *SOE in the Far East* (Oxford: Oxford University Press, 1983).

53. For more on Richmond's assignment to 101, see Eifler to Stilwell, 11 November 1942, NARA; "Major Eifler's Mission in Relation to S.O.E. India," [July 1942?], F 499, B 68, E 190, RG 226, NARA. For Richmond's correspondence, see correspondence to Colonel Wally Richmond and correspondence from Colonel Wally Richmond in F 010394, B 270, E 210, RG 226, NARA. Richmond and a later SOE officer, Colonel

Ottaway, had known each other from working in Burma before the war. Richmond was involved in the timber extraction industry around Myitkyina while Ottaway was involved in mining operations around Tavoy. Both would be quietly dismissed from the Detachment in late 1944 on account of graft through army contracts made by Ottaway's company, Leslie and Company. In SOE's defense, they at least partly warned Eifler about Ottaway (Colin MacKenzie to Carl F. Eifler, "Dear Eifler," 3 November 1942, F 197, B 23, E 165, RG 226, NARA). Eifler also made contact with V-Force. See Carl F. Eifler to Joseph W. Stilwell, 11 November 1942, F 364, B 58, E 190, RG 226, NARA.

54. Eifler to Donovan, "Report of Action to Date and Request for Instructions," 24 November 1942, NARA. Colin Mackenzie to Carl F. Eifler, 11 October 1942, F 499, B 68, E 190, RG 226, NARA, discusses Donovan's view of the agreement. Donovan expressed reservation that the Mackenzie/Eifler agreement was not in accordance with directives regarding OSS/SOE spheres of influence. These spheres were agreed upon by OSS/SOE on 26 June 1942 and confirmed by the Joint Chiefs of Staff (JCS) on 26 August 1942 (Roosevelt, *War Report*, 207); Frank D. Merrill to Benjamin G. Ferris, "Conference with D.M.O. and D.M.I. on Eifler Group," 16 March 1943, F 499, B 68, E 190, RG 226, NARA.

55. Detachment 101 also faced individual acts of obstruction. On 11 November 1942, Eifler sent a letter to Stilwell detailing such an obstruction. A Mr. Case was to provide Burmese agents for Eifler's consideration. However, upon hearing that the mission would be extremely dangerous, Case sabotaged the effort by telling the agents ahead of time that only the "stoutest" of them should accept. Eifler to Stilwell, 11 November 1942, F 364, B 58, E 190, RG 226, NARA.

56. Carl O. Hoffman to William J. Donovan, "Far East-Conference with Colonel Merrill" 5 May 1943, Donovan's personal correspondence microfilm, roll 110, A 3304, E 180, RG 226, NARA.

57. For more on P Division see Aldrich, *Intelligence and the War against Japan*, 178–186. For P Division's direct impact on Detachment 101, see F 1421, B 185, E 108B, RG 226, NARA; F 2158, B 119, E 154, RG 226, NARA; F 492–495, B 68 E 190, RG 226, NARA; F 10, B 59, E 99, RG 226, NARA.

58. Carl F. Eifler to Joseph W. Stilwell, 11 November 1942, F 27, B 191, E 92, RG 226, NARA

59. W. G. Wyman to Chief of Staff U.S.F.C.B.I. [Stilwell], "The Eifler Group," 23 August 1942, F 499, B 68, E 190, RG 226, NARA.

60. Eifler to Donovan, "Report of Action to Date and Request for Instructions," 24 November 1942, NARA.

61. "A History of the Assam Company," *OSS-101 Association Incorporated*, Winter 1995–1996, 9.

62. F. Kingdon-Ward, "Notes on Hill Jungle For Guerrillas," F 333, B 56, E 190, RG 226, NARA. Another similar-type report, compiled from sources in the New York

Public Library, can be found in "Notes On Burma," 1 June 1943, F 117, B 72, E 154, RG 226, NARA. In this case, the report deals with the "Nats," spiritual creatures of north Burma Kachin belief.

63. Peers and Brelis, "Original Draft," 42, USAHEC.

64. [Brief Chronology of OSSSU Detachment 101], F 74, B 42, E 190, RG 226, NARA.

65. Eifler to Donovan, "Report of Action to Date and Request for Instructions," 24 November 1942, NARA.

66. Brief Chronology of OSSSU Detachment 101, NARA.

67. Eifler to Donovan, "Report of Actions to Date and Request for Instructions," 26 December 1942, NARA.

68. Later, Detachment 101 expanded this school to teach Air Force personnel jungle survival.

69. [Harry W. Ballard], "Report on Casing of Chabua Aerodrome," 23 November 1942, Ballard Folder, B 52, E199, RG 226, NARA. Further reports of such test reconnaissance missions, as well as Ballard's personal file, are located in the same folder.

70. "Problem Report," [undated, but sometime in December 1942–January 1943], F "Aikman, John (Jinx)," B 52, E 199, RG 226, NARA.

71. Wally Richmond to Carl F. Eifler, 23 April 1943, F 358, B 57, E 190, RG 226, NARA.

72. Benjamin G. Ferris to Carl F. Eifler, 6 April 1943, F 499, B 68, E 190, RG 226, NARA.

73. Sample examples of these contracts can be found in Eifler to Donovan, "Report of Action to Date and Request for Instructions," 24 November 1942, NARA.

74. Ibid.

75. "History of Special Funds Branch Headquarters Detachment 101," [May–June 1945], F 1541, B 225, E 199, RG 226, NARA, provides a brief but excellent account of the branch.

76. Carl F. Eifler to William J. Donovan, "Report of Actions to Date and Request for Instructions," 26 December 1942, F 4, B 76, E 99, RG 226, NARA.

77. Carl F. Eifler to William J. Donovan, "Detailed Report of My Activities Covering the Period December 26 1942 to date," 6 April 1943, F49, B 39, E 190, RG 226, NARA.

78. Eifler to Donovan, "Detailed Report of My Activities Covering the Period December 26 1942 to date," 6 April 1943, NARA.

79. Eifler to Donovan, "Report of Action to Date and Request for Instructions," 24 November 1942, NARA.

80. Eifler to Donovan, "Report of Actions to Date and Request for Instructions," 26 December 1942, NARA.

81. Eifler to Donovan, "Detailed Report of My Activities Covering the Period December 26 1942 to date," 6 April 1943, NARA.

82. Ibid. Since Detachment 505 became a separate entity from 101, it is not covered in any great detail.

83. Eifler to Donovan, "Status of O.S.S. Detachment 101," 16 February 1943, NARA.

3. LONG-RANGE PENETRATION OPERATIONS

1. On 13 June 1942 the COI was dissolved by Roosevelt, and in its place the OSS was created. Donovan remained the director.

2. Carl F. Eifler, interviewed by Dr. Stanley Sandler, United States Army John F. Kennedy Special Warfare Center and School.

3. Kermit Roosevelt, *The Overseas Targets: War Report of the OSS (Office of Strategic Services)*, vol. 2 (New York: Walker, 1976), 361, 11–26; For an account of the OSS operations in North Africa, see Carlton S. Coon, *A North African Story: The Long-Mislaid Diary-Like Account of a Harvard Professor of Anthropology Turned Cloak-and-Dagger Operative for General Donovan and his OSS; 1942–3* (Ipswich, MA: Gambit, 1980).

4. Carl F. Eifler to William J. Donovan, "Report of Action to Date and Request for Instructions," 24 November 1942, Folder 49, Box 39, Entry 190, Research Group 226, National Archives and Records Administration, College Park, MD. The exact wording of this mission guidance can be found in a letter to Eifler that is in the author's possession: Joseph W. Stilwell to Carl F. Eifler, "Letter of Instruction," 15 September 1942.

5. [Jack Barnard], "Report on Secret Operations in Burma," [post-June 1943], F 447, B 30, E 154, RG 226, NARA.

6. Carl F. Eifler, "Report to General Ferris, Deputy Chief of Staff, thru Colonel Merrill, G-3," 11 February 1943, F 4, B 76, E 99, RG 226, NARA.

7. Letter from Oscar Milton to Troy J. Sacquety, 1 April 2006, in author's possession.

8. Barnard, "Report on Secret Operations in Burma," NARA.

9. Eifler to Donovan, "Report of Action to Date and Request for Instructions," 24 November 1942, NARA; Peers and Brelis, "Original Draft," 76.

10. Carl F. Eifler to William J. Donovan, "Detailed Report of My Activities Covering the Period December 26, 1942 to Date," 6 April 1943, F 49, B 39, E 190, RG 226, NARA.

11. Barnard, "Report on Secret Operations in Burma," NARA. A Group is among the Detachment 101 operations most documented in the literature, with no fewer than three accounts and one full-length memoir. See William R. Peers and Dean Brelis, *Behind the Burma Road: The Story of America's Most Successful Guerrilla Force* (Boston: Little, Brown, 1963), 68–98; Thomas N. Moon and Carl F. Eifler, *The Deadliest Colonel* (New York: Vantage, 1975), 98–99; and Richard Dunlop, *Behind Japanese Lines: With the OSS in Burma* (Chicago: Rand McNally, 1979), 147–199. John Beamish authored *Burma Drop* (London: Elek Books, 1958), but its many basic

inconsistencies with the original 1943 report leave it suspect. Oscar Milton has also written an unpublished memoir.

12. Peers and Brelis, "Original Draft," 123–124.

13. Detachment 101 was given the services of "Pop" Milligan, from the Air Transport Command. Milligan was a former barnstormer, steer-roper, and oilman, and, despite his age, had a good deal of experience in airborne operations.

14. Eifler to Donovan, "Detailed Report"; "Report-Red, Dennis, and Pat: Diary of Operations in and Trip Out of Burma," [undated but mid-1943], F 448, B 30, E 154, RG 226, NARA.

15. Barnard, "Report on Secret Operations in Burma," NARA.

16. Oscar Milton, email to Troy Sacquety, 28 September 2005.

17. Jack Barnard, Mission Diary, F OSS Reports, Box 4, OSS Detachment 101 Collection, USAHEC.

18. Ibid.

19. Ibid.

20. Ibid.

21. "Report-Red, Dennis, and Pat."

22. Beamish, *Burma Drop*, 59–60.

23. Barnard, Mission Diary.

24. Ibid.

25. Ibid.

26. "Pat Diary," [undated but mid-1943], Eifler to Donovan, "Detailed Report"; "Report-Red, Dennis, and Pat: Diary of Operations in and Trip Out of Burma," [undated but mid-1943], F 448, B 30, E 154, RG 226, NARA.

27. Cable to RED from Carl F. Eifler, [March–May 1943], F 447, B 30, E 154, RG 226, NARA.

28. Peers and Brelis, "Original Draft," 142.

29. Barnard, Mission Diary.

30. Ray [Peers] to JACK [Barnard], 7 March 1943, F 447, B 30, E 154, RG 226, NARA. This is a copy of a letter that was presumably dropped to the Barnard-led section of A Group in a resupply bundle.

31. "Message from Wilkinson," 2 June 1943, F 448, B 30, E 154, RG 226, NARA.

32. Ibid. Wilkinson was then the Detachment 101 officer in charge of the FORWARD group. From March 1944 on, SOE in the Far East was known as Force 136.

33. Casualty Report, 13 October 1944, F 372, B 58, E 190 RG 226, NARA. Note that this file has a mistake, and lists John Beamish of A Group as among the missing of B Group. In fact, it is John Clark (listed later in the report with the W Group personnel) who should be listed in Beamish's place. For further information on Clark, see F "Clark, John C (John)," B 54, E 199, RG 226, NARA.

34. Eifler to Donovan, "Detailed Report"; Peers and Brelis, *Behind the Burma Road*, 101–102.

35. Peers and Brelis, *Behind the Burma Road*, 102; Eifler to Donovan, "Detailed Report."

36. Peers and Brelis, *Behind the Burma Road*, 104.

37. Carl F. Eifler to William J. Donovan, "Report Covering the Period April 6 to April 30 1943," 30 April 1943, F 49, B 39, E 190, RG 226, NARA.

38. Peers writes in Peers and Brelis, "Original Draft," 168, that Stilwell was against the operation as it would not further his aims in North Burma. However, he did not wish to countermand Eifler's orders.

39. "Report of Investigation: Harry W. Ballard," 29 June 1945, F Ballard, Harry W. (Harry), B 52, E 199, RG 226, NARA.

40. Eifler to Donovan, "Report Covering the Period April 6 to April 30 1943"; William Slim, *Defeat into Victory: Battling Japan in Burma and India, 1942–1945* (New York: Cooper Square Press, 2000), 154.

41. Eifler to Donovan, "Detailed Report."

42. "Operation Maurice," 2 March 1943, F 49, B 39, E 190, RG 226, NARA.

43. Eifler to Donovan, "Report Covering the Period April 6 to April 30 1943."

44. John G. Coughlin to William J. Donovan, "Situation as of this date," 10 March 1943, F 49, B 39, E 190, RG 226, NARA.

45. Daniel Mudrinich, "Report of Investigation: Charles Morrell," 29 June 1945, B 54, E 199, RG 226, NARA; "Student Questionnaire" [for John Aikman], 30 October 1942, B 52, E 199, RG 226, NARA; a misfiled operational plan for the group can be located in F "Balls" 009505, B 214, E210, RG 226, NARA; Operation plan and summary of mission personnel, undated, F 009505, B 214, E 210, RG 226, NARA.

46. Roosevelt, *The Overseas Targets*, 378.

47. Moon and Eifler, *The Deadliest Colonel*, 118–119.

48. Allen Richter, telephone conversation with author, 25 September 2005.

49. Daniel Mudrinich, "Report of Investigation: John Aikman," 29 June 1945, F Aikman, John (Jinx), B 52, E 199, RG 226, NARA.

50. Carl F. Eifler to William J. Donovan, "Report covering period August 1 to August 31, 1943, inclusive," 1 September 1943, F 1, B 65, E 99, RG 226, NARA. A copy of the mission file is also located in F 412, Ball Group No 1 (Mellie), B 28, E 154, RG 226, NARA.

51. "Missing Agents—Detachment 101," 31 May 1945, F 398, B 54, E 199, RG 226, NARA; Eifler to Donovan, "Report covering period August 1 to August 31, 1943, inclusive" NARA. This prior reconnaissance is also discussed in Coughlin's personal correspondence in Coughlin to Eifler, 7 and 16 August 1943, F, 93, B 45, E 190, RG 226, NARA.

52. Eifler to Donovan, "Report covering period September 1 to October 31, 1943, inclusive," 1 November 1943, F 50, B 39, E190, RG 226, NARA; an additional copy is located in F 1, B 78, E 99, RG 226, NARA.

53. Kenneth Murphy Pier to Eifler, "Ball's Plan, Second Echelon," 16 February

1944, F 002155, B 76, E 210, RG 226, NARA. Copies of this report can be found in F 007282, B 175, E 210, RG 226, NARA, and F 411 "Ops Balls Group # II Closed June 22, 1945," B 28, E 154, RG 226, NARA.

54. Mudrinich "Report of Investigation: Vincent Darlington alias Vin," 13 June 1945, F Darlington, Vincent Geo (Vin), B 53, E 199, RG 226, NARA.

55. William R. Peers to William J. Donovan, "Report covering period November 1 to December 13, 1943 inclusive," 14 December 1943, F 4, B 78, E 99, RG 226, NARA.

56. Peers and Brelis, "Original Draft," 156.

57. Eifler to Donovan, "Report Covering Period July 1 to July 31, 1943, Inclusive," 1 August 1943, F 1, B 65, E 99, RG 226, NARA.

58. Eifler to Donovan, "Detailed Report."

59. For information on these missions, see Daniel Mudrinich, "Report of Investigation: Vincent Darlington alias Vin"; Peers to Donovan, "Report covering period November 1 to December 13, 1943 inclusive"; Eifler to Donovan, "Report covering period August 1." A copy of the mission file is also located in F 412, Ball Group No 1 (Mellie), B 28, E 154, RG 226, NARA; "Missing Agents—Detachment 101"; Eifler to Donovan, "Report covering period August 1"; John G. Coughlin to Carl F. Eifler, 7 and 16 August 1943, F 93, B 45, E 190, RG 226, NARA; Eifler to Donovan, "Report covering period September 1 to October 31, 1943, inclusive"; Kenneth Murphy Pier to Carl F. Eifler, "Ball's Plan, Second Echelon," 16 February 1944, F 002155, B 76, E 210, RG 226, NARA. Copies of this report can be found in F 007282, B 175, E 210, RG 226, NARA, and F 411 "Ops Balls Group # II Closed June 22, 1945," B 28, E 154, RG 226, NARA; "Interrogation of Thra," [June 1945?], F Rodriguez, Joseph E. M (Mellie), B 54, E 199, RG 226, NARA.

60. Peers and Brelis, "Original Draft," 198.

61. Ibid., 158.

62. Eifler to Donovan, "Detailed Report."

63. Ibid.; also recounted in Roosevelt, *The Overseas Targets*, 378.

64. Vince Trifletti, "Rocky Reardon's Airforce," *101 Association Incorporated* 5, no. 9 (April 1975): 3–5.

4. SHORT-RANGE PENETRATIONS MEET SUCCESS

1. William R. Peers, *Guerrilla Operations in Northern Burma* (Fort Leavenworth: Command and General Staff College, [date unknown]), 5. Also published in two parts in William R. Peers, "Guerrilla Operations in Northern Burma," *Military Review* 28 (June 1948): 10–16, and (July 1948): 12–20.

2. Carl F. Eifler to William J. Donovan, "Report of Actions to Date and Request for Instructions," 26 December 1942, F 49, B 39, E 190, RG 226, NARA.

3. Like many OSS operations, the files in the OSS records at NARA for Operation FORWARD are quite detailed. For the reports from FORWARD, see "Operation

Wilkie," F 444 and 445, B 29, E 154, RG 226, NARA. For an account from James C. Luce, see "Report on Tour of Duty with Office of Strategic Services Detachment 101: North Burma and Assam, November 1, 1943 to April 1, 1945," original in author's possession. For the Fort Hertz radio station that operated in conjunction with FORWARD, see F 428, B 28, E 154, RG 226, NARA. For an account of the Japanese POW captured near FORWARD, see "Wires on Japanese Prisoner of War Flown from Major Wilkinson's Area by Colonel Eifler, Japanese Interrogation POWs," F 407, B 61, E 190, RG 226, NARA, and "Testimony of Jap Prisoner Taken Fort Hertz," 19 November 1943, Japanese Interrogation POWs, F 407, B 61, E 190, RG 226, NARA. The first commander also penned a short report of lessons learned from this experiment in William C. Wilkinson, "Problems of a Guerrilla Leader," *Military Review* 32 (November 1952): 23–28.

4. Carl F. Eifler to Benjamin G. Ferris, "Report to General Ferris, Deputy Chief of Staff, thru Colonel Merrill, G-3," 11 February 1943, F 49, B 39, E 190, RG 226, NARA.

5. Eifler was also likely part of the problem. James Luce recalled some of the reactions he got from the British when he went to Fort Hertz after Eifler. "As nearly as we could determine, this was the result of Col. Eifler's rough-shod processes. As we later found out, Eifler had plenty of reason for disapproval of British methods and the treatment of him. At the same time, he was no politician and he repeatedly just added fuel to the fire." See James Luce, "Finally at His Duty Station," *OSS 101 Association Incorporated Newsletter*, Spring 1997, 5.

6. Ibid.

7. Carl F. Eifler to William J. Donovan, "Detailed Report of My Activities Covering the Period December 26, 1942 to Date," 6 April 1943, F 49, B 39, E 190, RG 226, NARA.

8. Colin MacKenzie to Carl F. Eifler, "No. 1889," 12 November 1942, F 197, B 23, E 165, RG 226, NARA, and N. A. Christopher, "Report: Christopher," 13 March 1943, F 444, B 29, E 154, RG 226, NARA; Eifler to Donovan, "Detailed Report of My Activities Covering the Period December 26 to Date." An example of one such report—including detailed sketch maps of Japanese dispositions—can be found in Agent Mac to Wilkinson, 21 November 1943, F 444, B 29, E 154, RG 226, NARA.

9. Carl F. Eifler to William J. Donovan, "Report Covering Period June 1 to June 30, 1943, Inclusive," 1 July 1943, F 1, B 65, E 99, RG 226, NARA.

10. [Carl F. Eifler] to William C. Wilkinson, 7 August 1943, F 444, B 29, E 154, RG 226, NARA.

11. William C. Wilkinson to William R. Peers, "Report Covering the Period October 35 [*sic*], 1943 to December 31,1943," 31 December 1943, F 3, B 78, E 99, RG 226, NARA.

12. William C. Wilkinson to William R. Peers, "Report for Period October 25, 1943 to December 31, 1943," 31 December 1943, F 445, B 29, E 154, RG 226, NARA.

13. Carl F. Eifler to William J. Donovan, "Report Covering the Period July 1 to July 31, 1943, Inclusive," 1 August 1943, F 1, B 65, E 99, RG 226, NARA.

14. Luce, "Report on Tour of Duty."

15. Luce, "Finally at His Duty Station," 4.

16. William C. Wilkinson to Carl F. Eifler, "Report for August," 31 August 1943, F 444, B 29, E 154, RG 226, NARA; William C. Wilkinson to Carl F. Eifler, [personal letter], 25 October 1943, F 444, B 29, E 154, RG 226, NARA.

17. Carl F. Eifler to William J. Donovan, "Report Covering Period November 1 to December 13 1943, Inclusive," 14 December 1943, F 50, B 39, E 190, RG 226, NARA.

18. Carl F. Eifler to William J. Donovan, "Report Covering Period August 1 to August 31, 1943, Inclusive," 1 September 1943, F 50, B 39, E 190, RG 226, NARA. See #12 cable, 16 August 1943.

19. [Carl F. Eifler] to Wally Richmond, 17 July 1943, F 010394, B 270, E 210, RG 226, NARA; William R. Peers to Wally Richmond, 16 June 1943, F 010394, B 270, E 210, RG 226, NARA.

20. William R. Peers and Dean C. Brelis, "Original Draft of Peers-Brelis Behind the Burma Road," 115, Box 1, Detachment 101 Collection, U.S. Army Historical and Education Center, Carlisle Barracks, PA.

21. James C. Luce, "Background, Historical, Military and Political of the Kachin Hills Area," 28 January 1944, original copy in author's possession. Regarding Japanese atrocities, see Peers to Donovan, "Report Covering Period 1 February to 29 February, 1944, Inclusive." Luce reports that the Japanese had raided Kachin villages. In so doing, they looted, carried off two women, and killed seven villagers. "Kachin" or "Jinghpaw" is a term for an amalgamation of several minor tribes, the largest being the Jinghpaw. For an anthropological account of the Kachins, see E. R. Leach, *Political Systems of Highland Burma: A Study of Kachin Social Structure* (London: Athlone Press, 1970), and U Min Thu, *Glimpses of Kachin Traditions and Customs* (Myitkyina, Burma: U Htun Hlaing, 2002). Small ethnographic background studies done by Detachment 101 personnel can be found in Peter K. Lutken, "Report on Kachin Contribution to the Allied War Effort in Burma," 1945, F 44, B 37, E 190, RG 226, NARA, and Luce, "Background, Historical, Military and Political." Although most Kachins were loyal, there are plentiful examples of Kachins who worked or spied for the Japanese. That meant that the OSS always had to keep a wary eye on their indigenous recruits until they had proved their loyalty.

22. Although it was unnecessary, OSS/SOE were prepared to defend Maddox's actions. See [Carl F. Eifler] to Wally Richmond, 8 November 1943, F 010394, B 270, E 210, RG 226, NARA. For Wilkinson's reaction to the shooting, see Wilkinson to Eifler, 25 October 1943, F 444, B 29, E 154, RG 226, NARA.

23. "Skittles," the chief agent of J Group, has penned a memoir of his experiences. This memoir represents one of the few published accounts of a native agent working on behalf of the OSS. Harry "Skittles" Hengshoon, *Green Hell: Unconventional Warfare in the CBI* (Huntington Beach, CA: B & L Lithograph, 2000).

24. Detachment 101 tried to insert the HATE group, led by Ernie de Valeris, but numerous—and probably made-up—problems prevented it. Years later, Detachment

101 veterans wrote "Ernie was a strange person, for sure. He and his gang always seemed to approach their mission relaxed—too relaxed some of us thought. We of 101 considered ourselves pretty loose too . . . but underneath was a code, a discipline, a direction, a strength that all subscribed to but never talked about." See "Ernie and His Gang," *101 Association Incorporated Newsletter* 5, no. 6 (June 1974): 1.

25. Eifler to Donovan, "Detailed Report of My Activities Covering the Period December 26, 1942 to Date"; Hengshoon, *Green Hell*, 35.

26. Hengshoon, *Green Hell*, 58.

27. Eifler to Donovan, "Detailed Report of My Activities Covering the Period December 26, 1942 to Date."

28. Draft History of Detachment 101, F 1, B 78, E 99, RG 226, NARA; "Brief Chronology of OSSSU Detachment 101," F 74, B 42, E 190, RG 226, NARA.

29. Peer and Brelis, *Behind the Burma Road*, 113.

30. "KNOTHEAD Group," F 48, B 38, E 190, RG 226, NARA.

31. "Interview with Hefty," F 48, B 38, E 190, RG 226, NARA.

32. "Interview with Jack Pamplin," 26 May 1945, F 48, B 38, E 190, RG 226, NARA.

33. "Interview with Hefty."

34. Peers and Brelis, "Original Draft," 16. Father James Stuart gives Zhing Htaw Naw's spelling as Zinghtung Naw.

35. "Interview with Jack Pamplin."

36. Peers and Brelis, "Original Draft," 173.

37. Eifler to Donovan, "Report Covering Period November 1 to December 13 1943, Inclusive."

38. "Interview with Jack Pamplin."

39. For more on Fathers McAlindon and Stuart, see Edward Fischer, *Mission in Burma: The Columban Fathers' Forty-Three Years in Kachin Country* (New York: Seabury Press, 1980), 61–70. Father Stuart's recollections can be found in "Statement of Father Stuart Dealing with Events in Area North of Myitkyina from May 1942 until March 1944," found in Thomas N. Moon and Carl F. Eifler, *The Deadliest Colonel* (New York: Vantage Press, 1975), 268–309.

40. "Interview with Jack Pamplin."

41. The cable traffic concerning the planning and extraction of this pilot can be found at "Wires on Japanese Prisoner of War Flown from Captain Curl's Area by Colonel Eifler," F 4, B 78, E 99, RG 226, NARA.

42. "Detailed Report by Father Stuart on His Attempt to Take Refugees to Shingbwiyang Evacuee Camp," F 433, B 29, E 154, RG 226, NARA.

43. Peers and Brelis, "Original Draft," 216.

44. Moon and Eifler, *The Deadliest Colonel*, 170–172.

45. "KNOTHEAD Group Report May 1944," 1 April, 1944, F 433, B 29, E 154, RG 226, NARA.

46. Tom Moon interview by Heidi Vion, 13 April 1995, Garden Grove, CA. Contained in Heidi Vion, "Booms from Behind the Lines": The Oral Histories of the

Covert Experiences of the Men of the Office of Strategic Services' Detachment 101 in the World War II China-Burma-India Theater," thesis, California State University, Fullerton, 2004.

47. William R. Peers to William J. Donovan, "Report covering period 1 March to 31 March, 1944, inclusive," 31 March 1944, F 53, B 40, E 190, RG 226, NARA.

5. RETHINKING OPERATIONS: THE DETACHMENT EVOLVES, FEBRUARY 1943–JANUARY 1944

1. Carl O. Hoffman to Milton Miles, "Eifler," 2 April 1943, Roll 78, M 1642, RG 226, NARA.

2. Carl F. Eifler to William J. Donovan, "Report Covering Period June 1 to June 30, 1943, Inclusive," 1 July 1943, F 1, B 65, E 99, RG 226, NARA.

3. Carl F. Eifler to William J. Donovan, "Report Covering Period September 1 to October 31, 1943, Inclusive," 1 November 1943, F 1, B 78, E 99, RG 226, NARA; "OSS-SU 101: Schools and Training; Report," November 1944, frames 376–393, Roll 88, M 1642, RG 226, NARA. This booklet, now on microfilm at NARA, was produced by the S&T staff at Detachment 101.

4. George D. Gorin to Douglas M. Dimond, 29 November 1943, F 393, B 53, E 199, RG 226, NARA; Detachment 101 had great success with its local recruits and in only a few cases did significant problems arise. One such case was Dennis Gomes, who deserted while on leave to Calcutta. He was apprehended and, lest he reveal the identities of those whom he had trained with and who were involved in operations behind Japanese lines, was incarcerated for the duration of the war. Supposedly, the OSS continued to pay his salary. See Floyd Frazee to Gavin Stewart, 21 June 1943, F 197, B 23, E 165, RG 226, NARA.

5. John G. Coughlin to William J. Donovan, "Situation as of This Date," 10 March 1943, F49, B 39, E 190, RG 226, NARA.

6. Carl O. Hoffman to Carl F. Eifler, "Yours of April 21 and 26, 1943," 26 May 1943, F 27, B 191, E 92, RG 226, NARA.

7. Carl F. Eifler to William J. Donovan, "Status of O.S.S. Detachment 101," 16 February 1943, F 49, B 39, E 190, RG 226, NARA.

8. Eifler to Donovan, "Report Covering Period September 1 to October 31, 1943, Inclusive," 1 November 1943.

9. William R. Peers to William J. Donovan, "Report Covering Period November 1 to December 13, 1943, Inclusive," 14 December 1943, F 4, B 78, E 99, RG 226, NARA; Theater Commander, Field Photo Unit #23, to Director of the History Project, "Narrative History, Field Photo Unit # 23; Period September 1943 to September 1944," 20 November 1944, F 627, B 70, E 144, RG 226, NARA; Guy Bolte to John Ford, "Activities of Unit 23 for December, 1943," 12 January 1944, F 366, B 22, E 90, RG 226, NARA.

10. Carl F. Eifler to William J. Donovan, "Status of O.S.S. Detachment 101," 16 February 1943, F 49, B 39, E 190, RG 226, NARA.

11. Eifler to Donovan, "Report Covering Period June 1 to June 30, 1943, Inclusive," 1 July 1943.

12. William C. Wilkinson to William R. Peers, "Report Covering the Period October 35 [*sic*], 1943 to December 31,1943," 31 December 1943, F 3, B 78, E 99, RG 226, NARA.

13. Carl F. Eifler to William J. Donovan, "Report Covering Period August 1 to August 31, 1943, Inclusive," 1 September 1943, F 1, B 65, E 99, RG 226, NARA.

14. William R. Peers and Dean C. Brelis, "Original Draft of Peers-Brelis Behind the Burma Road," 119, Box 1, Detachment 101 Collection, U.S. Army Historical and Education Center, Carlisle Barracks, PA.

15. William R. Peers to William J. Donovan, "Report Covering period 1 April to 30 April, 1944, Inclusive," 14 December 1943, F 54, B 110, E 190, RG 226, NARA.

16. Carl F. Eifler to Douglas M. Dimond, "Special Funds," 5 December 1943, F. Eifler Procurement, B 148, E 134, RG 226, NARA; George D. Gorin to Douglas Dimond, 29 November 1943, F 393, B 53, E 199, RG 226, NARA.

17. Eifler to Donovan, "Report Covering Period September 1 to October 31, 1943, Inclusive," 1 November 1943.

18. Peers to Donovan, "Report Covering Period November 1 to December 13, 1943, Inclusive," 14 December 1943; George D. Gorin, "Report of Finance Section for the Months of December/43 and January/44, [late January 1944], F 528, B 71, E 199, RG 226, NARA, reports an even sharper increase. He says that the increase for December was $100,000, a $60,000 increase from the previous month. For the sake of standardization, the lower increase cited in the monthly report is being used.

19. Eifler to Donovan, "Report Covering Period September 1 to October 31, 1943, Inclusive," 1 November 1943; Peers to Donovan, "Report Covering Period November 1 to December 13, 1943, Inclusive," 14 December 1943 details the sending of examples of Thai money for the same purpose.

20. George D. Gorin to Carl F. Eifler, "Report of Finance Section, OSSSU DET 101, for September and October, 1943," 31 October 1943, F 528, B 71, E 199, RG 226, NARA.

21. Peers to Donovan, "Report Covering Period November 1 to December 13, 1943, Inclusive," 14 December 1943; L Group was a short-lived intelligence-gathering mission headed by Agent Skittles that went into the upper Hukawng Valley in May 1943.

22. Samuel A. Schreiner, "The 101 Experience," *OSS 101 Association Incorporated Newsletter*, March 1988, 7.

23. Carl F. Eifler to William J. Donovan, "Detailed Report of My Activities Covering the Period December 26, 1942 to Date," 6 April 1943, F 49, B 39, E 190, RG 226, NARA; "Brief Chronology of OSSSU Detachment 101," [early 1945?], F 74, B 42, E 190, RG 226, NARA.

24. Carl F. Eifler to William J. Donovan, "Report Covering Period July 1 to July 31, 1943, Inclusive," 1 August 1943, F 1, B 65, E 99, RG 226, NARA.

25. Eifler to Donovan, "Report Covering Period August 1 to August 31, 1943, Inclusive," 1 September 1943.

26. Eifler to Donovan, "Report Covering Period September 1 to October 31, 1943, Inclusive," 1 November 1943.

27. Peers to Donovan, "Report Covering Period November 1 to December 13, 1943, Inclusive," 14 December 1943.

28. Eifler to Donovan, "Report Covering Period September 1 to October 31, 1943, Inclusive," 1 November 1943.

29. Eifler to Donovan, "Report Covering Period July 1 to July 31, 1943, Inclusive," 1 August 1943.

30. Eifler to Donovan, "Report Covering Period June 1 to June 30, 1943, Inclusive," 1 July 1943.

31. Peers to Donovan, "Report Covering Period November 1 to December 13, 1943, Inclusive," 14 December 1943.

32. John G. Coughlin, "Report of Drop to Ernie on November 26, 1943," [27 November 1943], F 315, B 56, E 190, RG 226, NARA.

33. Peers and Brelis, "Original Draft," 213.

34. Peers and Brelis, *Behind the Burma Road*, 147–148.

35. Peers to Donovan, "Report Covering Period November 1 to December 13, 1943, Inclusive," 14 December 1943.

36. Carlton F. Scofield to [Richard Heppner?], "Informal Report on Detachment 101," 13 March 1944, F Eifler, B 644, E 190, RG 226, NARA.

37. Kermit Roosevelt, *The Overseas Targets*, vol. 2 of *War Report of the OSS (Office of Strategic Services)* (New York: Walker, 1976), 364; [Eifler or Peers] to Wally Richmond, 14 February 1944, F 010394, B 270, E 210, RG 226, NARA.

38. Eifler to Donovan, "Report Covering Period September 1 to October 31, 1943, Inclusive," 1 November 1943; the correspondence with NCAC can be found at F 499, B68, E 190, RG 226, NARA. RG 493, the Army CBI records, does not have copies.

39. [Carl F. Eifler] to Wally Richmond, 21 July 1943, F 010394, B 270, E 210, RG 226, NARA.

40. E. L. Taylor to Albert C. Wedemeyer, "Coordination of Intelligence and Sabotage Activities," 30 October 1943, F 2158, B 119, E 154, RG 226, NARA. Taylor writes that Major General Cawthorn (British Army in India) said that the most "urgent problem facing his proposed committee was the coordination of the activities of Colonel Eifler's OSS team in Burma." In contrast to Detachment 101, which focused on using the Kachin ethnic group, SOE chose to work in the main with the Karen. An example of a report of a Karen agent working for SOE and sent through P Division channel can be found in "Report of I.S.L.D. Agent," presumably late 1943–early 1944, F 010394, B 270, E 210, RG 226, NARA.

41. Roosevelt, *The Overseas Targets*, 393–394. For more on QUADRANT, see Charles Romanus and Riley Sunderland, *United States Army in World War II: China-Burma-India Theater: Stilwell's Mission to China* (Washington, DC: Center of Military History, 1987), 357–367.

42. Benjamin G. Ferris to Henry Pownall, "Combined Liaison Committee," 18 November 1943, F 2158, B 119, E 154, RG 226, NARA.

43. The details of the arrangement can be found at "Integrations of S.O.E. With S.E.A. Command Suggested Procedure for Control and Direction," [October? 1943], F 2158, B 119, E 154, RG 226, NARA. The OSS found this proposal unacceptable in regard to Detachment 101. Their recommendation can be found in Richard P. Heppner, "Proposed Interim Procedure For Coordination of American and British Agencies in SEAC," [late 1943], F 2158, B 119, E 154, RG 226, NARA.

44. Stilwell's formal reservations can be found in "Project Combined Liaison Committee," 28 August 1943, F 2158, B 119, E 154, RG 226, NARA.

45. An example of this can be found at Richard P. Heppner to P Division, SEAC, "Projected OSS Operations in Northern Burma," 27 December 1943, F 10, B 59, E 99, RG 226, NARA. In this case, Detachment 101's entire brief for the British on operational plans for early 1944 consists of a single page.

46. As the OSS representative, Heppner was sent in part to give OSS more control over Detachment 101's operations. See Francis T. Devlin to R. Davis Hallowell, "Eifler Report 2/16/43—New Delhi India," 12 March 1943, F Eifler, B 644, E 190, RG 226, NARA.

47. Richard P. Heppner to E. L. Taylor, "Coordination of OSS in SEAC," 14 November 1943, F 2158, B 119, E 154, RG 226, NARA.

48. Carl O. Hoffman to William J. Donovan, "Far East Conference with General Merrill," 5 May 1943, F Eifler, B 644, E 190, RG 226, NARA, has a discussion on Stilwell's warning to OSS to keep from under British control.

49. E. L. Taylor to Albert C. Wedemeyer, "Memorandum for General Wedemeyer," 15 November 1943, F 2158, B 119, E 154, RG 226, NARA.

50. Richard P. Heppner to E. L. Taylor, "Coordination of Quasi Military Activities," 14 November 1943, F 2158, B 119, E 154, RG 226, NARA.

51. William R. Peers to Wally Richmond [personal letter], 21 December 1943, F 010394, B 270, E 210, RG 226, NARA.

52. Roosevelt, *The Overseas Targets*, 393–394.

53. William R. Peers to William J. Donovan, "Report Covering Period 31 May to 30 June, 1944," [30 June 1944], F 136, B 34, E 190, RG 226, NARA.

54. Letter to Captain D. Hunter, "U.S. Army Experimental Station Headquarters, Calcutta," 12 November 1943, F 010394, B 270, E 210, RG 226, NARA. In this instance the weapon being evaluated, the Welrod Mk 2, failed. Wally Richmond's correspondence and diary of events can be found at F 010394, B 270, E 210, RG 226, NARA; J. Q. Wood to Wally Richmond, "Subject: Employment-Lt. J. Girsham, A.B.R.O.," 27 September 1943, F 010394, B 270, E 210, RG 226, NARA.

55. Eifler to Donovan, "Report Covering Period July 1 to July 31, 1943, Inclusive," 1 August 1943.

56. Eifler to Donovan, "Report Covering Period June 1 to June 30, 1943, Inclusive," 1 July 1943.

57. James W. Kirk to Sidney Wheeler, "Official Code and Color Markings for OSS Overseas Shipments as Approved by Policy Committee," 30 September 1943, F 313, B 56, E 190, RG 226, NARA; [OSS Washington] to Richard P. Heppner, "Markings for All OSS Shipments," 30 October 1943, F 313, B 56, E 190, RG 226, NARA.

58. Eifler to Donovan, "Report Covering Period July 1 to July 31, 1943, Inclusive," 1 August 1943.

59. Eifler to Donovan, "Report Covering Period June 1 to June 30, 1943, Inclusive," 1 July 1943.

60. Eifler to Donovan, "Report Covering Period September 1 to October 31, 1943, Inclusive," 1 November 1943.

61. Ibid.

62. Eifler to Donovan, "Report Covering Period August 1 to August 31, 1943, Inclusive," 1 September 1943; Eifler to Donovan, "Report Covering Period September 1 to October 31, 1943, Inclusive," 1 November 1943; Detachment 101 to OSS Washington, "#AG 461 AMMDEL," 9 May 1943, F Eifler Procurement, B 148, E 134, RG 226, NARA.

63. Eifler to Donovan, "Report Covering Period September 1 to October 31, 1943, Inclusive," 1 November 1943.

64. William C. Wilkinson, "Need for OSS Special Items in Northern Burma," [1944–1945?], F 3997, B 273, E 139, RG 226, NARA.

65. Carl O. Hoffman to Richard Heppner, "Since you have departed," 13 September 1943, F 2119, B 117, E 154, RG 226, NARA.

66. Peers to Donovan, "Report Covering Period November 1 to December 13, 1943, Inclusive," 14 December 1943; Harold "Bud" Banker, telephone interview by author, Fayetteville, NC, 22 March 2007.

67. Hoffman to Heppner, 13 September 1943, NARA.

68. Eifler to Donovan, "Report Covering Period June 1 to June 30, 1943, Inclusive," 1 July 1943. For more on the OSS Free Thai, see E. Bruce Reynolds, *Thailand's Secret War: The Free Thai, OSS, and SOE during World War II.* (Cambridge: Cambridge University Press, 2005), and Nicol Smith and Blake Clark, *Into Siam: Underground Kingdom* (Indianapolis: Bobbs-Merrill, 1946).

69. Carl F. Eifler to Carl O. Hoffman, "SO," 15 July 1943, F Eifler Procurement, B 148, E 134, RG 226, NARA; Vince Trifletti, "Rocky Reardon's Airforce," *101 Association Incorporated* 5, no. 10 (April 1975): 5.

70. Charles N. Fisher to Carl F. Eifler, "FE-1 Personnel," 23 October 1943, F 371, B 58, E 190, RG 226, NARA.

71. Carl F. Eifler to Carl O. Hoffman [personal letter], 3 November 1943, F 267, B 16, E 146A, RG 226, NARA; to read about this crash and Eifler's ten-day walkout, see

Troy Sacquety, "Behind Japanese Lines in Burma," *Studies in Intelligence: Journal of the American Intelligence Professional* 11 (Fall–Winter 2001): 67–79.

72. Eifler to Hoffman, "SO," 9 July 1943.

73. Eifler to Donovan, "Report Covering Period September 1 to October 31, 1943, Inclusive," 1 November 1943.

74. Anonymous, "Sea Rescue," *101 Association Incorporated* 5, no. 10 (August 1975): 7; William B. Shepard, "Report on Rescue Mission," [November 1943], in Peers to Donovan, "Report Covering Period 14 December 1943 to 31 January, 1944, Inclusive," 31 January 1944, F 51, B 39, E 190, RG 226, NARA; Peers to Donovan, "Report Covering Period November 1 to December 13, 1943, Inclusive," 14 December 1943. A full accounting of this mission can be read in Thomas N. Moon and Carl F. Eifler, *The Deadliest Colonel* (New York: Vantage, 1975), 85–87. Eifler's faulty accounting has the rescue occurring a year earlier than it actually did. See Harry W. Little to Carl F. Eifler, "Preparation of Motor Boat for Sea Rescue Trip," 2 December 1943, F 630, B 70, E 144, RG 226, NARA; Richmond, "Preparations for Sea Rescue Trip," [early December 1943], F 630, B 70, E 144, RG 226, NARA; M. E. Miles, "Rescue Mission Commanded by Colonel Carl E. Eifler, AUS," 12 December 1943, F2538, B 192, E 139, RG 226, NARA. For the commendation letter from the Tenth Air Force, see Howard C. Davidson to Carl F. Eifler, "Commendation," 6 December 1943, F 3, B 5, E 165A, RG 226, NARA. To rescue the nine airmen, Eifler had the *Miami* loaded down with six crew members and an additional six passengers, including himself, Wally Richmond, and an indigenous agent. On board, they only had six Thompson submachine guns for antiaircraft protection. It was the *Miami*'s maiden voyage, the first time that the captain had driven it or a boat of its type, and the gas consumption for a long journey—910 miles—was an unknown.

75. Coughlin, "Report of Drop to Ernie on November 26, 1943," [27 November 1943].

76. Thomas Riley, "Air Drop to Curl on December 9, 1943-Personnel, Supplies, and Equipment," 11 December 1943, F 315, B 56, E 190, RG 226, NARA. Riley observed that ATC personnel often were unclear about which supplies went to what group during drops from a single sortie to multiple groups. This resulted in some groups getting more supplies than needed, while others received none. Jim Ward, "My Introduction to 101," *101 Association Incorporated*, April 1985, 3. Thomas Riley was later killed while on an airdrop mission to FORWARD. On 18 January 1944, the C-47 in which he was flying was shot down by Japanese fighter aircraft. Lieutenant Jim Ward, who arrived to become the next air drop officer, reported in as Riley's replacement. He was greeted by Peers with a stern warning: "No one can replace Tom Riley! You are not his replacement. You're his successor." Peers would keep a portrait of Riley over his desk for the duration of the war.

77. Jim Tilly, "Tilly's Tall Tales," *101 Association Incorporated Newsletter* 6, no. 4 (September 1976): 6.

78. D. V. Cavanaugh, "Air Drop: Part II-People, Parachutes, Problems," *101 Association Incorporated Newsletter* 6, no. 3 (June 1976): 6.

79. Peers to Donovan, "Report Covering Period November 1 to December 13, 1943, Inclusive," 14 December 1943.

80. James Luce, "Finally at His Duty Station," *OSS 101 Association Incorporated*, Spring 1997, 6.

81. James Luce, "Jim Luce (2nd Installment)," *OSS 101 Association Incorporated*, Winter 1997, 6.

82. Allen Richter to author, email, 29 November 2006.

83. Peers and Brelis, "Original Draft," 279–280.

84. William R. Peers and Dean Brelis, *Behind the Burma Road: The Story of America's Most Successful Guerrilla Force* (Boston: Little, Brown, 1963), 100.

85. Eifler to Donovan, "Report Covering Period June 1 to June 30, 1943, Inclusive," 1 July 1943.

86. Anonymous, "The Only Time General Donovan Got Behind the Lines," *101 Association Incorporated* 5, no. 10 (August 1975), 8. This article says that Eifler knew that Donovan wanted to go behind the lines as a way to build up his credibility. Other sources say the OSS chief did this so as not to back down from Eifler's invitation. Either way, the event demonstrates a profound lack of judgment for both parties. Had Eifler been captured, Detachment 101's existence would have been in jeopardy. Had the same happened to Donovan, the existence of the OSS itself would have been at risk.

87. Peers and Brelis, *Behind the Burma Road*, 132; [William R. Peers?],"My Dear General Richardson," 11 December 1943, F 2538, B 192, E 139, RG 226, NARA.

88. Carl O. Hoffman to Richard Heppner, "#62," 21 October 1943, F1053, B 164, E 134, RG 226, NARA. Donovan was already planning in October to remove Eifler—even before he came out to the Detachment. After a partial recovery—Eifler spent many postwar years dealing with his injuries—Donovan placed him in charge of the Field Experimental Unit, in mid-1944. Colonel John Coughlin briefly took over command until he was sent to take over OSS operations with the fledgling Detachment 202 in China. Colonel Ray Peers then took command of Detachment 101, and held it until the end of the war.

6. PEERS TAKES OVER: DETACHMENT 101 COMES OF AGE, JANUARY–MAY 1944

1. William R. Peers and Dean Brelis, *Behind the Burma Road: The Story of America's Most Successful Guerrilla Force* (Boston: Little, Brown, 1963), 132.

2. E. L. Taylor to William J. Donovan, 9 January 1944, Folder 2728, Box 193, Entry 146, Research Group 226, National Archives and Records Administration, College Park, MD.

3. Carlton F. Scofield to [Richard Heppner?], "Informal Report on Detachment 101," 13 March 1944, F Eifler, B 644, E 190, RG 226, NARA.

4. William R. Peers to William J. Donovan, "Report Covering Period 1 February to 29 February, 1944, inclusive," 29 February 1944, F 52, B 39, E 190, RG 226, NARA.

5. John G. Coughlin to Far East Theater Officer [OSS Washington], 12 May 1944, F 2536, B 192, E 139, RG 226, NARA.

6. Peers and Brelis, "Original Draft," 11.

7. Peers and Brelis, "Original Draft," 25.

8. "Theater Officer's Pouch Report," 2 May 1944, F 31, B 75, E 99, RG 226, NARA. Repeated searches have failed to uncover records of the American troops in V-Force prior to their joining Detachment 101. Many were on detached service from the 988th Signals Battalion.

9. See Michael Calvert, *Chindits: Long Range Penetration* (New York: Ballantine, 1973) and Shelford Bidwell, *The Chindit War: Stilwell, Wingate, and the Campaign in Burma: 1944* (New York: Macmillan, 1979); only five of the six Chindit brigades went into Burma. One was used to help blunt the Japanese U-GO offensive into India.

10. Joseph W. Stilwell, *The Stilwell Papers* (New York: William Morrow, 1975), 301.

11. Peers and Brelis, "Original Draft," 229.

12. Peers to Donovan, "Report Covering Period 1 February to 29 February, 1944, inclusive," 29 February 1944; [William R. Peers to William J. Donovan] "O.S.S.S.U. Detachment 101 Monthly Report," May 1944, F 12, B 34, E 190, RG 226, NARA. Unless Anglo-Burmese were of "definitely outstanding character," they were no longer a target for recruitment on account of the problems that the Detachment had in trying to employ them in north Burma. Various letters between Detachment 101 personnel relay confusion over Eifler's status, and he may have even been under the impression that he would soon return to command of Detachment 101.

13. William R. Peers to William J. Donovan, "Report Covering Period 14 December 1943 to 31 January, 1944, inclusive," 31 January 1944, F 51, B 39, E 190, RG 226, NARA.

14. William R. Peers to William J. Donovan, "Report Covering Period 1 April to 30 April, 1944, inclusive," 30 April 1944, F 54, B 110, E 190, RG 226, NARA.

15. "O.S.S.S.U. Detachment 101 Monthly Report," May 1944. This would become important later, when Detachment 404 began operations along the Arakan Coast. This was still an area that Peers saw as in the area of operations of Detachment 101.

16. John G. Coughlin to Carl [Hoffman?], 29 January 1944, F 2535, B 192, E 139, RG 226, NARA. One aspect of this was to uncover possible fraud on behalf of Harry W. Little, who was thought—wrongly—to have been mixed up in the affairs of Richmond and Ottaway.

17. Peers to Donovan, "Report Covering Period 1 February to 29 February, 1944, inclusive," 29 February 1944.

18. "O.S.S.S.U. Detachment 101 Monthly Report," May 1944.

19. Peers to Donovan, "Report Covering Period 1 April to 30 April, 1944, inclusive," 30 April 1944; "O.S.S.S.U. Detachment 101 Monthly Report," May 1944.

20. Peers to Donovan, "Report Covering Period 1 February to 29 February, 1944, inclusive," 29 February 1944.

21. Peers to Donovan, "Report Covering Period 14 December 1943 to 31 January, 1944, inclusive," 31 January 1944.

22. Ibid.

23. Peers to Donovan, "Report Covering Period 1 April to 30 April, 1944, inclusive," 30 April 1944. One problem that Peers pointed out in William R. Peers to John G. Coughlin, 6 March 1944, F 192, B 23, E 165, RG 226, NARA, was that other OSS units in theater, including what would become Detachment 404, poached on the OSS/SOS arrangement by requesting supplies under the guise of being from Detachment 101.

24. "O.S.S.S.U. Detachment 101 Monthly Report," May 1944.

25. Sherman Joost, "Situation at Air Drop," [early 1944?], F 314, B 56, E190, RG 226, NARA.

26. William R. Peers to William J. Donovan, "Report Covering Period 1 March to 31 March, 1944, inclusive," 31 March 1944, F 53, B 40, E 190, RG 226, NARA; "O.S.S.S.U. Detachment 101 Monthly Report," May 1944.

27. Dow S. Grones to Quinn, "Air Drop and Air Activities, January Report," 30 January 1945, F 20, B 34, E 190, RG 226, NARA.

28. Joseph E. Lazarsky, interview by Troy J. Sacquety, 26 March 2008, Middleburg, VA. For more on the Second Troop Carrier Squadron, see W. E. Smith, ed., *2nd Troop Carrier Squadron: AAF-CBI-WWII* (Cullman, AL: Gregath, 1987).

29. Lazarsky interview, 26 March 2008, Middleburg, VA. Lazarsky was later awarded the Distinguished Flying Cross for actions over Burma in which he took over control of a damaged C-47 from a wounded pilot.

30. Peers and Brelis, "Original Draft," 224.

31. Harold "Bud" Banker, telephone interview by Troy J. Sacquety, 14 April 2008, Fort Bragg, NC. Banker was the noncommissioned officer in charge of the Nazira supply warehouse. Banker has also authored a self-published manuscript called "Serving Military Time."

32. Peers to Donovan, "Report Covering Period 14 December 1943 to 31 January, 1944, inclusive," 31 January 1944.

33. Richard Dunlop, *Behind Japanese Lines: With the OSS in Burma* (Chicago: Rand McNally, 1979), 278; interview with Marje Luce (widow of James) by author, Fayetteville, NC, May 2007, notes. The next drop did not occur until 12 February as detailed in Peers to Donovan, "Report Covering Period 1 February to 29 February, 1944, inclusive," 29 February 1944.

34. James C. Luce, "Background, historical, military and political of the Kachin Hills area," 28 January 1944, personal papers in author's possession.

35. Peers to Donovan, "Report Covering Period 1 February to 29 February, 1944, inclusive," 29 February 1944.

36. Father James Stuart's account of his guiding a refugee column to Allied lines can be found in the KNOTHEAD report in Peers to Donovan, "Report Covering Period 1 April to 30 April, 1944, inclusive," 30 April 1944.

37. Peers to Donovan, "Report Covering Period 1 March to 31 March, 1944, inclusive," 31 March 1944; "O.S.S.S.U. Detachment 101 Monthly Report," May 1944.

38. "O.S.S.S.U. Detachment 101 Monthly Report," May 1944; in addition to two USAAF squadrons, the Second Troop Carrier and the Rescue Squadron, the Air Transport Corps (ATC), and the 5301st, 5302nd, and 5303rd Air Dropping Platoons assisted; Peers to Donovan, "Report Covering Period 1 March to 31 March, 1944, inclusive," 31 March 1944; "O.S.S.S.U. Detachment 101 Monthly Report," May 1944. For a look at how the USAAF cooperated with OSS in the European theater, see Troy Sacquety, "Supplying the Resistance: OSS Logistics Support to Special Operations in Europe," *Veritas: Journal of Army Special Operations History* 3, no. 1 (2007): 37–48.

39. William J. Slim, *Defeat into Victory: Battling Japan in Burma and India, 1942–1945* (New York: Cooper Square Press, 2000), 225–226.

40. Charles F. Romanus and Riley Sunderland, *United States Army in World War II: China-Burma-India Theater: Time Runs Out in CBI.* (Washington DC: Center of Military History, 1959), 97.

41. Charles F. Romanus and Riley Sunderland, *United States Army in World War II: China-Burma-India Theater: Stilwell's Command Problems* (Washington, DC: Center of Military History, 1987), 108–109.

42. Ibid., 105.

43. Lazarsky interview, 26 March 2008, Middleburg, VA.

44. FORWARD Daily Log January 23 to April 8 [1944], 9 March [1944], copy in author's possession.

45. FORWARD Daily Log, 10 March [1944], copy in author's possession. As an aside, one of the air drop officers relayed that on night flights, signal fires popped up along their flight path. However, they dropped only on the pattern used by Detachment 101. The fires were probably set by villagers hoping to get a free bonanza of supplies. See D. V. Cavanaugh, "Air Drop: Part II-People, Parachutes, Problems," *101 Association Incorporated Newsletter* 6, no. 3 (June 1976): 6.

46. Peers to Donovan, "Report Covering Period 1 March to 31 March, 1944, inclusive," 31 March 1944.

47. R. T. Shelby to KNOTHEAD, "Dear Pamplin and Knothead Group," 12 April 1944, F 453, B 30, E 154, RG 226, NARA.

48. Mike Council to Raymond T. Shelby, 22 April 1944, F 456, B 65, E 190, RG 226, NARA. In Mike Council to Raymond T. Shelby, 17 March 1944, F 456, B 65, E 190, RG 226, NARA, Council reported that his section alone consumed 447½ pounds of rice per day—illustrating the large amount of provisions required monthly.

49. Peers to Donovan, "Report Covering Period 1 February to 29 February, 1944, inclusive," 29 February 1944; at the time, Detachment 101 possessed no air assets. Both the Gypsy Moth and one of the Piper Cubs had crashed. A second Piper Cub was out of commission with a cracked propeller that could not be replaced.

50. "O.S.S.S.U. Detachment 101 Monthly Report," May 1944. The acquisition of the additional liaison planes might have been helped by USAAF General John F.

Egan, who in March agreed to help Detachment 101 by having additional airplanes assigned to him, for use by the Detachment. See William R. Peers to John G. Coughlin, 24 March 1944, F 93, B 45, E 190, RG 226, NARA.

51. G. Edward Buxton (Acting Director OSS) to Commanding Officer, Detachment 101, "Designation of Parachute Jumping School and Parachute Unit," 7 April 1944, F 2728, B 193, E 146, RG 226, NARA. Opening a parachute school was not common for OSS, but it was done, and other schools included Kunming, China, and North Africa.

52. Peers to Donovan, "Report Covering Period 14 December 1943 to 31 January, 1944, inclusive," 31 January 1944.

53. Robert Baker to William R. Peers, "Cooperation of Detachment 101 with ATC," 20 August 1944, F 3, B 5, E 165A, RG 226, NARA.

54. Peers to Donovan, "Report Covering Period 1 February to 29 February, 1944, inclusive," 29 February 1944.

55. See "Plans" in Peers to Donovan, "Report Covering Period 14 December 1943 to 31 January, 1944, inclusive," 31 January 1944; [Carl F. Eifler or William R. Peers] to Wally Richmond, 14 February 1944, F 010394, B 270, E 210, RG 226, NARA.

56. Peers to Donovan, "Report Covering Period 1 February to 29 February, 1944, inclusive," 29 February 1944. The officer chosen was Lieutenant Charles Stelle, previously of the R&A section in New Delhi. Detachment 101 had proposed Operation DEMOS, but it was turned down because Wingate would be operating in the same area. With liaison established, the same men could go in as originally proposed, but under Wingate's direction.

57. [Eifler or Peers] to Richmond, 14 February 1944. For more on the First Air Commandos, see Herbert A. Mason Jr., Randy G. Bergeron, and James A. Renfrow Jr., *Operation THURSDAY: Birth of the Air Commandos* (Washington, DC: United States Air Force History and Museums Program, 1994).

58. Peers to Donovan, "Report Covering Period 1 February to 29 February, 1944, inclusive," 29 February 1944.

59. [Eifler or Peers] to Richmond, 14 February 1944. Cooperation was not acquired from every U.S. Army officer. In late February, Brigadier General Frank Dorn, Stilwell's deputy chief, informed Detachment 101 that he was going to "withdraw any connection with your group," on account of some agents that he thought were unsavory characters and possibly Japanese agents. See Frank Dorn to John G. Coughlin, "Memo for Colonel Coughlin," 21 February 1944, F 453, B 30, E 154, RG 226, NARA.

60. Peers to Coughlin, 24 March 1944.

61. Peers to Donovan, "Report Covering Period 1 April to 30 April, 1944, inclusive," 30 April 1944.

62. Peers to Coughlin, 24 March 1944.

63. Peers to Donovan, "Report Covering Period 14 December 1943 to 31 January, 1944, inclusive," 31 January 1944.

64. William R. Peers to Faulkner, "I have just read . . . ," 14 February 1944, F 192,

B 23, E 165, RG 226, NARA. Peers further went on to say, "This helps a great deal and proves conclusively to us that our information is highly desirable to the combat units. We have had five men assigned to us by General Merrill with promises of more to come."

65. Peers to Donovan, "Report Covering Period 14 December 1943 to 31 January, 1944, inclusive," 31 January 1944.

66. "O.S.S.S.U. Detachment 101 Monthly Report," May 1944.

67. Peers to Donovan, "Report Covering Period 14 December 1943 to 31 January, 1944, inclusive," 31 January 1944.

68. Peers to Donovan, "Report Covering Period 1 April to 30 April, 1944, inclusive," 30 April 1944.

69. "O.S.S.S.U. Detachment 101 Monthly Report," May 1944.

70. Peers to Donovan, "Report Covering Period 1 March to 31 March, 1944, inclusive," 31 March 1944.

71. William R. Peers to Harry L. Bearno, 2 February 1944, F 313, B 56, E 190, RG 226, NARA.

72. "O.S.S.S.U. Detachment 101 Monthly Report," May 1944.

73. Peers to Donovan, "Report Covering Period 1 February to 29 February, 1944, inclusive," 29 February 1944. Having no metal or telephone poles available, the group substituted betel nut trees.

74. Charles Fisher to John G. Coughlin, "Personnel and Supplies," 3 March 1944, F 373, B 59, E 190, RG 226, NARA. Peers seems to have been a bit dubious about the utility of pigeons. He wrote in March, "I don't know who ordered them initially if they were ordered or somebody is trying to shove them down our throats." See Peers to Coughlin, 24 March 1944.

75. Kermit Roosevelt, *The Overseas Targets* [special title], vol. 2 of *War Report of the OSS (Office of Strategic Services)* (New York: Walker, 1976), 212–215. Even when the Morale Operations (MO) Branch was represented in the Far East, its growth was very slow. For more on MO, see Elizabeth P. McIntosh, *Sisterhood of Spies: Women of the OSS* (Annapolis, MD: Naval Institute Press, 1998),

76. Joint Chiefs of Staff 312/1 (Revised), "Joint Chiefs of Staff Special Military Plan for Psychological Warfare in Burma," 4 June 1943, F 93, B 546, E 190, RG 226, NARA. Also see Carl O. Hoffman to Harry W. Little, "MO Plan for the Far East," 30 October 1943, F 1929, B 143, E 139, RG 226, NARA.

77. E. L. Taylor to William R. Peers, "MO Possibilities and Needs at 101," 2 January 1944, contained in Peers to Donovan, "Report Covering Period 14 December 1943 to 31 January, 1944, inclusive," 31 January 1944, and Taylor to Donovan, 9 January 1944.

78. Peers to Donovan, "Report Covering Period 14 December 1943 to 31 January, 1944, inclusive," 31 January 1944.

79. Edgar Sallinger to Harley C. Stevens, "Burmese Evil Spirits," 20 March 1944, F 3, B 524, E 92, RG 226, NARA. In this case, the MO product was a sound device that

emitted shrieks and wails. The intent was to play on Burmese fears of jungle spirits.

80. Carleton F. Scofield to Herbert Little, 24 February 1944, F 24, B 191, E 92, RG 226, NARA.

81. See Charles Fenn, *At the Dragon's Gate: With the OSS in the Far East* (Annapolis, MD: Naval Institute Press, 2004) 15–19; Peers to Donovan, "Report Covering Period 1 February to 29 February, 1944, inclusive," 29 February 1944.

82. OWI was charged with "white," or overt, propaganda, while MO was responsible for "black" propaganda—in which the true source is hidden; Peers to Donovan, "Report Covering Period 1 April to 30 April, 1944, inclusive," 30 April 1944, and Charles H. Fenn to Harry W. Little, "MO Operations From 101," 10 April 1944, F 4, B 192, E 92, RG 226, NARA. A brief account of Fenn's trip into KNOTHEAD can be found in "KNOTHEAD Group-Report April," 1 April 1944, F 433, B 29, E 154, RG 226, NARA.

83. Peers to Donovan, "Report Covering Period 1 March to 31 March, 1944, inclusive," 31 March 1944. Because of the black nature of MO propaganda, its leaflets could not be printed on the same high-quality paper as that used by OWI. Instead, and with difficulty, MO had to find the "worst paper" it could—usually newsprint, to duplicate the effect that the leaflets were being printed by dissident Burmese factions. See Charles H. Fenn to Harry W. Little, "MO Developments," 19 April 1944, F 4, B 192, E 92, RG 226, NARA.

84. "O.S.S.S.U. Detachment 101 Monthly Report," May 1944.

85. William R. Peers to William J. Donovan, "Report Covering period 31 May to 30 June, 1944," [30 June 1944], F 136, B 34, E 190, RG 226, NARA.

86. Peers to Donovan, "Report Covering Period 1 March to 31 March, 1944, inclusive," 31 March 1944.

87. Charles H. Fenn to Harry W. Little, "MO at 101," 9 May 1944, F 4, B 192, E 92, RG 226, NARA.

88. Peers to Donovan, "Report Covering Period 14 December 1943 to 31 January, 1944, inclusive," 31 January 1944; Carlton Scofield to Kennett Hinks, 15 March 1944, F Eifler, B 644, E 190, RG 226, NARA. The R&A Branch is considered one of the most—if not the most—valuable branches and contributions that the OSS made during the war. When the OSS was dissolved on 6 October 1945, the R&A Branch was retained for use by the U.S. State Department. This branch could be considered the founding organization of both the State Department's Bureau of Intelligence and Research and the CIA's Directorate of Intelligence.

89. Peers to Donovan, "Report Covering Period 14 December 1943 to 31 January, 1944, inclusive," 31 January 1944; Scofield to Kennett Hinks, 15 March 1944, NARA.

90. Peers to Donovan, "Report Covering Period 1 February to 29 February, 1944, inclusive," 29 February 1944.

91. Ibid., see Charles Stelle to Robert Hall, "R & A Possibilities at 101."

92. Coughlin to Far East Theater Officer [OSS Washington], May 1944, NARA.

93. Wally Richmond to "John" [Coughlin?], 28 January 1944, F 010394, B 270, E 210, RG 226, NARA.

94. It is actually called "Secret Intelligence." Apparently, Detachment 101 was not up on the latest terms from Washington. Peers to Donovan, "Report Covering Period 14 December 1943 to 31 January, 1944, inclusive," 31 January 1944.

95. Stelle to Hall, "R & A Possibilities at 101," in Peers to Donovan, "Report Covering Period 1 February to 29 February, 1944, inclusive," 29 February 1944. For the first of the weekly intelligence reports that were separated into the eight areas, see "Headquarters Detachment 101: Weekly Information Summary to Jan, 29/44," in William B. Shepard, "Report on Rescue Mission," [November 1943], in Peers to Donovan, "Report Covering Period 14 December 1943 to 31 January, 1944, inclusive," 31 January 1944. These reports would include such items as Japanese troop movements, as well as traffic tallies for specific roads. In June 1944, the 101 summaries went to the Commanding General USAAF, CBI, Commanding General Chinese Army in India, 'Y' Task Force, General Dorn, Chindits, Commanding General S.O.S., Commanding General ATC, ATC Station #6, Forward Area Intel and Security, Third Tactical Air Force, 443 Troop Carrier Group, Third Combat Cargo Resupply Group, USA Experimental Bureau, Coughlin, Tenth Air Force, Heppner, Seventh Bomb Group, Burma Government, Eighth Photo Group, First Air Commando, G-2 CBI, Eleventh Combat Carrier Group, Twelfth Bomb Group, and Second Troop Carrier Squadron. Notice the large number of USAAF groups receiving the intelligence reports.

96. Peers to Donovan, "Report Covering Period 14 December 1943 to 31 January, 1944, inclusive," 31 January 1944.

97. Peers to Donovan, "Report Covering Period 1 February to 29 February, 1944, inclusive," 29 February 1944; in February, the group identified its first Japanese hydrogen cyanide gas chemical grenade. The Japanese used chemical weapons, though rarely, in the Burma Campaign. An example of a chemical grenade use in early July 1944 can be found in Louis J. Allen, *Burma: The Longest War 1941–45* (London: Phoenix Press, 2001), 301–302.

98. Peers to Donovan, "Report Covering Period 14 December 1943 to 31 January, 1944, inclusive," 31 January 1944.

99. Peers to Coughlin, 6 March 1944; Peers to Donovan, "Report Covering Period 1 February to 29 February, 1944, inclusive," 29 February 1944.

100. Peers and Brelis, *Behind the Burma Road*, 138.

101. Peers to Coughlin, 24 March 1944. Peers correctly concluded that the directive to increase the number of indigenous troops meant that Stilwell had "a lot of faith in our activities."

102. R. T. Shelby to KNOTHEAD, "Dear Knothead," 4 March 1944, F 453, B 30, E 154, RG 226, NARA. Shelby also sent a similar letter to Luce of FORWARD, in R. T. Shelby to James C. Luce, 4 March 1944, F 456, B 65, E 190, RG 226, NARA.

103. R. T. Shelby to James C. Luce, 23 March 1944, F 455, B 65, E 190, RG 226, NARA.

104. William R. Peers to Carl O. Hoffman, 11 May 1944, F 192, B 23, E 165, RG 226, NARA.

7. DETACHMENT 101 AND THE CAMPAIGN FOR MYITKYINA: FEBRUARY–AUGUST 1944

1. Myitkyina is the capital of Kachin State, Burma. In 1944, it only had 7,328 people as opposed to 134,950 in Mandalay and 398,967 in Rangoon.

2. Louis Allen, *Burma: The Longest War: 1941–45* (Phoenix Press: London, 1984), 661.

3. Meirion Harries and Susie Harries, *Soldiers of the Sun: The Rise and Fall of the Imperial Japanese Army* (New York: Random House, 1991), 412. For a biography of Sato, see Richard Fuller, *Shōkan: Hirohito's Samurai; Leaders of the Japanese Armed Forces, 1926–1945* (London: Arms and Armour, 1992), 191–192. For a detailed description of the U-GO offensive, see Allen, *Burma: The Longest War*, 191–314; William Slim, *Defeat Into Victory: Battling Japan in Burma and India, 1942–1945* (New York: Cooper Square Press, 2000), 285–346. For the Japanese individual soldier's perspective see John Nunneley and Kazuo Tamayama, *Tales by Japanese Soldiers of the Burma Campaign, 1942–1945* (London: Cassell, 2000), 152–212. Unfortunately, this work does not cover the Japanese perspective of the north Burma campaign.

4. Charles F. Romanus and Riley Sunderland, *United States Army in World War II: China-Burma-India Theater: Stilwell's Command Problems* (Washington, DC: Center of Military History, 1987), 130; 220; Allen, *Burma: The Longest War 1941–45*, 662.

5. Charles F. Romanus and Riley Sunderland, *United States Army in World War II: China-Burma-India Theater: Stilwell's Mission to China* (Washington, DC: Center of Military History, 1987), 366.

6. Romanus and Sunderland, *Stilwell's Command Problems*, 35. The Marauders were composed of volunteers from combat veterans of Guadalcanal and New Guinea, or from training areas in the Caribbean Defense Command and the United States. They were all supposed to have received jungle training. None had seen combat in Burma.

7. Only five of the brigades participated in Operation THURSDAY; one was held back to assist in a similar role against the Japanese Fifteenth Army in its U-GO offensive.

8. Lack of air superiority did not stop the Japanese from conducting near-daily bombing and strafing runs on the Chindit stronghold of BROADWAY. On 30 March, and again on the 31st, they even attempted an aerial resupply to their besieging forces. In June, the Japanese shot down eight C-47 and two C-46 cargo aircraft in the vicinity of Myitkyina, although some of this might have been from ground-fire; even though aerial resupply had already been accomplished with Detachment 101 groups, the first Chindit mission in particular had shown that aerial resupply of large troop formations was possible. For more on the Air Commando, see Herbert A. Mason Jr., Randy G. Bergeron, and James A. Renfrow Jr., "*Operation THURSDAY: Birth of the Air Commandos* (Washington, DC: United States Air Force History and Museums Program, 1994). Aerial extraction of wounded personnel was a huge improvement

from the first Chindit expedition, when the wounded were left behind with "five days rations and a compass." See Pop and Red to John Ford, 28 March 1944, Folder 627, Box 70, Entry 144, Research Group 226, National Archives and Records Administration, College Park, MD.

9. Carleton F. Scofield, "Informal Report on Detachment 101," 13 March 1944, F 1920, B 181, E 136, RG 226, NARA.

10. William R. Peers to William J. Donovan, "Report Covering Period 1 March to 31 March, 1944, Inclusive," 31 March 1944, F 53, B 40, E 190, RG 226, NARA.

11. William R. Peers to William J. Donovan, "Report Covering Period 1 February to 29 February, 1944, Inclusive," 29 February 1944, F 52, B39, E 190, RG 226, NARA. The USAAF flew as many as 170 sorties per day in the Hukawng Valley. According to an interview with a Lieutenant Jenkins, a P-40 pilot who crashed and was picked up by Detachment 101, the pilots often did not know why they were bombing through tree cover and had no idea that they were causing so much damage. In fact, they preferred other missions to such a "dull assignment," so that they would know that they were doing damage to the Japanese. "KNOTHEAD Group-Report April," 1 April 1944, F 433, B 29, E 154, RG 226, NARA.

12. "Theater Officer's Pouch Report," 2 May 1944, F 31, B 75, E 99, RG 226, NARA.

13. Peers to Donovan, "Report Covering Period 1 February to 29 February, 1944, Inclusive," 29 February 1944.

14. William R. Peers to William J. Donovan, "Report Covering Period 1 April to 30 April, 1944, Inclusive," 30 April 1944, F 54, B 110, E 190, RG 226, NARA. Under a policy set up by the previous Detachment 101 commander, Colonel Carl F. Eifler, the families of the Lightning Force were to be taken care of by Detachment 101. In a scene much like what would occur later in the Central Highlands of Vietnam, the families clustered around the Detachment 101 main field camp at KNOTHEAD. Food supplies were stretched to the limit, and Eifler's successor, Peers, ordered the practice to stop because it interfered with operations. The refugees were given the option of being led to Allied lines. The "care and welfare of the Kachin refugees was not in any way to influence the actions or policy of this unit." "KNOTHEAD Group-Report April," 1 April 1944. An account of the group making their way to Allied lines can be found at James Stuart, "Detailed Report by Father Stuart in His Attempt to Take Refugees to Shingbwiyang Evacuee Camp," [March 1944], F 433, B 29, E 154, RG 226, NARA.

15. "KNOTHEAD Group," [March–May 1944], F 48, B 38, E 190, RG 226, NARA.

16. Peers to Donovan, "Report Covering Period 1 February to 29 February, 1944, Inclusive," 29 February 1944; Peers advised Merrill not to have the Marauders march 125 miles to their jumping-off point, but instead be trucked or fly. Merrill said that he wanted them to march in order to condition his men. Merrill's decision contributed to the Marauders' fatigue and exhaustion; see William R. Peers and Dean Brelis, *Behind the Burma Road: The Story of America's Most Successful Guerrilla Force* (Boston: Little, Brown, 1963), 141–142.

17. Peers to Donovan, "Report Covering Period 1 April to 30 April, 1944, Inclusive," 30 April 1944. The Marauders, however, were behind schedule, and in the meantime, Detachment 101 still had a representative with the Marauders in the form of Lieutenant Waters, a liaison officer who had been with the group since 19 February.

18. Chester Chartrand to William H. Shepardson, "My Dear Mr. Shepardson," 16 November 1959, F 16, B 119A, William J. Donovan Papers, U.S. Army Historical and Education Center, Carlisle Barracks, PA.

19. Peers to Donovan, "Report Covering Period 1 March to 31 March, 1944, Inclusive," 31 March 1944.

20. "Statement of Father Stuart Dealing with Events in Area North of Myitkyina from May 1942 until March 1944," found in Thomas N. Moon and Carl F. Eifler, *The Deadliest Colonel* (New York: Vantage Press, 1975), 298.

21. Peers to Donovan, "Report Covering Period 1 April to 30 April, 1944, Inclusive," 30 April 1944.

22. "KNOTHEAD GROUP," [March–May, 1944], NARA.

23. "KNOTHEAD Group-Report April," 1 April 1944, F 433, B 29, E 154, RG 226, NARA.

24. Peers to Donovan, "Report Covering Period 1 March to 31 March, 1944, Inclusive," 31 March 1944.

25. Peers to Donovan, "Report Covering Period 1 April to 30 April, 1944, Inclusive," 30 April 1944.

26. Ibid.

27. James Tilly, untitled report, [March 1944], F 433, B 29, E 154, RG 226, NARA.

28. "KNOTHEAD Group Report," May 1944, F 433, B 29, E 154, RG 226, NARA.

29. Peers to Donovan, "Report Covering Period 1 April to 30 April, 1944, Inclusive," 30 April 1944.

30. James Tilly, "Lt. Tilly's Report," [March 1944], F 486, B 67, E 190, RG 226, NARA.

31. Jack Pamplin complained to Peers that he needed Stuart on account of the great help that he had given with the Kachins. Pamplin, while recognizing that the Marauders held Stuart in "high regard," tried to remind them that Stuart was successful only because of the Kachins and "hinted that they should realize that it was the work of the organization of this unit—not any one individual—which was proving of such value to them." See the 12 April entry in "KNOTHEAD Group Report," May 1944, NARA.

32. Peers to Donovan, "Report Covering Period 1 April to 30 April, 1944, Inclusive," 30 April 1944.

33. Jack Pamplin to William R. Peers, "Dear Col. Peers," 30 March 1944, F 453, B 30, E 154, RG 226, NARA.

34. "KNOTHEAD Group-Report April," 1 April 1944, F 433, B 29, E 154, RG 226, NARA.

35. William R. Peers to William J. Donovan, "Report Covering Period 30 September to 31 October, 1944," [1 November 1944], F 17, B 34, E 190, RG 226, NARA. See "Report by Father Stewart [*sic*]."

36. Ibid.

37. Ibid.

38. Ibid.

39. *The Merrill's Marauders War in Burma*, vol. 1 (Merrill's Marauders Association, 1995), 25.

40. Anonymous, *Merrill's Marauders* (Washington, DC: United States Army Center of Military History, 1990), 75–76.

41. "KNOTHEAD GROUP," [March–May 1944], NARA.

42. Stelle was also to provide OSS intel to Wingate; place OSS equipment and personnel at Wingate's disposal; find possibilities for morale operations, special operations, and secret intelligence work; and perform a tactical research and analysis (R&A) function. To perform this mission, Stelle had a crash course in the area that Wingate would go into, as well as familiarization with enemy equipment and the operations of Detachment 101. Charles C. Stelle to Hall, "Activities as OSS Liaison Officer with General Wingate's Forces," [June 1944], F 2010, B 109, E 154, RG 226, NARA.

43. Peers to Donovan, "Report Covering Period 1 March to 31 March, 1944, Inclusive," 31 March 1944. Per Charles C. Stelle, "Report on Operations of Unit A Group," [March 1944], F 486, B 67, E 190, RG 226, NARA, the code names of the Kachins were Petru, Pom, Htem, Ching, Raw, and Long. For more on the CG-4A, see Troy Sacquety, "The CG-4A Waco Glider," *Veritas: Journal of Army Special Operations History* 3, no. 2 (2007): 35–37.

44. Peers to Donovan, "Report Covering Period 1 April to 30 April, 1944, Inclusive," 30 April 1944. Detachment 101 later occupied BROADWAY in August after it was abandoned by the Chindits, and used it as an operations base and landing strip to infiltrate/exfiltrate personnel.

45. Stelle to Hall, "Activities as OSS Liaison Officer," [June 1944].

46. Sherman P. Joost to Peers, "On or about January . . . ," 28 May 1944, F 466, B 66, E 190, RG 226, NARA. Another copy can be found in F 2010, B 109, E 154, RG 226, NARA. Joost was the "jack of all trades" in Detachment 101 during the Myitkyina Campaign. As liaison officer to the Air Commando, he went into BROADWAY by glider, was later given command of the DEMOS group, and accompanied a Chindit column called the "Dah" force. He later replaced James C. Luce as the commanding officer of FORWARD.

47. Pamplin noted that General Stilwell and his son flew into KNOTHEAD on 25 April to confer with Merrill. Since Merrill was not present, they visited the OSS camp, had lunch, and spoke with KNOTHEAD's personnel. See "KNOTHEAD Group Report," May 1944.

48. James Luce, "Jim Luce (2nd Installment)," *OSS 101 Association Incorporated Newsletter*, Winter 1997, 6.

49. [William R. Peers to William J. Donovan] "O.S.S.S.U. Detachment 101 Monthly Report," May 1944, F 12, B 34, E 190, RG 226, NARA.

50. James C. Luce, "Report on Tour of Duty with Office of Strategic Services Detachment 101: North Burma and Assam, November 1, 1943 to April 1, 1945," [April 1945], original in author's possession.

51. Peers to Donovan, "Report Covering Period 1 April to 30 April, 1944, Inclusive," 30 April 1944.

52. Roger Hilsman, *American Guerrilla: My War behind Japanese Lines* (Washington, DC: Brassey's, 1990), 170–171.

53. "Operations," [June 1944], F 486, B 67, E 190, RG 226, NARA.

54. "Personal Field Report of Lysle E. Wilson PHM 1/C," [late 1944], F 78, B 43, E 190, RG 226, NARA.

55. Peers to Donovan, "Report Covering Period 1 April to 30 April, 1944, Inclusive," 30 April 1944.

56. William R. Peers to "P" Division, "Processing of Current and Future Operational Plans," 5 April 1944, F 340, B 57, E 190, RG 226, NARA.

57. Thomas J. Davis to Operations, "Report of Field Operations for Period April 7 to July 1, 1944," July 1944, F 415, B 28, E 154, RG 226, NARA.

58. Luce, "Report on Tour of Duty," [April 1945]; Joseph E. Alderdice to Charles S. Cheston, "Casualties and Illness of Personnel," 31 August 1944, F 209 A, B 26, E 165, RG 226, NARA; a Kachin after-action report of this engagement can be found at Sima Kawng to Major [Sherman P. Joost], 4 September 1944, F 46, B 38, E 190, RG 226, NARA. The group miscalculated and originally estimated that there were thirty-five Japanese in the village. See James C. Luce, "Report on Action at Sadon; May 15 to June 24," [July 1944], F 450, B 64, E 190, RG 226, NARA. The chaotic nature of the campaign troubled FORWARD's guerrillas. U.S. Navy Pharmacist's Mate R. B. Walter reported on 13 May that a large group of Japanese were headed right for the jungle headquarters where he was. However, before the Japanese got to Walter, they were intercepted by another group under Sergeant Keber, who "killed and disorganized them to such an extent that they had to retreat." "Personal Field Report of R. B. Walter," [December 1944], F 78, B 43, E 190, RG 226, NARA.

59. "Interview with Maj. Drown," 16 May 1945, F 46, B 38, E 190, RG 226, NARA.

60. Anonymous, *Merrill's Marauders*, 94–97.

61. William J. Martin interview by James C. Luce, 8 August 1988, Oregon.

62. Major Fred Huffine, "Operations of the 150th Chinese Regiment from 1 April 1944 to 4 August 1944," contained in Hayden Boatner papers, copy in the USASOC History Office Classified Files, Fort Bragg, NC.

63. "1st Lieutenant William John Martin," 11 June 1945, F 47, B 38, E 190, RG 226, NARA; Richard Dunlop, *Behind Japanese Lines: With the OSS in Burma* (Chicago, IL: Rand McNally, 1979), 304–306.

64. "O.S.S.S.U. Detachment 101 Monthly Report," May 1944; repeated in Kermit Roosevelt, *The Overseas Targets* [special title], vol. 2 of *War Report of the OSS (Office of Strategic Services)* (New York: Walker, 1976), 386.

65. Each American officer assigned to a Chinese regiment has a different story. However, it is clear that there was a high level of friendly fire between separate Chinese regiments even before the 150th's assault into the center of the city. As a whole, observers often commented on the Chinese tendency to expend incredible amounts of ammunition if they thought that enemy forces were in contact. For more on the individual Chinese regiments, see Robert L. Waters, "The Operations of the 88th and 89th Regiments (30th Chinese Division) at Myitkyina, Burma 26 May–3 August, 1944" (India-Burma Campaign), Donovan Research Library, Fort Benning, GA, found online at http://www.benning.army.mil/library/content/Virtual/Donovan papers/wwii/index.htm; and Major Thomas L. Kesley, "Liaison with 1st Bn 150th Regt," copy in USASOC History Office Classified Files, Fort Bragg, NC.

66. Waters, "The Operations of the 88th and 89th Regiments (30th Chinese Division) at Myitkyina, Burma 26 May–3 August 1944."

67. Major Fred Huffine, "Operations of the 150th Chinese Regiment from 1 April 1944 to 4 August 1944," contained in Hayden Boatner papers, copy in the USASOC History Office Classified Files, Fort Bragg, NC.

68. "1st Lieutenant William John Martin," 11 June 1945.

69. Hazelwood was later a possible sufferer of combat fatigue, now called post-traumatic stress disorder (PTSD). He was shipped back to OSS Washington in August because he "broke down completely." William J. Peers to Carl O. Hoffman, "Reference my Cable . . . ," 20 August 1944, F 192, B 23, E 165, RG 226, NARA.

70. "O.S.S.S.U. Detachment 101 Monthly Report," May 1944. Also see Charles C. Stelle to William R. Peers, "Operations of Group at Broadway, Group 10, March–May 1944," [May 1944], F 438, B 29, E 154, RG 226, NARA; Thomas J. Davis to William R. Peers, [28 June 1944], F 415, B 28, E 154, RG 226, NARA.

71. "Interview with Conley," 17 May 1945, F 46, B 38, E 190, RG 226, NARA.

72. Thomas J. Davis to William R. Peers, "Situation Report," 31 May 1944, F 415, B 28, E 154, RG 226, NARA; a brief description of the ADAMS group's activities in this period can be found in "Personal Field Report of Capt. Alan G. Adams; May to October," 15 November 1944, F 78, B 43, E 190, RG 226, NARA. For more on the DIXIE mission, see David D. Barrett, *Dixie Mission: The United States Army Observer Group in Yenan, 1944* (Berkeley: University of California Press, 1979); Carolle J. Carter, *Mission to Yenan: American Liaison with the Chinese Communists, 1944–1947* (Lexington: University Press of Kentucky, 1997); John Colling, *The Spirit of Yenan: A Wartime Chapter of Sino-American Friendship* (Hong Kong: API, 1991).

73. "O.S.S.S.U. Detachment 101 Monthly Report," May 1944. Unit records indicate that 207 Japanese were killed and an indeterminate number wounded from 20 April to 31 May. Two supply-carrying elephants also fell to the Detachment's guns. In return the Detachment had five killed and five wounded.

74. William R. Peers to William J. Donovan, "Report Covering Period 31 May to 30 June, 1944," [30 June 1944], F 13, B 34, E 190, RG 226, NARA; Detachment 101 had one other major element in the field: Operation TRAMP, collecting intelligence and harassing Japanese forces attacking toward Imphal. Formed out of the RED group under Pat Maddox, TRAMP had been augmented in April by the DOW and PETE groups (named after their commanders) and composed of Americans that had been in V-Force, a British-led intelligence unit. These V-Force personnel were extremely valuable to Detachment 101. They brought with them a wealth of experience on the operating environment including several, such as Captain Peter K. Lutken of PETE, who had learned to speak Kachin, and was well respected by the local population. The TRAMP reports can be found in F 438 and 439, B 64, E 190, RG 226, NARA.

75. Luce, "Report on Tour of Duty," [April 1945]; reports from Detachment 101 officers in the area place the number of Chinese killed at around 400. See "Interview with Maj. Drown," 16 May 1945, F 46, B 38, E 190, RG 226, NARA. Relations with the Chinese troops were so poor that members of Detachment 101 were given a standing order that they were to keep themselves and their troops well away from them unless a specific liaison task was given. This was not the only incident between Kachin guerrillas and Chinese soldiers.

76. Peers to Donovan, "Report Covering Period 31 May to 30 June, 1944," [30 June 1944]; despite the rains, the air drop section of Detachment 101 managed to get some 251,000 pounds of supplies in the field; TRAMP operations under PETE were also singularly successful when on 22 June the group killed 150 Japanese who were floating on rafts down the Namting River.

77. Ibid.

78. [Robert R. Rhea?], "handwritten notes starting with 'July 5th LT Comdr Pier . . . ,'" [August 1944?], F 349, B 21, E 90, RG 226, NARA; Peers to Donovan, "Report Covering Period 31 May to 30 June, 1944," [30 June 1944].

79. Phone Interview by author with Blaine Headrick, Fayetteville, NC, 3 June 1945.

80. William R. Peers to William J. Donovan, "Report Covering Period 30 June to 31 July, 1944," [31 July 1944], F 14, B 34, E 190, RG 226, NARA.

81. William R. Peers to William J. Donovan, "Report Covering Period 31 July to 31 August, 1944," [31 August], F 14, B 34, E 190, RG 226, NARA. See William H. Cummings to Carl O. Hoffman, "SO Operations, August Report," 1 September 1944.

82. Peers to Donovan, "Report Covering Period 30 June to 31 July, 1944," [31 July 1944].

83. Ibid., in particular, see William H. Cummings to Carl O. Hoffman, "S O Operations, July Report," 1 August 1944; Area #1 headquarters were at Sadon.

84. [Interview of Ted Barnes], 1 December 1944, F 78, B 43, E 190, RG 226, NARA. One of these screening groups was the DAVIS group, which had another "A" Group veteran, Saw Judson, as radio operator and interpreter. The DAVIS Group armed Kachin villagers to serve as a militia of sorts as well as agents, and organized local

labor to build an airstrip and to serve as stretcher bearers. These Kachins later served as the nucleus for several new groups. See Thomas J. Davis to Opero, radio message 22, 23 June 1944, F 415, B 28, E 154, RG 226, NARA; Thomas J. Davis to Operations, "Report of Field Operations for Period April 7," [July 1944], NARA.

85. "Harry S. Hengshoon (Skittles)," [May 1945?], F 46, B 38, E 190, RG 226, NARA; Area #2 groups also harassed Japanese stragglers north and south of Myitkyina. A small group of Kachins under Lieutenant Evan J. Parker also killed fifty-four and captured eighteen enemy troops.

86. Shelford Bidwell, *The Chindit War: Stilwell, Wingate, and the Campaign in Burma, 1944* (New York: Macmillan, 1979), 274. The legend is that Stilwell's staff then proceeded to ask where on the map the village of Umbrage was located.

87. Romanus and Sunderland, *Stilwell's Command Problems*, 233–236. A Japanese Regimental Combat Team of the Fifty-third Division was under way to relieve Myitkyina, but was turned back by the Allied advance on Mogaung.

88. Peers to Donovan, "Report Covering Period 30 June to 31 July, 1944," [31 July 1944]. See Cummings to Hoffman, "S O Operations, July Report," 1 August 1944.

89. [Interview of Ted Barnes], 1 December 1944.

90. Interview of Pete Lutken by author, 2 July 2007, Fort Bragg, NC, notes. Also see Reginald Thorlin, "Pete Group," 28 August 1944, F 439, B 64, E 190, RG 226, NARA.

91. Peers to Donovan, "Report Covering Period 31 July to 31 August, 1944," [31 August]; "Mission Report"; "Interview with 1st Lt. James R. Ward," 28 June 1945, F 46, B 36, E 190, RG 226, NARA; William Martin interviewed by Mrs. Marje Luce, 1995, Oregon; "Leonard Report on Field Activities," 16 November 1944, F 78, B 43, E 190, RG 226, NARA.

92. Peers to Donovan, "Report Covering Period 31 July to 31 August, 1944," [31 August]. See Cummings to Hoffman, "SO Operations, August Report," 1 September 1944.

93. Peers to Donovan, "Report Covering Period 30 June to 31 July, 1944," [31 July 1944]. See Cummings to Hoffman, "S O Operations, July Report" 1 August 1944. When Myitkyina fell, Detachment 101 also received a number of Gurkha recruits. See William R. Peers to Edmund Taylor, 20 August 1944, F2152, B119, E 154, RG 226, NARA.

94. Peers to Laurence F. Grimm, 11 August 1944, F 438, B 64, E 190, RG 226, NARA.

95. Peers to Donovan, "Report Covering Period 31 July to 31 August, 1944," [31 August]. See "Mission Report."

96. Robert Rodenberg to William R. Peers, "Casualties of Detachment 101 Personnel," 31 August 1944, F 209A, B 26, E 165, RG 226, NARA. At that time, over the course of its entire operation, from 1942 on, Detachment 101 was roughly responsible for killing nearly 2,000 Japanese. More than half of these occurred over the months of May–August 1944. Therefore in four months after Peers had taken over

command from Eifler, the Detachment succeeded in inflicting more direct damage on the enemy in terms of personnel that in the entire previous year of field operations. It is also possible that these numbers are low. According to "KNOTHEAD GROUP," F 48, B 38, E 190, RG 226, NARA, Japanese dead were counted only if a body was seen, or if a Japanese was seen to fall after being shot.

97. Peers to Donovan, "Report Covering Period 31 July to 31 August, 1944," [31 August]. See Howard Davidson to William J. Donovan, "Contribution of Detachment 101, OSS, to USAAF in Northeastern Assam and North Burma," 1 August 1944.

98. Three of the Marauders that joined Detachment 101 were Philip Weld, Roger Hilsman, and Thomas Chamales. See Philip Weld, *Moxie: the American Challenge* (Boston: Little, Brown, 1981); Hilsman, *American Guerrilla*; and Tom Chamales, *Never So Few* (New York: Charles Scribner's Sons, 1957). *Never So Few* was later made into a feature film starring Frank Sinatra, Gina Lollobrigida, Steve McQueen, and Charles Bronson.

99. "Psychological Warfare in the Battle of Myitkyina," [late July 1944], F 1855, B 137, E 144, RG 226, NARA. OWI managed to sow surrender leaflets over Japanese lines beginning in June, and had loudspeaker teams that used Nisei to broadcast news, music, and surrender appeals to the defenders. The result was lowered morale, and at least one successful attempt to surrender. Other possible surrender attempts may have been killed by trigger-happy Chinese and American troops. On other occasions, supply drops were deliberately made to cut-off Japanese forces in the hopes that they might surrender. See William R. Peers to Demas, "Dr. Telburg Letter to Lt. Commander Hinks—Japanese Comment on '101,'" 29 June 1944, F 373, B 59, E 190, RG 226, NARA.

100. R. T. Shelby to KNOTHEAD, "Dear Pamplin and 'Knothead' Group," 12 April 1944, F 453, B 30, E 154, RG 226, NARA.

101. Jack Pamplin to R. T. Shelby, 30 March 1944, F 453, B 30, E 154, RG 226, NARA. Robert W. Rhea had been attached to KNOTHEAD for seven months, and photographed the Marauders as they pushed from Wallabum to Myitkyina. Rhea had the singular honor of having been made an official member of Merrill's Marauders. See Peers to Donovan, "Report Covering Period 31 July to 31 August, 1944," [31 August]; "Mission Report."

102. Peers and Brelis, *Behind the Burma Road*, 171.

103. William R. Peers and Dean C. Brelis, "Original Draft of Peers-Brelis Behind the Burma Road," 317, Box 1, Detachment 101 Collection, USAHEC.

104. Anonymous, *Merrill's Marauders*.

105. Mischa Titiev to Conyers Read, "Merrill's Marauders," 17 May 1945, F 1, B 75, E 99, RG 226, NARA.

106. Conyers Read to Walter L. Wright, "Merrill's Marauders (American Forces in Action Series)," 27 June 1945, F 1, B 75, E 99, RG 226, NARA. Walter L. Wright was the U.S. Army's first chief historian.

107. Romanus and Sunderland, *Command Problems*, 176.

108. Joseph W. Stilwell to William H. Shepardson, "Dear Mr. Shepardson," 14 September 1960, F 16, B 119A, William J. Donovan Papers, USAHEC.

109. Samuel V. Wilson to Joseph W. Stilwell, "Wilson Comments on Shepardson Correspondence," 4 August 1960, F 16, B 119A, William J. Donovan Papers, USAHEC.

110. R. M. Cannon, "Citation: Commanding General, India-Burma Theater," 28 February 1945, F 16, B 119A, William J. Donovan Papers, USAHEC.

111. Joseph W. Stilwell Jr, "Presidential Citation," 26 February 1945, F 16, B 119A, William J. Donovan Papers, USAHEC.

8. PEERS CONTINUES HIS REFORMS: JUNE–AUGUST 1944

1. Herbert S. Little to Harley C. Stevens, "Answer to your pouch letter No. 3," 26 August 1944, Folder 1295, Box 174, Entry 108B, Research Group 226, National Archives and Records Administration, College Park, MD; Herbert S. Little to Robert Wentworth, 14 July 1944, F 1295, B 174, E 108B, RG 226, NARA. The Calcutta branch later split off from Detachment 101 to form Detachment 505. Detachment 303 in New Delhi, which operated as a rear echelon and administrative base for Detachment 404, did have a small MO staff.

2. Herbert S. Little to John G. Coughlin, "MO-101," 7 September 1944, F 1295, B 174, E 108B, RG 226, NARA; Little to Harley Stevens, "Answer to your pouch letter No. 3," 26 August 1944, NARA.

3. Robert J. Wentworth to Betty MacDonald, 8 August 1944, F 1193, B 116, E 144, RG 226, NARA.

4. William R. Peers to William J. Donovan, "Report Covering Period 31 May to 30 June, 1944," [30 June 1944], F 13, B 34, E 190, RG 226, NARA.

5. Betty MacDonald to Charles H. Fenn, 26 July 1944, F 1193, B 116, E 144, RG 226, NARA; for OWI's reaction, see Wentworth to MacDonald, "Dear Betty," 8 August 1944, NARA.

6. Peers to Donovan, "Report Covering Period 31 May to 30 June, 1944," [30 June 1944].

7. William R. Peers to William J. Donovan, "Report Covering Period 30 June to 31 July, 1944," [late July 1944], F 14, B 34, E 190, RG 226, NARA.

8. William R. Peers to William J. Donovan, "Report covering period 31 July to 31 August, 1944," [31 August 1944], F 15, B34, E 190, RG 226, NARA. See "Mission Report" and "Monthly Report for August."

9. Peers to Donovan, "Report Covering Period 31 July to 31 August, 1944," [31 August 1944]. See "Mission Report"; Peers to Donovan, "Report Covering Period 30 June to 31 July, 1944," [late July 1944]. In Peers to Donovan, "Report Covering Period 30 June to 31 July, 1944," [late July 1944], see Charles W. Cox to William L. Langer, "R&A Report," 29 July 1944, and Robert E. Adams to Weston Howland, "Security Branch, July Report" and Robert E. Adams, "Security Office Functions"; Peers to

Donovan, "Report Covering Period 31 May to 30 June, 1944," [30 June 1944]. An example of one of Washington's requests for information can be found at McClure to Hollis, "Urgent Request for Information on Burma," 9 August 1944, F 470, B 80, E 106, RG 226, NARA. A R&A compilation report of the strategic situation in Burma can be found at OSS/R&A New Delhi Office, "Burma: Situation Report No. I," [March 1944?], F 1418, B 81, E 154, RG 226, NARA; an example of how the R&A section trained outgoing personnel to report on intelligence matters can be found in Peers to Donovan, "Report Covering Period 31 July to 31 August, 1944," [31 August 1944]. See "Intelligence Message Reporting," 25 August 1944.

10. Peers to Donovan, "Report Covering Period 31 May to 30 June, 1944," [30 June 1944]; Peers to Donovan, "Report Covering Period 30 June to 31 July, 1944," [late July 1944]. See George Bolte to FP OSS Washington, "Report of Activities for July."

11. The SUGARLOAF II mission file can be found at F 489, B 67, E 190, RG 226, NARA. An operational report can be found at John Achelis to William R. Peers, "Report on Operation Sugar Loaf II," 20 June 1944, F 465, B 30, E 154, RG 226, NARA. Detachment 101 also had additional inter-theater cooperation with Detachment 404 when Lieutenant James Tilly was ordered from the field and sent to Ceylon to establish a school and training program similar to that at Nazira. See Peers to Donovan, "Report Covering Period 31 May to 30 June, 1944," [30 June 1944].

12. Peers to Donovan, "Report Covering Period 31 May to 30 June, 1944," [30 June 1944].

13. Peers to Donovan, "Report Covering Period 30 June to 31 July, 1944," [late July 1944]. See William H. Cummings to Quinn, "Air Drop and Air Activities," 1 August 1944.

14. Peers to Donovan, "Report Covering Period 31 May to 30 June, 1944," [30 June 1944]; "Detachment 101 to Supply, #4387," 8 August 1944, F 1016, B 157, E 134, RG 226, NARA.

15. Peers to Donovan, "Report Covering Period 30 June to 31 July, 1944," [late July 1944]. See Cummings to Quinn, "Air Drop and Air Activities," 1 August 1944. The more nimble and faster B-25s were used in locations in which the slower and unarmed C-47s might be subjected to great danger on account of enemy air action or ground fire.

16. Peers to Donovan, "Report Covering Period 31 July to 31 August, 1944," [31 August 1944]. See William H. Cummings to Quinn, "Air Drop and Air Activities, August," 1 September 1944.

17. "Personal Field Report of H. H. Ramsey, PHM. 2/C," [December 1944], F 78, B 43, E 190, RG 226, NARA.

18. Peers to Donovan, "Report Covering Period 30 June to 31 July, 1944," [late July 1944]. See George D. Gorin to Special Funds Branch, "July Report-Finance."

19. Peers to Donovan, "Report Covering Period 31 July to 31 August, 1944," [31 August 1944]. See George D. Gorin, "Report of the Finance Section for August," 31 August 1944.

20. Carl O. Hoffman to William R. Peers, "Dear Colonel Peers," 25 May 1944, F 192, B 23, E 165, RG 226, NARA.

21. Peers to Donovan, "Report Covering Period 30 June to 31 July, 1944," [late July 1944]. See "Status of Personnel"; Peers to Donovan, "Report Covering Period 31 May to 30 June, 1944," [30 June 1944]. In July, the group received another thirty-two men, more in one month than they had in all of 1942 and most of 1943. William R. Peers and Dean Brelis, *Behind the Burma Road: The Story of America's Most Successful Guerrilla Force* (Boston: Little, Brown, 1963), 130, relates that the group only had twenty-five Americans in late 1943.

22. Peers to Donovan, "Report Covering Period 31 July to 31 August, 1944," [31 August 1944]. See "Mission Report."

23. Peers to Donovan, "Report Covering Period 30 June to 31 July, 1944," [late July 1944]. See L. Coffey to William R. Peers, "July Report-Recruiting." While the system worked relatively smoothly, there were occasional flare-ups with the British, who in some cases did not like the high salaries that the OSS could pay to the indigenous recruits. For an example of this, see L. Coffey to the Governor of Burma, "Major E. Leach, C.A.S.," 29 August 1944, F 182, B 21, E 165, RG 226, NARA. This incident came right about the same time that an SOE representative showed up at Myitkyina on a P Division matter, even though it had not been coordinated through Peers, the NCAC P Division lead. This series of letters can be found at F 2152, B 119, E 154, RG 226, NARA. The incident, called the "Dilwyn Plan," ruffled the feathers of 101, especially when the SOE representative informed the Kachins that anyone who joined the Americans would be "unfavorably regarded" by the British and that any old Burma Rifles veterans would lose their pensions and not receive service credit for the time with 101. Eventually SOE encouraged the Kachins to serve with 101. See Sherman P. Joost, "Report on Field Conditions," 8 June 1945, F 26, B 74, E 99, RG 226, NARA. SOE also tried one more time to get the SO Branch of OSS to integrate with them, as had been done in the ETO. Both Detachments 101 and 404 were adamant that this not happen. For the series of exchanges on this between Peers and other officers, see F 192, B 23, E 165, RG 226, NARA. Also see William Peers to E. L. Taylor, "Dear Ed," 20 August 1944, F 2152,B 119, E 154, RG 226, NARA, where when speaking of SOE and its implications for Detachment 101 actions, Peers writes, " Our unit has done much for the people of Northern Burma. We fed them, protected them, etc, not with the idea of political gain but only that they would not die of starvation or be killed by the Japs. It gripes me more than a little when someone raises an issue such as this. I wish people would start fighting the war and stop fighting amongst themselves, or trying to cut someone else's throat."

24. Peers to Donovan, "Report Covering Period 31 July to 31 August, 1944," [31 August 1944]. The new system was a drastic improvement over the old, where agents were recruited without extensive background checks. The fear was that the Japanese could easily infiltrate an agent into the Detachment 101 training program. See BH/001 to SAINT, "Possible Penetration of OSS at Calcutta," 6 May 1944, F 1447, B 192, E

108B, RG 226, NARA. The locally recruited Anglo-Indians and Anglo-Burmans, many recruited under Colonel Carl F. Eifler, were almost universally found inadequate. Exceptions were "Skittles" and "Betty." Although the reports concerning field concerns with these agents are many, see James C. Luce to William R. Peers, 25 April 1944, F 455, B 65, E 190, RG 226, NARA.

25. The number recruited was not small, with 1,119 students for the Nazira jungle school recruited from 1 January 1944 to 1 December 1944. See Don Callahan, "Major Callahan's First Report," 27 December 1944, F 550, B 38, E 148, RG 226, NARA.

26. Peers to Donovan, "Report Covering Period 30 June to 31 July, 1944," [late July 1944]. See "Mission Report."

27. Peers to Donovan, "Report Covering Period 31 July to 31 August, 1944," [31 August 1944]. See "Mission Report."

28. Peers to Donovan, "Report Covering Period 30 June to 31 July, 1944," [late July 1944]. See James C. Luce to Sylvester Missal, "Medical Report for July 1944."

29. For more on Seagrave, see Gordon Seagrave, *Burma Surgeon* (New York: Norton, 1943), and *Burma Surgeon Returns* (New York: Norton, 1946).

30. Peers to Donovan, "Report Covering Period 31 July to 31 August, 1944," [31 August 1944]. See Carl Hook to L. W. Lowman, "Communication August Report."

31. Peers to Donovan, "Report Covering Period 31 May to 30 June, 1944," [30 June 1944].

32. Peers to Donovan, "Report Covering Period 31 July to 31 August, 1944," [31 August 1944]. See Hook to Lowman, "Communication August Report."

33. "Interview with Capt. [Thomas] Baldwin," 29 May 1945, F 46, B 38, E 190, RG 226, NARA.

34. Peers to Donovan, "Report Covering Period 31 July to 31 August, 1944," [31 August 1944]. See "Mission Report"; also see Peers to Donovan, "Report Covering Period 31 May to 30 June, 1944," [30 June 1944]. The two-week course syllabus can also be found here; previously, there had been thirteen weeks of instruction with fifty-six courses. Hours of instruction per course ranged from 1 to 120 hours each. See Carleton F. Scofield, "Informal Report on Detachment 101," 13 March 1944, F 1920, B 181, E 136, RG 226, NARA.

35. [William R. Peers to William J. Donovan], "O.S.S.S.U. Detachment 101 Monthly Report," May 1944, F 12, B 34, E 190, RG 226, NARA; Kermit Roosevelt, *War Report of the OSS* (New York: Walker, 1976), 230–231. From letters between John G. Coughlin and William R. Peers, it is very apparent that they did not know why Carl F. Eifler was coming back to the CBI; they even supposed that perhaps Eifler was coming to be the theater OSS officer, replacing Coughlin. See John G. Coughlin to William R. Peers, 18 March 1944, F 93, B 45, E 190, RG 226, NARA; Thomas N. Moon and Carl F. Eifler, *The Deadliest Colonel* (New York: Vantage Press, 1975), 323. Eifler took some of the original members of Detachment 101, including Aitken, Chang, Curl, Frazee, Huston, and Richmond. They trained on Catalina Island for an

infiltration of Korea, with the possibility of conducting operations on the Japanese mainland. The war ended before they could be employed.

36. Roosevelt, *War Report of the OSS*, 155.

37. Peers to Donovan, "Report Covering Period 30 June to 31 July, 1944," [late July 1944]. See Lucy to Lovell, "July Report-R&D." The first representative to Detachment 101, Captain Lee Tolman, had the additional duties of instructing students at the jungle camp in the use of OSS devices. He was followed in July by Major Samuel G. Lucy.

38. Peers to Donovan, "Report Covering Period 31 July to 31 August, 1944," [31 August 1944]. See Sam Lucy, "R&D monthly Report," August 1944.

39. "Area One Headquarters, 23 to 29 December (Inclusive)," F 452, B 65, E 190, RG 226, NARA.

40. D. V. Cavanaugh, "Air Drop: Part I-Three Tragedies," *101 Association Incorporated Newsletter* 6, no. 2 (March 1976): 3.

41. Peers to Donovan, "Report Covering Period 30 June to 31 July, 1944," [late July 1944].

42. Roosevelt, *War Report of the OSS*, 190. Although there had previously been a security function under SI, this was subsumed by the X-2 branch. This was reflected at Detachment 101 as well.

43. The agreement can be found at F 1421, B 185, E 108B, RG 226, NARA.

44. HH/001 to SAINT, "SCI Field Units-Northern Burma Front," 5 May 1944, F 1466, B 194, E 108B, RG 226, NARA. HH/001 is an X-2–given code name and is likely Major Roger A. Pfaff.

45. John J. McDonough to Eric Timm, "Assam Trip," 14 August 1944, F 1421, B 185, E 108B, RG 226, NARA.

46. HH/001 to SAINT, "SCI Field Units-Northern Burma Front," 5 May 1944, F 1466, B 194, E 108B, RG 226, NARA.

47. Peers to Donovan, "Report Covering Period 30 June to 31 July, 1944," [late July 1944]. For more on Peers's embarrassment, see John J. McDonough to Eric Timm, "Assam Trip," 14 August 1944, F 1421, B 185, E 108B, RG 226, NARA. Much controversy still surrounds the activities of the head of the X-2 branch in New Delhi, George D. White. After the war, White is alleged to have worked on "Manchurian Candidate"-like substances, such as LSD, on behalf of the CIA. This period remains one of those that continue to attract a number of allegations and conspiracy theories. However, while he was in New Delhi, White, a former narcotics agent for the FBI, was very concerned with the illegal drug trade.

48. BH/001 to SAINT, "Enemy Espionage Operations in Assam," 6 May 1944, F 1477, B 194, E 108B, RG 226, NARA. Many X-2 reports assigned code names to the personnel writing and receiving the report.

49. McDonough, "Relations of the X-2 India-SEAC (404) with Det. 101," 29 July 1944, F 1420, B 185, E 108B, RG 226, NARA.

50. John J. McDonough to Baird Helfrich, "X-2 Possibilities at 101," 28 August 1944, F 1422, B 185, E 108B, RG 226, NARA; Peers to Donovan, "Report Covering Period 31 July to 31 August, 1944," [31 August 1944]. See "Mission Report."

9. REORGANIZING AFTER MYITKYINA: SEPTEMBER–DECEMBER 1944

1. William R. Peers and Dean C. Brelis, "Original Draft of Peers-Brelis Behind the Burma Road," 430, Box 1, Detachment 101 Collection, USAHEC.

2. William R. Peers to William J. Donovan, "Report Covering Period 30 September to 31 October, 1944," [1 November 1944], Folder 17, Box 34, Entry 190, Research Group 226, National Archives and Records Administration, College Park, MD. See Charles W. Cox to Research and Analysis, "R & A Report for October 1944"; William R. Peers to William J. Donovan, "Report Covering Period 31 August to 30 September, 1944," [1 October 1944], F 16, B 34, E 190, RG 226, NARA. See "Mission Report." In September, the Detachment managed to account for 192 Japanese killed and 17 wounded, and 5 Burmese auxiliaries killed. The number was off from August because all the enemy forces the Detachment was encountering at the time were stragglers fleeing north Burma.

3. William R. Peers to William J. Donovan, "Report Covering Period 31 October to 30 November, 1944," [1 December 1944], F 11102, B 273, E 210, RG 226, NARA. See William R. Peers to Headquarters, India-Burma Theater, "Office of Strategic Services Detachment 101." The operations section also acquired a new role, when it agreed to become the primary organization responsible for Allied prisoners of war who were located along the route of advance. In this role, the Detachment worked to secure intelligence on the whereabouts of POWs and attempted to secure them before the enemy could retreat with, or dispose of, them.

4. Peers to Donovan, "Report Covering Period 31 August to 30 September, 1944," [1 October 1944]. The 475th, a component of the MARS Task Force, was the follow-on U.S. ground element to Merrill's Marauders.

5. Peers to Donovan, "Report Covering Period 30 September to 31 October, 1944," [1 November 1944]. See Charles W. Cox to Research and Analysis, "R & A Report for October 1944." The photos were supplied to Detachment 101 field units and used to grid enemy targets for bombing.

6. Peers to Donovan, "Report Covering Period 31 October to 30 November, 1944," [1 December 1944].

7. Hugh R. Conklin, "I Entered 101 by the Back Door," *101 Association Incorporated Newsletter*, May 1987, 4.

8. Peers to Donovan, "Report Covering Period 30 September to 31 October, 1944," [1 November 1944]. See Michael P. Georges to Schools and Training, O.S.S., Washington D.C., "Schools and Training Report for October."

9. Peers to Donovan, "Report Covering Period 31 August to 30 September, 1944," [1 October 1944]; exit briefings would also relay the penalties under the India Security Act if discharged personnel violated the unit's secrecy.

10. Robert E. Crowley, "Dentistry for Native Agents at Detachment 101," [January 1945], F 2131, B 118, E 154, RG 226, NARA.

11. Peers to Donovan, "Report Covering Period 30 September to 31 October, 1944," [1 November 1944]. See "Security Report for October 1944."

12. [Peers to Donovan], "O.S.S.S.U. Detachment 101 Monthly Report November 1944," [1 December 1944], NARA. See Claude V. Wadsworth to Communication Branch, "Communications Report for November."

13. Peers to Donovan, "Report Covering Period 31 August to 30 September, 1944," [1 October 1944]. See Allen Richter, "Communications Report for September." At the time the pigeon section had eighty breeding pairs. See Morris Y. Lederman to Carl O. Hoffman, "Activities of the Pigeon Section."

14. Peers to Donovan, "Report Covering Period 30 September to 31 October, 1944," [1 November 1944]. See Morris Y. Lederman to Carl O. Hoffman, "Activities of the Pigeon Section."

15. Peers to Donovan, "Report Covering Period 31 October to 30 November, 1944," [1 December 1944].

16. Peers to Donovan, "Report Covering Period 30 September to 31 October, 1944," [1 November 1944].

17. Peers to Donovan, "Report Covering Period 31 October to 30 November, 1944," [1 December 1944].

18. [Peers to Donovan], "O.S.S.S.U. Detachment 101 Monthly Report November 1944," [1 December 1944]. See Claude V. Wadsworth to Communication Branch, "Communications Report for November."

19. [Peers to Donovan], "O.S.S.S.U. Detachment 101 Monthly Report December 1944," 31 December 1944, F 19, B 34, E 190, RG 226, NARA. See Claude V. Wadsworth to Communications Branch, "Communications Report for December."

20. Peers to Donovan, "Report Covering Period 30 September to 31 October, 1944," [1 November 1944]. See "Personnel Report October."

21. Peers to Donovan, "Report Covering Period 30 September to 31 October, 1944," [1 November 1944]. See James C. Luce to S. C. Missal, "Detachment Surgeon, Detachment 101."

22. James C. Luce, "Report of Activities of U.S. Naval Group China Medical Personnel Attached to Detachment 101," [mid-late 1945], F 389, B 60, E 190, RG 226, NARA.

23. [Peers to Donovan], "O.S.S.S.U. Detachment 101 Monthly Report November 1944," [1 December 1944]. See James C. Luce to S. C. Missal, "Medical Report." [Peers to Donovan], "O.S.S.S.U. Detachment 101 Monthly Report December 1944," 31 December 1944. See James C. Luce to Chief, Medical Services, OSS, Washington, D.C., "Medical Services Report for December, 1944."

24. Peers to Donovan, "Report Covering Period 31 August to 30 September, 1944," [1 October 1944]. Seventy-six C-47 and twelve B-25 loads came from Dinjan for a total of 467,384 pounds, and thirty-two C-47 loads out of Myitkyina, for a total of 75,000 pounds.

25. Peers to Donovan, "Report Covering Period 30 September to 31 October, 1944," [1 November 1944]. The total dropped in November was much the same: 942,418 pounds were dropped from 190 C-47 flights and 4 of B-25s. See [Peers to Donovan], "O.S.S.S.U. Detachment 101 Monthly Report November 1944," [1 December 1944], NARA. See William E. Cummings to Quinn, "Air Drop and Air Activities, November."

26. Peers to Donovan, "Report Covering Period 30 September to 31 October, 1944," [1 November 1944]. See R. T. Walsh to Procurement & Supply, "Supply Report for October." [Peers to Donovan], "O.S.S.S.U. Detachment 101 Monthly Report December 1944," 31 December 1944. See R. T. Walsh to Supply & Procurement, "Supply Report for December 1944."

27. D. V. Cavanaugh, "Air Drop: Part II-People, Parachutes, Problems," *101 Association Incorporated Newsletter* 6, no. 3 (June 1976): 4.

28. Bernard Brophy, telephone interview by author, 9 April 2008, Fort Bragg, NC.

29. "Leonard Report on Field Operations," 16 November 1944, F 78, B 43, E 190, RG 226, NARA.

30. Peers and Brelis, "Original Draft," 438.

31. [Peers to Donovan], "O.S.S.S.U. Detachment 101 Monthly Report December 1944," 31 December 1944. See Dow S. Grones, "Air Drop and Air Activities, December Report"; Francis J. Reardon to William R. Peers, "Air Operations."

32. Peers to Donovan, "Report Covering Period 31 August to 30 September, 1944," [1 October 1944]. Flights were conducted between Nazira and Dinjan and Chabua; and Myitkyina and Combat Headquarters at Shaduzup.

33. [Peers to Donovan], "O.S.S.S.U. Detachment 101 Monthly Report November 1944," [1 December 1944]. See George D. Gorin to Chief Special Funds Branch, "Special Funds Report for November 1944."

34. Peers to Donovan, "Report Covering Period 30 September to 31 October, 1944," [1 November 1944]. See George D. Gorin to Chief Special Funds Branch, "Special Funds Report for October 1944."

35. Peers to Donovan, "Report Covering Period 31 August to 30 September, 1944," [1 October 1944]. See Charles W. Cox to R&A, "R & A Report for September 1944."

36. [Peers to Donovan], "O.S.S.S.U. Detachment 101 Monthly Report December 1944," [1 January 1945]. See Charles W. Cox to Research and Analysis, "R & A Report for December 1944."

37. Carlton F. Scofield to T. J. McFadden, 8 October 1944, F 2111, B 117, E 154, RG 226, NARA.

38. Peers to Donovan, "Report Covering Period 31 August to 30 September, 1944," [1 October 1944]. See Robert Wentworth to Herbert W. Little, "Morale Operations

Report for September"; George H. Boldt, "Report on MO Operations, Detachment 101," [July 1945], F 4, B 552, E 92, RG 226, NARA.

39. Milton to Bill, "Dear Bill," 8 October 1944, F 410, B 28, E 154, RG 226, NARA.

40. George H. Boldt, "Report on MO Operations, Detachment 101," [July 1945], F 27, B 35, E 190, RG 226, NARA; also see GOLD DUST folder, F 2053, B 151, E 139, RG 226, NARA.

41. Herbert S. Little to John G. Coughlin, "MO-101," 7 September 1944, F 1295, B 174, E 108B, RG 226, NARA.

42. [Peers to Donovan], "O.S.S.S.U. Detachment 101 Monthly Report November 1944," [1 December 1944]. See Edward B. Hamm to Herbert S. Little, "[MO] Report for November 1944."

43. [Peers to Donovan], "O.S.S.S.U. Detachment 101 Monthly Report December 1944," 31 December 1944. See Edward B. Hamm CO/MO FE, "MO/101 Report for December." Several of the MO weekly idea sheets can be found at F 3, B 552, E 92, RG 226, NARA.

44. Peers to Donovan, "Report Covering Period 30 September to 31 October, 1944," [1 November 1944]. See Sam G. Lucy to Research and Development, "R&D Report for October"; [Peers to Donovan], "O.S.S.S.U. Detachment 101 Monthly Report November 1944," [1 December 1944]. See Sam G. Lucy to Research and Development, "R&D Report for November."

45. [Peers to Donovan], "O.S.S.S.U. Detachment 101 Monthly Report December 1944," [1 January 1945]. See Sam G. Lucy to Research and Development, "R&D Report for December." Drawings of camouflaged explosive devices can be found in T. B. Pitman to Watts Hill, "Camouflage Suggestions," 11 December 1944, F 601, B 54, E 134, RG 226, NARA.

46. Peers to Donovan, "Report Covering Period 31 August to 30 September, 1944," [1 October 1944]. See Baird V. Helfrich, "Report on X-2-September."

47. Peers to Donovan, "Report Covering Period 30 September to 31 October, 1944," [1 November 1944]. See Baird V. Helfrich, "October Report X-2."

48. Ibid. Examples of interrogations and trial reports of black hats can be found at F 510, B 70, E 190, RG 226, NARA; a memorandum describing the form, utility, and structure of a CIT can be found at F 1499, B 192, E 108B, RG 226, NARA; the CIT weekly reports can be found at F 509, B 70, E 190, RG 226, NARA.

49. [Peers to Donovan], "O.S.S.S.U. Detachment 101 Monthly Report November 1944," [1 December 1944]. See Baird V. Helfrich to James Murphy, "X-2 Report for November." A letter from the wife of a suspected bad/black hat that was disposed of can be found at Ma Saw Hman to W. F. D. Gebhart, 27 November 1944, F 1366, B 181, E 108B, RG 226, NARA.

50. [Peers to Donovan], "O.S.S.S.U. Detachment 101 Monthly Report December 1944," 31 December 1944. See Charles W. Cox to Research and Analysis, "R & A Report for December 1944"; Baird V. Helfrich to James Murphy, "X-2 Report for December 1944."

51. William R. Peers, "Operating Plans for Detachment 101," September 1944, F 2152, B 119, E 154, RG 226, NARA.

52. [Peers to Donovan], "O.S.S.S.U. Detachment 101 Monthly Report November 1944," [1 December 1944]. See Chester R. Chartrand to Chief, SI Branch, "SI Report for November."

53. [Peers to Donovan], "O.S.S.S.U. Detachment 101 Monthly Report December 1944," 31 December 1944. See Chester R. Chartrand to Chief, SI Branch, "SI Monthly Report Nov. 25 to Dec. 25, 1944."

10. THE LAST OSS BRANCHES ARRIVE: JANUARY–MARCH 1945

1. William R. Peers to William J. Donovan, "Mission Report, Detachment 101," 28 January 1945, Folder 20, Box 34, Entry 190, Research Group 226, National Archives and Records Administration, College Park, MD; Charles W. Cox to Research and Analysis, "R & A Report for January 1945," [1 February], F 20, B 34, E 190, RG 226, NARA; [William R. Peers to William J. Donovan], "Monthly Report February," [1 March 1945], F 21, B 34, E 190, RG 226, NARA. See Dow S. Grones to Carl O. Hoffman, "SO Operations, February 1945"; John I. Howell to Chief, Secretariat, Office of Strategic Services, "Report on Detachment 101's contribution to the Lashio campaign," 22 March 1945, F 22, B 34, E 190, RG 226, NARA.

2. Peers to Donovan, "Mission Report, Detachment 101," 28 January 1945.

3. [Peers to Donovan], "Monthly Report February," [1 March 1945]. See William R. Peers to William J. Donovan, "Mission Report for Detachment 101 for February 1945."

4. Peers to Donovan, "Mission Report, Detachment 101," 28 January 1945.

5. George D. Gorin to Chief Special Funds Branch, "Special Funds Report for January 1945," 27 January 1945, F 20, B 34, E 154, RG 226, NARA.

6. George D. Gorin to William R. Peers, "Special Funds Report, March 1945," 23 March 1945, F 23, B 35, E 190, RG 226, NARA; [George D. Gorin], "History of Special Funds Branch Headquarters Detachment 101," [July 1945], F 528, B 71, E 199, RG 226, NARA.

7. W. R. Peers to James F. Whisenand, "Air Operations, Detachment 101," 25 March 1945, F 401, B 60, E 190, RG 226, NARA.

8. Francis J. Reardon to William R. Peers, "Monthly Report on Air Operations," 27 January 1945, F 20, B 34, E 190, RG 226, NARA.

9. Vince Trifletti, "Rocky Reardon's Airforce," *101 Association Incorporated Newsletter* 5, no. 9 (April 1975): 5.

10. John P. Willey to William R. Peers, "Commendation," 11 January 1945, F 20, B 34, E 190, RG 226, NARA.

11. [Peers to Donovan], "Monthly Report February," [1 March 1945]. See Francis J. Reardon, "Monthly Air Operations Report."

12. Francis J. Reardon to William R. Peers, "Air Operations Monthly Report, March 1945," 24 March 1945, F 23, B 35, E 190, RG 226, NARA.

13. Dow S. Grones to Quinn, "Air Drop and Air Activities, January Report," 30 January 1945, F 20, B 34, E 190, RG 226, NARA.

14. D. V. Cavanaugh, "Air Drop: Part II—People, Parachutes, Problems," *101 Association Incorporated Newsletter* 6, no. 3 (June 1976): 4.

15. [Peers to Donovan], "Monthly Report February," [1 March 1945]. See Dow S. Grones to Quinn, "Air Drop and Air Activities, February Report."

16. "Area One Headquarters Weekly Report February 1 to 7 Inclusive," 8 February 1945, F 10162, B 277, E 210, RG 226, NARA.

17. R. T. Walsh to Supply and Procurement, "Supply Report for January 1945," [1 February 1945], F 20, B 34, E 154, RG 226, NARA.

18. Ibid.

19. William R. Peers and Dean C. Brelis, "Original Draft of Peers-Brelis Behind the Burma Road," 437, Box 1, Detachment 101 Collection, U.S. Army Historical and Education Center, Carlisle Barracks, PA.

20. R. T. Walsh to William R. Peers, "Supply and Air Drop Monthly Report," 24 March 1945, F 23, B 35, E 190, RG 226, NARA; D.V. Cavanaugh to William R. Peers, "Operational Summary, Air Drop Monthly Report, March 1945," 25 March 1945, F 23, B 35, E 190, RG 226, NARA. A breakdown of the pounds dropped per group can be found at Wesley S. Bogdan to William R. Peers, "Air Drop Monthly Report, March 1945," 24 March 1944, F 23, B 35, E 190, RG 226, NARA.

21. Oliver A. Ryder, telephone interview by author, 9 April 2008.

22. Ibid.

23. Ibid.

24. Ibid.

25. Dennis Cavanaugh, "Jumpin In," *101 Association Incorporated Newsletter*, April 1982, 7.

26. Wayne Marling, "Stories Heard in Atlanta," *OSS 101 Association Incorporated Newsletter*, Fall 2001, 8.

27. John Breen, "Some of My Experiences in Detachment 101," *OSS 101 Association Incorporated Newsletter*, Winter 1999–2000, 2.

28. Claude V. Wadsworth to Communications Branch, "Communication Report for July," 26 January 1945, F 20, B 34, E 190, RG 226, NARA. Prior to January 1945, the cryptographic section's workload had not been broken down in the monthly reports.

29. John W. Brunner, *OSS Weapons*, 2nd ed. (Williamstown, NJ: Phillips, 2005), 243.

30. [Peers to Donovan], "Monthly Report February," [1 March 1945]. See Claude V. Wadsworth to Communications Branch, "Communications Report for February, 1945."

31. [Peers to Donovan], "Monthly Report February," [1 March 1945]. See M. Y. Lederman to Carl O. Hoffman, "Activities of the Pigeon Section."

32. M. Y. Lederman to Carl O. Hoffman, "Activities of the Pigeon Section," 28 January 1945, F 20, B 34, E 154, RG 226, NARA; Grones to Hoffman, "SO Operations, January Report," 25 January 1945.

33. James C. Luce to Chief of Medical Services, OSS, Washington D.C., "Medical Services Report for January, 1945," [1 February 1945], F 20, B 34, E 154, RG 226, NARA.

34. Douglas J. King, "Medical Services Monthly Report March, 1945," [1 April 1945], F 23, B 35, E 190, RG 226, NARA.

35. Luce to Chief of Medical Services, OSS, Washington D.C., "Medical Services Report for January, 1945," [1 February 1945]; these cases were not a full accounting for the field groups, but represent an estimate of the cases treated.

36. Robert B. C. Franklin to Noah B. Levin, "Area 1 Medical Report, 1 February to 11 March 1945," 25 April 1945, F 24, B 25, E 190, RG 226, NARA.

37. [Peers to Donovan], "Monthly Report February," [1 March 1945]. See there James C. Luce to Chief of Medical Services, OSS, Washington, D.C., "Medical Services Report for February, 1945"; Lyman D. Burtch, "Malaria Control."

38. Cox to Research and Analysis, "R & A Report for January 1945," [1 February].

39. Charles W. Cox to Research and Analysis, "R & A Report for February 1945," [1 March 1945], F 21, B 34, E 154, RG 226, NARA.

40. G. H. Owen, "DET 101 R&A Serial Report #39," 1 March 1945, F 1329, B 79, E 154, RG 226, NARA.

41. [Peers to Donovan], "Monthly Report February," [1 March 1945]. See Charles W. Cox to Research and Analysis, "R & A Report for February 1945."

42. Charles W. Cox to William R. Peers, "R & A Monthly Report, March 1945," 20 March 1945, F 23, B 35, E 190, RG 226, NARA.

43. [Peers to Donovan], "Monthly Report February," [1 March 1945]. See Peers to Donovan, "Mission Report for Detachment 101 for February 1945."

44. E. L Taylor to John G. Coughlin, "Monthly Report of SI Branch," 13 March 1945, F 2753, B 161, E 154, RG 226, NARA.

45. Chester R. Chartrand to William R. Peers, "SI Monthly Report, March 1945," 24 March 1945, F 23, B 35, E 190, RG 226, NARA.

46. John I. Howell to William R. Peers, "Reports Section Final Monthly Report, June–July 1945," 6 July 1945, F 1, B 33, E 190, RG 226, NARA.

47. [Peers to Donovan], "Monthly Report February," [1 March 1945]. See Peers to Donovan, "Mission Report for Detachment 101 for February 1945"; Hugh R. Conklin to Russell Livermore, "OG Report, February 1945,"

48. Peers to Donovan, "Mission Report, Detachment 101, March 1945," 25 March 1945; Chartrand to Peers, "SI Monthly Report, March 1945," 24 March 1945.

49. Richard F. Kranstover, "I Got into the OSS by Ringing Their Doorbell," *OSS 101 Association Incorporated Newsletter*, Fall 1992, 3.

50. Baird V. Helfrich to James Murphy, "January Report," 1 February 1944, F 20, B 34, E 154, RG 226, NARA.

51. FB/001 to DH/001 and DH/005, 23 January 1945, F 1362, B 181, E 108B, RG 226, NARA.

52. [Peers to Donovan], "Monthly Report February," [1 March 1945]. See Baird V. Helfrich to James Murphy, "February Report"; Helfrich to William R. Peers, 15 February 1945. Both the CIC head and X-2 head that did not get along were removed from the CIT program.

53. [Report of Liaison with Thirty-sixth Division, British], July 1945, F 78, B 43, E 190, RG 226, NARA.

54. Jim Wilcox to "Mac," 1 March 1945, F 1445, B 191, E 108B, RG 226, NARA.

55. San G. Lucy, "R&D Report January 1945," 16 February 1945, F 20 B 34, E 190, RG 226, NARA; Newton J. Jones to Ray Kellogg and Sam Lucy, "Summary of Progress on Personal Camouflage Assignment in CB&I," [February 1944], F 20 B 34, E 190, RG 226, NARA; more on War Paint can be found in F 2260, B 1298, E 154, RG 226, NARA.

56. Peers to Donovan, "Mission Report, Detachment 101, March 1945," 25 March 1945; Thomas H. Daugherty to William R. Peers, "R&D Monthly Report, March 1945," 24 March 1945, F 23, B 35, E 190, RG 226, NARA.

57. G. H. Boldt to Commanding Officer, MO/FE, "MO/101 Report for January, 1945," [1 February 1945], F 20, B 34, E 154, RG 226, NARA.

58. "Personal Field Report of Fulton D'Gois (Fully)," 22 April 1945, F 78, B 43, E 190, RG 226, NARA.

59. Norman R. Sturgis Jr. to Chief, S&T Branch, OSS, Washington, D.C., "Monthly Report," 21 February 1945, F 1565, B 147, E 136, RG 226, NARA; another copy is at F 2121, B 159, E 139, RG 226, NARA; Harold Gullixson, "Report of Experiences Encountered While Procuring a Mobile Reproduction Unit for Detachment 101," 1 February 1945, F 27, B 35, E 190, RG 226, NARA; another copy is located at F 1295, B174, E 108B, RG 226, NARA; George H. Boldt to William J. Donovan, "MO/101 Operations," 1 July 1945, F 3027, B 175, E 154, RG 226, NARA. More on the surrender order can be found at K. D. Mann to William J. Donovan, "False Surrender Order," 26 March 1945, F 2042, B 151, E 139, RG 226, NARA; F 2053, B 151, E 139, RG 226, NARA.

60. [Peers to Donovan], "Monthly Report February," [1 March 1945]. See George H. Boldt to Commanding Officer MO/FE, "MO/101 Report for February, 1945."

61. Boldt to Commanding Officer, MO/FE, "MO/101 Report for January, 1945," [1 February 1945].

62. [Peers to Donovan], "Monthly Report February," [1 March 1945]. See George H. Boldt to Commanding Officer MO/FE, "MO/101 Report for February, 1945."

63. George H. Bolte to Commanding officer MO/FE, "MO/101 Report for March, 1945," [1 April 1945], F 23, B 35, E 190, RG 226, NARA.

64. "Personal Account of Lt. Norman R. Sturgis, Jr., 14 Apr to 15 May 1945," 19 May 1945, F 46, B 36, E 190, RG 226, NARA.

65. K. D Mann to William J. Donovan, "Report of Trip to China, India-Burma and SEAC Theaters," 28 March 1945, F 2042, B 151, E 139, RG 226, NARA.

66. Target studies for the employment of OSS Operational Groups in Burma can be found at F 1420 and F 1421, B 81, E 154, RG 226, NARA.

67. Hugh R. Conklin to Russell Livermore, "Report of O.G. Group, Det. 101," 28 January 1945, F 20, B 34, E 190, RG 226, NARA. See organizational chart attached to the report; Hugh R. Conklin to Russell Livermore, "OG Report, February 1945," F 21, B 34, E154, RG 226, NARA; Michael P. Georges to Schools and Training, O.S.S., Washington D.C., "Schools and Training Report for January 1945," [1 February 1945], F 20, B 34, E 154, RG 226, NARA; Charles G. Hutter to William R. Peers, "A Critical Analysis of the Medical Problems of O.S.S. Unit 101," 29 May 1945, F 27, B 35, E 190, RG 226, NARA.

68. Hugh R. Conklin to Russell Livermore, "OG Report, February 1945," F 21, B 34, E 154, RG 226, NARA; Wadsworth to Communications Branch, "Communication Report for July," 26 January 1945.

69. Douglas J. King to William R. Peers, "Personnel Report," 12 July 1945, F 1, B 33, E 190, RG 226, NARA.

70. Grones to Hoffman, "SO Operations, January Report," 25 January 1945.

71. Jay [Julian] Niemczyk, "Recruitment by OSS and DET 101," *OSS 101 Association Incorporated Newsletter*, Winter 1989, 7.

72. Howell to Chief, Secretariat, Office of Strategic Services, "Report on Detachment 101's contribution to the Lashio campaign," 22 March 1945.

73. [Peers to Donovan], "Monthly Report February," [1 March 1945]. See Douglas J. King to Personnel Officer, "Personnel Report, February 1945"; Michael P. Georges to Schools and Training, "Schools and Training Report for February, 1945."

11. THE SHAN STATES: AUGUST 1944–MARCH 1945

1. William R. Peers to William J. Donovan, "Report Covering Period 30 September to 31 October, 1944," [1 November 1944], F 17, B 34, E 190, RG 226, NARA.

2. Charles F. Romanus and Riley Sunderland, *United States Army in World War II: China-Burma-India Theater: Time Runs Out in the CBI* (Washington, DC: United States Army Center of Military History, 1999), 102.

3. Ibid., 123.

4. Peers to Coughlin, "Message #236," 7 April 1945, F 2482, B 141, E 154, RG 226, NARA.

5. William R. Peers and Dean C. Brelis, "Original Draft of Peers-Brelis Behind the Burma Road," 453, Box 1, Detachment 101 Collection, USAHEC.

6. "Leonard Report on Field Operations," 16 November 1944, F 78, B 43, E 190, RG 226, NARA.

7. William E. Cummings to Carl O. Hoffman, "SO Operations, August Report," 1 September 1944, F 486, B 67, E 190, RG 226, NARA.

8. Jervis-Read, "South of the Namkham Road," USAHEC.

9. William H. Cummings to Carl O. Hoffman, "SO Operations, October Report," 1 November 1944, F 486, B 67, E 190, RG 226, NARA.

10. Ibid.

11. An example of an agent recruiting to form a guerrilla group is found in "Personal Field Report of Fulton D'Gois (Fully)," 22 April 1945, F 78, B 43, E 190, RG 226, NARA, or "Harry S. Hengshoon (Skittles)," [May 1945?], F 46, B 38, E 190, RG 226, NARA. In this latter case, Skittles recruited 800 men in three weeks.

12. Peers and Brelis, "Original Draft," 441, USAHEC.

13. Ibid, 469.

14. Cummings to Hoffman, "SO Operations, October Report," 1 November 1944, NARA.

15. Peers and Brelis, "Original Draft," 376, USAHEC.

16. [William R. Peers to William J. Donovan], "O.S.S.S.U. Detachment 101 Monthly Report November 1944," [1 December 1944], F 18, B 34, E 190, RG 226, NARA. See William E. Cummings to Carl O. Hoffman, "SO Operations, November Report."

17. "Area One Monthly Report November 1944," F 452, B 65, E 190, RG 226, NARA.

18. "Personal Field Report of Pvt. George McNally," 30 December 1944, F 78, B 43, E 190, RG 226, NARA.

19. William H. Cummings to Carl O. Hoffman, "SO Operations, November Report," 1 December 1944, F 486, B 67, E 190, RG 226, NARA.

20. Ibid.

21. "Area One Monthly Report November 1944," F 452, B 65, E 190, RG 226, NARA.

22. James R. Ward, "Field Report of 'WARD' Group," [December 1945], F 78, B 43, E 190, RG 226, NARA.

23. William H. Cummings to Carl O. Hoffman, "SO Operations, November Report Addenda," 1 December 1944, F 486, B 67, E 190, RG 226, NARA.

24. Ward, "Field Report of 'WARD' Group," [December 1945], NARA.

25. John I. Howell, "Aspects of Detachment 101's Contribution to the Lashio Campaign," 19 March 1945, F 2151, B 116, E 154, RG 226, NARA.

26. Dow S. Grones to Carl O. Hoffman, "SO Operations, December Report," 28 December 1944, F 486, B 67, E 190, RG 226, NARA.

27. "Area One Headquarters, 23 to 29 December (Inclusive)," F 452, B 65, E 190, RG 226, NARA.

28. Joseph Lazarsky, "The Death of Lieutenant Berg," *101 Association Incorporated Newsletter* 6, no. 3 (June 1976): 1–2.

29. Ibid.

30. "Area One Headquarters, 23 to 29 December (Inclusive)," F 452, B 65, E 190, RG 226, NARA.

31. Dennis V. Cavanaugh, "The Rest of the Story of the Death of Maje Waldo," *OSS 101 Association Incorporated Newsletter*, June 1991, 2.

32. "Field Report of Lt. Philip S. Weld," 11 April 1945, F 46, B 38, E 190, RG 226, NARA.

33. Peter Lutkin to Pete Joost, 17 February 1945, F 452, B 65, E 190, RG 226, NARA.

34. "Lt. Douglas B. Martin interview," July 1945, F 46, B 38, E 190, RG 226, NARA.

35. "Interview with 1st. Lt. Edward D. Poole and SGT. Neil Barrett," 10 June 1945, F 46, B 36, E 190, RG 226, NARA.

36. Grones to Hoffman, "SO Operations, December Report," 28 December 1944, NARA.

37. Ibid.

38. Thomas Chamales to Commanding Officer Brigade Headquarters, Mongwi, 29 January 1945, F 452, B 65, E 190, RG 226, NARA.

39. Ralph Henderson, "Jump-In to Adventure," *Reader's Digest*, June 1945, 47.

40. Dow S. Grones to Carl O. Hoffman, "SO Operations, January Report," 25 January 1945, F 486, B 67, E 190, RG 226, NARA.

41. Li-Jen Sun to Commanding General, Chinese Army in India, "Conflict between Chinese Guerrilla and Cochin Forces," 16 January 1945, F 463, B 65, E 190, RG 226, NARA. Another copy is in F 191, B 24, E 165, RG 226, NARA.

42. "Area One Headquarters Report, January 5 to 31, 1945," 1 February 1945, F 452, B 65, E 190, RG 226, NARA.

43. William R. Peers and Dean Brelis, *Behind the Burma Road: The Story of America's Most Successful Guerrilla Force* (Boston: Little, Brown, 1963), 209.

44. Richard Dunlop, *Behind Japanese Lines: With the OSS in Burma* (Chicago: Rand McNally, 1979), 348.

45. Charles P. Rockwood Jr. to M. D. Shulman, "Relations of Chinese Troops with Local Population," 11 February 1945, F 496, B 67, E 190, RG 226, NARA.

46. "Area One Headquarters Weekly Report February 8 to 14 Inclusive," 15 February 1945, F 10162, B 277, E 210, RG 226, NARA.

47. Grones to Hoffman, "SO Operations, January Report," 25 January 1945, NARA.

48. Peers and Brelis, "Original Draft," 419, USAHEC.

49. William R. Peers to William J. Donovan, "Mission Report, Detachment 101," 28 January 1945, F 20, B 34, E 190, RG 226, NARA.

50. Grones to Hoffman, "SO Operations, January Report," 25 January 1945, NARA.

51. Ernest Easterbrook, "Commendation, 101 Detachment," 31 January 1945, and John F. Willey, "Commendation," 6 February 1945, in Dow S. Grones to Carl O.

Hoffman, "SO Operations, February Report," 25 February 1945, F 486, B 67, E 190, RG 226, NARA.

52. Lieutenant Colonel Cumming to Brigadier, General Staff (Operations) ALFSEA, 2 January 1945, contained in Hugh Tinker, ed., *Burma, The Struggle for Independence 1944–1948*, vol. 1 (London: Her Majesty's Stationery Office, 1983), 136. "Interview with Capt. Roger Hilsman Jr.," [July 1945], F 46, B 38, E 190, RG 226, NARA, also confirms this. Indeed, this came at a time when Detachment 101 was concerned that Force 136 was trying once again to secure a place in its operations. See John Coughlin to Harry Little, "Dear Harry," 4 October 1944, F 2759, B 82, E 210, RG 226, NARA; and Harry Little to John Coughlin, "Dear Colonel Coughlin," 30 September 1944, F 2759, B 82, E 210, RG 226, NARA.

53. "Interview with HEFTY, Second Trip in," 10 June 1945, F 46, B 38, E 190, RG 226, NARA.

54. Gerald E. Larsen, "'MM' Operation," 30 December 1944, F 437, B 29, E 154, RG 226, NARA. Milton's experience on the team can be found in "Interview with Billy Milton," 13 May 1945, F 46, B 36, E 190, RG 226, NARA.

55. Grones to Hoffman, "SO Operations, January Report," 25 January 1945, NARA.

56. "DET. 101 Operational Summary 1200 6 March to 1200 7 March Area #1," 7 March 1944, F 454, B 65, E 190, RG 226, NARA.

57. "Harry S. Hengshoon (Skittles)," [May 1945?], F 46, B 38, E 190, RG 226, NARA; "Photo of the Evacuation of the Sabwa of Hsenwi," *101 Association Incorporated Newsletter* 8, no. 3 (August 1980): 10.

58. Grones to Hoffman, "SO Operations, February Report," 25 February 1945, NARA.

59. Dow S. Grones, "Long Range Agent Groups," contained in Dow S. Grones to William R. Peers, "SO Monthly Report, March 1945," 25 March 1945, F 486, B 67, E 190, RG 226, NARA.

60. "Temple R. Kennedy interview," July 1945, F 46, B 38, E 190, RG 226,NARA.

61. [Report of Liaison with 36th Division, British], July 1945, F 78, B 43, E 190, RG 226, NARA.

62. "Interview with Capt. Parker," 28 April 1945, F 46, B 38, E 190, RG 226, NARA.

63. "Field Report of Lt. Philip S. Weld," 11 April 1945, F 46, B 38, E 190, RG 226, NARA (as in note 34).

64. Grones to Peers, "SO Monthly Report, March 1945," 25 March 1945, NARA.

65. "Interview with 1st. Lt. Edward D. Poole and SGT. Neil Barrett."

66. Grones to Peers, "SO Monthly Report, March 1945," 25 March 1945, NARA; Romanus and Sunderland, *Time Runs Out in the CBI*, 227.

67. "Area One Headquarters Weekly Report February 15 to 21, Inc.," 22 February 1945, F 10162, B 277, E 210, RG 226, NARA.

68. Howell, "Aspects of Detachment 101's Contribution to the Lashio Campaign," 19 March 1945, NARA.

69. "Interview of Quentin M. Enos," 9 June 1945, F 46, B 38, E 190, RG 226, NARA.

70. "Interview with 1st. Lt. Pierre Mead," 11 June 1945, F 46, B 36, E 190, RG 226, NARA.

71. William R. Peers to William J. Donovan, "Mission Report, Detachment 101, March 1945," 25 March 1945, F 002145, B 76, E 210, RG 226, NARA.

72. William R. Peers to William J. Donovan, "Mission Report, Detachment 101, March 1945," 25 March 1945, F 23, B 35, E 190, RG 226, NARA.

73. "Interview with 1st. Lt. James R. Ward," 28 June 1945, F 46, B 36, E 190, RG 226, NARA.

74. "Interview with 1st. Lt. Wallace C. Welch," 11 April 1945, F 46, B 38, E 190, RG 226, NARA.

75. Daniel J. Barnwell, "Burma Days," *OSS 101 Association Incorporated Newsletter*, August 1987, 6.

76. Walter E. O'Brien, "An Affair with China," *101 Association Incorporated Newsletter* 5, no. 7 (October 1974): 3. O'Brien also discusses this in "Report, Tour of field duty, Capt Walter E. O'Brien, March 22, 1945 to April 18, 1945," 18 April 1945, F 78, B 43, E 190, RG 226, NARA.

12. THE ARAKAN FIELD UNIT: FEBRUARY–JUNE 1945

1. Kermit Roosevelt, *The Overseas Targets* [special title], vol. 2 of *War Report of the OSS (Office of Strategic Services)* (New York: Walker, 1976), 358, 381, 398–399.

2. Stanley S. Brotman to [Warren L.?] Barnette, "Anti-American Propaganda," 9 October 1945, Folder 1404, Box 81, Entry 154, Research Group 226, National Archives and Records Administration, College Park, MD (NARA).

3. Solon to William J. Donovan, "Additional British Opinions on Burma," 3 July 1945, F 9658, B 228, E 210, RG 226, NARA.

4. Manly Fleischmann to Cora DuBois, "Notes on the First Two Weeks of the British Reoccupation of Akyab, Burma," 13 February 1945, F 1176, B 74, E 154, RG 226, NARA.

5. [Gregory?] Bateson and Carleton F. Scofield to David G. Mandelbaum, "Report on Expedition to Sat Tha Village," 26 January 1945, F 9058, B 231, E 210, RG 226, NARA.

6. Maurice P. Coon to Charles J. Trees, 29 March 1945, F 905, B 231, E 210, RG 226, NARA.

7. Headquarters Supreme Allied Commander South East Asia Supreme Allied Commander's Meetings, 30 January 1945, F 492, B 68, E 190, RG 226, NARA. AFL-OSS cooperation is an interesting study, and the Detachment 101 X-2 section sent in numerous reports of its contacts with AFL members. Although the OSS tried to act on the potential cooperation, in the words of X-2 member Stuart Power, when contact

was established with Aung Sang, the OSS was told by the G-2 of the British Fourteenth Army "to butt out." See Stu Power, "How I Got into the OSS to Far Away Places with Strange Sounding Names," *101 Association Incorporated Newsletter*, March 1990, 10. For more on the Fourteenth Army interaction with the AFL, see General Slim's description in William Slim, *Defeat into Victory: Battling Japan in Burma and India, 1942–1945* (New York: Cooper Square Press, 2000), 515–520. Also see Baird Helfrich, "X-2 Experience with Burma Anti-Fascist League," [June 1945], F 24791, B 6, E 214, RG 226, NARA.

8. James H. Mysbergh, "Report on the Arakan Front," 12 November 1944, F 1495, B 200, E 108B, RG 226, NARA.

9. Guy Martin to Harry L. Berno, "Planning Developments," 28 November 1944, F2010, B 106, E 154, RG 226, NARA.

10. Harriet W. Sabine, "History of Detachment 404 Operations," [21 September 1944], F 1, B 64, E 99, RG 226, NARA.

11. A good general survey on the Arakan Field Unit can be found in Martin J. Waters, "The Operations of a Provisional OSS Platoon, Night Reconnaissance Operations, The Arakan Coast, Burma, Oct. 1944–Apr. 1945," Infantry School General History Section Military History Committee, Fort Benning, Georgia: Advanced Officers Course, 1946–1947.

12. For clarification, the time of the AFU under Detachment 404 will be denoted as BITTERSWEET, while under 101, it will be referred to as the Arakan Field Unit (AFU). Many of the BITTERSWEET mission files and directives can be found at F 2480, B 141, E 154, RG 226, NARA. The Detachment 404 MU section was originally under Detachment 101 and had been set up by former commanding officer Colonel Carl F. Eifler.

13. David G. Mandelbaum, "Notes on Penetration Groups in the Arakan," 24 December 1944, F 2135, B 118, E 154, RG 226, NARA. Prior to its inclusion in Detachment 101, the MU section conducted thirteen operations along the Arakan Coast. See "MU Operations from the Arakan," F 3525, B 238, E 139, RG 226, NARA; Lloyd E. Peddicord to Amos D. Moscrip, "Situation Report," 1 March 1945, F 2482, B 141, E 154, RG 226, NARA.

14. Carleton F. Scofield to James R. Withrow, 31 December 1944, F 2111, B 117, E 154, RG 226, NARA; Bateson and Scofield to Mandelbaum, "Report on Expedition to Sat Tha Village," 26 January 1945; [Gregory?] Bateson to Carleton F. Scofield, "Weekly Report Jan 7–Jan 14," 14 January 1945, F9059/008, B 231, E 210, RG 226, NARA.

15. Evelle J. Younger to John J. McDonough, "Weekly Report 24–31 December 1944," 31 December 1944, F 1431, B 187, E 108B, RG 226, NARA; another copy is located at F 2145, B 119, E 154, RG 226, NARA.

16. Evelle J. Younger to John J. McDonough, "Weekly Report 1–7 January 1945," 7 January 1945, F 1430, B 187, E 108B, RG 226, NARA.

17. Evelle J. Younger to Joseph P. McCarthy, "Informants, AFU," 31 March 1945, F 1436A, B 189, E 108B, RG 226, NARA.

18. Lloyd E. Peddicord to Commanding Officer, BITTERSWEET MISSION, "Operations Report for the Period 6–11 February, 1945," 11 February 1945, F 2140, B 118, E 154, RG 226, NARA.

19. L. H. to Isadore Burstein, "Mobile Assessment and Training Unit in the Arakan," 26 January 1945, F 554, B 38, E 148, RG 226, NARA.

20. Evelle J. Younger, "Operation 'Charlene,'" 22 February 1945, F 90601010, B 231, E 210, RG 226, NARA.

21. Sabine, "History of Detachment 404 Operations," [21 September 1944].

22. Trimble C. Condict to Daniel I. Sultan, "Semi-Monthly Operational Report, 1 May 1945 to 15 May 1945," 15 May 1945, F 2140, B 118, E 154, RG 226, NARA.

23. Philip K. Crowe to John G. Coughlin, "SI Plan for Burma," 12 December 1944, F 2010, B 109, E 154, RG 226, NARA.

24. William R. Peers to Strategic Services Officer Headquarters India Burma Theater, "Monthly Report," 25 February 1945, F 002141, B 76, E 210, RG 226, NARA. Target studies for the employment of OSS Operational Groups in southwest Burma, which were most likely put together by the R&A section, can be found at F 1420, B 81, E 154, RG 226, NARA.

25. William R. Peers to John G. Coughlin, 17 February 1945, F 228, B 20, E 110, RG 226, NARA.

26. Don S. Packer to Commanding Officer, Detachment 404, 28 March 1945, F 1367, B 203, E 199, RG 226, NARA.

27. T. H. Daugherty to Sam G. Lucy, 4 April 1945, F 2255, B 129, E 154, RG 226, NARA; F. R. Loetterle to T. H. Daugherty, 16 March 1945, F 2260, B 129, E 154, RG 226, NARA.

28. Intelligence debriefs and reports can be found at F 76, B 43, E 190, RG 226, NARA.

29. "Maritime Unit Arakan," [June 1945], F 13, B 549, E 92, RG 226, NARA.

30. The OSS created a new command structure for SEAC when Donovan flew to New Delhi, India, in November 1943 to meet with Vice Admiral Mountbatten. They set up P Division, a joint supervisory panel that deconflicted both British and American clandestine operations in the region. As the P Division coordinator for north Burma, Colonel William R. Peers retained autonomy of Detachment 101's operations. Operation BOSTON cleared P Division on 16 February. Moscrip to Farr, Priority Cable, 16 February, F 2482, B 141, E 154, RG 226, NARA; Operation "BOSTON" Operation Order and "Questionnaire No. 20 Foul Island," [19 February 1945], Box 1, Folder "Misc Mission Reports from SE Asia," Dr. Christian Lambertsen Collection, United States Army Special Operations Command History Office, Fort Bragg, NC (USASOC).

31. Maritime Unit Arakan, [June 1945], F 13, B 549, E 92, RG 226, NARA. The P-564 had been involved in Operations CLEVELAND (25–26 January 1945), TARGET (1–2 February), SNATCH (6 February), NORTH CAROLINA (11–13 February), and SOUTH DAKOTA (16 February).

32. Walter Mess, interview by author, 24 March 2008.

33. Operation "Boston" Operation Order, 19 February 1945, Box 1, Folder "Misc Mission Reports from SE Asia," Dr. Christian Lambertsen Collection, USASOC.

34. Walter Mess interview, 24 March 2008.

35. Ibid.

36. Ibid.

37. LCDR Derek Lee and LT John E. Babb to LTC Harry Berno, "Report on Operation 'BOSTON' (Reconnaissance of Foul Island)," 21 February 1945, F 2141, B 118, E 154, RG 226, NARA; also in Box 1, Folder "Maritime Units in the Arakan," LCDR Derek A. Lee "Report of Proceeding," [late February 1945], Dr. Christian Lambertsen Collection, USASOC. Also see Box 1, Folder "Misc Mission Reports from SE Asia," Dr. Christian Lambertsen Collection, USASOC.

38. Lee, "Report of Proceeding," [late February 1945]. Also see Box 1, Folder "Misc Mission Reports from SE Asia," Dr. Christian Lambertsen Collection, USASOC.

39. LT Louis A. O'Jibway, "Operation 'RUGBY,'" [22 February 1945] , Box 1, Folder "Misc Mission Reports from SE Asia," Dr. Christian Lambertsen Collection, USASOC. Operation RUGBY was the OG nomenclature for Operation BOSTON.

40. Lee, "Report of Proceeding," [late February 1945]. Also see Box 1, Folder "Misc Mission Reports from SE Asia," Dr. Christian Lambertsen Collection, USASOC.

41. O'Jibway, "Operation 'RUGBY,'" [22 February 1945].

42. Walter Mess interview, 24 March 2008. The photographers were Captain T. Johnson (OG-Army), Lieutenant John E. Babb (MU-USN), and Lieutenant Commander Derek A. Lee (MU-Royal Navy Volunteer Reserve). The OSS Field Photo Branch opted not to cooperate. Lee, "Report of Proceeding," [late February 1945].

43. Walter Mess interview, 24 March 2008.

44. LT John E. Babb, "Answers to Questionnaire No. 20 on Foul Island," 22 February 1945, Box 1, Folder "Maritime Units in the Arakan," Dr. Christian Lambertsen Collection, USASOC.

45. Booth and Eubank interview, March 1998, USASOC.

46. "AFU DET 101 and the Arakan Campaign," [May 1945?], F 76, B 43, E 190, RG 226, NARA.

47. James H. Mysbergh to Herbert Avedon, "Diary March 15–23," 24 March 1945, F 905, B 231, E 210, RG 226, NARA.

48. Herbert Avedon to Charles J. Trees, "Morale Operations in the Arakan and Sothern Burma," 29 May 1945, F 76, B 43, E 190, RG 226, NARA. A clandestine radio broadcast, JN27, which had begun under BITTERSWEET, was kept in operation. However, since its target was the Malayan Peninsula, it will not be covered.

49. Charles J. Trees, "Conference Noted P Div., HQ. XV Corps," 30 March 1945, F 905, B 231, E 210, RG 226, NARA.

50. Herbert Avedon to Charles J. Trees, "Monthly Report March 1945," 28 March 1945, F 2050, B 151, E 139, RG 226, NARA.

51. D. B. Higgenbottom to E. J. Younger, "Monthly Report, X-2 Branch, AFU," [1 May 1945], F 1470, B 194, E 108B, RG 226, NARA.

52. "Extract: Letter from Lt. James Hamilton to Dr. Robert C. Tryon," 30 March 1945, F 2011, B 109, E 154, RG 226, NARA.

53. Alan F. Laidlaw to John G. Coughlin, "Parachute Training for Operational Group," 19 April 1945, F 90, B 45, E 190, RG 226, NARA.

54. "Det 101, Arakan Field Unit Report April 26, 1945," [27 April 1945], F 1919, B 181, E 136, RG 226, NARA.

55. Amos D. Moscrip to William R. Peers, "Monthly Report [OSS Detachment 101 BA]," 29 April 1945, F 400, B 60, E 190, RG 226, NARA.

56. Trimble C. Condict to Charles J. Trees, "Semi-Monthly Operational Report; 1 April to 15 April 1945," 15 April 1945, F 2140, B 118, E 154, RG 226, NARA.

57. "AFU DET 101 and the Arakan Campaign," [May 1945?].

58. "Det 101, Arakan Field Unit Report April 26, 1945," [27 April 1945].

59. Trimble C. Condict to Charles J. Trees, "Semi-Monthly Operational Report; 1 April to 15 April 1945," 15 April 1945, F 481, B 66, E 154, RG 226, NARA. The number of agents in the field added to the AFU communications duties. In March, the number of coded groups received stood at 101,138 groups. See Fred A. Chastain, "History of Commo AFU," 26 May 1945, F 76, B 43, E 190, RG 226, NARA.

60. "AFU DET 101 and the Arakan Campaign," [May 1945?].

61. Herbert Avedon to Charles J. Trees, "Proposed Operations," 14 April 1945, F 1117, B 107, E 144, RG 226, NARA; another copy is located at F 2050, B 151, E 139, RG 226, NARA.

62. "Det 101, Arakan Field Unit Report April 26, 1945," [27 April 1945]. November 1944 report located in Mysbergh, Report on the Arakan Front, F 1495, B 200, E 108B, RG 226, NARA.

63. K. D. Mann to William J. Donovan, "Report of Trip to China, India-Burma and SEAC Theaters," 28 March 1945, F 2042, B 151, E 139, RG 226, NARA.

64. John G. Coughlin to Charles J. Trees, 4 May 1945, F 2140, B 118, E 154, RG 226, NARA.

65. William R. Peers to John G. Coughlin, 1 May 1945, F 228, B 20, E 110, RG 226, NARA.

66. Baird V. Helfrich, "Special Snatch Unit Arms," 25 April 1945, F 490, B 67, E 190, RG 226, NARA.

67. "Directive for Organizing a Rangoon City Team," 21 March 1945, F 390, B 60, E 190, RG 226, NARA. The U.S. Army had followed a similar intelligence exploitation program in Europe with "S-Forces" (Italy) and "T-Forces" (northwest Europe).

68. Trimble C. Condict to Daniel I. Sultan, "Semi-Monthly Operational Report, 1 May 1945 to 15 May 1945," 15 May 1945, F 481, B 66, E 154, RG 226, NARA; Moscrip to Peers and Coughlin, "Message #209," 11 May 1945, F 2482, B 141, E 154, RG 226, NARA.

69. David G. Mandelbaum to Charles J. Trees, "Preliminary Report City Documents Team-Operation Jean," 16 May 1945, F 76, B 43, E 190, RG 226, NARA; David G. Mandelbaum to Charles J. Trees, "Final Report, City Documents Team, Op. Jean," 25 May 1945, F 76, B 43, E 190, RG 226, NARA.

70. "MO Report on Operation JEAN/DRACULA," 15 May 1945, F 6315, B 137, E 210, RG 226, NARA; Herbert Avedon to Charles J. Trees, "Monthly Report, Morale Operations Branch, May 1945," 26 May 1945, F 2050, B 151, E 139, RG 226, NARA; Avedon to Trees, "Morale Operations in the Arakan and Sothern Burma," 29 May 1945.

71. Baird V. Helfrich to William R. Peers, "14th Army X-2 Team for Rangoon," 6 May 1945, F 490, B 67, E 190, RG 226, NARA.

72. Baird V. Helfrich to Commanding Officer, Br Hq, Det 404, "X-2 Monthly Report, June 1945," 20 June 1945, F 24794, B 6, E 214, RG 226, NARA; John J. McDonough to John G. Coughlin, "Rangoon Trip," 22 June 1945, F 1393, B 184, E 108B, RG 226, NARA. The only example that the OSS uncovered of the Japanese trying to send indigenous agents behind Allied lines can be found in Evelle J. Younger to John J. McDonough, "Jap Espionage Attempt, TAUNGUP to SANE," 21 February 1945, F 2141, B 118, E 15, RG 226, NARA. For more on Japanese intelligence see Stephen C. Mercado, *The Shadow Warriors of Nakano: A History of the Imperial Japanese Army's Elite Intelligence School* (Washington D.C., Brassey's, 2002).

73. Baird V. Helfrich to Joseph P. McCarthy, "Weekly X-2 Report, Det. 101 AFU, 21–28 May 1945," 28 May 1945, F 1470, B 194, E 108B, RG 226, NARA.

74. Baird V. Helfrich to Charles J. Trees, "X-2 Monthly Report, May 1945," 20 May 1945, F 1470, B 194, E 108B, RG 226, NARA; Baird V. Helfrich, "Memorandum on Conference," 1 July 1945, F 2011, B 109, E 154, RG 226, NARA. At the time, the cost of X-2 operations in Rangoon was $1,500 per month, FB/001 to JJ/001 and DH/005, 19 July 1945, F 1471, B 194, E 108B, RG 226, NARA.

75. David G. Mandelbaum to Cora DuBois, "Accomplishments of R&A Branch, Arakan Field Unit, 14 December to 14 June 1945," 2 July 1945, F 2142, B 118, E 154, RG 226, NARA; Mandelbaum to Trees, "Final Report, City Documents Team, Op. Jean," 25 May 1945, NARA.

76. John G. Coughlin to William R. Peers, 22 June 1945, F 228, B 20, E 110, RG 226, NARA.

77. William R. Peers to John G. Coughlin, 18 June 1945, F 228, B 20, E 110, RG 226, NARA.

78. Mandelbaum to DuBois, "Accomplishments of R&A Branch, Arakan Field Unit," 2 July 1945.

79. Waller B. Booth to John G. Coughlin, "Visit to AFU," 2 May 1945, F 2134, B 118, E 154, RG 226, NARA.

80. "AFU DET 101 and the Arakan Campaign," [May 1945?].

13. THE LAST MONTHS: APRIL–JULY 1945

1. Coughlin to Peers for Sultan, info Heppner and Cheston, "Message #20527," 24 April 1945, Folder 2482, Box 141, Entry 154, Research Group 226, National Archives and Records Administration, College Park, MD (NARA).

2. William R. Peers to Strategic Services Officer, OSS, China Theater, 21 April 1945, F 3027, B 175, E 154, RG 226, NARA. To account for the fact that Detachment 101 was still operating south of Lashio, the NCAC AOR for clandestine operations was extended to 250 miles south of the city. The OSS had already prepared for the invasion of Thailand, which would be conducted by the British South-East Asia Command. OSS Special Operations (SO) and Secret Intelligence (SI) teams had infiltrated as early as December 1944, with the assistance of politicians high in the Thai government who had formed a quasi-resistance group. The OSS trained nascent Thai guerrilla groups, but the war ended before they rose up. Thailand, a nominal Japanese ally, had played their political cards well. See E. Bruce Reynolds, *Thailand's Secret War: The Free Thai, OSS, and SOE during WWII* (Cambridge: Cambridge University Press, 2005), and Nicol Smith and Blake Clark, *Into Siam: Underground Kingdom* (New York: Bobbs-Merrill, 1946). Although Thais were technically allied with the Japanese, the Detachment 101 guerrilla groups were ordered to treat them on friendly terms. See Cummings to Peers, "Message #02497," 10 April 1945, F 2482, B 141, E 154, RG 226, NARA.

3. John G. Coughlin to William J. Donovan, "Your Cable #2046," 24 April 1945, Frame 750, Roll 88, M 1642, RG 226, NARA.

4. William R. Peers to William J. Donovan, "Mission Report, Detachment 101, May 1945," 24 May 1945, F 26, B 35, E 190, RG 226, NARA.

5. Robert B. Moore to William R. Peers, "SO Monthly Report, April 1945," 25 April 1945, F 24, B 35, E 190, RG 226, NARA.

6. Ibid.

7. William J. Slim to Daniel I. Sultan, "My Dear General," 19 April 1945, F 392, B 60, E 190, RG 226, NARA.

8. E. M. Koch to Daniel I. Sultan, "Assaults and Affrays with Civilian Population," 14 February 1945, F 392, B 60, E 190, RG 226, NARA.

9. Reginald Thorlin to William R. Peers, "Affrays with Civilian Population," 26 February 1945, F 496, B 67, E 190, RG 226, NARA.

10. "Interview with Sgts. Jack Tweedy and George Triska," 1 June 1945, F 46, B 36, E 190, RG 226, NARA.

11. Roger Hilsman, *American Guerrilla: My War behind Japanese Lines* (Washington, DC: Brassey's, 1990), 187.

12. William R. Peers to William J. Donovan, "Mission Report, Detachment 101, April 1945," 20 April 1945, F 24, B 35, E 190, RG 226, NARA.

13. William R. Peers to John G. Coughlin, "Dear John," 3 June 1945, F 3028, B 175, E 154, RG 226, NARA.

14. "Interview with Capt. Roger Hilsman, Jr.," [July 1945], F 46, B 38, E 190, RG 226, NARA. Hilsman's description is echoed in "Interview with T/4 Edward Arida and Sgt. Elbert Van Arsdale," 6 July 1945, F 46, B 38, E 190, RG 226, NARA.

15. "DET. 101 Operational Summary 1000 10 June to 1000 11 June," 11 June 1944, F 453, B 65, E 190, RG 226, NARA.

16. Robert B. Moore to William R. Peers, "SO Monthly Report, May 1945," 25 May 1945, F 486, B 67, E 190, RG 226, NARA; Robert B. Moore to William R. Peers, "Operational Report, 23 May–8 July1945," 8 July 1945, F 486, B 67, E 190, RG 226, NARA.

17. Peers and Brelis, "Original Draft," 469.

18. "Interview with T/SGT Edward S. Maslowsky," 30 May 1945, F 46, B 36, E 190, RG 226, NARA.

19. "Interview with 1st. Lt. Edward D. Poole and SGT. Neil Barrett," 10 June 1945, F 46, B 36, E 190, RG 226, NARA.

20. "Interview of Staff Sergeant Constantine C. Brelis," [March 1945], F 47, B 38, E 190, RG 226, NARA.

21. "Interview with Jacko," 11 May 1945, F 46, B 38, E 190, RG 226, NARA.

22. Robert B. Moore to William R. Peers, "SO Monthly Report, May 1945," 25 May 1945, F 486, B 67, E 190, RG 226, NARA.

23. Moscrip to Peers and Coughlin, "Message #209," 11 May 1945, F 2482, B 141, E 154, RG 226, NARA.

24. Robert B. Moore to William R. Peers, "Operational Report, 23 May–8 July 1945," 8 July 1945, F 486, B 67, E 190, RG 226, NARA.

25. Robert B. Moore to Raymond A. Wheeler, "Operational Report, 15 June to 30 June," 30 June 1945, F 2153, B 119, E 154, RG 226, NARA.

26. Robert B. Moore to William R. Peers, "Operational Report, 23 May–8 July 1945," 8 July 1945, F 486, B 67, E 190, RG 226, NARA.

27. "Statistical Summary Detachment 101 Activities 10 April 1945 to 15 June 1945," F 2155, B 119, E 154, RG 226, NARA. The same document places the number of estimated enemy killed during this period at 2,500.

28. William R. Peers to Richard P. Heppner, "Dear Dick," 27 June 1945, F 3028, B 175, E 154, RG 226, NARA.

29. William R. Peers to John G. Coughlin, "Dear John," 3 June 1945, F 3028, B 175, E 154, RG 226, NARA.

30. Peers to Donovan, "Mission Report, Detachment 101, April 1945," 20 April 1945.

31. Hugh R. Conklin, "I Entered 101 by the Back Door!" *101 Association Incorporated Newsletter*, May 1987, 5.

32. Francis J. Reardon to William R, Peers, "Air Operations Monthly Report, April 1945," F 24, B 35, E 190, RG 226, NARA. In all, the squadron evacuated nineteen Japanese and Burman auxiliary troops in April for interrogation back at Detachment 101 headquarters.

33. Francis J. Reardon to William R. Peers, "Air Operations Monthly Report, May 1945," 24 May 1945, F 26, B 35, E 190, RG 226, NARA.

34. Francis J. Reardon to William R. Peers, "Monthly Report of Air Operations, June 1945," 5 July 1945, F 1, B 33, E 190, RG 226, NARA; Charles G. Hutter to William R. Peers, "Report of the Medical Services of Detachment 101 for June 1945," 7 July 1945, F 1, B 33, E 190, RG 226, NARA.

35. R. T. Walsh to William R. Peers, "Supply and Air Drop Report, April 1945," 27 April 1945, F 24, B 35, E 190, RG 226, NARA; D. V. Cavanaugh to William R. Peers, "Operational Summary, Air Drop Monthly Report, April 1945," 25 April 1945, F 24, B 35, E 190, RG 226, NARA.

36. D. V. Cavanaugh to William R. Peers, "Operational Summary, Air Drop Monthly Report, May 1945," 25 May 1945, F 26, B 35, E 190, RG 226, NARA.

37. Earl E. Walker to William R. Peers, "Air Drop Monthly Report, June 1945," 22 June 1945, F 1, B 33, E 190, RG 226, NARA; J. M. Garrett to William R. Peers, "Air Drop Final Report," 12 July 1945, F 1, B 33, E 190, RG 226, NARA.

38. Leroy Thompson to William R. Peers, "Communications Monthly Report, April 1945," 25 April 1945, F 24, B 35, E 190, RG 226, NARA.

39. Claude V. Wadsworth to William R. Peers, "Communications Report as of 25 May 1945," 25 May 1945, F 26, B 35, E 190, RG 226, NARA.

40. Claude V. Wadsworth to William R. Peers, "Communications Monthly Report for Period 26 May 1945 to 8 July 1945," 8 July 1945, F 1, B 33, E 190, RG 226, NARA.

41. Thompson to Peers, "Communications Monthly Report, April 1945," 25 April 1945.

42. George H. Boldt to William R. Peers, "MO/101 Report for April, 1945," [1 May 1945], F 24, B 35, E 190, RG 226, NARA. Peers to Donovan, "Mission Report, Detachment 101, April 1945," 20 April 1945, NARA. The Fourteenth Army wished to have MO products, but did not want MO personnel operating in their areas. The Detachment took eleven Japanese prisoners of war in April, and British Fourteenth Army had numbers of Japanese soldiers surrender to them in the Mandalay area (where Detachment 101 propaganda products were also used).

43. Chester R. Chartrand to William R. Peers, "Final Monthly Report, SI Branch," 11 July 1945, F 1, B 33, E 190, RG 226, NARA.

44. George H. Owen to William Peers, "R & A Monthly Report, April 1945," 20 April 1945, F 24, B 35, E 190, RG 226, NARA.

45. Peers to Donovan, "Mission Report, Detachment 101, April 1945," 20 April 1945.

46. James Tilly, "Report on Bark Drop," 31 March 1945, F 413, B 28, E 154, RG 226, NARA.

47. Baird V. Helfrich to William R. Peers, "Combat Interrogation Reports for Week Ending 30 April," 1 May 1945, F 1470, B 194, E 108B, RG 226, NARA; Baird V. Helfrich to John J. McDonough, "Specific Target Information for X-2 Agents Operating in Lower Burma," 7 April 1945, F 61, B 8, E 110A, RG 226, NARA. Instructions to AFL X-2 agents can also be found in this folder; an initial report on the BARK group can be found at Baird V. Helfrich to William R. Peers, "April 1945 Report on X-2," 25 April 1945, F 512, B 70, E 190, RG 226, NARA; the BARK group mission file can be found at F 413, B 28, E 154, RG 226, NARA; Evelle J. Younger to David Hunter, "Comparison of X-2 and CIC Mission," 7 May 1945, F 1445, B 191, E 108B, RG 226, NARA; Baird V. Helfrich to William R. Peers, "X-2 Monthly Report, April 1945," 25 April 1945, F 24, B 35, E 190, RG 226, NARA.

48. John D. Maharg to William R. Peers, "X-2 Monthly Report, May 1945," [1 June 1945], F 26, B 35, E 190, RG 226, NARA; Baird V. Helfrich to David Hunter, "Experience with British, 17 March–1 July 1945," 29 June 1945, F 15765, B 434, E 210, RG 226, NARA; "X-2 Combat Interrogation Teams, Burma," 15 June 1945, F 007335, B 193, E 210, RG 226, NARA.

49. Claude Constable to William R. Peers, "Field Photographic Monthly Report, May 1945," 21 May 1945, F 26, B 35, E 190, RG 226, NARA; Peers to Donovan, "Mission Report, Detachment 101, May 1945," 24 May 1945, NARA; R. T. Walsh to William R. Peers, "Supply and Air Drop Monthly Report, April 1945," 22 May 1945, F 26, B 35, E 190, RG 226, NARA; Charles G. Hutter to O.S.S. Headquarters, "Monthly Medical Report," 23 May 1945, F 26, B 35, E 190, RG 226, NARA.

50. Robert B. Moore to William R. Peers, "Operational Report, 23 May–8 July 1945," 8 July 1945, F 486, B 67, E 190, RG 226, NARA; W. R. Peers to All Battalion Commanders, Detachment 101, 5 June 1945, F 379, B 59, E 190, RG 226, NARA.

51. W. R. Peers to Raymond A. Wheeler, "Dear Sir," 5 July 1945, F 383, B 59, E 190, RG 226, NARA. Another copy is located in F 6063, B 231, E 210, RG 226, NARA.

52. Charles P. Henderson to John G. Coughlin, "Report of the Theater Counsel for July 1945," 26 July 1945, F 1, B 83, E 99, RG 226, NARA; George D. Gorin to John G. Coughlin, 1 November 1945, F 25, B 3, E 140, RG 226, NARA.

53. Team rosters for several of the Detachment 202 teams and the Mercy Missions can be found in Francis B. Mills, Robert Mills, and John W. Brunner, *OSS Special Operations in China* (Williamstown, NJ: Phillips Publications, 2002), 491–532; William R. Peers to William J. Donovan, "Mission Report, Detachment 101, 1 June 1945 to 12 July 1945," 12 July 1945, F 1, B 33, E 190, RG 226, NARA. The numbers of personnel transferred: 325 to China, 101 to Detachment 404, and 123 to the U.S., can be found in William R. Peers to John G. Coughlin, "Sitrep," 12 July 1945, F 2481, B 141, E 154, RG 226, NARA.

54. Hale H. Knight, "The Operations of a Guerrilla Company (OSS DET 101) at Lawksawk, Burma 6 May–12 May 1945," 1948–1949, Advanced Infantry Officers Course, Infantry School, Fort Benning, Georgia.

55. Robert B. Moore to William R. Peers, "Operational Report, 23 May–8 July 1945," 8 July 1945, F 1, B 33, E 190, RG 226, NARA; Robert B. Moore to William R. Peers, "SO Monthly Report, May 1945," 25 May 1945, F 26, B 35, E 190, RG 226, NARA; Douglas J. King to William R. Peers, "Personnel Report," 12 July 1945, F 1, B 33, E 190, RG 226, NARA; William E. Cox to Daniel I. Sultan, "Commendable Operations of O.S.S., Detachment 101," 16 July 1945, F 1, B 33, E 190, RG 226, NARA.

56. John Coughlin to William R. Peers, "Inactivation of Detachment 101," 25 July 1945, F 2155, B 119, E 154, RG 226, NARA.

57. Doering to William J. Donovan, 17 June 1945, Frame 700, Roll 88, M 1642, RG 226, NARA.

CONCLUSION

1. Phone interview with Richard Kranstover by author, 20 November 2007, Fort Bragg, NC.

2. [OSS Special Operations Branch history], "This Phase of SO," Folder 4, Box 101, Entry 99, Research Group 226, National Archives and Records Administration, College Park, MD (NARA).

3. William R. Peers to William J. Donovan, "Mission Report, Detachment 101, 1 June 1945 to 12 July 1945," 12 July 1945, F 1, B 33, E 190, RG 226, NARA.

4. Thomas J. Davis, "OSS Plans for Burma," 29 November 1944, F 2010, B 109, E 154, RG 226, NARA.

5. S. P. Joost to Chief, SI, "Report on Field Conditions," 8 June 1945, F 26, B 74, E 99, RG 226, NARA.

6. Douglas J. King to William R. Peers, "Personnel Report," 12 July 1945, F 1, B 33, E 190, RG 226, NARA.

7. William R. Peers to William J. Donovan, "Mission Report, Detachment 101, March 1945," 25 March 1945, F 002145, B 76, E 210, RG 226, NARA.

8. Kermit Roosevelt, *The Overseas Targets* [special title], vol. 2 of *War Report of the OSS (Office of Strategic Services)* (New York: Walker, 1976), 391–392; William R. Peers and Dean Brelis, *Behind the Burma Road: The Story of America's Most Successful Guerrilla Force* (Boston: Little, Brown, 1963), 217.

POSTSCRIPT: THE LASTING RELATIONSHIPS OF DETACHMENT 101

1. For more on the creation of Special Forces, see the excellent study Alfred H. Paddock Jr., *U.S. Army Special Warfare: Its Origins* (Lawrence: University Press of Kansas, 2002).

2. For more on this see Frank Holober, *Raiders of the China Coast: CIA Covert Operations during the Korean War* (Annapolis, MD: Naval Institute Press, 1999).

3. For more information see W. R. Peers, *The My Lai Inquiry* (New York: W. W. Norton, 1979).

4. "101 Awarded the Green Beret," *101 Association Incorporated Newsletter*, Fall 1966, 3.

5. The Institute of Heraldry, "Special Forces Tab," found online at http://www.tioh.hqda.pentagon.mil/UniformedServices/Tabs/Special_Forces_Tab.aspx.

6. William R. Peers and Dean C. Brelis, "Original Draft of Peers-Brelis Behind the Burma Road," 458, Box 1, Detachment 101 Collection, U.S. Army Historical and Education Center, Carlisle Barracks, PA (USAHEC).

7. Niemczyk in later years retired from the U.S. Air Force as a colonel and served as ambassador to Czechoslovakia from 1986 to 1989.

8. "Twenty Years Ago and Today," *101 Association Incorporated Newsletter*, April 1965, 1.

9. Peers and Brelis, "Original Draft," 454.

10. Wilkie to Peers, "Dear Ray," 28 August 1944, F 192, B 23, E 1665, RG 226, NARA.

11. Peers and Brelis, "Original Draft," 172.

12. William R. Peers to William J. Donovan, "Dear General," 21 September 1948, Files 917-939, Book No 52, B 75B, William J. Donovan Papers, USAHEC.

13. Newsletter, "American Veterans of DET.101 American-Jinghpaw Rangers," 9 March 1947, copy in author's possession.

14. Art Aubry, "How Our Association Got Started," *101 Association Incorporated Newsletter* 5, no. 10 (August 1975): 4.

15. Sam Schreiner, "Dear 101er," 20 October 1961, copy in author's possession.

16. For more on the Far East in post-WWII see Christopher Bayly and Tim Harper, *Forgotten Wars: Freedom and Revolution in Southeast Asia* (Cambridge, MA: Belknap Press, 2006).

17. John P. Breen, "OSS-101 Association Membership Meeting," *OSS 101 Association Incorporated Newsletter*, Fall 1999, 3.

18. James E. Brooks and Peter K. Lutken letter to Thane Han, 6 October 1994, in *OSS 101 Association Incorporated Newsletter*, Winter 1994–95, 6.

19. James E. Brooks, letter to Mr. O. B. Klien, 29 January 1992, reprinted in *OSS 101 Association Incorporated Newsletter*, Winter 1992, 4.

20. Peter Lutken, "Agricultural Program (Crop Substitution) Effort for Kachin Progressess," *OSS 101 Association Incorporated Newsletter*, Summer 2006, 3.

21. Mickey Kaliff, "Crop Substitution Program on its Way," *OSS 101 Association Incorporated Newsletter*, Fall 1996, 8.

22. John P. Breen, "Minutes: OSS-101 Assoc. Membership Meeting September 29, 2001," *OSS 101 Association Incorporated Newsletter*, Fall 2001, 4.

23. Mickey Kaliff, "Dallas Veteran Meeting," *OSS 101 Association Incorporated Newsletter*, Winter 2011, 7.

24. Brian Ferry, "Veteran Efforts, Association Dues, Help Educate Young Burmese," *OSS 101 Association Incorporated Newsletter*, Summer 2009, 1.

25. Dan Tarter, "OSS 101 Kachin Ranger Myitkyina Schools Project," *OSS 101 Association Incorporated Newsletter*, Fall 2008, 5.

26. "Reflections on 101's Impact in Burma," *OSS 101 Association Incorporated Newsletter*, Summer 2011, 2.

A NOTE ON SOURCES

1. When the OSS was dissolved in 1945, the Research and Analysis (R&A) section and its records went to the State Department, while the other branches deemed

worthy of saving formed the Strategic Services Unit (SSU). The records now in RG 226 formed the basis of the initial files of the Central Intelligence Agency (CIA) when it was created under the National Defense Act in 1947. The CIA held these records in its custody and began releasing them to the National Archives and Records Administration (NARA) only in the early 1980s. For more on the transition of the records to NARA, see Lawrence H. McDonald, "The OSS and Its Records," in *The Secrets War: The Office of Strategic Services in World War II*, ed. George C. Chalou (Washington, DC: National Archives and Records Administration, 1992).

2. An explanation for the lack of correspondence was found in a letter dated 26 May 1943 in which the OSS headquarters area operations officer for the Far East relays to Colonel Eifler that all that Donovan required of him in the way of correspondence was to continue sending in monthly reports. (Carl O. Hoffman to Carl F. Eifler, "Yours of April 21 and 26, 1943," 26 May 1943, Folder 27, Box 191, Entry 92, Research Group 226, National Archives and Records Administration, College Park, MD.) The only direct correspondence to Eifler from Donovan was a 2 June 1943 letter congratulating him on his excellent job. William J. Donovan to Carl F. Eifler, National Archives microfilm, Roll 110, A 3304, E 180, RG 226, NARA. A copy of Donovan's records is also held by the U.S. Military History Institute at Carlisle, PA.

3. The only substantial inclusion of the OSS in RG 493 concerned the Detachment 202 OSS "Mercy" missions to protect the prisoners from Japanese retaliation.

4. Thomas N. Moon and Carl F. Eifler, *The Deadliest Colonel* (New York: Vantage Press, 1975) and William R. Peers and Dean Brelis, *Behind the Burma Road: The Story of America's Most Successful Guerrilla Force* (Boston: Little, Brown, 1963).

5. Richard Dunlop, *Behind Japanese Lines: With the OSS in Burma* (Chicago: Rand McNally, 1979).

6. Thomas Chamales, *Never So Few* (New York: Scribners, 1957); Roger Hilsman, *American Guerrilla: My War behind Japanese Lines* (Washington: Brassey's, 1990); Dean Brelis, *The Mission* (New York: Random House, 1958).

7. Bill Brough, *To Reason Why . . .* (Whickham, UK: Hickory Tree Press, 2001); Thomas Baldwin, *I'd Do It All Again: The Life and Times of Tom Baldwin* (Tustin, CA: Wambtac, 1996); Harry "Skittles" Hengshoon, *Green Hell: Unconventional Warfare in the CBI* (Huntington Beach, CA: B & L Lithograph, 2000).

8. Maochun Yu, *OSS in China: Prelude to Cold War* (New Haven, CT: Yale University Press, 1996); E. Bruce Reynolds, *Thailand's Secret War: The Free Thai, OSS, and SOE during World War II* (Cambridge: Cambridge University Press, 2005); Dixee R. Bartholomew-Feis, *The OSS and Ho Chi Minh: Unexpected Allies in the War against Japan* (Lawrence: University Press of Kansas, 2006); Richard J. Aldrich, *Intelligence and the War against Japan: Britain, America, and the Politics of Secret Service* (Cambridge: Cambridge University Press, 2000); Kermit Roosevelt, ed., *War Report of the OSS*, 2 vols. (New York: Walker and Company, 1976); Charles Cruickshank, *SOE in the Far East* (Oxford: Oxford University Press, 1983).

References

ARCHIVES CONSULTED

National Archives and Records Administration, College Park, MD (NARA).

RG 226. *Records of the Office of Strategic Services.*

RG 493. *Records of the China Burma India Theater.*

M1642. *Records of the Office of Strategic Services, 1941–1945.*

Preston Goodfellow Collection, Hoover Institute Archives, Stanford University, CA.

United States Army Historical and Education Center (USAHEC), Carlisle Barracks, PA.

Detachment 101 Collection.

William J. Donovan Papers.

United States Army Infantry School, Donovan Research Library, Fort Benning, GA.

Knight, Hale H. "The Operations of a Guerrilla Company (OSS DET 101) at Lawksawk, Burma 6 May–12 May 1945." 1948–1949, Advanced Infantry Officers Course, Infantry School, Fort Benning, GA.

Waters, Martin J. "The Operations of a Provisional OSS Platoon, Night Reconnaissance Operations, the Arakan Coast, Burma, Oct. 1944–Apr. 1945." 1946–1947, Advanced Infantry Officers Course, Infantry School, Fort Benning, GA.

United States Army Special Operations Command (USASOC) History Office, Fort Bragg, NC.

Huffine, Fred. "Operations of the 150th Chinese Regiment from 1 April 1944 to 4 August 1944." Contained in Hayden Boatner papers, copy in the USASOC History Office, Fort Bragg, NC.

Kesley, Thomas L. "Liaison with 1st Bn 150th Regt." Copy in USASOC History Office, Fort Bragg, NC.

United States Special Operations Command (USSOCOM) History Office, MacDill Air Force Base, FL.

Wilson, Lieutenant General Samuel V. Interviewed by Dr. J. W. Partin, Rice, Virginia, 11 July 1988, USSOCOM History Office.

IN AUTHOR'S COLLECTION

Aubrey, Arthur. Memoir of experiences in DET 101.

Colling, John. Memoir of V-Force/OSS 101.

Correspondence with OSS Detachment 101 Veterans.

Eifler, Carl F. Personal papers.

Luce, James. Personal papers.

Murray, John M. *The China I've Seen.* Self-published, 1992.

101 Association Incorporated Newsletter, various.

Tottori, Calvin. *The OSS Niseis in the China-Burma-India Theater.* Self-published.

OTHER SOURCES CONSULTED

Aldrich, Richard J. *Intelligence and the War against Japan: Britain, America and the Politics of Secret Service.* Cambridge: Cambridge University Press, 2000.

Allen, Louis. *Burma: The Longest War 1941–45.* London: Phoenix Press, 2001.

Alsop, Steward, and Thomas Braden. *Sub Rosa: The O.S.S. and American Espionage.* New York: Reynal & Hitchcock, 1946.

Anonymous. *Merrill's Marauders.* Washington, DC: United States Army Center of Military History, 1990.

Asprey, Robert B. *War in the Shadows: The Guerrilla in History.* Vols. 1 and 2. New York: Doubleday, 1975.

Baldwin, Thomas. *I'd Do It All Again!* Tustin, CA: Wambtac, 1996.

Bank, Aaron. *From OSS to Green Berets: The Birth of Special Forces.* Novato, CA: Presidio Press, 1986.

Barnard, Jack. *The Hump: The Greatest Untold Story of the War.* London: Souvenir Press, 1960.

Barrett, David D. *Dixie Mission: The United States Army Observer Group in Yenan, 1944.* Berkeley: University of California Press, 1979.

Barrett, Neil H. *Chinghpaw.* New York: Vantage Press, 1962.

Bartholomew-Feis, Dixee R. *The OSS and Ho Chi Minh: Unexpected Allies in the War Against Japan.* Lawrence: University Press of Kansas, 2006.

Bayly, Christopher, and Tim Harper. *Forgotten Armies: The Fall of British Asia, 1941–1945.* Cambridge, MA: Belknap Press, 2004.

———. *Forgotten Wars: Freedom and Revolution in Southeast Asia.* Cambridge, MA: Belknap Press, 2006.

Beamish, John. *Burma Drop.* London: Elek Books, 1958.

Beaumont, Roger A. *Military Elites: Special Fighting Units in the Modern World.* New York: Bobbs-Merrill. 1974.

Bidwell, Shelford. *The Chindit War: Stilwell, Wingate, and the Campaign in Burma, 1944.* New York: Macmillan, 1979.

Bowen, John. *Undercover in the Jungle*. London: William Kimber, 1978.
Bower, Ursula Graham. *Naga Path*. London: John Murray, 1952.
Brelis, Dean. *The Mission: A Novel of War and Brotherhood*. New York: Random House, 1958.
Brough, Bill. *To Reason Why . . . .* Whickham, UK: Hickory Tree Press, 2001.
Brown, Anthony Cave. *Wild Bill Donovan: The Last Hero*. New York: Times Books, 1982.
Brunner, John W. *OSS Weapons*. 2nd ed. Williamstown, NJ: Phillips Publications, 2005.
Calvert, Michael. *Chindits: Long Range Penetration*. New York: Ballantine, 1973.
Carter, Carolle J. *Mission to Yenan: American Liaison with the Chinese Communists, 1944–1947*. Lexington: University Press of Kentucky, 1997.
Chalou, George C., ed. *The Secrets War: The Office of Strategic Services in World War II*. Washington, DC: National Archives and Records Administration, 1992.
Chamales, Tom T. *Never So Few*. New York: Charles Scribner's Son, 1957.
Chambers, John W. *OSS Training in the National Parks and Service Abroad In World War II*. Washington, DC: U.S. National Park Service, 2008.
Chan, Won Loy. *Burma: The Untold Story*. Novato, CA: Presidio Press, 1986.
Churchill, Winston S. *The Second World War: Closing the Ring*. Cambridge, MA: Riverside Press, 1951.
———. *The Second World War: The Hinge of Fate*. Cambridge, MA: Riverside Press, 1950.
Colling, John. *The Spirit of Yenan: A Wartime Chapter of Sino-American Friendship*. Hong Kong: API, 1991.
Cook, Haruko Taya, and Theodore F. Cook. *Japan at War: An Oral History*. London: Phoenix Press, 1992.
Coon, Carlton S. *A North African Story: The Long-Mislaid Diary-Like Account of a Harvard Professor of Anthropology Turned Cloak-and-Dagger Operative for General Donovan and His OSS; 1942–3*. Ipswich, MA: Gambit, 1980.
Cruickshank, Charles. *SOE in the Far East*. Oxford: Oxford University Press, 1983.
Défourneaux, René J. *The Winking Fox: Twenty-Two Years in Military Intelligence*. Indianapolis: Indiana Creative Arts, 1997.
Department of the Army. Field Manual 31-21, *Organization and Conduct of Guerilla Warfare*. Washington DC: Government Printing Office, 1951.
Dorn, Frank. *Walkout: With Stilwell in Burma*. New York: Thomas Y. Crowell, 1971.
Drea, Edward. *Japan's Imperial Army: Its Rise and Fall, 1853–1945*. Lawrence: University Press of Kansas, 2009.
Dunlop, Richard. *Behind Japanese Lines: With the OSS in Burma*. Chicago: Rand McNally, 1979.
———. *Donovan: America's Master Spy*. New York: Rand McNally, 1982.
Enriquez, C. M. *In Quest of Greatness*. Kachin State, Burma: CC Naw Ja.
Fenn, Charles. *At the Dragon's Gate: With the OSS in the Far East*. Annapolis, MD: Naval Institute Press, 2004.

Fischer, Edward. *Mission in Burma: The Columban Fathers' Forty-Three Years in Kachin Country*. New York: Seabury Press, 1980.

Ford, Corey. *Donovan of OSS*. Boston, MA: Little, Brown, 1970.

Ford, Corey, and Alastair MacBain. *Cloak and Dagger: The Secret Story of the Office of Strategic Services*. New York: Grosset & Dunlap, 1946.

Fuller, Richard. *Shōkan: Hirohito's Samurai; Leaders of the Japanese Armed Forces, 1926–1945*. London: Arms and Armour, 1992.

Hansen, James H. *Japanese Intelligence: The Competitive Edge*. Washington, DC: NIBC Press, 1996.

Harries, Meirion, and Susie Harries. *Soldiers of the Sun: The Rise and Fall of the Imperial Japanese Army*. New York: Random House, 1991.

Henderson, Ralph. "Jump-In to Adventure." *Reader's Digest*, June 1945, 47.

Hengshoon, Harry. *Green Hell: Unconventional Warfare in the CBI*. Huntington Beach, CA: B & L Lithograph, 2000.

Hilsman, Roger. *American Guerrilla: My War behind Japanese Lines*. Washington, DC: Brassey's, 1990.

Hinsley, F. H. *British Intelligence in the Second World War: Its Influence on Strategy and Operations*. Vols. 1–4. London: Her Majesty's Stationery Office, 1981, 1986, 1988, 1990.

Hodgson, Lynn Philip. *Inside-Camp X*. Port Perry, Canada: Friesens, 2002.

Holober, Frank. *Raiders of the China Coast: CIA Covert Operations during the Korean War*. Annapolis, MD: Naval Institute Press, 1999.

Hopkins, James E. T. *Spearhead: A Complete History of Merrill's Marauder Rangers*. Baltimore, MD: Galahad Press, 1999.

Howard, Michael. *British Intelligence in the Second World War*. Vol. 5: *Strategic Deception*. London: Her Majesty's Stationery Office, 1990.

Kappel, Roy. *Whispering Wings over Burma: The Jungle Angels; 5th Liaison Squadron*. Self-published, 1998.

Leach, E. R. *Political Systems of Highland Burma: A Study of Kachin Social Structure*. London: Athlone Press, 1970.

Mason, Herbert A., Jr., Randy G. Bergeron, and James A. Renfrow Jr. *Operation THURSDAY: Birth of the Air Commandos*. Washington, DC: United States Air Force History and Museums Program, 1994.

McIntosh, Elizabeth P. *Sisterhood of Spies: Women of the OSS*. Annapolis, MD: Naval Institute Press, 1998.

Mercado, Stephen C. *The Shadow Warriors of Nakano: A History of the Imperial Japanese Army's Elite Intelligence School*. Washington, DC: Brassey's, 2002.

Meyer, Milton Walter. *G.I. Joe 1943–1945*. Claremont, CA: Paige Press, 2003.

Mills, Francis B., Robert Mills, and John W. Brunner. *OSS Special Operations in China*. Williamstown, NJ: Phillips Publications, 2002.

Moon, Thomas N., and Carl F. Eifler. *The Deadliest Colonel*. New York: Vantage Press, 1975.

Moon, Tom. *This Grim and Savage Game: O.S.S. and the Beginning of U.S. Covert Operations in WWII*. Los Angeles, CA: Burning Gate Press, 1991.

Nunneley, John, and Kazuo Tamayama. *Tales by Japanese Soldiers of the Burma Campaign*. London: Cassell, 2000.

Office of Strategic Services. *Assessment of Men: Selection of Personnel for the Office of Strategic Services*. New York: Rinehart, 1948.

Paddock, Alfred H., Jr. *U.S. Army Special Warfare: Its Origins*. Lawrence: University Press of Kansas, 2002.

Peers, William R. "Guerrilla Operations in Northern Burma." *Military Review* 28 (June 1948): 10–16, and (July 1948): 12–20.

———. *Guerrilla Operations in Northern Burma*. Fort Leavenworth: Command and General Staff College, n.d.

———. "Intelligence Operations of OSS Detachment 101." *Studies in Intelligence: Journal of the American Intelligence Professional* 4 (1960): 1–13.

———. *The My Lai Inquiry*. New York: W. W. Norton, 1979.

Peers, William R., and Dean Brelis. *Behind the Burma Road: The Story of America's Most Successful Guerrilla Force*. Boston: Little, Brown, 1963.

Phillips, Bob. *KC8 Burma: CBI Air Warning Team, 1941–1942*. Manhattan, KS: Sunflower University Press, 1992.

Phillips, C. E. Lucas. *The Raiders of Arakan*. London: Heinemann, 1971.

Rasor, Eugene L. *The China-Burma-India Campaign, 1931–1945: Historiography and Annotated Bibliography*. Westport, CT: Greenwood Press, 1998.

Reynolds, E. Bruce. *Thailand's Secret War: The Free Thai, OSS, and SOE during World War II*. Cambridge: Cambridge University Press, 2005.

Romanus, Charles F., and Riley Sunderland. *United States Army in World War II: China-Burma-India Theater: Stilwell's Command Problems*. Washington, DC: United States Army Center of Military History, 1987.

———. *United States Army in World War II: China-Burma-India Theater: Stilwell's Mission to China*. Washington, DC: United States Army Center of Military History, 1987.

———. *United States Army in World War II: China-Burma-India Theater: Time Runs Out in CBI*. Washington, DC: United States Army Center of Military History, 1959.

Roosevelt, Kermit, ed. *War Report of the OSS (Office of Strategic Services)*. Vol. 1. New York: Waller, 1976.

———. *The Overseas Targets* [special title]. Vol. 2 of *War Report of the OSS (Office of Strategic Services)*. New York: Walker, 1976.

Sacquety, Troy J. "Behind Japanese Lines in Burma." *Studies in Intelligence: Journal of the American Intelligence Professional* 11 (Fall–Winter 2001): 67–79.

———. "The CG-4A Waco Glider." *Veritas: Journal of Army Special Operations History* 3, no. 2 (2007).

———. "Supplying the Resistance: OSS Logistics Support to Special Operations in

Europe." *Veritas: Journal of Army Special Operations History* 3, no. 1 (2007): 37–48.

Seagrave, Gordon. *Burma Surgeon.* New York: Norton, 1943.

———. *Burma Surgeon Returns.* New York: Norton, 1946.

Sinclair, William Boyd. *Confusion beyond Imagination: China-Burma-India in World War II.* Book 7 of 10: *Under Wraps for Eyes Alone.* Coeur d'Alene, ID: Joe F. Whitley, 1990.

Slim, William J. *Defeat into Victory: Battling Japan in Burma and India, 1942–1945.* New York: Cooper Square Press, 2000.

Smith, Bradley F. *The Shadow Warriors: O.S.S. and the Origins of the C.I.A.* New York: Basic Books, 1983.

Smith, Nicol, and Blake Clark. *Into Siam: Underground Kingdom.* Indianapolis: Bobbs-Merrill, 1946.

Smith, R. Harris. *OSS: The Secret History of America's First Central Intelligence Agency.* Los Angeles: University of California Press, 1972.

Smith, W. E., ed. *2nd Troop Carrier Squadron: AAF-CBI-WWII.* Cullman, AL: Gregath, 1987.

Spector, Ronald H. *Eagle against the Sun: The American War with Japan.* New York: Vintage Books, 1985.

Stilwell, Joseph W. *The Stilwell Papers.* New York: William Morrow, 1975.

Stratton, Roy Olin. *The Army-Navy Game.* Falmouth, MA: Volta, 1977.

———. *SACO: The Rice Paddy Navy.* New York: C. S. Palmer, 1950.

Studies in Intelligence, Journal of the American Intelligence Professional. *Office of Strategic Services, 60th Anniversary.* Washington, DC: Central Intelligence Agency, 2002.

Thompson, Julian. *The Imperial War Museum Book of War behind Enemy Lines.* Washington, DC: Brassey's, 1998.

Thu, U Min. *Glimpses of Kachin Traditions and Customs.* Myitkyina, Burma: U Htun Hlaing, 2002.

Tinker, Hugh, ed. *Burma: The Struggle for Independence, 1944–1948.* Vol. 1. London: Her Majesty's Stationery Office, 1983.

Troy, Thomas F. *Donovan and the CIA: A History of the Establishment of the Central Intelligence Agency.* Washington, DC: Central Intelligence Agency, 1981.

Tucker, Shelby. *Among Insurgents: Walking through Burma.* New York: Radcliff Press, 2000.

Vion, Heidi. "'Booms from behind the Lines': An Oral History of the Covert Experiences of the Men of the Office of Strategic Services' Detachment 101 in the World War II China-Burma-India Theater." Thesis, California State University, Center for Oral and Public History, 2004.

Waller, Douglas. *Wild Bill Donovan: The Spymaster Who Created the OSS and Modern American Espionage.* New York: Free Press, 2011.

Warner, Michael. *The Office of Strategic Services: America's First Intelligence Agency.* Washington, DC: Central Intelligence Agency, 2000.

Weld, Philip. *Moxie: The American Challenge.* Boston, MA: Little, Brown, 1981.

Wilkinson, William C. "Problems of a Guerrilla Leader." *Military Review* 32 (November 1952).

Wiriyawit, Wimon. *Free Thai: Personal Recollections and Official Documents.* Bangkok, Thailand: White Lotus Press, 1997.

Yu, Maochun. *OSS in China: Prelude to Cold War.* New Haven, CT: Yale University Press, 1996.

Index